Communication and Society
Today and Tomorrow

Many Voices
One World

**Towards a new
more just and more efficient
world information and communication order**

Kogan Page, London/Unipub, New York/Unesco, Paris

First published in 1980 and reprinted 1981
by the United Nations
Educational, Scientific and Cultural Organization
Place de Fontenoy, Paris
and Kogan Page Ltd
120 Pentonville Road, London
and Unipub
345 Park Avenue South
New York

© Unesco, 1980

Printed by The Anchor Press Ltd and bound by Wm Brendon & Son Ltd
both of Tiptree, Colchester, Essex

ISBN 0 85038 348 X (Kogan Page)
ISBN 0 89059-008-7 (Unipub)
ISBN 0 92-3-101802-7 (Unesco)

Printed in Great Britain

Members of the Commission

Sean MacBride (Ireland), President

Elie Abel (USA)
Hubert Beuve-Méry (France)
Elebe Ma Ekonzo (Zaire)
Gabriel Garcia Marquez (Colombia)
Sergei Losev (USSR)
Mochtar Lubis (Indonesia)
Mustapha Masmoudi (Tunisia)
Michio Nagai (Japan)

Fred Isaac Akporuaro Omu (Nigeria)
Bogdan Osolnik (Yugoslavia)
Gamal El Oteifi (Egypt)
Johannes Pieter Pronk (Netherlands)
Juan Somavia (Chile)
Boobli George Verghese (India)
Betty Zimmerman (Canada)

Secretariat

Members: Asher Deleon (Executive Secretary), Pierre Henquet,
Ahmed Kettani, John G. Massee, William Syad,
Suzanne Do Dinh, Daphne Mullett, Sheila de Vallée,
Jane Wright

Collaborating Consultants: Francis Balle, James Halloran, John Lee,
Fernando Reyes Matta, Mrs Deba Wieland, Yassen Zassoursky

Editorial Advisor to the President: Mervyn Jones

Translators: John Crombie, Gilles Philibert

Contents

Part V: Communication Tomorrow

Appendices

Foreword

Amadou-Mahtar M'Bow
Director-General of Unesco

Communication is at the heart of all social intercourse. Whenever men have come to establish regular relations with one another, the nature of the systems of communication created between them, the forms these have taken and the measure of effectiveness they have attained have largely determined the chances of bringing communities closer together or of making them one, and the prospects for reducing tensions or setting conflicts wherever they have arisen.

At the beginning, permanent communication was possible only within circumscribed communities, groups of people living side by side or forming part of the same political unit. Nowadays, however, as a result of the speed at which the information media operate and of the network of relations of all kinds that have been developed throughout the world, communication has grown until it is essentially of planetary scope.

Henceforward, apart from a very few groups in areas to which access is particularly difficult, people cannot live in isolation. Every nation now forms part of the day-to-day reality of every other nation. Though it may not have a real awareness of its solidarity, the world continues to become increasingly interdependent.

This interdependence, however, goes hand in hand with a host of imbalances and sometimes gives rise to grave inequalities, leading to the misunderstandings and manifold hotbeds of tension which combine to keep the world in ferment.

It is true that the patterns of domination and the conflicts of interests stemming from them cannot be made to disappear merely because the scope for communication has been broadened, but the increased possibilities of communicating can help to soften their impact by making every individual more alive to the problems and aspirations of others and every nation more conscious of the dangers lying in wait for the world community as a whole.

In these circumstances, the importance of communication is fundamental. Moreover, as a result of the tremendous strides taken by science and technology, the means now exist of responding to that need. Mass communication in the satellite era offers all peoples the possibility of simultaneously witnessing the same events, exchanging full information, understanding one another better notwithstanding their specific features, and valuing each other while acknowledging their differences.

At the same time, the media are in the process of transforming the basic data of social communication within individual nations, setting up new exchange systems, completely changing the conditions governing the transmission of knowledge, opening up a whole range of possibilities for making formal and non-formal education generally available, bringing culture to the people at large, and promoting knowledge and knowhow. They are creating conditions which allow of constant individual enrichment and enable the populations of all nations to take part in their own advancement and to broaden their outlook to take in the whole international community.

It is not, then, wishful thinking to imagine that, as people come to feel more and more that their national destinies are closely intertwined, they will, in future, seek to develop ties of growing fellowship with one another and to establish little by little relationships based on mutual respect and co-operation.

These, however, are only some of the prospects offered by an age which is equally capable of producing the best for the future, or the worst. They will be realized only if the temptation to enlist the mass media in the service of narrow sectarian interests and to turn them into new instruments of power, justifying assaults on human dignity and aggravating the inequalities which already exist between nations and within individual nations themselves is resisted. And, also, only if everything possible is done to prevent tendencies towards a concentration of the mass media from progressively curtailing the scope of inter-personal communication and from ultimately destroying the multiplicity of channels, whether they be traditional or modern, by which individuals can exercise their right to freedom of expression.

The information media can contribute to commanding respect in all quarters for human beings as individuals, with all the manifold differences they display, and to winning acceptance of the aspirations common to all peoples in place of self-centred nationalisms. They can also foster uninterrupted dialogue between communities, cultures and individuals, in a bid to promote equality of opportunities and two-way exchanges. This presupposes, first, that information in all fields should go unfettered. But we shall never cease to affirm that such freedom cannot be fully effective until it becomes a reality for everybody.

Unesco has devoted its efforts to bringing about such conditions ever since it was founded on the authority of its Constitution, which enjoins it to work for "the unrestricted pursuit of objective truth and the free exchange of ideas and knowledge ..." and, to that end, "to increase the means of communication between peoples".

It is chiefly over the past two decades, however, with the increasing importance that the mass media have assumed in the life of modern societies and with the growing awareness of the role they are called upon to play, particularly in the development of the newly-independent nations, that the Organization has been prompted to give more penetrating thought to the matter and to strengthen its action. It has accordingly made an active contribution to highlighting the need for a more balanced flow of information, both world-wide and within individual societies.

It was with this in view that the General Conference, at its nineteenth session, held in Nairobi in 1976, instructed me to undertake a review of all the problems of communication in contemporary society seen against the background of technological progress and recent developments in international relations with due regard to their complexity and magnitude. I therefore deemed it advisable, in undertaking this task, to set up a "brains trust" composed of highly competent, prominent figures from various backgrounds, and I accordingly established the International Commission for the Study of Communication Problems, under the presidency of Mr. Sean MacBride and comprising the following members:
Elie Abel (United States of America); Hubert Beuve-Méry (France); Elebe Ma Ekonzo (Zaïre); Gabriel Garcia Marquez (Colombia); Sergei Losev (USSR); Mochtar Lubis (Indonesia); Mustapha Masmoudi (Tunisia); Michio Nagai (Japan); Fred Isaac Akporuaro Omu (Nigeria); Bogdan Osolnik (Yugoslavia); Gamal el

Oteifi (Egypt); Johannes Pieter Pronk (Netherlands); Juan Somavia (Chile); Boobli George Verghese (India) and Betty Zimmerman (Canada).

The Commission, which had complete intellectual freedom and the widest possible latitude with regard to the conditions and procedures whereby it conducted its inquiry into the problems and went about its work, immediately tackled the task before it. Despite the short time available to it for carrying out such an undertaking, it succeeded, in eight sessions spread over two years—altogether two months of work—in drafting the final report which I have great pleasure in presenting to you here.

May I, on this occasion, say publicly how grateful I am to Mr. MacBride and all the members of the Commission who drawn from all the regions of the world and having the most varied professional and political backgrounds, strove, with unfailing intellectual integrity and tolerance, to deal collectively with a particularly wide range of questions, and to identify their most important implications in the world today.

This report may therefore be regarded as a first stage in the endeavour to be made by the international community as a whole to consider in practical terms the challenges we have to face and the ways in which we might act in concert to meet them, in accordance with the principles set forth in the Declaration on the media unanimously adopted by the General Conference at its twentieth session in 1978.

The problems arising in connexion with communication, when the diversity of contemporary societies is considered, are not of a kind that can be dealt with exhaustively in a single study, however thorough and comprehensive it may be. The work of the Commission must therefore be continued and taken deeper.

For these reasons, the report will be made available not only to the authorities responsible for communication and the institutions which are concerned, on various grounds, with its development, but also to administrators and research workers in all branches of study, non-governmental and intergovernmental international organizations, and the general public in all countries. It will be published initially in the working languages of Unesco's deliberative bodies, that is to say in English, French, Spanish, Arabic, Russian and Chinese, but we shall do all we can to assist its publication in other languages.

It is essential that all men and women, in all social and cultural environments, should be given the opportunity of joining in the process of collective thinking thus initiated, for new ideas must be developed and more positive measures must be taken to shake off the prevailing inertia. With the coming of a new world communication order, each people must be able to learn from the others, while at the same time conveying to them its own understanding of its own condition and its own view of world affairs. Mankind will then have made a decisive step forward on the path to freedom, democracy and fellowship.

Preface

Sean MacBride
President

The International Commission for the Study of Communication Problems began its work in December 1977. My feelings then, at the outset of our long journey in the world of communications, were a mixture of excitement and trepidation: excitement at the opportunity to preside a sixteen-member group from all corners of the globe in the exploration of a subject so basic to peace and human development; trepidation because of the vast range of topics and the crucial nature of the problems to be studied.

Nor did the background to the establishment of the Commission permit any optimistic temerity in anticipating the difficulties of the task ahead or of reaching agreed conclusion.

In the 1970s, international debates on communications issues had stridently reached points of confrontation in many areas. Third world protests against the dominant flow of news from the industrialized countries were often construed as attacks on the free flow of information. Defenders of journalistic freedom were labelled intruders on national sovereignty. Varying concepts of news values and the rôle, rights and responsibilities of journalists were widely contended, as was the potential contribution of the mass media to the solution of major world problems.

Given this divisive atmosphere which surrounded the start of the Commission's work, my concern from the beginning was how to achieve a balanced, non-partisan, objective analysis of today's communication scene and how to meet the challenge of reaching the broadest possible consensus in our views on the major issues before us.

Another primary concern was the breadth of our mandate: "to study the totality of communication problems in modern societies". Among all the documentation and literature in the field which this Commission perused during the course of its work, none attempted such an all-encompassing review. Ours does not purport to be anything near a definitive work, but we have tried to transcend the conventional issues and to come close to the terms of our mandate.

Hence, ours is not simply a report on the collection and dissemination of news or on the mass media, although the major problems in these areas were starting-points for our discussion. We have been immediately involved in a wider historical, political and sociological perspective. Likewise, concentration on information had to be broadened to include all aspects of communication, considered in an overall socio-economic, cultural and political context. Moreover, as communication is so central to all social, economic and political activity at community, national and international levels, I would paraphrase H. G. Wells and say human history becomes more and more a race between communication and catastrophe. Full use of communication in all its varied strands is vital to assure that humanity has more than a history . . . that our children are ensured a future.

The Commission's sixteen members — largely representative of the world's ideological, political, economic and geographical spectrum — reached what I consider a surprising measure of agreement on major issues, upon which opinions heretofore had seemed irreconcilable. It was not simply a matter of reaching conclusions; more important, perhaps, was the identification and analysis of the problems and the possible solutions. In the inevitable continuing debates on facets of the developing new world information and communication order we hope that these may be of assistance.

For me, and I venture to think that this also applies to all my colleagues on the Commission, the most rewarding experience was the mutual sense of respect and friendship which we developed for each other in the course of our work. I hope that the constructive effort which dominated our work will persist when our report comes to be examined by Governments and others.

When the final draft of the report came before us for approval I felt impelled by a desire to rewrite it from beginning to end. I am sure that all my colleagues and Members of the Secretariat felt the same impulse. The style of writing varied, parts were prolix. Apart from the fact that we did not have the time necessary to undertake such a task, we felt that, despite the stylistic imperfection the report conveyed our views clearly. The reader must bear in mind the many linguistic, cultural and philosophical strands that were woven into this vast mosaic on communication.

Despite the large area of consensus reached on most major issues, it is obvious that many questions remain open; in addition, many subjects require further analysis. Many difficulties lie ahead, particularly in organizing and implementing concrete measures to help to construct the new order, which call for continuing review. There are many varying views as to the meaning of the "New Order" and as to what it should encompass, just as there are diverse opinions on ways and means of achieving it. But, in spite of these divergences, there was nobody in the Commission not convinced that structural changes in the field of communication are necessary and that the existing order is unacceptable to all.

There is obviously no magic solution to efface by a single stroke the existing complicated and inter-connected web of communication problems. There will be many stages, strategies and facets in the patient step-by-step establishment of the new structures, methods and attitudes which are required. Thus, the "New World Information and Communication Order" may be more accurately defined as a process than any given set of conditions and practices. The particulars of the process will continually alter, yet its goals will be constant — more justice, more equity, more reciprocity in information exchange, less dependence in communication flows, less downwards diffusion of messages, more self-reliance and cultural identity, more benefits for all mankind.

The Commission's analysis and its consensus on major guidelines for the development of a New World Information and Communication Order were themselves the result of a lengthy process. We owe much to Ambassador Mustapha Masmoudi and to Dr. Bogdan Osolnik, not only for their persistent advocacy of the "New Order" but for their constructive elucidation of its major aspects. But besides rich discussions between the Members of the Commission, during eight sessions from December 1977 to November 1979, our basic approach was constantly to reach outwards, to the extent practically feasible, to examine broad subjects directly with professionals and specialists involved, representing national, regional and international participation.

We started by organizing a large international gathering on issues such as contents of information, accuracy and balance in facts and images presented, infrastructures for news supply, rights and responsibilities of journalists and organizations engaged in news gathering and distribution, as well as technical and economic aspects of their operations. For that purpose an International Seminar on the Infrastructures of News Collection and Dissemination held in April 1978 in Stockholm, with the generous assistance of the Swedish government, attended by some 100 representatives of news agencies, broadcasting organizations, major newspapers, research institutes and international non-governmental organizations of regional or world-wide scope.

Apart from meetings held at Unesco Headquarters in Paris, the Commission held four sessions in countries as various as Sweden, Yugoslavia, India and Mexico. This permitted a closer insight into disparate cultural and social issues involved. It also permitted contacts with professionals and researchers sharing different views on basic aspects of communication in divergent societies. Round tables were organized on topics which were of particular importance for the Commission; with Yugoslav media and government representatives, we discussed the interaction between society and communication media; we had another debate on cooperation among developing countries on the same occasion. Our Indian hosts organized a wide ranging discussion on the relationship between communication and development; we also discussed with them the impact of future technological advances. With a large group of Latin American writers, professors and media personnel we focused on the correlation between culture and communication.

These direct consultations on central themes provided us with invaluable insights into the interlocking nature of fundamental issues in communications; particularly, they confirmed that these issues are structurally linked to wider socio-economic and cultural patterns. Thus, finally — and inevitably — communication problems assume a highly political character which is the basic reason why they are at the centre of the stage today in national and international arenas.

Further background material for our deliberations was provided by some one hundred descriptive and opinion papers prepared on specific aspects of communication by specialists from around the world. This represented particularly valuable substantive material for purposes of comparative analysis and for stimulating rethinking on communication issues.

Our professional contacts were further enriched by the opportunities afforded myself and other Members of the Commission and the Secretariat to attend more than a score of conferences, meetings, seminars and discussion groups organized by international organizations, international professional associations, the Non-Aligned countries, regional and national institutions concerned with various aspects of information and communication.

In addition, during the course of the Commission's work, dozens of international, regional and national institutions — research and documentation centres, schools of journalism, universities, professional associations and similar bodies — collaborated actively by the generous supply of research findings, topical documentation and substantive commentary.

Finally, we had the benefit of hundreds of individual, institutional and governmental comments on our Interim Report, which was submitted in 1978 to the Twentieth Session of Unesco's General Conference.

Thus, while our report represents the Commission's collective vision of the communication scene it has been based on a virtually worldwide survey of opinions, both individual and institutional, and a mountain of documentation from myriad sources. This wealth of information covered the widest possible spectrum of ideological, political, socio-economic and cultural colourings. Each member of the Commission considered it from his or her own viewpoint, then it was collectively reviewed in our deliberations.

The resulting distillation makes up our Report. Generally it is a consensus of how the Commission sees the present communication order and foresees a new one. Where there were differences those are reflected by way of comment or dissent. But given its broad base, plus its formulation by a representative international group which the Commission was, our Report — its presentations, findings and proposals — will, I trust, reach a wide like-minded audience. With this belief, my initial trepidations have been dissipated. I am confident that, with good will governing future dialogues, a new order benefiting all humanity can be constructed.

Part I

Communication
and Society

Chapter 1
The Historical Dimension

Communication maintains and animates life. It is also the motor and expression of social activity and civilization; it leads people and peoples from instinct to inspiration, through variegated processes and systems of enquiry, command and control; it creates a common pool of ideas, strengthens the feeling of togetherness through exchange of messages and translates thought into action, reflecting every emotion and need from the humblest tasks of human survival to supreme manifestations of creativity — or destruction. Communication integrates knowledge, organization and power and runs as a thread linking the earliest memory of man to his noblest aspirations through constant striving for a better life. As the world has advanced, the task of communication has become ever more complex and subtle — to contribute to the liberation of mankind from want, oppression and fear and to unite it in community and communion, solidarity and understanding. However, unless some basic structural changes are introduced, the potential benefits of technological and communication development will hardly be put at the disposal of the majority of mankind.

1. A Past Still Present

Generously endowed with diverse innate faculties for communication, mankind owes its success as a species both to its organizational capacity and to the capacity it has displayed for improving, developing and extending these natural gifts, thereby influencing its own biological evolution. One of man's earliest preoccupations has been to increase the impact, diversity and intelligibility of his messages while simultaneously developing his capacity to intercept and decipher them.

Throughout history, human beings have sought to improve their ability to receive and assimilate information about their surroundings and at the same time to increase the speed, clarity and variety of their own methods for transmission of information. This was necessary first to create awareness of dangers that might be lurking and then to share a vision of the social possibilities of meeting those dangers.

Starting with the simplest vocal and gestural signals rooted in their physical structure, human beings developed a whole range of non-verbal means for conveying messages: music and dance, drum messages, signal fires, drawings and other forms of graphic symbols, including the pictogram, followed by the ideogram, important especially because it associated the representation of an object with an abstract idea. But what rendered human communication particularly powerful, and gave Mankind its pre-eminent position in the animal world, was the development of language, important for the potential scope and depth it gave to the content of communication, as well as for the precision and detail of expression it allowed. All these means and ways of communication were simultaneously in use, indispensable to the survival of individuals who were organizing themselves into societies of different sorts and therefore required both interpersonal and intercommunal methods for exchanging information.

There is, in fact, virtually no limit to the variety and the ingenuity of the modes of communication employed by human beings. The forms and content of communication developed and varied continuously. Different languages arose because of lack of contact among peoples of distant regions, but especially because societies with distinct economic, moral and cultural traditions required specific vocabularies and linguistic structures. But at the same time, even within communities, distinctions between social groups — especially between a dominant elite and the mass of the population — came to be reflected in differences in idiom and vocabulary, in the meaning given to certain words, as well as in pronunciation. Millions of people today speak languages that are not understood by neighbouring groups, even though close social and economic links have been established and populations have intermingled. Thus, paradoxically, the very richness and diversity of languages can render communication difficult, just as its elaboration can perpetuate privilege.

Certain languages came to acquire a special status introduced by religious leaders, scholars or conquerors, sometimes becoming the basis of power and privilege. A language spoken by a small minority — such as Sanskrit in India or Latin in medieval Europe — could become the medium of scholarship, of record-keeping and of religious ceremony. A language introduced by conquerors, who became a ruling and landed elite, would be used in commerce, administration and law. During the era of imperialism, the languages of the colonial powers became the languages of administration, codified laws, higher education, science and technology in their colonies, thus holding back the development of older languages excluded from these spheres. To a varying extent, languages such as English and French still hold this position in some of the now independent nations of Asia and Africa. This can create problems within these States, as well as between neighbouring countries — notably in West Africa and the Caribbean — which have emerged from subjection to different alien powers.

Words being symbols of human experience, the perceptions underlying them have undergone change over time and in response to new situations. Moreover, all languages are in a state of incessant change — sometimes gradual, sometimes rapid. They respond to new needs arising from developments in thought and knowledge, in productive techniques, in social relationships, in political and economic structures. Words, therefore, change their meanings and acquire fresh applications; specialized technical terms pass into general usage; and new words are invented. There is, at any given time, a difference between formal language and everyday colloquial speech, and between the speech of the older and of the younger generation. The process reminds us that language is not a corpus of learning, but an instrument adapted to human purposes.

Writing, man's second major achievement, gives permanence to the spoken word. Long ago, laws and prescriptions for ceremonial rites and observances — designed to express and to ensure the continuity of a community — were durably recorded on clay tablets, stone carvings, or scrolls. The development of writing permitted the preservation of the most meaningful, symbol-laden messages, those ensuring the community's permanent existence. Books, in handwritten and copied form, have a history that goes back thirty centuries. By extension, the book became an invaluable repository of thought and knowledge in many of the great civilizations of classical times. More than two thousand years ago, Chinese emperors initiated the project of recording all the knowledge then available — chiefly scientific and historical — in a series of books; this was to be the first encyclopaedia. It should be noted, though, that the great libraries of ancient times were intended for the use of scholars, both lay and religious, and for the convenience of administrators. It was a long time before diffusion of books outside this privileged circle was attempted.

Very early on, communication as a social function was subordinated to traditions, rules, rites and taboos peculiar to a given society or sector of society; hence, the traditional means of communication and its codes came to vary in innumerable respects from one civilization or culture to another. The study of traditional societies — both those of the past and those which have endured to the present — shows that traditional communication was shaped by the different way in which cultural, legal, moral and religious institutions evolved.

For many centuries, and even millenia in some places, the vast majority of the earth's inhabitants lived completely within the context of their own small social unit — the tribe or the village — with interpersonal communication being their main form of social contact. Only the rare appearance of strangers (travellers, pilgrims, nomads, soldiers) briefly interrupted the routine of this rather hermetic existence. Arrival of news from outside was important to various aspects of public life and consequently to private life. Such interpersonal communication has been ever-present, unceasing and, especially within a small community, unrivalled in its importance. In the past, it must have served to strengthen values of comradeship and cooperation to counterbalance the fragmentation imposed by subjection to external authority. In any case, it has always had a socializing dimension, encouraging work, harmonious group living, banding together in the struggle against natural forces and in collective decision making. It remains an irreplaceable facet of human communication.

Gradually, communication became institutionalized within traditional — as it has been in later — societies. Interpersonal communication and public institutional communication, in the form of the transmission of norms and customs, existed in superimposition. As communication became thus institutionalized, there arose professional categories as guardians of collective memory and responsible for the transmission of certain types of message: griots, bards, sorcerers, tribal chiefs, travelling merchants, panchayat serpanches, local administrators, dancers, scribes and so on. The initial institutionalization of communication paralleled the development of increasingly more complex societies and promoted that development.

But in the dimension of space, communication was limited by the slowness of its pace. The human voice reached only those within its range, and the written message travelled no faster than a runner, a horse, a bird, or a sailing-ship. It is true that, despite this leisurely pace, knowledge and ideas could be deeply implanted at a great distance from their origins. The Hindu temples in the countries of south-east Asia are striking evidence of this mobility of ideas and flow of information; the teachings of Buddha, of Christ and Mohammed were effectively carried to remote places at a time when travel was slow, arduous and dangerous. No electromagnetic waves were needed to achieve changes in the thinking and the beliefs of millions of people. Nevertheless, the slow pace of change in most societies — even those of high cultural attainment — has to be connected with the slowness of communication, both within these societies and from one to another.

However, even at this early stage, the circulation of news was an aspect of every organized society, covering many spheres of social life. It is difficult to imagine that all the advances in administration, trade, education, economic and military development could have been made without the dissemination of news. But the news that arrived was limited in scope, haphazard both as to its source and its audience, and especially reinforcing tradition, hence authority, encouraging passivity and fatalism, strengthening the established order — the power of the ruler, of the gods, or not infrequently of the ruler invested with the attributes of divinity. Communication, therefore, had, within and among societies, a definite importance for the diffusion of great ideas, for the relationship between the authorities and the majority of inhabitants, as well as for the conservation and stabilization of societies.

This brief glance back at the past is not a gratuitous exercise. It is designed to show that the ills as well as the benefits of modern communication are rooted in the distant past, but a past that is still with us today, both in means of communication still used in different parts of the world, and in a social legacy that is a result of and a cause of the evolution of communication. Traditional forms of communication may not only still be useful in themselves in certain conditions, but may also have a corrective influence on the distortions of modern communication in general. A more generous appreciation of the ways in which communication developed, of the forms it took in the past, its goals as well as its means, could hold promise for the future. It is also possible, even at this early stage of our survey, to identify the issues that will be recurrent themes in our Report. These are (a) the power possessed by those who control and direct communication; (b) its influence on social assumptions and therefore on social action; (c) the inequalities between various groups or classes within each society; (d) the domination that has been conferred by colonial rule, or at least by the advantages derived from a faster and earlier process of development. But as we confront these problems, we can restate them in a more positive and hopeful direction. It is possible to think of (a) the diffusion of power through broader access to and participation in the communication process; (b) the benefits of communication used as an educational and socializing force; (c) the reduction of inequalities through democratization; (d) the abolition of the vestiges of domination as full national liberation becomes a reality.

2. The Roots of the Present

The modern age of communications is generally considered to date from the invention of printing. While this assumption is legitimate, two reservations must be made. First, it is important to note that the technique of multiple reproduction by the printing of images and writings initially engraved on stone or wood first appears almost twenty-five centuries back. Secondly, the impact of this invention was at first more spectacular in promoting the spread and proliferation of knowledge and ideas (through books) than in developing mass information as this came to be understood later.

In such civilizations as the Chinese, the Indian, the Egyptian, or the Greco-Roman, the invaluable repository of thought and knowledge was the book. It provided a means of collating a considerable store of information in a small space and in durable form. The first important advance in book production came with the invention of paper, a material which superseded the older papyrus or parchment. Paper came into use in China in the first century A.D., in the Arab world in the eighth century, and in Europe in the fourteenth century. Paper books consisted of bound pages instead of scrolls, which made it easier to use them as works of reference. The technique of reproduction by images and writings engraved on stone or wood dates from about 500 B.C. The next great step forward was the invention of printing, a technique evolved in China in the ninth century and then in Europe in the fifteenth. It now became possible to produce numerous copies of the same book without resorting to the laborious process of hand-copying. Certain influential books gradually became the shared intellectual equipment of many above a certain level of education; and their availability was a stimulus to literacy, which in some countries extended by the sixteenth century to fairly wide sections of at least the urban population.

These changes did not come about without a rearguard action by the guardians of religious or political doctrines. Freedom of thought and freedom of expression have always been contested ground between public and private authorities and the independent spirit. Debates on the possible boundaries of freedom in the India of Asoka are known to have taken place; dissident Hebrew sects took refuge in caves and hid their scrolls; in Athens, Socrates paid with his life for "corrupting the young". With the advent of printing and the prospect that "dangerous thoughts" might be circulated far beyond the immediate influence of their originators, the issue was sharpened. The technological advance as such was often seen as a threat; printing-presses were frequently forbidden and generally permitted only under licence, sometimes actually destroyed. Innovatory thinking in philosophy or the natural sciences was stigmatized as impiety or heresy. Many men who are now revered as pioneering intellects, were forbidden to publish, dismissed from universities, ordered to renounce their ideas under threat of dire penalties, imprisoned, or even put to death. The obscurantism of medieval Europe had long erected effective barriers against intellectual discoveries first made in the Arab or Persian world. When the age of printing and the widespread diffusion of books arrived, no edicts from authority could stem the tide, and the way was open for the transformations which led to the Renaissance and the Reformation.

Books were followed in the seventeenth century by topical pamphlets, and then by newspapers. Some of the early newspapers were founded to give information about trade, commodities, shipping movements and the like; they performed a service rendered necessary by the nascent capitalist system. Others offered disclosures, scandals, and satirical comment on the social and political scene. Others, again, set out to mobilize opinion in support of a popular or democratic cause. Thus, we can trace the origins of types of journalism that we recognise today: the business press, the sensational press, the opinion press, and the campaigning or crusading press. But when there was a state of political conflict — and, expecially, a challenge to established order — the press often assumed the role of spokesman for a popular cause. Tom Paine's *Common Sense,* for example, gave moral sustenance to the revolt of the American colonies against British rule. In Latin America, similarly, the content and responsibility of a part of the press were closely connected with the struggle against Spanish domination which was to lead to independence. This historical link can still be perceived today both in the content of reporting and in the way in which newspapermen conceive their social and political responsibilities in this region of the world.

The early newspapers had a distinctively personal tone; many links existed between readers and the writers, editors and publishers (who might well be the same individual). A publication written by one author from beginning to end and openly attributed to him could exert an extraordinary influence. Whether well-informed newsmongers or gossip writers, the legislators and architects of tomorrow's society, the virulent lampooners of the morals of the age and the vices of the powerful, or the enemies of superstition and the clergy, such journalists were for the most part courageously and sincerely devoted to the public good. They were certainly disrespectful of authority, and their activities were an irritant — or even a threat — to power. Governments hit back with seizures, proscriptions, prosecutions under restrictive laws, and sometimes the imprisonment of editors.

In Britain, in the United States, and in revolutionary France, the battle for the freedom of the press had in principle been won by the end of the eighteenth century, though attempts to contain and limit it continued long afterwards, as they continue even to this day. It is worth taking a closer look at the historical circumstances in which this concept of press freedom emerged. In defiance of authority, which claimed the right to control, by prior censorship or otherwise, the chief medium for the spreading of ideas — the printing-press — its opponents demanded free use of the printing-press and free dissemination of its products. Thus, from the very outset, the political dimension of communication became prominent, the aim being to wrest from the established powers one of their means of action. To win possession of the crucial technique was to deprive authority of its monopoly of influence.

The essential demand was for the expression and dissemination of "thoughts and opinions", to cite the language of the Declaration of the Rights of Man proclaimed in France in 1789. The freedom in question was essentially freedom for ideas, for those who create and propagate them. Hence it was an elitist form of freedom, permitting "top-down" communication from political and intellectual leaders to the public, but one which nevertheless served the large numbers of those with access to printed materials. By offering to each reader an ideological spectrum, it made individual choice and critical discernment possible. Nor was this freedom, at this early period, reserved to the well-to-do. The artisanal nature of printing equipment placed it within the reach even of men who were far from wealthy, as is witnessed by the proliferation of handbills, pamphlets and manifestos published in those days. Accordingly, at that stage in the development of technology, the fight for freedom of the press was predominantly a battle against authoritarian rulers fully aware of the dangers to which they were exposed by the free dissemination of unorthodox opinions and ideas. In the nineteenth century and the early years of the twentieth, there was still no freedom of the press in nations under autocratic rule, such as Czarist Russia. Nor was there any real press freedom in the vast regions of Asia and Africa which had been reduced to a colonial status. The newspapers that were started in the subject countries were owned and edited by Europeans and existed to serve the information needs and reflect the outlook of the ruling community. Gradually, newspapers owned by Asians and Africans appeared, making a contribution to the struggle for democratic rights and national liberation. They encountered all kinds of repressive measures, and were often seized or banned in periods of unrest. Moreover, colonial rule exerted a strong influence over structures of communication, patterned on those of European nations. Such influences continued even when political independence was secured, or when another metropolitan power, wielding an increasing economic and cultural influence obtained, to a greater or lesser extent, control of the avenues of communication. These patterns, where they still exist, are at the root of many of today's problems.

Yet, despite all the handicaps, journals of nationalist, radical or revolutionary opinion made their impact, acting as spokesman for socialist movements in the capitalist world, for democratic opposition to autocracies, and for the growing revolt against colonialism. Cavour's Il *Risorgimento,* Lenin's *Iskra,* Gandhi's *Harijan,* among many others spearheaded a revolution of ideas, and helped to bring down established power structures by awakening and mobilizing the hitherto passive millions. Journalism, in these conditions, became more of a mission, not just a profession. Not only were these papers passed from hand to hand, but they were also read aloud by the literate to the illiterate, so that their influence far exceeded their nominal circulation.

In the wealthier nations, newspapers were now produced in such large numbers as to bring about the emergence of what is called the mass-circulation press. Advances in education had made literacy progress and more and more people were able to buy newspapers, both because wages had risen and because the newspapers were cheaper. Other factors favouring the mass press included the adoption of printing techniques which introduced "long runs"; circulation by railway; the financial support provided by advertising; and, not least, the increased flow of up-to-date news transmitted by telegraph.

A good deal of the news was provided by news agencies, which developed early in the nineteenth century and extended their operations on an international scale. The pioneering efforts of these news agencies simultaneously contributed to and followed the emergence of the mass daily press. They had their own marked effects on the opening up of further trade and commerce, and on making the world a much smaller place. At the same time, since this was the heyday of colonialism, they promoted the interests of the colonial powers, helped to sustain the existing political and economic order and to expand the commercial and political interests of the metropolitan powers.

Where the mass press was developing, its influence was intermingled with changing social processes and structures which were bringing to an end the long ages in which the majority of the population was excluded by sheer ignorance from political life. Working-class people, in the densely packed industrial towns and even in villages, became better informed than ever before and could form their opinions on issues of controversy. Public opinion, as we speak of it today, became a growing reality. The press — the Fourth Estate, as it came to be called — established itself as an integral part of the modern constitutional state, in which governments normally changed as a result of elections and not simply through manoeuvres within an elite or at the whim of a monarch. Also, newspapers were now strong enough to defy pressure from the authorities; the idea that they had a right, and indeed a duty, to maintain their independence became accepted doctrine.[1] However, this independence from governmental interference, which established the press as a power in itself, was not always accompanied by equal independence from the private interests that controlled it.

But the new situation also saw the emergence of a gulf between, on the one hand, "serious" or "quality" newspapers read mainly by well-educated people and exerting an influence out of proportion to their circulation, and on the other hand, "popular"

---

(1) This doctrine was formulated by John Delane, editor of *The Times,* in 1852: "We cannot admit that a newspaper's purpose is to share the labours of statesmanship or that it is bound by the same limitations, the same duties and the same liabilities as the Ministers of the Crown. The purpose and duties of the two powers are constantly separate, generally independent, sometimes diametrically opposite. The dignity and freedom of the press are trammelled from the moment that it accepts an ancillary position. To perform its duties with entire independence, and consequently to the utmost public advantage, the press can enter into no close or binding alliances with the statesmen of the day".

papers which gave space predominantly to crimes, scandals and sensational events, at the expense of political or social developments. Proprietors, for the most part, were in the business to win readers and to make money, and often had a low estimate of the interests and the intelligence of their customers.

In countries where the socialist politico-economic system was established in the 20th century, press ownership, character and objectives changed accordingly, to a varying degree. That led not only to extending readership to the masses of the population, but also to the development of a mass press without commercial motives; it also led to a press one of whose primary aims became to educate and mobilize opinion, to rally support for governmental and political objectives formulated by the ruling powers, rather than to extension of varied information, diffusion of diverging viewpoints and promotion of critical independent readership.

While the mass-circulation press was still rising towards its apogee, another important feature of the period was the emergence and growth of communication media developing from applications of electricity — the telegraph, telephone, radio and cinema. More rapidly than the press, and benefiting from the existence and experience of its established infrastructures, the new technologies entered directly into the industrialized era of mass communication and mass consumption. The growth of these technologies has coincided with broader political and economic changes, both within many countries and on a world scale.

In this short historical survey, we have seen the extension of written communication from minorities to majorities; we have seen the press expanding from its elitist origins to a democratic style, at least in range and appeal; and we have also seen, in the countries where the mass press originated, the increasing predominance of a commercial structure and a commercial outlook. However, the pace of all these changes led to harmful disparities both between countries and within them, as well as towards diversity, pluralism and a great variety of communication patterns, both at various development levels and inside countries belonging to different socio-political systems. We may also conclude that such an evolution — in fact the roots of the present — merits close study and reflexion, as a stimulus for action at national and international levels.

3. The Future in the Making

The modern age has seen an accelerating development of new resources, techniques and technological devices in communication, particularly for transmitting and receiving signals and messages. One discovery followed another with increasing speed. The phonograph was invented by Edison early in the second part of last century. Telegraphy was invented around 1840 by Sir Charles Wheatstone and Samuel Morse. The first public telegraphic message was transmitted in 1844; in 1876 Bell sent the first telephone message by wire. Around 1895, Marconi and Popoff succeeded independently of one another in transmitting and receiving wireless messages. In 1906, Fessender transmitted the human voice by radio. In 1839 Daguerre devised a practical method of photography. The first film was screened in 1894. Already in 1904, the first photographs were transmitted by phototelegraphic apparatus (Belin system), while the first picture was televised in 1923. The first radio broadcasting networks were installed in the 1920s, television broadcasting began in the 1930s, and regular transmission of colour television began in 1954. Rapid intercontinental communication was initiated with the under-water telegraph cable between America and Europe laid in 1857. While the first transatlantic telephone cable entered into service only in 1956, intercontinental radio telephone and telegraph systems were already functioning regularly by 1920; teleprinting began to be operational at the start of the 1930s. Finally, Early Bird, the first commercial communication satellite, was launched in 1962.

The invention of radio in the first decade of the twentieth century produced a means of long-distance communication that did not depend — like the press — on printing and surface transport, and that could even reach its audience without the requirement of literacy. National leaders, especially in times of crisis, soon discovered the advantages of speaking directly to the population instead of waiting for their utterances to be reported in the newspapers. Radio in the early days was principally a medium of entertainment; especially, it created a vast new public for music and drama. But news-reporting by radio had begun to be important by the 1930s, bringing into existence a new branch of the journalistic profession.

Television — though delayed by the second world war — was a feature of life in developed countries by the late 1940s or early 1950s. Like radio, it secured and held its audience largely by offering entertainment in a cheap and convenient form. However, television newscasts make a powerful impression by enabling viewers to see events as they actually occur; while documentary programmes (whether made as films or on videotape) shape the popular perception of realities, including the realities of distant countries. Improvements in definition, the advent of colour pictures and the invention of the video cassette in the last two decades have increased the vividness of the perception and the range of television use.

The last century and a half thus brought tremendous change in technological facilities for communication. The recent decade and a half was particularly inventive, productive and imaginative. Two big international satellite systems, Intelsat and Intersputnik, started respectively in 1965 and 1971. Space technology, both manned and un-manned space vehicles which made the moon landing possible in 1969, and more recently the vehicles landing on Venus and Mars, opened new possibilities for communication purposes. The world's first domestic synchronous orbit satellite system for telecommunication purposes and for the distribution and reception of television programmes, through low-cost earth stations and low-powered transmitters was inaugurated in 1973 in Canada. The following year the USA was launching the WESTAR I which is capable of relaying 8 million words per second and has capacity for voice, video, facsimile and data transmission. In 1977 the facility was created for a different kind of satellite network that would, unlike existing systems, carry voice, facsimile and data directly to the end user, thus completely bypassing common carrier telephone lines. Quite distinct transmission techniques have been invented: a gallium arsenide laser which may enable numerous television programmes to be transmitted along a fibre no thicker than a human hair was tested in 1970; in 1976 optical fibre cables for telephone traffic and for television signals were given field trials; at the same time a fibre optic interactive computer-controlled network was designed in Japan to carry two-way video information to and from households. In another field, videocassettes have been invented in 1969, the audio-visual cassette became a marketable reality in 1971, and a first videodisc system became available to consumers in 1979. The manufacturing of machines for facsimile transmission of small electronic calculators, and particularly of a variety of micro-processors represented during the last ten years a major input to data collection, storage, retrieval and diffusion.

The amount of information available to those with access to present-day technologies has been immensely increased by developments in the new science of informatics. Computers and data-banks can be used to collate, store and transmit millions of items of information. The invention of the silicon chip has reduced the space required to minute proportions. Binary codes of transmission have created a new language, virtually eliminating delays. These developments have multiplied, to a degree that would have been unthinkable in the past, the resources not only of information and entertainment but also of science, medicine, all branches of scholarship and professional life, and social organization in general.

These new technologies, use of which is at present mainly concentrated in a few industrialized countries, open paths for a new era in communication. Distance has ceased to be an obstacle, and the possibility exists — if there were a collective will — of a universal communication system linking any point on the planet with any other. The equipment, cumbersome and costly in its early days, has become rapidly cheaper and is by its nature extremely flexible. Electronic communications, for a long time restricted to communication between individuals, are increasingly available for use in collective communication. Conversely, it is feasible to envisage, instead of global systems, a web of communication networks, integrating autonomous or semi-autonomous, decentralized units. The content of messages could be diversified, localized and individualized to a large extent. New techniques exist which make it possible to multiply information centres and to foster exchanges between individuals. Tele-processing, or telematics, and the establishment of links and relays between two or more satellites, are likely to open up almost limitless possibilities of systematic integration. However, under present social structures, the poor and marginal groups — which in many societies account for a large percentage of the population — will have no contact with this "new era" for a long time to come. Their main problems are more to satisfy their basic needs and improve living conditions, rather than to solve issues related to the global communication system.

The importance and originality of this process lies not only in transmission facilities and the size of coverage, but chiefly in the fundamental transformation of the nature of the language of human communication. As man moved from food gathering and hunting to agriculture, he simultaneously evolved from a communication system directly phased with nature to an analogical system. In the industrial age, he learned to handle alphanumerical information and communication systems. He has now entered a quite new era, increasingly dominated by informatics, with the consequent need to convert rapidly from present-day analogical techniques to various forms of binary language. This does not mean that analogical languages are doomed to disappear as such, any more than men have lost the capacity for natural communication. Communication is, by and large, a cumulative faculty, each new language adding itself to — without obliterating — preceding languages.

Many changes, both at national and international levels, will have to be made before the majority of developing countries are able to take advantage of all these technological advances which, for them, remain largely theoretical. In fact, they could, under certain conditions, or, rather, if certain conditions are created, yield major benefits to men and women and to communities everywhere, and to developing as well as developed nations. However, for the time being, they are at the disposal of only a few countries and of a few people within them. The few countries in which these discoveries originated still enjoy a massive advantage over other countries, where the development is still proceeding in tortuous ways, hampered by a poverty which enforces a lack of the necessary infrastructure. Indeed, since information and communication may today become — as never before — the sources of the creation of wealth, the system responsible for the existing communication gaps and the inequality in this sphere threaten to widen the gulf between the rich and the poor.

Developments in communication take place, not only because of technological discoveries, but also because there is a consciousness of opportunities and needs — social, political, economic, cultural or spiritual. The gap is growing between minorities who control communication and the public which is exposed to its impact. At the same time, society and the State become increasingly intermeshed, and both government agencies and the media encroach on what had been the domain of private life. Needs for contact and for the exchange of knowledge and ideas, within nations and between nations, become ever more imperative; yet dangers are seen in the power possessed by those with great technical resources to impose their ideas on others. In the developing nations, communication has been a weapon in the struggle for independence, and then in efforts to transform social structures and solve economic problems. Many people, looking towards cultural as well as political independence, have become dissatisfied with the manner in which communication systems work. They want greater access to the media, both individual and collective. This aspiration is often thwarted by vested interests and by various forms of oppression. This complex situation has in many places generated a mood of rejection and criticism — rejection of the mass media by individuals, discontent with the functioning of information systems at community and national levels, and protests against external domination.

In the sphere of communication, the problem of the present and the near future is to open up the opportunities which exist in principle but are still denied to the majority of the world's population. The productive sectors of society will increasingly depend on the intelligently planned organization of labour, on understanding and experience, and on the use of information where and when it is needed. While shortages of food, energy and many materials present major anxieties, the resources of communication are constantly growing; the scarcity of all previous history has been turned into abundance. The world of the 1980s and beyond will be a world of opportunity. Yet the life of many millions of people, especially in developing countries, is still one of hard and wasteful toil and of rudimentary subsistence — precisely as though these immense resources did not exist. Whether the resources of communication will indeed be mobilized for human benefit depends on decisions now due to be taken. It depends, also, on who will take these decisions, from what motives, and in whose interests. Each society will have to make its own choices and find ways of overcoming the material, social and political constraints that impede progress. But the basic decisions in order to forge a better future for men and women in communities everywhere, in developing as well as in developed nations, do not lie principally in the field of technological development: they lie essentially in the answers each society gives to the conceptual and political foundations of development.

Chapter 2

The Contemporary Dimension

1. The Functions of Communication

If communication is considered in its broadest sense, not only as the exchange of news and messages but as an individual and collective activity embracing all transmission and sharing of ideas, facts and data, its main functions in any social system may be identified as the following:

—Information: the collection, storage, processing and dissemination of news, data, pictures, facts and messages, opinions and comments required in order to understand and react knowledgeably to personal, environmental, national and international conditions, as well as to be in a position to take appropriate decisions.

—Socialization: the provision of a common fund of knowledge which enables people to operate as effective members of the society in which they live and which fosters social cohesion and awareness thereby permitting active involvement in public life.

—Motivation: the promotion of the immediate and ultimate aims of each society, and the stimulation of personal choices, and aspirations; the fostering of individual or community activities, geared to the pursuit of agreed aims.

—Debate and discussion: the provision and exchange of facts needed to facilitate agreement or to clarify differing viewpoints on public issues; the supply of relevant evidence needed to foster greater popular interest and involvement in all local, national and international matters of common concern.

—Education: the transmission of knowledge so as to foster intellectual development, the formation of character and the acquisition of skills and capacities at all stages of life.

—Cultural promotion: the dissemination of cultural and artistic products for the purpose of preserving the heritage of the past; the development of culture by widening the individual's horizons, awakening his imagination and stimulating his aesthetic needs and creativity.

—Entertainment: the diffusion, through signs, symbols, sounds and images, of drama, dance, art, literature, music, comedy, sports, games, etc. for personal and collective recreation and enjoyment.

—Integration: the provision to all persons, groups and nations of access to the variety of messages which they need in order to know and understand each other and to appreciate others' living conditions, viewpoints and aspirations.

Besides these functions which are seen essentially from the individuals's standpoint, emphasis should also be laid on a new phenomenon, or at least one whose importance is rapidly increasing: communication has become a vital need for collective entities and communities. Societies as a whole cannot survive today if they are not properly informed about political affairs, international and local events, or weather conditions, etc. Governments need varied information from all corners of their respective countries as well as from every quarter of the earth, concerning trends in population growth, harvest results, water supplies, etc., if they are to be able to plan dynamically for the future. Without sufficient data on world commodity and money markets, public authorities are handicapped in their international activities and negotiations. Industrial enterprises also need rapid information from many sources in order to increase their productivity and to modernize their production processes; banks depend more and more on world networks for data on currency fluctuations, etc. The armed services, political parties, airline companies, universities, research institutes and all kinds of other bodies could not function today without daily, efficient information exchanges. However, in many cases the collective information and data systems do not correspond to the needs of the public authorities or private bodies. Apart from main government services, and the biggest enterprises and banks, which are usually well-informed, many local bodies, factories, firms and agencies lack ready access to organized information. So, in many instances, the emphasis is still on information systems whose purpose it is to satisfy individual communication needs. It is vitally important to correct this situation which is liable to affect adversely the development prospects of millions of people, especially in developing countries.

This is particularly so as communication functions are linked to all people's needs, both material and non-material. Man does not live by bread alone; the need for communication is evidence of an inner urge toward a life enriched by cooperation with others. People want to add aspirations toward human growth to the satisfaction of material needs. Self-reliance, cultural identity, freedom, independence, respect for human dignity, mutual aid, participation in the reshaping of the environment — these are some of the non-material aspirations which all seek through communication. But higher productivity, better crops, enhanced efficiency and competition, improved health, appropriate marketing conditions, proper use of irrigation facilities are also objectives — among many others — which cannot be achieved without adequate communication and the provision of needed data.

It must also be recognized that each of these functions may, depending on environmental conditions, display different and even contradictory characteristics. Information is easily corrupted into the dissemination of half-truths and even falsehoods; persuasion into manipulation and propaganda. Similarly, institutionalized communication may serve to inform, to control, or to manipulate citizens. While the content often serves to sustain personal identity, it may lead to the standardizing of attitudes and aspirations. Information systems which use a variety of sources and messages help to foster open-mindedness (albeit with the attendant risk of alienation in extreme cases), while systems ignoring this need may lead to a taming of the mind, or indoctrination. The simple truth that the functions of communication are essentially relative and related to varied needs of different communities and countries is often overlooked or underestimated, yet without recognition of it there can be no realistic approach to communication problems in a divergent, divided but interdependent world. Hence, communication effects vary according to the nature of each society. There is, indeed, no such thing as contemporary society, but only contemporary societies.

Another element involved in the thinking about the functions of communication is the debate concerning the respective significance of content, context, and media. Some theorists maintain that the means of communication, and in particular the mass media, exert more influence than the content; in fact, that the medium is the message. Others regard content as paramount, conceding to the medium only a marginal influence on its effect. Others, again, see the social context in which the message is transmitted as the determining factor. This approach, more rounded and more sociological, appears to be the most fruitful in answering questions about the role of communication.

Although the first impression may be that such issues are principally the concern of theoreticians and researchers, they do merit consideration by a wider cross-section of the community — politicians, decision-makers, planners, professionals and the public itself — who should be actively involved in the search for solutions. Indeed, such a trend is beginning to emerge. Today's thinking is centred less on the media, the modernization of technologies and the expansion of infrastructures and more on social, political and cultural environment as well as on the message itself — its nature, role and content, whether it is hidden or evident, implicit or explicit.

This is the direction in which reflection and discussion might best be pursued, and it is the purpose of this Report to encourage all those concerned with the development of human communication to direct their efforts along these lines.

2. A Social Need

In the past the communication system has often been seen as an isolated phenomenon within society, related essentially to technology, divorced more or less from other aspects of society. Its place in the political system, its convergence with social structures and its dependence upon cultural life were seldom given adequate thought. Society might thus be led into wrong choices or mistaken priorities, selecting inappropriate infrastructures or devoting efforts to technical innovations for which there was no real need. Today, it is much more widely recognized as a social process to be studied from every angle, not in isolation but in an extremely broad social context. In the modern world, awareness of these interlinks has become more widespread than ever before.

As a corollary, communication has frequently been seen as a force invested with absolute and omnipresent powers. Such over-simplification has been made obsolete by modern research. Communication's ability to activate, socialize, homogenize and even adapt people to their own culture has always been over-estimated, while at the same time the standardizing and distorting consequences of audio-visual media have been under-valued. Other observers were convinced that the media had such a powerful socializing effect that they could tell their audiences how to think and behave. No doubt, the mass media — press, radio and television — do have a capacity not only to reflect but also to shape opinion, and to play a part in forming attitudes. But many observers think that the media generate an illusory perception of the real world, instead of offering a broader range of knowledge and a choice of viewpoints. Up to a certain point, deliberately or otherwise, they can give rise to cultural alienation and social uniformity; no part of the world is immune to these risks. Especially, this pressure toward uniformity has become more intense since the media have taken on an industrialised character. Efforts to reach wider markets and give the public what it wants, or is believed to want, tend often, if not invariably, to lower the quality of what is purveyed. The growing dependence on advertising, whether the media are publicly or privately owned, tends to produce a commercial mentality in which consumption becomes an end in itself. Instead of fostering a culture based on the plurality of views and the increasing spread of knowledge, many say that the media generate a mythical vision of the world. In some cases, the uniformity and standardization of the messages reflect the constraints of the laws of the market. Similar effects happen where the power to inform lies in the hands of a minority possessing both the data and the sources of information and who in addition control the instruments of communication. In other words, political or bureaucratic measures may lead to intellectual sterility. Where the flow is predominantly from the top downwards, the media are likely to promote the acceptance of approved ideas at the expense of independent thought and critical judgement. Operating in a one-way direction, the media sometimes succeed in transmitting the values and norms fostered by the dominant group to a public which, in a large measure, fails to find in them any reflection of its own vital concerns and aspirations. It is equally true that the media, particularly television, have on occasion given the public a vivid account of alternative lifestyles and aspirations, though not in every case with deliberate intent. The effect has been to legitimize dissent, counter-cultural values and various forms of protest.

This is, nevertheless, somewhat of a black-and-white picture, greatly modified by recent studies, which point out that many factors and many cross-currents are at work, reacting upon one another. It is becoming increasingly clear that reference to the misdeeds or distortions of communication means in effect reference to the contradictions inherent in contemporary societies. The process of socialization has many effects — real or apparent, deep or shallow, lasting or ephemeral — which can be ascribed to various influences, of which communication is only one. To take the media at their face value is to accept an inaccurate picture of what is really going on. One needs to ask exactly how communication, and mass communication in particular, functions as an agent of social change — and within what limitations. It seems exaggerated to exalt the media as the begetter of all beneficent change, or yet as the guardian of all that should be cherished; it seems overstated on the other hand to echo the outcries of those who accuse the media of causing the decay of the quality of life, the extinction of local traditions, and the reduction of culture to an elementary level. Despite the considerable influence of communication, it would be wrong to attribute to it more virtues, more faults, or greater powers than it truly possesses.

Thus to draw the conclusion that communication is a good in itself or an evil in itself is apparently a mistake. The structures of communication are no more neutral than the messages transmitted by the media. Deciding on the infrastructures and technologies to be used is as much based on value judgements as the selection of news, data and programme content. Another illusion is to invest the messages disseminated with an absolute objectivity: most of the time the messages are qualified or result from individual judgements which are implicit in the terms used to convey them. The picture of reality as seen by those who put their sole or even primary trust in the media is inaccurate. It must also be remembered that communication is powerful but not all-powerful: it cannot transform the tenor of interpersonal relationships nor the substance of social life. Communication is most effective when its impact is strengthened by other social factors and the messages conveyed are already reflected in public opinion or in emerging interests. As Aesop said of the tongue, all facility in communication can be used for better or for worse. It is the responsibility of the communication policy-makers and professionals to see that such risks are limited and distortions corrected. But in all societies there are other forces to be reckoned with that cannot be reduced to a state of passivity.

Furthermore, many societies contain forces which have a responsibility to guard against the risks and to correct the distortions. Many governments adopt policies designed to protect the nation's cultural identity. The dangers of political manipulation meet resistance from grass-roots action, from "alternative" channels of communication, or simply from the turning of deaf ears. The resources of resistance and opposition are much wider than the official systems of communication. This is not to deny that a significant role is played by the controllers of communication policy and by professionals employed in the system. However, the last word belongs to social forces once they are awakened and mobilised.

It is along these lines that our thinking is taking us. From the outset, two main conclusions merit a mention. On the one hand, the fact that diversity and pluralism are values to be fostered, not discouraged. Both at the regional and world levels, there are various social models and socio-economic systems. Both within nations and among them, different levels of development and different roads toward development exist, just as there are differences in the conception and use made of communication resources. On the other hand, the success of measures to improve communication, in both form and content, is inextricably linked with steps to make society itself less oppressive and unequal, more just and democratic. This fact should be highlighted rather than concealed.

3. A Political Instrument

Communication, taken as a whole, is incomprehensible without reference to its political dimension, its problems, and cannot be resolved without taking into account political relationships. Politics, to use the word in the "elevated" sense, has an indissoluble relationship with communication.

Two distinct, though related, questions, demand consideration. How much, and in what ways, does politics influence communication? And then how much, and in what ways, can communication influence politics? The crucial relationships are those between communication and power, and between communication and freedom. Various conceptions of what these relationships should be are upheld in different parts of the world, responding to various traditions, resources, social systems and development needs. There may nevertheless be some prospect of broad general agreement, especially if more realism and less rhetoric, more flexibility and less bias are introduced into the argument — which has too often been inward-looking and intolerant.

The modes of exercising freedom are, and must inevitably be, as varied as national legal systems or constitutions. It is widely recognised that freedom must be reconciled with an obligation to obey the law and must not be exploited to injure the freedom of others; also that the exercise of freedom has a counterpart which is the need to exercise it with responsibility, which in the field of communication means primarily a concern for truth and the legitimate use of the power it conveys. We need to ask, moreover, on what grounds a claim for freedom is being made. The freedom of a citizen or social groups to have access to communication, both as recipients and contributors, cannot be compared to the freedom of an investor to derive profit from the media. One protects a fundamental human right, the other permits the commercialization of a social need. Yet when all these reservations are made, the principle of freedom of expression is one that admits of no exceptions, and that is applicable to people all over the world by virtue of their human dignity.[1] This

_____

(1) The UN Declaration of Human Rights uses repeatedly, and specifically in connection with freedom of expression, the phrase: "Everyone has right . . ." The Unesco Declaration of 1978

freedom is one of democracy's most precious acquisitions, frequently secured through arduous struggles with political and economic powers and authorities and at the cost of heavy sacrifice, even of life itself, and is at the same time a vital safeguard of democracy. The presence or absence of freedom of expression is one of the most reliable indications of freedom in all its aspects in any nation. Today, in many countries throughout the world, freedom is still trampled upon and violated by bureaucratic or commercial censorship, by the intimidation and punishment of its devotees, and by the enforcement of uniformity. The fact that there is said to be freedom of expression in a country does not guarantee its existence in practice. The simultaneous existence of other freedoms (freedom of association, freedom to assemble and to demonstrate for redress of grievances, freedom to join trade unions) are all essential components of man's right to communicate. Any obstacle to these freedoms results in suppression of freedom of expression.

Even where freedom is not openly attacked by authority, it may be limited by self-censorship on the part of communicators themselves. Journalists may fail to publish facts which have come into their possession for several reasons: sheer timidity, an excessive respect for the power structure or in some instances lest they give offence to officialdom and thus risk losing access to their sources of information. Self-censorship, like censorship itself, if adopted as a regular practice, grows more and more restrictive. Nevertheless, there is room for debate on this delicate issue of self-censorship, or restraint as it might more favourably be called.[1][2]

In any case, the concept of freedom is central to all political debate in the modern

---

speaks of "the exercise of freedom of opinion, expression and information, recognised as an integral part of human rights and fundamental freedoms."

(1) Katherine Graham, Proprietor of the *Washington Post,* has written: "If any limits on the disclosure of information are to be imposed, it is for the law-makers to say so and not for us. Journalists are not elected by the people; their only job in the public arena is to tell what is happening. Of course, this doctrine is based on a conviction that, at the end of the day, and in any society, ignorance of facts is *always* harmful." (*L'Express*)

(2) In a recent text, **Mr. Hubert Beuve-Méry,** one of our Commission's members, posed the same problem in the following terms and dealt with it in a similar manner: ". . . Can reporters, journalists in the widest understanding of their profession and of the means available to them, feel justified, whatever they do, by virtue of the principle: 'The law, the whole law, but nothing but the law'? Or must they, on the contrary, themselves extend the scope of their responsibilities and consider the possible or probable consequences of publishing information which they nevertheless know to be true? . . . Pending a legal solution (and even after one is found, for the law could do no more than assert a principle, without letting itself be swamped by the complexity of the facts), it must indeed be recognized that the journalist then ceases to be only a reporter for whom 'all is grist to the mill' and becomes in good faith a judge of what is expedient, at least in the here and now, for it is generally only a matter of delaying publication, with all the difficulties which this entails . . . Information is not, and cannot be, entirely neutral. Moreover, we must be careful not to fall out of the frying pan into the fire! For it would then be all too easy to shun responsibilities on so-called moral grounds. It must indeed be admitted that this approach to the debate is fraught with consequences. Either the journalist is, as many people believe, but a man like other men, whose business is purely and simply to publish what he knows, or else the exercise of this profession entails both obligations and privileges which do not, to be sure, pertain to a public *service*— which would make him the equivalent of a public servant — but to what might be termed, and the distinction is primordial, the public interest. In this respect, I fully concur with the rules laid down, as early as 1946, by the Japanese Association of Newspaper Publishers.

This *interest* derives, as the British Royal Commission of Inquiry would seem to admit, from the public's right to be informed, this right establishing, by reference to human rights, the legitimacy and necessity of the profession . . ." (CIC Document No. 90ter *Freedom and Responsibility of Journalists*) world, and is involved in innumerable controversies concerning policies and decisions. It has won so much respect — even if, in some cases, this is only the tribute paid by vice to virtue — that every kind of political system claims to incarnate it, or at least to move towards it. True, the word "freedom" (along with other words such as "democracy", "socialism" and "peace") is interpreted in diverse ways. While it seems, thus, hardly possible to define in a universally acceptable way, freedom in general, or even freedom of expression, it is not without interest to have a look into the interpretations of freedom that have taken concrete shape in recent history.

The emphasis in the pioneering period was placed on freedom for "thoughts and opinions". With the development of the press on a more stable basis and on a larger scale, the stress shifted to the diffusion of information — of facts, and of news about current events. Freedom of information was, in the first place, the citizen's right to information — the right to be kept informed of whatever might affect his daily life, help him to make decisions, and contribute to his thinking. The scope of this right to information broadened as new techniques gave improved access to information on a nation-wide and then a world-wide scale. The other aspect of this freedom was the journalist's freedom to acquire knowledge in the shape of facts and documents, clearing away the secrecy in which the conduct of political affairs had been shrouded, and the freedom to publish the information that he obtained.

But developed technology also transformed the setting within which the basic principles could be implemented, and introduced new dangers for freedom. The hallmark of each new invention was that it required an investment on a scale feasible only for the possessors of considerable capital, whether from private or public funds. In most countries, this privileged access to the increasingly costly printing-presses, and especially to the new media of radio and television, meant that people of limited wealth could compete, at best, on disadvantageous terms. In theory everyone enjoyed the right to freedom of expression, but not everyone could exercise it equally. Meanwhile, the State, with public funds at its disposal, took cognisance of new opportunities offered by the media to influence the thinking of the citizen, and replaced the old strategy of clamping down on freedom of expression by a more active policy (already initiated by some autocratic monarchs by such means as they had at their disposal) of harnessing the new techniques to its own ends. Nor is it only at the national level that these inequalities make their impact; on an international scale, they have created the present imbalance in the sphere of communication between rich and poor countries.

Thus the problems of communication — successively presented as freedom of the press, freedom of information, and right to information — have become more and more political, economic and social in character. And they have been marked by a basic contradiction. In every nation throughout the world, literacy campaigns, consciousness-raising, and the achievement of national independence have greatly increased the number of individuals who now seek information and who are even potential message-transmitters. However, parallel to this growth, there has been a movement of concentration, related to the financial requisites of technical progress. As a result of this concentration, the number of message-transmitters, at least relatively speaking, has been reduced. At the same time, the strength of the surviving transmitters has been reinforced.

One thing is certain: communication has taken on such overwhelming importance that even in societies with privately owned media systems, the State imposes some degree of regulation. It can intervene in all kinds of ways, ranging from total political control to measures for promotion of pluralism. Some governments find it natural to assume total control over the content of information, justifying themselves by the ideology in which they believe. Even on purely pragmatic standards, it is doubtful whether this system can be called realistic. Experience shows that the effects of commercial or political monopolies on information means, or the indoctrination pursued by the State are never total, and that the incessant monologue cannot extinguish critical intelligence or independent judgement. The media are blanketed by a dull monotony which evokes distrust rather than confidence.[1] When dissident voices are silenced, credibility of the media is suffering; the State appears to be afraid of controversy and to feel unsure of the version of reality which it puts forward as truth. Anyway, the monopoly of the controlled media is broken by other methods of communication: news is passed on by word of mouth, illegal leaflets are circulated. These methods may be rudimentary, but they retain their vitality, and repression merely adds to their credibility. Finally, foreign broadcasts make inroads on the monopoly enforced by any State within its frontiers.

Some governments, while reserving to the State certain regulatory functions, not only permit but encourage alternative media, citizen participation, public access to information sources, group communication, decentralization of information means, etc.

Radically different is the idea that the State should make itself the guardian of pluralism, providing subsidies to some financially weak — but representative groups — even if their political outlook is critical of the established authority — in order to free them from the domination of financial interests and thus to secure the widest possible diversity of ideas and of information. This policy is not without its problems (of which some are technical, such as the allocation of a limited number of radio wavelengths). Any community defines a basic framework of acceptable ideas; it can scarcely be maintained that the most liberal State should, in the name of pluralism, be obliged to subsidize a racist publication. Nor would it be acceptable to preclude a democratically organized State itself, as spokesman for agreed national aims, to explain its policies and its actions via the media, according to the regulations that prevail nationally for such media use. This, indeed, is an obvious necessity when national goals demand a collective effort. Progress and development must be based on such a collective effort, which in turn requires a large degree of informed consent and support from the public.

The framework within which communication takes place is ultimately determined by the political and social struggles which have shaped the prevailing social consensus in a given society. The way communications are organized in a democratic society is basically a political decision reflecting the values of the existing social system. At a pragmatic level, solutions to the political problems of communication depend on finding a balance between the legitimate interests of the State and the rights of access to information that may be extended to diverse sections of opinion. These solutions will necessarily vary according to the political structure, the degree of development, and the size and resources of each nation. But neither practical necessities nor the claims of ideology should be invoked to exclude freedom of expression from its proper place.

Yet, even if this balance is struck, it will still be necessary to guard against certain dangers. One of these is elitism, a concern even in the early days of the free press.

---

(1) "A free press may be good or bad, but a press without freedom can only be bad. For the press as for mankind, freedom is the opportunity for improvement; slavery is the certainty of deterioration." (Albert Camus).

Communication which is overwhelmingly from the top downward — amplifying the voices of political leaders, persons occupying powerful positions in other sectors of national life, or of prominent intellectuals — often reduces the private citizen to the role of passive receiver and overshadows his concerns, his wishes and his experience. Clearing an upward as well as a downward path for communication is a difficult task. Hand in hand with the danger of elitism, moreover, goes that of over-centralization. If access to the media is confined to politically or culturally dominant groups, whether at the national or the international level, there is a grave risk of imposing patterns in conflict with the values of ethnic, cultural and religious minorities. The need to give them a voice to permit affirmation of these values is another demand for pluralism.

Another danger arises when those enjoying access to the media demand total freedom for themselves, while rejecting any degree of responsibility to the public, the function of information being considered as absolute. All too frequently, the two concepts, freedom and responsibility, are seen and posited as being at variance with one another, whereas in fact they are both key factors of civilization. Sometimes the consequences of disseminating information are not taken into consideration, nor are they viewed as involving any kind of accountability. Such a position obscures the intimate relationship which makes freedom and responsibility inseparable, in the field of communication, as in all other areas. The best weapon against abuses of freedom is the responsibility exercised by those who enjoy freedom in their action and their conduct. It stands to reason that there can be no responsibility when the absence of freedom prevents every individual from choosing his course of action. However, it is also true that one of the essential dimensions of liberty is denied when the consequences of a given action are ignored. Freedom of information can be reconciled with ethical demands by steering a difficult course between respect for individual rights and the prerogatives of society as a whole. Responsibility must be founded more in the concern to respect truth than in the existence of a constitutional right.

Although these considerations have a world-wide application, it is impossible to remain indifferent to changes which tend to show the relativity of and modify the concepts of freedom and responsibility to give them new dimensions which take into account: (a) the course of history; (b) the fact that the right of expression is increasingly governed by the patterns of industrialized communication; (c) the transformation of the respective roles played by the individual and society in the social process. It is also useless to prescribe universal remedies without taking account of national or regional circumstances. At the risk of engendering sharp controversy, it may be said that an essential criterion of freedom of information is diversity of sources, coupled with free access to these sources. A concentration of such sources under the control of dominant groups, tends, whatever the political system, to make a mockery of freedom. A wide spectrum of information and opinion is necessary to equip the citizen to make well-founded judgements on public issues, and is thus a vital ingredient of any communication system in a democratic society; and access to a diversity of sources is as desirable on an international as on a national level. Two cautions, nevertheless, are in order. Firstly, a diversity of sources is no automatic guarantee of the reliability of information, even though it does make deliberate falsifications more difficult. Secondly, diversity is not in every case the same thing as pluralism — in particular, pluralism of opinion. Communication networks and outlets should be as diversified, and as independent one from another, as the sources; if they are not, diversity is only a facade.[1]

There are also varying ideas on the relationship between communication and power. One view is that information is a vital instrument for keeping a check on authority, and even a counterweight to power, in that the mission of the media is to hold up a mirror to governments.[2] The contrasting view is that information should be at the service of the State, so that it may contribute to providing new socio-political systems with strength and stability. Experience in many countries since the end of World War II certainly shows that the freedom of the media is still a keystone of democratic renewal, but it is important to understand the direction of changes which are in progress. These changes have made the relationship between communication and power a more central issue than ever before. The classical antagonism between the leaders and the led has been complicated by another basic conflict — between enterprises which control huge areas of information and individuals whose lives are influenced by decisions over which they have no control. Making use of data is the fundamental role of many institutions which compose the infrastructure of information (press agencies, public opinion institutes, centres of documentation) and also of many disciplines (statistics, economics, sociology, psychology, operational research, systems analysis). To a great extent, communication has thus become an arsenal of signals and instructions, tending to reinforce the power of large organisations — public or private, national or transnational. Such an organisation has capabilities of advance planning and decision-making, and therefore of command, far greater than those of disunited groups of citizens who possess only fragments of information. All information that can be used is therefore, a source of power. For this reason, there is a need for changes in the outlook and the behaviour of those who control the sources of information and the means of transmission.

The current world debate on communication is inevitably political, because the anxieties, the aims and the arguments have a primarily political character. Nothing is gained by concealing the real nature of the problems, nor by failing to recognise the threats to the status quo. If we are to reach practical and realistic solutions, we must take account of every element in the debate.

4. An Economic Force

Both in its structures and its content, communication intermeshes with, and is dependent on, the economy in many ways. A constant flow of information is vital for economic life. As well as being a great economic force with incalculable potentialities, it is a decisive factor in development. As an element of increasing importance in all national economies, communication represents a growing segment of a country's

---

(1) For example, in some countries, as many as five television channels are operated by a single company; in some others, newspapers and broadcasting stations may be under the same ownership; in other situations, the benefits of diversity are lost when several media under the same ownership speak with one voice.

(2) 'But let us have no naive illusions. While the press can check on, or in any case oppose and irritate, the Establishment, the latter has ways of defending itself and indeed asserting itself without infringing the legal framework. Journalists must know how to resist cunning pressures, favours, honours, and of course bribes. Liberty, even when recognized, is *never* altogether a free gift; we must be willing to pay the price for it. It can also, alas, be abused. Under the Front Populaire government (in France in 1936) certain weeklies waged such a violent campaign against a Minister that he was driven to suicide. That was the unhappy reverse side of liberty.' (**Mr. Hubert Beuve-Méry,** member of the CIC, speech in Tokyo, October 1979.)

gross national product and has direct repercussions on productivity and employment. In particular, advances in telecommunications bring about instant transmission of information and thus, in some places, dispense with skilled labour, while in others modify its nature. It is communication that now holds out the best prospects of growth in industrial societies and can be seen as the pivot of the world economy. Modern communication means make the site of enterprises often irrelevant, permit transfers to distant areas of many factories, or a freer choice of locations for different industries and other sorts of activities, such as trade, banking and airlines. The ordinary man feels, even though he does not control, the crucial part played in the economy by communication and information. And all this is sure to become more emphatically true in the coming decades.

True, various forms of communication and information have always been linked, at least implicitly, to work and production, but now it has become easier to see the connections.

Thus, information — and more specifically the ability to transmit, store and use information — is a key resource on a par with energy or raw materials. But in some societies, or for limited groups in almost all societies, communication becomes in a certain sense perverted or distorted: people, as expressed by an economist, can no longer communicate otherwise than by exchanging monetary signs and material goods. On an international level, new structures of communication reflect the life-styles, values and models of a few societies, spreading to the rest of the world certain types of consumption and certain development patterns in preference to others. In this there is a grave danger of the distorting power of communication.

By under-estimating these factors, some developing countries neglect the protection of their independence in the sphere of communication. And the economic imbalances in this sphere, as between nations and regions, are a cause for concern. Unless they are overcome, they will be made still more glaring by technical progress. In developed countries, the introduction of the new technology followed the industrial revolution with an ample breathing-space; but developing countries cannot repeat this sequence, partly because they have a pressing need to speed up their development, partly because the industrial revolution and the informatic revolution are impinging on them at the same time. Many countries have strong reasons to work out concrete development strategies for communication, and to devote added resources to the creation of appropriate infrastructures.

Development in this field demands a better utilization of resources which are at present under-employed. As things stand, there is no doubt that communication resources are unequally distributed on a world scale. Some countries have a full capacity to collate information regarding their needs; many have little capacity to do so, and this is a major handicap in their development.[1]

These disparities are especially marked, and have the most serious consequences, in the scientific and technological sphere. Problems of information about scientific research and its applications have taken on a new dimension, because of the exponential growth in the volume of information available and also because of its increasing complexity, which gives so many research projects and potentialities a

---

(1) One specialist in communication economics writes: "The third world's information infrastructure is impoverished. There is a dearth of scientific, technical, professional, and managerial talent; and even that which exists is often trained abroad in European and US universities. The third world, at present, cannot afford to produce its own information" (Marc Uri Porat, "Policy in an information society", in *Communications for Tomorrow*, Aspen Institute for Humanistic Studies, Praeger Publishers, New York, 1978).

broad interdisciplinary character. STI (the current abbreviation for "scientific and technical information") is today a vital economic resource which ought to be more generously and widely shared, since it derives from the efforts and the thinking of men and women in many countries, in the past and in the present. It is certainly the key to all independent national development, while it is also a basic factor in the co-ordinated progress of mankind. Informatics obviously governs the gathering, classification and analyses of scientific data. However, although it is a guarantee of speed and often of reliability, it does not always ensure the relevance of the data. So the organisation of STI on a world scale requires a strategy at the service of the users of information, devoted to the evaluation and synthesis of information related to the solving of concrete problems and translated into directly applicable knowledge relevant to different societies. But again the question arises of who controls, and how the process of selection and distribution of information is organized. There is a special need to concentrate on the development of national infrastructures with access to world resources of STI. To the global store of information, they can add knowledge of local origin, for this is one factor in making a success of independent national development.

These problems are compounded by the fact that although unit costs of many communication products have tended to decrease, the investments necessary to produce them are increasing. Capital-rich nations have, for this reason, a built-in structural advantage in this situation for the future. This economic reality links communication problems to the new international economic order. The changes necessary in the field of economics and communications are closely interwoven as part of the same process towards a more equitable and just international division of labour.

These issues have a practical as well as a theoretical value. Communication, whether considered as a tool in economic development or as a subject of economic research, calls for new and relevant studies, which should be made so far as possible on comparative lines. But these studies should lead to political actions. There is no longer any room for uncertainty either about the role that communication should play in economic planning, nor about its place in development strategy, nor about the need for the resources that should be devoted to it by every nation and by the international community.

5. An Educational Potential

The rapid development of communication in most countries, the expansion of various forms of mass communication and in particular of audio-visual communication, combined with the spread of informatics, open up new horizons and multiply the linkages between education and communication. There is an evident increase of the educational potential of communication. Endowed with a greater educational value, communication generates an "educational environment". While the educational system loses the monopoly of education, communication becomes itself a vehicle for and a subject of education. Meanwhile, education is an essential tool for teaching men to communicate better, and to draw greater benefits from the exchanges established between them. Thus, there is a growing reciprocal relationship between communication and education.

Firstly, the educational value of information and communication, and their impact on intellectual development are considered to be of primary importance by many thinkers, research workers and government authorities, in particular in the Third

World. For innumerable deprived men, women and children, the school is equated with the media, even if they can only draw from it those elements least rich in significance and with the most simple content, thus picking up but the crumbs from the feast. Witness the educational significance of the messages and news transmitted throughout the world, or, conversely, their anti-educational or anti-social import. It would be difficult to deny the educational — and not simply didactic in the strict sense of the term — impact of the media and of communication in general, even in cases where the content of the messages is not of an educational nature. The educational and socializing role pertaining to communication implies that it should correspond to the utmost to society's development needs, and be treated as a social good.

Secondly, the omnipresence of communication in modern society[1] is a sign of the emergence of a new framework for the personality, with a strong educational flavour. The bombarding of citizens with an ever-growing volume of information, and above all the extension of news flows to new social or geographical categories, has created the impression that access to knowledge is now free, and that social distances could be eliminated and professional secrets revealed. Concepts such as the "video civilization", "alternative schooling", "the computerized society" and the "global village" reflect the growing awareness that the technical environment creates a permanent form of news presentation and access to knowledge. There is talk of the emergence of a "new man" capable to varying degrees of being fashioned day by day in his habits of thinking, his critical attitudes and his technical know-how by this environment.

Thirdly, the knowledge thus presented and amassed daily by the various media of communication is in the nature of a "mosaic", which no longer corresponds to traditional intellectual categories. Without denying the implicit or explicit value of the knowledge amassed in this way, it may not be superfluous to stress the chaotic nature of the information presented, the priority given to the dissemination of trivial or sensational news, increasing "noise" at the cost of the real message. In addition, mass communication tends to strengthen and enrich our common symbolic systems, expressed and interpreted in new ways. By doing so, it diminishes the distinctive qualities of groups and reinforces stereotypes. Intellectual standardization becomes entrenched, generally to a higher degree than at the start of the process. However, nothing in research on current experiments suggests that this trend towards standardization, which is today a feature of the communication industries, is either inexorable or irreversible. The way such information is imposed, stresses the impression by the user of being subjected to it rather than controlling it (a sense of

---

(1) This wealth of information in highly developed countries has led to a reversal of the customary priorities and hierarchies. In Europe, a 10-year-old spends an average of 24 hours per week watching television, i.e. as much time as at school. In the USA, today's 16-year-old has spent a minimum of 15,000 hours of his life watching television. In many countries, a large number of young people already have a natural and practical familiarity with a whole continuum of cameras, miniaturized electronic appliances, video tape-recorders and pocket calculators. By contrast, adults, accustomed to drawing distinctions between functions (television, computer, telephone) have trouble grasping the way in which the different functions are now interlinked (the television screen becoming a computer display screen and video games area while at the same time serving to carry cinematic images; the pocket calculator serving as a clock and the radio as a morning coffee-maker), and frequently feel helpless before the constant "sound-effects" and the flood of messages of all kinds and from every origin. (These figures are based on findings made by several organizations and researchers, e.g. The Council of Europe, L. Porcher, J. Arbois, J. Mousseau, Thollon Pommerol, etc.)

impotence which he also feels vis-à-vis the programmed environment of informatics). From the point of view of the individual's training, the lack of coherence of the elements of knowledge acquired is probably of less importance than the constraints imposed by mass communication.

At the same time, in many countries broadcasting stations have developed interesting, useful and imaginative educational programmes, some of a "formal" nature (as complements or enrichments to school curricula, or to university studies), others of an "informal" pattern (particularly for farmers, adults and people in need of technical knowledge). Some countries, both developed and developing, dedicate separate broadcasting channels in radio and television to educational programmes, while others reserve shorter or longer periods of their general broadcasting schedules for educational, training and learning purposes. Usually, these programmes are prepared by educators and broadcasters together, although such cooperation is sometimes missing, which affects the nature or style of educational broadcasting.

The sudden extension of the use of communication technologies for educational purposes first led to an analysis of the "effects", "impact" and direct influence of ever more stimuli upon individuals and groups, and generated discussion of the media's "educational impact" upon cognitive development or behaviour patterns in mechanistic terms of stimulus response. Today, a less hard-and-fast, more sophisticated approach is leading to the conclusion that communication forms part of a broader set of transformations caused by gradual changes in the environment, and that the impact of technologies differs according to the psychological, intellectual, social and cultural circumstances of the individuals exposed to them. From this point of view, the interpretation of the "non-formal" educational action of the media is following the same trend as educational thinking in general: stress is laid on the role of interpersonal relations and the influence of the group's shared values, as well as on longterm effects whose nature is still not fully known.

Fourthly, schools and colleges in virtually all societies have been obliged to renounce their monopoly on education, now that communication is doing so much of the school's traditional job. This raises the question of rethinking the school's function.

Until the start of this century the school was, even in industrial societies, the primary source of knowledge, and the teacher its licensed dispenser. The individual depended on the school for his knowledge of the world and his ability to master the patterns of behaviour, which enabled him to find his place therein. In most societies today the two systems operate in competition, either openly or under-cover, thereby generating contradictions and even major difficulties in the individual mind. The educational system, founded as it is on values of order and technique, programming, personal effort and concentration, and competition, stands opposed to the communication system which offers all that is topical and novel, reflecting the turmoil of the world, easy understanding, and hedonistic values. This opposition, tolerable in wealthy societies where waste is frequently the rule, is today considered incompatible with the situation of developing countries. Yet, at the practical level, the media represent such a powerful capacity for spreading information and knowledge that no community can afford to do without them.

The school has something of an epistemological function, which consists in teaching how to integrate, structure and analyse knowledge and the data derived from experience, and to understand the languages which describe and interpret the world. But it is partly a communication function: teaching is essentially a process of transmitting signs, of working on and with signs. Although it teaches how to use verbal language, the present-day school tends to neglect the other forms of corporal, graphic and pictorial communication. Thus the language of images is virtually the preserve of the mass communication system.

The school is expected to pass on the ability to master the transformation of the message into meaning, especially by finding adequate expression for a given concept. Even if the message has no meaning as such, it leads to a meaning, or rather to any number of meanings[1]. Meaning is in fact created by the receiver in the light of the experience which he already possesses. Experience and language are thus the preconditions of all acts of communication. The school's role, as indeed that of alternative schooling or of non-formal ways of education and learning, is to help to construct meaning, and not to impose it. Therein lies the only path in responsibility, tolerance, social awareness, the enjoyment of creative activity and the pleasures of communicating.

The effort to strike a balance between education and communication takes very different forms: some consider that the media serve to supply contemporary knowledge, while education is responsible for transmitting the heritage accumulated by tradition. For others, the school should devote itself to generating more effective social awareness, equipping the individual to fill responsible positions, and assisting the economic growth of the nation, while communication should be at the service of leisure and pleasure, and also of international exchange and understanding. Yet others feel that the school's function is to provide, in face of the hubbub of communication, a haven of silence, reflection, intellectual exercise and integration. There are others, lastly, for whom the essential function of educational systems should be to introduce order into the elements of knowledge scattered in all directions by the communication networks, since such systems are founded on an order of values and on methods which teach the pupil how to pick out essentials — in short, they teach him how to learn. So the school must now devise new strategies for learning, tying in with a body of practical experience already acquired elsewhere.

This redistribution of functions has not yet, it would seem, become the subject of any systematic policy-making, the two systems still tending to hold aloof from one another or to negotiate, each from a position of strength. Quite clearly, such an operation necessarily entails the retraining of all categories of teaching staff for new tasks, as well as a genuine openness on the part of communicators to educational issues.

In practice, educational institutions tend to take most of the modern forms of communication under their wing, making their own decisions and choices. Certain countries have begun to take initiatives to introduce the knowledge and use of means of communication from primary school age and throughout secondary schooling, particularly by introducing the press into schools. This initiative is aimed at teaching children to react critically to information, and also to choose their reading matter, programmes and leisure activities, particularly television, according to qualitative and cultural criteria. Countless other alternative experiments and approaches have been and continue to be tried out, with varying degrees of success, in all parts of the world and at all levels of the educational systems. It has been noted that the major media-based educational campaigns have often been over-optimistic in their aims, underestimating the difficulties, the complications, and the bulkiness of the necessary equipment. Renewed interest is being shown today in the use of more light-weight techniques of storage and distribution (local radio transmitters, tape recorders,

---

(1) According to the term used by René La Borderie.

portable video cameras with play-back capabilities, etc.). Nevertheless, the absence of any consistent cultural policy and the rigidity of educational strategies diminish the potential for effective application of the media.

The increasing weight of communication in society is compelling it to vest a new responsibility in educational systems: that of teaching the proper use of communication, while pointing out the dangers of an audio-visual pseudo-knowledge and the illusion of the power of informatics. What is called for here is a more critical form of education, capable of freeing the individual from his fascination with technology, of rendering him more wary and more demanding, and enabling him to choose more discriminatingly between the different products of the communication process. It is now taken for granted that the trend towards an improvement in the quality of the press and radio and television programming is fostered by such education. In paving the way for a future approach to truly participatory communication, the various institutions of formal and non-formal education are aiming at an ideal world in which everyone could be simultaneously a producer and consumer of information.

Finally, the most crucial aspect of the interdependence of communication and education is perhaps this: the process of learning as such, for pupils and students at all levels, must become an experience of communication, of human relations, of give-and-take and association, instead of a one-way transmission of knowledge. It must be a means of breaking through the obstacles between individuals, classes, groups and nations. This is the best contribution that knowledge of and experience in communication can make to enriching learning, training and education, since the essential significance of both is an exchange, a form of social interaction working through symbols.

Education is both more and less than communication. In its absence illiteracy persists, limiting communication abilities at the threshold; its expansion becomes a basis for further communication. Any discussion of the need to remedy communication imbalances cannot therefore ignore the importance of universal education and upgrading the quality of education and educational opportunities. Similarly, discussion of the communication handicap faced by developing nations cannot ignore the potential of education as a factor in human development and the transfer of technology. Likewise, if popular participation is to become a reality in the communication field, the educational and training potential must be better understood by those called upon to play a bigger role in the organization of communication as participants, subjects, consumers, managers and decision-makers in all areas and at all levels.

These increasing links between communication and education force us to ask how the relationship can be made more fruitful and positive. But it remains necessary to take account of the specific nature of each process. By its very nature, education cannot be indifferent to tradition and to the transmission of cultural values inherited from the past. It has to function, nevertheless, in a world that is less and less obedient to authority and respectful of tradition, a world conscious of the task of creating a new future. The basic task of the school is to teach young people what the world is, and this necessarily involves a perspective drawn from the past. Communication turns its eyes more naturally to modernisation and to fitting young people to take their place in a world that is being remade. Its mission is to bring to light social possibilities which have not yet been explored or applied. Thus, individuals, groups and communities are encouraged to work out their own values and their own culture. To remind them that they cannot do so without some equipment in the form of knowledge and ideas is the province of education.

6. An Impulse and Threat to Culture

The inter-dependence of culture and communication is even more pronounced. Particularly if the term "culture" is used to mean the entire achievement of human creativity — "all that man has added to nature" — if it is seen to embody everything that raises human life above the animal level, and to embrace all aspects of life and all ways of understanding. In that light, communication — both between people and nations — is a major component of all ways of life, and thus of every culture. The role of communication may be regarded as that of a major carrier of culture. The media of communication are cultural instruments which serve to promote or influence attitudes, to motivate, to foster the spread of behaviour patterns, and to bring about social integration. They play, or should play, a major role in implementing cultural policies and in helping to democratize culture. For millions of people, they are the principal means of access to culture and to all forms of creative expression. Communication is involved, too, in the management of knowledge, the organisation of the collective memory of society, and in particular the collection, processing and use of scientific information. Potentially at least, it can recast the cultural mould of society. But in this sphere, as much as in others, the rapid development of new technology and the growth of industrialized structures, which extend their grasp over culture as well as over information, introduce problems and dangers.

Although a great body of cultural expression maintains its traditional and inter-personal forms, it is also true that in the modern world the mass media supply the cultural fare, and shape the cultural experience, of many millions of people. For coming generations, they are creating a new culture; it is not easy to define its character, still less to judge its value. Masterpieces of creativity, both from the past and from the present, have been introduced to new audiences on an international as well as national scale. Entertainment in various forms has been made far more readily available, and undoubtedly responds to human needs and demands. But a great deal of this entertainment is so banal and stereotyped that it dulls instead of stimulating the imagination. The influence of commercial and advertising interests, and also the sterile conformism of culture approved by bureaucrats of all kinds, carry threats of a levelling, impoverishment and hollowness of cultural life. Nor are these the only contradictions. Individual creativity has sometimes been aroused by new opportunities, and sometimes replaced by the imitativeness and the passivity of the spectator. The cultural identity of ethnic and other minorities has sometimes been confirmed by taking advantage of fresh avenues of expression, but has often been overwhelmed by external influences. For good or for ill, the mass media have a vast responsibility, because they do not merely transmit and disseminate culture but also select or originate its content.

Mass communication and mass culture are phenomena characteristic of, at most, the last two centuries. Their development can be defined from an economic standpoint as the application to the cultural sphere of the changes brought by the industrial revolution. The outcome is the large-scale production and distribution, through the appropriate techniques and institutions, of a constant flow of messages and stimuli. Mass culture is certainly not the same thing as popular culture, which often has to fight a difficult battle against cultural forms generated by a dominant minority and then disseminated on a mass scale. Still, the concept of mass culture is not without ambiguity. It may have overtones of approval when we think of its general acceptability, or a pejorative ring when we deplore its shallowness. Nor is it easy to say whether a given cultural product is part of "mass culture" or not: should more attention be paid to its origins or to present-day forms of dissemination? An old ballad, surely, does not become a piece of mass culture because it is heard on transistor radios.

Another danger that has assumed considerable proportions is that of cultural domination, which takes the form of dependence on imported models reflecting alien life-styles and values. Cultural identity is endangered by the overpowering influence on and assimilation of some national cultures though these nations may well be the heirs to more ancient and richer cultures. Since diversity is among the most precious qualities of culture, the whole world is the poorer. To hold at bay the forces of possible influences which may lead to cultural dominance is today an urgent task. Yet the problem is not a simple one. History shows that a narrow parochialism leads to cultural stagnation. A culture does not develop by retreating into its shell; much more by free exchange with other cultures and by maintaining the link with all the forces of human progress. But a free exchange must also be an equal exchange based on mutual respect. To secure this, it will often be necessary to protect and strengthen the threatened culture, develop communication at a local level, and open up alternative forms of communication as an antidote to the pressure of the big media. It should be stressed, too, that the problem does not arise solely in the relationships between one nation and another; often, it takes its sharpest form and presents the most pressing dangers within nations whose population includes cultural minorities.

We can conceive of a richer cultural future only in a pluralistic form, in which cultures representing the world's diversity connect with one another while sedulously preserving their originality. No doubt, specific contributions to culture will take on a somewhat hybrid form as traditions mingle and fuse; indeed, that has happened throughout cultural history. However, because of the rapid pace of change and the dangers of standardization, it will be necessary to ensure that the emerging forms preserve what is most distinctive and most developed in each culture, rather than what is most elementary and commonplace. Cultural evolution is inevitable; the question of incalculable importance is one of what elements it should draw upon in order to be as fruitful as possible.

7. The Technological Dilemma

The technological progress in general — and more particularly the increasing use of communication and information technology — is now sufficiently well advanced for it to be possible to forecast trends and to define prospects, as well as to identify likely risks and stumbling-blocks. Science and technology are constantly making such advances which may one day facilitate breaking down barriers between persons and nations. That trend is without doubt irreversible. But the consequences which can now be foreseen are not necessarily beneficial.

To be sure, in all industrialized countries and in a growing number of developing countries interest is focused on the extraordinary new opportunities being opened up by technological innovations in this field. However, these opportunities are not yet, for political and economic reasons, within the reach of everyone. For many scientific discoveries and technological innovations were initiated, and may be controlled for a long time to come, by a small number of countries and by a few transnational firms. It is therefore vital to determine how these technological developments can be of greatest benefit to all nations and, within each nation, to each community and, ultimately, to all men and women; and how they can help to reduce inequalities and injustices.

Moreover, the feeling that technological progress is running ahead of man's capacity to interpret its implications and direct it into the most desirable channels — expressed by many thinkers for over a century — is becoming more and more widespread. The gap is disturbingly evident in such areas as biology, genetics, nuclear physics and cybernetics. New technologies, advancing by their own momentum or due to political pressures and economic requirements, impose themselves before they can be assimilated, and elude both ethical and social control.[1]

The new technologies have ambiguous consequences since they bring with them the risk of making the existing communication systems more rigid and exaggerate their faults and dysfunctions. In setting up ever more powerful, homogeneous and centralized networks, there is a danger of accentuating the centralization of the public or institutional sources of information, of strengthening inequalities and imbalances, and of increasing the sense of irresponsibility and powerlessness both in individuals and communities. The multiplication of radio-broadcasting channels made available by direct broadcast satellites could bring about a diversification of objectives and audiences; however, by intensifying competition, it may lead to the standardization of content and, at the international level, accentuate cultural dependence by increasing the use of imported programmes. Again, as distance becomes an increasingly irrelevant factor in transmission costs (in particular in the case of transmission by satellite, but also in broadband digital transmission by microwave, light conductors and cables), the inequalities between developed and developing countries can diminish; but they may be intensified as a result of the concentration of these resources in the hands of a minority. It may also be that the creation of data banks linked up with computers will lead to an increasing gulf between countries and regions by reducing the poorest countries' means of access of information, or that the emergence of vast communities interlinked by tele-informatics may intensify the already evident contradiction between the growing interdependence of countries and their sovereignty. Depending on circumstances, and on the way it is used, the computer may become a servant or a master; tele-informatics may be used to make society more hierarchical and bureaucratic, to strengthen technocracy and centralization, to increase the social control exercised by the powers that be (political or financial), and perpetuate inequalities (both intranational and international). It could, on the other hand, make social life freer, more spontaneous and open, and more democratic, by safeguarding the diversity of decision-making and media centres. We cannot rule out this possibility.

It is no less vital to safeguard the human dimension of communication and its techniques since new technological facilities and the overwhelming influence of big structures lead in a certain sense to the dehumanization of communication. It is to this end that some countries appear to favour light-weight and audio-visual media.

---

(1) "Discovery now follows discovery at an ever-increasing pace not only because of man's need to create, his desire to penetrate the secrets of nature and the great hopes he sets on the power of science to contribute to his own happiness, but also under the stimulating pressure of economic demands. Technical innovation has become one of the incentives to production. What has declined is the mental and cultural ability of society to control the effects of progress. Man no longer endeavours to obstruct the forces of change, but he does not always succeed in taming them."
(Address by Amadou-Mahtar M'Bow, Director-General of Unesco at the closing session of "Informatics and Society Week", 1979).

Designed for small groups sharing a community of interests, and playing an effective role in joint decision-making, light-weight audio-visual techniques are becoming an integral part of social action: economic redeployment projects, the organization of independent information circuits in local and professional communities, cultural studies and cultural expression. The development of light-weight, easy-to-handle and relatively cheap video techniques which can be adapted to different types of production appears likely to put an end to the divorce between a cultural industry geared to mass production of goods and the scattered islands of group communication. It is to this end as well that some countries promote active participation of users in communication media, in information exchange, democratic people's involvement, participation in media management, etc. Such breakthroughs may pave the way for a decentralization and democratization of the structures of production and distribution in the field of social communication.

To resolve this dilemma, bold decisions and options will have to be taken: the choices to be made are economic and technological, but also political in the first instance. Political decisions must be made in order to avoid some of the unforeseen economic and technological implications, to safeguard the needs of all social strata and national entities, and to preserve the interests of future generations and of the world as a whole.[1]

This complex of questions, linked to the emergence of new technologies, brings out the basic issues which all societies will have to face or are already facing. For while modern technology offers new prospects for the development of communications, it also creates problems and dangers. We must beware of the temptation to regard technology as an all-purpose tool capable of superseding social action and eclipsing efforts to make structural transformations in the developed and developing countries. The future largely depends upon an awareness of the choices open, upon the balance of social forces and upon the conscious effort to promote optimum conditions for communications systems within and between nations.

---

(1) A warning from the Secretary-General of the United Nations may be relevant here: ". . . failure to assert the primacy of policy over technology is an alarming and increasingly dangerous phenomenon in the modern world. This danger is present in the area of communication. Unless it is removed, further communications developments may well produce consequences which were neither foreseen nor desired from a more comprehensive national or international perspective. . ." (Kurt Waldheim).

Chapter 3

The International Dimension

Most of the many questions raised in, or arising out of, the preceding chapters have an international dimension, and have increasingly tended to become the focus of a world-wide debate among policy-makers, researchers and professionals alike.

1. The Issue

Probably the major phenomenon of the second half of the twentieth century has been the accession to independence of almost eighty nations, thanks to which over two billion people have been liberated from colonial domination. Despite this, present-day world conditions — political, economic, scientific, technological and military as well as social and cultural — tend to foster the position and influence of certain countries, and to perpetuate the dependence of a large number of other countries. Political independence is thus restricted, and even undermined, by economic dependence, and especially by the nature of relationships and the international division of labour between developed and developing countries. Moreover, it has become increasingly clear that the effects of intellectual and cultural dependence are as serious as those of political subjection or economic dependence. There can be no genuine, effective independence without the communication resources needed to safeguard it. The argument has been made that a nation whose mass media are under foreign domination cannot claim to be a nation. Unfortunately, in today's world, communication has all too frequently become an exchange between unequal partners, allowing the predominance of the more powerful, the richer and the better equipped. Discrepancy in power and wealth, by its own weight or by deliberate action, has an impact and influence on communication structures and communication flows. Herein lie many of the underlying causes of the inequalities, disparities and imbalances so characteristic of international communications, in particular between industrialized and developing countries.

Thanks to technological advances, nations can become more interlinked than ever before in history. The global web of electronic networks can, potentially, perform a function analogous to that of the nervous system, linking millions of individual brains into an enormous collective intelligence. Political, economic and cultural factors are working toward this inter-dependence; but unless major structural changes are achieved it is difficult to expect the free exchange, the equality, and the balance beneficial to all. The crucial question is whether there exists the political will to overcome the factors which can be recognised as obstacles.

Communication's role in international relations is also important, and indeed vital, because it governs the ability of international opinion to come fully to grips with the problems which threaten mankind's survival — problems which cannot be solved without consultations and cooperation between countries: the arms race, famine, poverty, illiteracy, racialism, unemployment, economic injustice, population growth, destruction of the environment, discrimination against women. These are but the principal problems, and it is essential to highlight how very serious, deep-rooted and far-reaching they are, and even more, how the same challenges and the same dangers affect all nations. The mass media have a vital role to play in alerting international public opinion to these — and other — problems, in making them better understood, in generating the will to solve them, and equipping ordinary people, if necessary, to put pressure on authorities to implement appropriate solutions. Only if the media put more stress on what joins people together rather than on what divides them will the peoples of the world be able to aid one another through peaceful exchange and mutual understanding.

The importance of communication in pursuing these objectives is increasingly recognised, and professional communicators are, on the whole, taking their responsibilities more and more seriously. There are, nevertheless, divergent views concerning the extent of these responsibilities and the ways of discharging them. The problem is that of reconciling two imperatives. The first is the positive contribution expected of the organs of information — which some would wish to make an actual obligation — in mobilising or alerting public opinion in connexion with the major questions which condition man's development and upon which the survival of mankind depends. The second is the freedom of the press — which has also to be regarded as an obligation — to make facts known simply because they are facts. Difficult choices must constantly be made, as professional communicators well know. However, the Commission takes the view that in principle there is no insuperable dilemma, and no insoluble conflict between these two concepts.

2. Imbalances and Inequalities

The international dimension of communication issues has its origins in the realities of the new world situation. More particularly, the concerns, claims and conflicts which generate the current international debate stem from certain negative repercussions of principles adopted long ago, which have taken the form of imbalances and inequalities.

At the period of the foundation of the UN and of Unesco, the international community set itself a certain objective: to guarantee and to foster freedom and free flow of information. This principle is solemnly proclaimed in various international instruments dealing with human rights and fundamental freedoms.[1] Their validity deserves to be re-emphasized and reaffirmed.

---

(1) The most important among them are the following: The Article 19 of the *Universal Declaration of Human Rights* (1948) states that the right to freedom of opinion and expression includes "freedom to hold opinions without interference and to seek, receive and impart information and ideas through any media and regardless of frontiers". Likewise, the *International Covenant on Civil and Political Rights* (1966) stipulates that the right to freedom of expression "comprises the freedom to seek out, to receive and to communicate information and ideas of all kinds, regardless of frontier whether in oral, printed or artistic form, or by any other means of the individual's choice." The governments of the States party to *Unesco's Constitution*, believing "in the unrestricted pursuit of objective truth, and in the free exchange of ideas and knowledge, "declared themselves "agreed and determined to develop and to increase the means of communication between their peoples and to employ these means for the purposes of mutual understanding and a truer and more perfect knowledge of each other's lives." Furthermore, the *Declaration of the Principles of International*

However, the obvious imbalances in communication supported the view that "free flow" was nothing more than "one-way flow", and that the principle on which it was based should be restated so as to guarantee "free and balanced flow". The somewhat hazy origins of these concepts date back to the 1950s; they became more clearly defined between the late 1960s and the early 1970s. By that time, the imbalance in the flow of news and information between industrialised and developing countries was a major topic in international meetings, as an issue in the debate on fundamental political and economic issues in the contemporary world. Today, virtually no one disputes the reality of this imbalance. There is no general agreement, however, about concrete applications of the concept, still less about remedies to the problem and desirable policies. It is for this reason that the concepts of free flow and one-way flow, balance and imbalance, have become issues of the debate and indeed of international contention.

The imbalance in news circulation is a complex and varied phenomenon. Alike quantitative and qualitative, it may occur at different levels and in different forms: (a) between developed and developing countries, insofar as the information flow is governed by the existence or non-existence of appropriate infrastructures; (b) between countries having different political and socio-economic systems; (c) between developed countries belonging to the same political system, particularly between smaller and bigger ones; (d) between the Third World countries themselves; (e) between political news and news concerning the social, economic and cultural life of countries battling with the ills of underdevelopment; (f) between what is conventionally called 'good' news and 'bad' news, i.e. news of catastrophes, failures, conflicts, set-backs, follies and excesses; and finally (g) between topical news of current events and information dealing in greater depth with issues important in the daily lives of peoples and nations. Doubtless there is no single, universal criterion by which to measure these imbalances and disparities, since news values differ from one country to another and from culture to culture, and even sometimes within a single country. Hence any generalization on news values is bound to remain rather loose, even if professional communicators do frequently agree on a number of factors considered to make for news.

Such imbalances are today not only limited to news flows in the usual sense. They also affect, to an increasingly serious extent, the collection and diffusion of data necessary for scientific purposes, technological innovations, commercial needs, trade development, exploitation of natural resources, meteorological forecastings, military purposes, etc. In short, there is an imbalance regarding strategic information for political and economic decision-making.

The gap between the fully-informed and the under-informed continues to widen as the imbalance between those imparting and those receiving information becomes accentuated. Although it is only fair to recognise that the international flows have enormously increased and that communication sources have enormously increased their output, it is necessary also to stress that communicators have strengthened their

Cultural Cooperation adopted by the General Conference of Unesco (1966) states that "broad dissemination of ideas and knowledge, based on the freest exchange and discussion, is essential to creative activity, the pursuit of truth and the development of the personality." In the most recent *Declaration on Fundamental Principles concerning the Contribution of the Mass Media to Strengthening Peace and International Understanding, to the Promotion of Human Rights and to Countering Racialism, Apartheid and Incitement to War* (Unesco) (Adopted on 28 November 1978) it is stated that "The exercise of freedom of opinion, expression and information recognized as an integral part of human rights and fundamental freedoms, is a vital factor in the strengthening of peace and international understanding." (Article II).

power to control the impact of the messages transmitted, as well as the selection of information available. Also, the attendant distortions and imbalances reflect in some way the dominant interests of the societies from which they emanate.

This situation cannot continue without detriment both to international understanding and to cooperation between nations, without affecting the socio-political and socio-cultural conditions prevailing in different countries and without prejudicing the efforts to satisfy the basic needs, to solve the essential problems of the world's populations and to safeguard world peace.

3. The International Debate

Thus, it was around 1970 that the concepts upon which today's international debate is focused first began to be formulated in clear-cut terms. Without retracing every stage in the history of this debate, it may nevertheless be useful to recall the major themes on which a wide range of protagonists are now joining issue: governments, and non-governmental organizations, specialised agencies, regional organizations, research centres, political movements, professional associations, mass media, journalists and politicians, etc.

First of all, the criticisms formulated in many developing countries reiterated by certain socialist countries and supported by many researchers and journalists in western countries, start from the observation that certain powerful and technologically advanced States exploit their advantages to exercise a form of cultural and ideological domination which jeopardizes the national identity of other countries. The problems raised by the one-way information flow and by the existence of monopolistic and oligopolistic trends in international flows[1] have been widely discussed in many international instances, gatherings and seminars. It has been frequently stated, in particular, that due to the fact that the content of information is largely produced by the main developed countries, the image of the developing countries is frequently false and distorted. More serious still, according to some vigorous critics, it is this false image, harmful to their inner balance, which is presented to the developing countries themselves. The dangers and fears created by the potentialities of direct satellite broadcasting stimulated the demand for a balanced flow of information. It was when these questions first came to be discussed that increasing anxiety arose about the content and quality of the information transmitted, together with a dawning awareness of the lag in developing countries in news production and transmission.

On the other hand, many media professionals consider that, while the existence of these imbalances and the dangers which they entail cannot be denied, stressing the one-way news flow can lead to further restrictions on freedom of information and to strengthening the hand of those in favour of reducing the inflow of information; the

---

(1) A major international study made at that period stated: "It must also be recognized that international information dissemination has long formed the subject of discriminatory practices ... Public opinion in the industrialized countries will not have real access to full information on the Third World, its demands, aspirations and needs, until such time as information and communication patterns are liberated from the market-oriented sensationalism and news presentation which characterize them at present and until they are consciously stripped of ethnocentric prejudices. The widening of the capacity to inform must be viewed as an essential component of attempts to create a new international order and, as such, the monopolistic and discriminatory practices inherent in current international information dissemination must be deemed as one of the worst, though subtle, characteristics of the present system." (RIO, Reshaping the International Order, A Report to the Club of Rome, Jan Tinbergen, Coordinator, 1977).

consequence would be a radical break with the concept of free flow. Assuming that the diversity of opinions, news, messages and sources is a precondition for truly democratic communication, this school of thought also considers that the "decolonization of information" must not serve as a pretext for bringing information under the exclusive control of government authorities, and thereby allowing them to impose their own image of reality on their peoples.

In the debate on international communication, the role played by the transnationals has become crucial.[1] Not only do these conglomerates mobilise capital and technologies and transfer them to the communication market; they also market countless socio-cultural consumer goods which serve as a vehicle for an amalgam of ideas, tastes, values and beliefs. The transnationals exert a direct influence on the economic production apparatus of the countries in which they operate, as well as playing a part in commercializing their culture, and can thus modify the socio-cultural focus of an entire society.

Transformations in the structures of international communications, as a factor inherent in the conceptual foundations of international relations and of development, are frequently called for. It is argued that a world built on mutual understanding, acceptance of diversity, promotion of détente and coexistence, encouragement of trends towards real independence, not only needs but makes room for new, different patterns in international communication. If the conception of development as a linear, quantitative and exponential process, based on transfers of imported and frequently alienating technology, is beginning to be replaced by that of an endogenous qualitative process focused on man and his vital needs, aimed at eradicating inequalities and based on appropriate technologies which respect the cultural context and generate and foster the active participation of the populations concerned, then there can be no doubt that communication between people and nations will become different.

The non-aligned countries have played a major role in the evolution of ideas concerning the dependence of the media, the imbalance in news flows and global communication patterns and the negative effects of this imbalance. They have advanced the view that the vast majority of countries are reduced to the state of passive receivers of information put out by a few centres.[2]

This is how the call for a "new order"[3] as distinct from the "old order" in the field

---

(1) A study submitted to the Seventh Special Session of the United Nations General Assembly, points out that "the essential factor of the present hierarchical pattern of the centers' ideological and cultural dominance is the virtual monopoly on international communication — even communication between the various Third World countries — exercised by the multinationals, their dominance over a large number of the mass media of Third World countries and their influence over almost all the mass media". (This study was prepared by a research team of the Dag Hammarskjöld Foundation in cooperation with the United Nations Environmental Programme, published under the title "what Now? Another Development".)

(2) The IVth Conference of Heads of State and Government of the Non-Aligned Countries which met in Algiers in 1973 was the first meeting at which these countries raised the problem in clear-cut terms and gave forceful expression to their common interest — 'born of the immense vacuum left by the UN' — in information. Three years later, a Symposium on communication, held in Tunisia, paved the way for the first Conference of Ministers of Information of the Non-Aligned Countries which adopted a draft declaration ratified in Colombo some weeks later by the Summit Conference of Non-Aligned Countries, stressing that a "new world communication order" was no less important than a new economic order.

(3) It should be noted here that the new order in the field of communication has been variously termed: "new world information order","new international information order", "new international

of communication and information came into being. The feeling that such a new order is today a necessity stems from the conviction that information and communication are an essential factor of international relations in all fields and particularly in the establishment of a new system founded on the principle of equality of rights and the independence and unfettered development of countries and peoples. Thus, transformations in communications are related to the conceptual foundations of the new international economic order. In certain respects, development and communication do follow or are based on the same principles. It is vital that the present state of dependence of the developing world, in its economy and its communications alike — a dependence which both generates ever greater inequalities and is wasteful of natural (and in particular non-renewable) material and human resources — be replaced by relations of interdependence and cooperation between national systems as they become progressively autonomous and capable of endogenous development. The new communication order must be considered as an element of the new economic order, and the same methods of analysis may be applied to both. In particular, both call for a global, universal — albeit necessarily pluralist — approach, since the major problems besetting mankind can be solved only at the world level. There is a coherent correlation between these two orders stemming from the fact that information is now a specific kind of basic economic resource (and not just a commodity) which performs an essential social function but which is today unequally distributed and badly used. In some other respects, the new communication order is a pre-condition of the new economic order, just as communication is the *sine qua non* of all economic activities between groups, peoples and nations.

At the present stage of the debate, a new world information and communication order is an open-ended conceptual framework which may direct the attention of those concerned towards (a) cataloguing and defining the problems affecting the building of a freer, more just, more effective and better balanced international communications system, based on democratic principles designed to establish egalitarian relations between sovereign entities; (b) facilitating coherent discussion at the international level by focusing it initially on the more urgent and practicable tasks; (c) clarifying the political options involved. In reality, it is a matter of initiating a long-term process at the national, regional and international levels, one involving not only those primarily concerned but all societies and geared less to academic discussion and more to effective, practical action. However, we must not ignore the fact that the establishment of a new order will bring major transformations in national as well as international structures of communication. Designed to meet the basic needs of the poorer sections of the world's population, it pre-supposes a new distribution of available resources in accordance with their vital rights and needs.

These concerns, and many other related claims, fuel the international debate. The contentions and opinions discussed above are, naturally, fiercely defended by some and no less fiercely disputed by others. However, it should be stressed that such claims and counter-claims directly or indirectly underlie a number of decisions and resolutions adopted by Unesco, in particular the decision which led to the creation of the International Commission.

---

information and communication order", etc. At the 1978 General Conference of Unesco and General Assembly of the United Nations two Resolutions have been adopted and consensus was reached on the term "new more just and more efficient world information and communication order" which indicates not only the aim but also its major parameters. For conciseness and completeness, the term "new world communication order" will be used in this Report.

4. A forum open to the World: Unesco

In the field of communication, Unesco has become a forum where issues can be raised and discussions pursued in depth. It is largely thanks to its action and initiatives that the international community has in recent years become aware of the problems involved, has measured their complexity and understood how vital it is to inquire more deeply into the matter so as to concert and focus efforts as effectively as possible. There has been a marked rapprochement in evaluations of the situation in matters of international communication.

In the early 1960s, Unesco endeavoured to conclude, in cooperation with pre-eminent professional organizations, arrangements relating to the international exchange of news. Projects were worked out to set up national news agencies and to establish links between them in order to increase the developing world's means of expression and to gather and exchange news, films and various broadcasts for the mutual benefit of these countries. Various possibilities of regional cooperation were explored with a particular view to establishing regional press agencies and satellite broadcasting systems for education and development. It was more particularly at the sixteenth session of the General Conference (1970) that the delegations of several developing countries referred explicitly to what might be called the issue of the unequal distribution of the media, asking that better adapted and balanced international news exchange systems be organized and stressing the right to cultural identity.[1] Two years later, delegates from a majority of Member States emphasized more forcefully still the potential dangers of news flow imbalance. The Director-General was authorized to continue to assist in developing communications research, in particular research of potential value for the formulation of communication policies and national strategies aimed at placing communication in the service of development. At its eighteenth session in 1974, in order to facilitiate communication between nations and between peoples and to promote a better understanding of the role played by the media in the implementation of national development policies and plans, the General Conference recommended that a first Intergovernmental Conference on communication policies be organized in Latin America in 1975 and that a similar intergovernmental conference by prepared and held in Asia in 1977.

The first Conference on Communication Policies was held in San Jośe de Costa Rica in July 1976. It unanimously recommended the formulation of new national and international communication policies, urging in particular that national communication councils be set up, scientific research in this field be developed and national and regional news agencies be established. The San José Declaration adopted on that occasion highlights the fact that communication has today come to be accepted as a pre-eminent factor of national renascence, and at the same time serves as a powerful force in relations between nations. It urged that "national communication policies should be conceived in the context of national realities, free

---

(1) The report of the Programme Commission specifically states that the delegates of a number of these countries urged that the programme continue to focus upon the right of the less advantaged countries to preserve their culture. At the same session, the General Conference authorized the Director-General to help Member States to formulate their communications policies in the light of experience gained in the elaboration of cultural policies. In 1972 the stress was on eventual negative impacts of information expansion "Because of their impact, the media of communication — whose scope is considerably widened by the utilization of communication satellites — demand of those who use them an acute sense of their responsibilities . . . If the dissemination of information is the monopoly of a few countries, and if the international circulation of information is a one-way process only, the cultural values of most of the remaining countries may be seriously harmed."

expression of thought and respect for individual and social rights." A similar conference held in Kuala Lumpur in February 1979 studied, in the context of Asia and Oceania, all aspects of communication policy and stressed that communication, considered both as a means of affirming a nation's collective identity and an instrument of social integration, has a decisive role to play in the democratization of social relations insofar as it permits the multidirectional flow of both horizontal and vertical messages, both from the media to their public and from this public to the media. This effort to define overall, coherent communication policies at the national and regional levels is to be extended in the coming years to the other regions of the world.

All these issues, necessarily controversial in the present-day world, have given rise to heated arguments and even to fierce confrontations. Although most of the decisions taken in Unesco on such matters were reached by consensus, their actual formulation was a painful process. Sharp controversies arose around certain initiatives taken concomitantly over the same period to draw up general norms and principles which might serve to inspire the mass media to play a more positive role in alerting public opinion to the major problems facing mankind and to their possible solutions. The idea was to adopt a normative instrument which, while not legally binding upon Member States, would comprise a set of principles constituting a statement of the intellectual and moral unity of the international community. The process of preparing this document was a lengthy and arduous one.

Many objections and new suggestions have been made by governmental representatives and professionals, both in developed and developing countries. Many professionals, especially journalists, in western countries expressed misgivings, criticism, and outright opposition to the trend of thought embodied in the draft Declaration. They were concerned lest certain governments, openly or covertly opposed to press freedom, might take measures — in the name of correcting imbalance — which would be equivalent to imposing control of information and the media, establishing censorship and in particular hampering or even terminating the work of foreign correspondents. These critics objected to references to the responsibilities of journalists, which could enable governments to discriminate against those arbitrarily labelled "irresponsible". They found that the draft Declaration lacked any positive reference to human rights, did not guarantee free access by journalists to diverse news sources and failed to mention the desirability of a multiplicity of news outlets. Finally, they objected to the role assumed by Unesco, interpreted its aims as a desire to "control the news flow", and charged it with confusing the real issues. Some organs of information went so far as to denounce Unesco as an enemy and published calls to "stop Unesco before it is too late".

Several drafts were successively presented and heatedly discussed and criticized, first in expert meetings and subsequently at government level. Not only was there opposition to the content of the instrument, the formulation of the principles it was to proclaim and the means of applying these principles, but there was also scepticism regarding the possibility of drafting a text of this kind in a world so divided as ours. This opposition, which came both from certain governments and from the professional communities of many countries, was so strong that, at the nineteenth session of the General Conference (Nairobi, 1976), the only realistic solution appeared to be to pursue the study of the problem and to defer all decision. This decision to decide nothing proved to be a wise and fruitful one, since it was possible at the following session (Paris, 1978) to adopt by consensus the text of the

Declaration on Fundamental Principles Concerning the Contribution of the Mass Media to Strengthening Peace and International Understanding, to the Promotion of Human Rights and to Countering Racialism, Apartheid and Incitement to War. Member States had also given unanimous support to the expansion of Unesco's programme in the field of communication.

Nevertheless, agreement by governments does not automatically bring the support of all the professional and other interests concerned, nor of all sections of opinion. There are still concerns about interpretations of the principles and guidelines embodied in the Declaration, as well as about its possible misuse. Some, while conceding Unesco's good faith, still think that the Declaration is likely to do more harm than good, and may legitimate interferences with press freedom. In this field, it is essential to take fears and anxieties seriously and to secure the widest possible measure of conviction in the support of news ideas. It is thus, natural that the debate still continues. It is also right and necessary, therefore, that the debate should continue.

Despite all political and ideological differences, this debate has highlighted the scale of communication problems and the many repercussions which they necessarily have. It is these problems which are outlined, in all their diversity and complexity, in the first part of this Report, and which will be described and analysed in greater depth and detail in its subsequent parts.

It was in the context of this debate that the representatives of all countries meeting in Nairobi urged that the study of communication problems in modern society be pursued in more detailed and systematic fashion and a synthesis made of them. In response, the Director-General stated in his address to the closing meeting: "You have, indeed, asked the Secretariat to take action but you have also asked it to inquire more deeply into the role, aims and conditions of communication. As I had occasion to state earlier during the discussion on this item, I intend, within the framework of the mandate you have laid upon me, to undertake wide-ranging consultations in support of the work we have been asked to do, making use, if necessary, of a discussion group."

Some months later, the Director-General decided to entrust an international commission, with Mr. Sean MacBride of Ireland as its President, with the task of carrying out a study of all communication problems in present-day society. The Commission's mandate specified the four main lines of inquiry and discussion to be pursued, namely:

(a) to study the current situation in the fields of communication and information and to identify problems which call for fresh action at the national level and a concerted, overall approach at the international level. The analysis of the state of communication in the world today, and particularly of information problems as a whole, should take account of the diversity of socio-economic conditions and levels and types of development;

(b) to pay particular attention to problems relating to the free and balanced flow of information in the world, as well as the specific needs of developing countries, in accordance with the decisions of the General Conference;

(c) to analyse communication problems, in their different aspects, within the perspective of the establishment of a new international economic order and of the measures to be taken to foster the institution of a "new world information order";

(d) to define the role which communication might play in making public opinion aware of the major problems besetting the world, in sensitizing it to these problems and helping gradually to solve them by concerted action at the national and international levels.

In accordance with these terms of reference the International Commission submitted an Interim Report to the twentieth session of the General Conference of Unesco (Paris, October-November 1978). After taking note of this Report, the General Conference adopted resolution 4/9.1/3 whose operative paragraph 1. clarifies the Commission's mandate by inviting the Director-General "to request the members of the International Commission for the Study of Communication Problems to address themselves, in the course of preparing their final report to the analysis and proposal of concrete and practical measures leading to the establishment of a more just and effective world information order."

To sum up, the establishment of the International Commission occurred at a time when various trends were emerging and converging. These reflect: (a) the increasing importance attached to communication as a social phenomenon and the consequent interest shown in the development of the communication media; (b) the growing impact and repercussions of technological progress in this field; (c) the re-examination of international news flows with a view to eliminating situations of political, economic and cultural dominance and dependence; (d) the growing concern of many developing countries to reduce their dependence in matters of communication following the process of political and economic decolonization during the 1960s; (e) the increasing potential of communication in fostering international understanding and awareness of major world problems. These trends have led to the questioning of certain received or preconceived ideas relating to communication. At the same time, many doubts and questions have arisen out of actual political and social experience in various parts of the world. Many people have come to realize that sovereignty, identity and independence do not only arise from formal political decisions, but are also, and perhaps even more, contingent upon the conditions of cultural and economic life, in short, upon circumstances which affect, in an increasingly interlocking fashion, the overall development of each and every nation.

Part II
Communication Today

Chapter 1

Means of Communication

The spectrum of communication in contemporary society almost defies description because of the immense variety and range of its components. It includes: human capacities; simple communication tools and media serving individuals, groups and masses; complex infrastructures and systems; advanced technologies, materials and machines which collect, produce, carry, receive, store and retrieve messages; innumerable individual and institutional partners and participants in the communication world.[1]

The symbols which make up messages and the means that carry them are simply two facets of one reality. Symbols, gestures, numbers, words, pictures, all are in themselves a means of communication, and the medium, be it a hand, printed page, radio or television, not only carries the message but is simultaneously another symbol of communication. Hence communication is an all-encompassing "global" phenomenon, which in essence cannot be reduced to or described in terms of isolated, independent parts, each element being an integral part of the whole. But all these elements are present — obviously in different proportions and with different significance and impact — in every part of the world.

1. Signs and Words

Since time immemorial, the human race has used primitive, simple forms of communication, which have been enhanced, extended, refined, and are still in use today in all societies despite the continuous invention of new technologies and the increasing sophistication and complexity of interaction between people. To be able to externalize their feelings and needs, individuals first used their bodies to communicate. "Body language" and other non verbal languages[1] while being used

---

(1) N.B.: Throughout this review, some statistical data are presented, which call for a word of caution. First, available statistics in the many fields related to communication vary widely in their abundance and accuracy or verifiability. Second, statistical presentations usually involve a selection, which by nature is necessarily subjective. Third, statistics often express aggregate totals or averages which sometimes mask wide variations in the separate units of the composite. Fourth, data published in a given year often refer to statistics assembled several years earlier which may be outdated. However, some relatively complete data are available in certain areas, allowing more or less valid assumptions or conclusions; in other fields or for different regions of the world, more selective, yet indicative, figures can be given. Despite these disclaimers, the data presented illustrate the situations examined and may help in understanding them.

(1) e.g. facial expression, gesture, mime, dance, images, music, songs, drawings, paintings, sculptures, sport, etc. Of special value are lip-reading and sign languages used by millions of handicapped persons.

for millenia in traditional societies for a variety of purposes, have lost none of their validity and importance today, despite their obvious limitations. Hence, messages and ideas are also transmitted in many countries by means of itinerant dance and mime groups, puppet shows and other folk media which serve not only to entertain but to influence attitudes and behaviour.

Images often preceded and precede words. But language marks an immense step forward in human communication, especially in the ability to memorize and pass on knowledge and in the expression of relatively complex conceptions. It is not, indeed, the only tool in interpersonal communication, but it is indispensable; speech still has powers which cannot be replaced either by technology or by the mass media. It is the lifeblood of innumerable networks of contact.

In communities where isolation or smallness of scale, or indeed persistent illiteracy, have encouraged the survival of tradition, speech, performance and example remain the most common, if not the only, means of transmitting information. While in industrialized countries, traditional channels for direct communication have virtually disappeared as sources of information, except in the most isolated areas, the same cannot be said for other interpersonal communication networks which include provision or exchange of information in the family or extended family, in the neighbourhood, in communities and ethnic groups, in various clubs and professional associations, and in conferences and meetings which are convened by governments, by organizations of all kinds, or by commercial enterprises.[1] All these and many others provide occasions to exchange information, elucidate issues, ventilate grievances, resolve conflicts or assist in opinion-forming and decision-making on matters of common interest to individuals, groups or society as a whole. These forms of interpersonal communication are sometimes overlooked by professional observers and investigators, whose focus is narrowed predominantly to the mass media, as the purveyors of news, facts, ideas, and indeed of all vital information.

While interpersonal communication is not a primary or even major concern of this review, some of the issues it raises should not be overlooked for a number of important reasons. First, traditional forms of communication, and particularly interpersonal communication, maintain a vital importance in all parts of the world, both developing and developed, and are even expanding. Second, the majority of people in the world, particularly the rural inhabitants of developing countries, comprising as much as 60 to 70 per cent of the world's population, continues to impart, receive and, what is more, accept messages through these channels of communication. Third, it is impossible to comprehend completely the advantages and limitations of modern media if they are treated as factors separate from the interpersonal communication, for clearly communication networks grow cumulatively, with each new form adding to but not eclipsing the older systems. On the contrary, interpersonal communication takes on a whole new significance in the face of the depersonalizing effects of modern technology and it remains an essential feature in the furtherance of democracy within societies.

---

(1) To give but one example of the order of magnitude of such activities, it is estimated that every year some two million scientists, technicians and specialists participate in international congresses alone; if national and regional scientific gatherings are taken into account, probably more than five million individuals are annually involved.

2. Languages

The number of languages used in verbal communication is high, with some 3,500 identified throughout the world. However, while speech is common to all societies and writing is not, the number of written languages is much lower, with one estimate indicating not more than 500.[1]

Over the centuries, the course of history has led to steady expansion in the use of some languages. Some of these languages have a predominant place in the circulation of information, programmes and materials.[2] It is estimated that there are at least 16 languages which are spoken by more than 50 million people: the family of Chinese languages, English, Russian, Spanish, Hindi, Portuguese, Bengali, German, Japanese, Arabic, Urdu, French, Malay-Bahasa, Italian, Teluga, Tamil.

About 1,250 languages are spoken on the African continent: some of these, such as Swahili, Wolof and Hausa, cover large areas and indeed different nations. In Europe, there are 28 official national languages. The people of south Asia use 23 principal languages. Although the Arab region is, in a certain sense, monolingual, vernacular languages there vary to some extent from classical Arabic, and Berber tongues which are distinct from Arabic are spoken in some countries of north Africa. Latin America uses two principal languages, Spanish and Portuguese, but there are hundreds of Indian languages and dialects; some of them, like Quechua in Peru and Guarani in Paraguay, being spoken by large local populations. In addition, English, French and Dutch continue to predominate in ex-colonies of the region and in the Caribbean. Many countries have a surprising number of languages: in the USSR there are 89; India recognizes 15 for official and educational use alone, with a total number of languages and dialects exceeding 1,650; for Ghana the total is 56 and Mexican Indians have more than 200. Many of these tongues have now been transcribed, but the majority have not.

The proliferation of a great number of languages and dialects had numerous historical, ethnological, religious and social reasons. But in the course of time, the creation of new nation states, coupled with hegemonistic pressures and imperialist domination over large parts of the world led frequently to linguistic modifications in many countries and the gradual disappearance of some dialects and local patois. Conversely, colonialism ensured that a few European languages were spread right across the globe. Assimilating tendencies over small and weak cultures are still continuing.

The multiplicity of languages, each the incarnation of long traditions, is an expression of the world's cultural richness and diversity. The disappearance of a language is always a loss, and its preservation is the consequence of the struggle for a basic human right. Moreover, in the modern mass media as well as in traditional communication, the use of a variety of languages is an advantage, bringing a whole

---

(1) These figures (their source being *Languages of the World,* Kenneth Katzner, Toronto 1975) are only indicative, since they are contested on various grounds. The mapping of different languages has not yet been completed. Divergences in differentiation between languages and dialects are still common among scientists. General census has not yet covered large areas in several countries. Some political considerations have also made some distinctions rather difficult. In the current literature, for instance, the number of languages ranges from two thousand to around four thousand. As far as written languages are concerned, divergences also arise from the fact that out of 500 with a script, only 200 are judged to have written and literary traditions, another 200 to have only a written tradition, while around 100 have little more than alphabets and some form of primer.

(2) It is estimated (by Unesco services) that more than two-thirds of printed materials are produced in English, Russian, Spanish, German and French.

population on to equal terms of comprehension. This does not mean that there are no problems arising from multiplicity. The choice of a national "link language", or the relationship between one language and another, has been a source of difficulty and conflict (in India, in Canada, in Belgium, to take only three examples). The multiplicity of languages presents obvious barriers to communication, gives rise to cultural problems, and can hamper scientific and technical development. The world-wide use of a small number of languages leads to a certain discrimination against other languages and the creation of a linguistic hierarchy; thus, most of the world's population lacks the linguistic means to take full advantage of much of modern research and technology.[1]

This concentration of key languages might encourage the view that the problem of "language barriers" is overrated, but the fact is that, beyond the native speakers of such languages and the relatively small number of bi or multilingual people, who belong mainly to narrow local elites, millions of people all over the world do indeed face an incomprehensible barrier. They are discriminated against, since currently the spread of information tends to take place in the terms, and the idiom, of the linguistically powerful.

Looking to the future, there are several possible avenues of development. Many national languages could become more widely used, particularly in print and electronic media, which at present often confine themselves to the language of the local elite. Or alternatively the rapid spread of technology could concentrate and decrease the number of languages, at least for some specific purposes. Plurilingualism is an attractive solution, probably the only realistic one in most countries, yet the diffusion of one simple, universal tongue, comprehensible and accessible to all, might also strengthen national cohesion and quickly demolish the barriers to communication between different peoples. Again, improved teaching of foreign languages and extensions of learning opportunities, particularly through use of radio and recordings, offers broad potential. All these possibilities are meaningful only if one basic principle is respected: that all languages are regarded as equal in dignity and as instruments of communication. In formulating its linguistic policy, each country has an option between various alternatives, and its decision cannot be postponed or circumvented for long without harm.

The use of many languages in modern communication has also been hampered until now because not all languages have been adapted to modern means of printing, processing and transmitting messages and information. Priority has been given to languages using latin or cyrillic script. However, recent advances in standardization, codification and printing technologies now make it possible to adapt such languages as Japanese, Chinese and Arabic to all modern means of communication. A Shanghai language research institute, using the 26 letter Roman alphabet, has developed a 4-letter code for each of some 2,000 ideograms, called "on-site encoding" for use in computing processing [2] For Arabic, a system called ASV-

---

(1) It is estimated that about 60% of scientific communication is conducted in English. Even in French-speaking countries, according to some estimates, 70% of researchers use English sources.

(2) It is interesting to note however that this did not effectively solve the problem of producing input-output software, which in most computer printing still uses typewriter-like impact printing, a mechanism ill-suited to accommodate 2,000 characters. Now, new electromechanical, micro-processing technologies have been used to develop what is called "ink-jet printing", in which each character is broken down into an array of minute drops of ink which have been squirted from a nozzle and electronically steered inflight to form the desired printed character. (Various methods of ink-jet printing have been devised; one device prints 45,000 lines per minute!)

CODAR has been developed which standardizes codes and reduces the number of letter forms to permit easy use of the Arabic script for typewriting, printing, data processing and telecommunications. The same may and indeed should be done for many other languages.

We are thus concerned about language problems for these particular reasons: (a) the development of truly national communication systems covering the entire population cannot be achieved unless more languages are used for information and cultural activities; (b) language policy should be an intrinsic part of communication policies, since the choice and promotion of languages opens up or eliminates possibilities for wider and equal communication; (c) additional efforts are needed to achieve transcription of various national and local languages, as well as adaptation of various language groups to communication machines (typewriters, linotypes, teleprinters, computers, etc); (d) the use of a few so-called world languages is essential in international communications, yet this poses sensitive questions concerning the individuality and even the political and cultural development of some countries.

3. Reading and Writing

If language, both spoken and written, is the primary code of human communication, illiteracy is the major obstacle to the development of communication. The lack of reading and writing skills drastically limits the expansion of a person's overall capacities and abilities.[1]

There are several reasons for illiteracy: millions speak non-transcribed languages; many live in environments and particular conditions where written communication is not yet necessary or available; many more have not had, in their childhood or adulthood, the chance to learn to read and write; some acquired that skill but reverted, for various reasons, to illiteracy during their lifetime; restricted resources hamper the establishment of widespread literacy programmes; there is often a lack of political will, at decision making levels, to step up efforts to eradicate illiteracy.

Illiteracy exists to a greater or lesser extent in almost all countries, although it is difficult to define precisely or to determine its worldwide dimensions. The concept of a literate person varies from country to country, ranging from the ability to decipher a simple test to the completion of full primary schooling, or to the ability of using literacy skills for "functional" purposes in working, civic and social life. However, indicative estimates are available to provide generally acceptable national, regional and global pictures of illiteracy around the world.

The latest available figures and estimates show a continuing reduction in the illiteracy rates among the world's population aged 15 years and over, which dropped from 40 per cent in 1950 to 36 per cent around 1960, and which should fall from 32.4 per cent in 1970 to 28.9 per cent in 1980 and to 25.7 per cent in 1990. This is

---

(1) "Most people think of waste in physical terms, such as waste of resources, energy, or money. Indeed, the global problematique has focused attention on the wasteful misuse of non-renewable physical resources...But another kind of waste has an even more serious impact on the whole knot of global problems: the waste of human learning potential. In this context, waste can result not only from the misuse that relegates people to marginal positions, but also from the lack of use or neglect of human capacities...Unacceptably large numbers of people find themselves excluded from all but the most rudimentary, informal opportunities to develop their learning processes...Illiteracy, both a symptom and a cause of the downward spiral of ignorance and poverty, epitomizes the waste of human learning potential." (*The Human Gap,* The Learning Project Report to the Club of Rome, 1979, pages 106–107).

essentially the result of a gradual expansion of schooling, and partly of adult literacy programmes in a number of countries, as well as instruction by mass media, carried out by the press and broadcasting systems, with or without international assistance, which significantly helped campaigns against illiteracy in various parts of Asia and Africa. While percentage-wise illiteracy is decreasing in absolute terms, projections indicate that the number of illiterates will continue to increase, rising from 742 million in 1970 to 814 million in 1980 and 884 million in 1990. This discouraging development is, nevertheless, partly counterbalanced by the fact that the absolute number of literates will increase by 456 million between 1970 and 1980 and by 556 million in the next decade.

The following graph regarding the proportion of literates and illiterates aged 15 and over, from 1970 to 1990, shows that while the number of literate persons will grow by 1,000 million, the number of illiterates will increase by almost 150 million as well:[1]

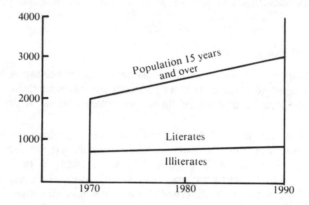

Thus, despite reductions in the rate of illiteracy, the absolute number of illiterates continues to grow. It now stands at the shocking figure of 800 million, or almost one-third of the world's adult population. This is enough to demonstrate the enormous size of the problem.

The fact is that the advance of literacy does not keep pace, on a world scale, with the high rate of population growth. Equally disquieting is that, at present, nearly one young person in four enters employment without having received minimum education.

In many countries there is a marked disparity between the proportions of male and of female literates. Tradition often dictates that women should confine their interests to the domestic sphere, should not compete with men for work except at an unskilled manual level, and therefore should have no need to read and write. Girls sometimes receive a briefer and inferior education, compared to boys, and are expected to prepare themselves only for marriage. Among people who acquire a basic literacy in youth and then lose it because they find no opportunity to make use of it, the majority are probably women. When governments initiate adult literacy campaigns women are sometimes deterred from participation by their husbands, or

(1) *Source* for figures on illiteracy: Unesco Office of Statistics. Particularly the recent publication *Estimates and Projections of Illiteracy*, Unesco, Sept. 1978 (Figures do not include China, Democratic People's Republic of Korea and Vietnam).

discouraged by prevailing customs and social norms. On a world scale, it is estimated that 60% of all illiterates are women, and their numbers are increasing faster than these of male illiterates. The elimination of this disparity is a complex task, requiring a deep-rooted change in social and psychological attitudes, and involves all the issues of full human liberation.

It has been suggested that illiteracy is not so great a social and cultural evil, since new media can bring even illiterate people into the orbit of communication by the use of spoken word and image. But it is evident — without denying the power of audio-visual means of communication — that language, in both its spoken and written forms, is an irreplaceable way of communication. At the same time, literacy is not just a reading habit. We share the view that literacy means much more "reading the world, rather than reading the word".[1] Thus, illiteracy means that eight hundred million human beings remain second-class citizens, excluded from truly full participation in their societies and in the world.

Denial of vital communication tools to many hundreds of millions of men and women makes a mockery of the right to inform or be informed. It is therefore necessary to assemble all possible means, educational, cultural and social, along with various communication technologies and mass media, whose powerful potential may lead to the eradication of this blot on the landscape of all countries in the world. And, at the same time, since the number of illiterate people will unfortunately grow for decades, adequate communication channels, particularly audio-visual vehicles, have to be developed to bring those who cannot be reached by the printed word into the mainstream of social and economic life.

4. Post and Telephone

Interpersonal communication remains an indispensable segment of the communication network in both developed and developing countries. As already mentioned, there are innumerable ways and channels of interpersonal communication in all societies, using symbols, languages and other modes of human expression. In the contemporary world, interpersonal communication is supported or made easier by modern media and various services offered by telecommunications.

MAIL TRAFFIC (Millions)

	1968	1976
Africa	3.029	4,293
North America	85,522	96,630
South America	2,236	3,350
Asia	23,488	26,117
Europe	60,073	70,420
USSR	6,954	7,923
Oceania	3,169	2,980
WORLD	184,471	211,713

SOURCE: Based on figures in the *Statistical Yearbook* 1977, United Nations. (The figures for South America include only nine countries; the figures for the U.S.S.R. are official figures communicated directly to the statistical office of the United Nations.)

---

(1) As expressed by Paulo Freire, Brazilian educationist.

The largest organised system for delivery of point-to-point messages is the postal system. Postal services had their beginnings thousands of years ago. Today they represent a vital network in each society. The preceding table indicating the volume of postal operations and its growth from 1968 to 1976 shows a general trend towards expansion.

While postal services are well-established in developed countries, they continue to be inadequate in most developing countries, partly because of the remoteness of millions of villages and the poor quality of road and rail networks. There are still many centres of population which have no post office.[1] Progress in this field could be a factor for social cohesion, and contribute to the infrastructure of commerce and industry. Post offices can also serve a useful purpose as government information centres, and as focal points for activity in the fields of development and public health.

A surprising trend in recent decades has been the deterioration of postal services in certain developed countries. One reason is that the excellent services of the past depended on lavish use of manpower. Another reason is that communication authorities now prefer to invest in improvement of the telephone system, which is profitable, rather than on maintenance of the postal system, which is not; hence, the deterioration of postal services between persons, nations and continents. The faster the aeroplanes, it seems, the slower the post. This deterioration often causes serious disruptions in individual and commercial communication. There are grounds for thinking, indeed, that the decline in the habit of letterwriting has been a factor in reducing the ability of many people to express themselves in a literate manner, and this also represents a cultural loss.

The second largest organized interpersonal communication network is the world-wide telephone system. It has been rightly said that the telephone is a sophisticated extension and amplifier of traditional oral communication. No other media can match the telephone for direct, spontaneous dialogue.[2]

There are at present some 400 million telephones in the world, an increase of about 1,000 per cent since 1945. Virtually all nations are linked together, many by direct dialling systems, in the international web, the largest integrated machine ever built. Eighty per cent of the world's telephones are in only ten countries of North America and Europe, for a total population of about 750 million; approximately half of all telephones are in the United States alone, where several cities have more phones than people. The socialist world has 7% of the world's telephones for a population of 1,300 million, and the developing world has 7 per cent for population of 2,000 million.[3]

---

(1) On the average worldwide there is one post office for every 7,000 persons; some European countries (e.g. Norway, Portugal), have fewer than 1,000 persons per post office, but in some African and Asian countries there is only one for hundreds of thousands (e.g. one per 300,000 in Rwanda) (Source: *Encyclopaedia Britannica* 1974).

(2) Because the telephone has become such a commonplace feature in industrialized societies, its vital role is often simply taken for granted and its socio-economic impact insufficiently analysed, particularly as a potentially powerful, indeed essential, tool for development in the Third World. It was quite rightly stated: "How important was the telephone's specific technology in these processes of change? It is extraordinary how little has been written exploring this question. Social scientists have neglected the telephone not only along with, but also relative to, other technologies. As a cause of social change, transportation has been much more studied than communication. And among communication media, TV, radio, movies, even the telegraph have been studied more than the telephone." (*The Social Impact of the Telephone*, Ithiel de Sola Pool, Editor, The MIT Press, Cambridge, Massachusetts, 1977).

(3) *The Role of Telecommunications in Socio-Economic Development*, Hudson, Goldschmidt, Parker and Hardy, Keewatin Publications, 1979.

The growth of telephone communications has been equally rapid. According to ITU figures about 440 billion telephone calls are made per year (some 50% in the United States). Particularly revealing is the number of international calls; for example, in 1950 overseas messages to and from the United States totalled 773,000, but in 1977 the number was more than 50 million outgoing calls alone. Since the first transatlantic underwater cable was laid in 1956 with the capacity to carry 50 telephone calls at one time, five more have been brought into use, the last capable of handling 4,000 calls simultaneously. In all, there are 30 international submarine cables, with a total capacity of 17,074 telephone circuits. Meanwhile, in the past decade, the capacity of international satellite communications has jumped from 150 to more than 10,000 circuits; the latest generation of satellite used for transmitting telephone messages can handle 6,000 calls simultaneously.

Such increased traffic has been caused by social and economic needs for direct contacts between persons, firms and public authorities as well as by technological improvements in facilities. Another influence has been the rate reduction which has defied the usual inflationary spiral and actually reduced the cost of telephone use. It is these rapid advances in facilities, continuously decreasing costs and higher quality service which lie behind the upsurge in the use of the telephone and no limit to its utility can be seen.

It appears to us that the slow development in many countries of postal and telecommunication facilities and services is a real obstacle both to persons and societies. It is not sufficiently recognised that these facilities and services are not only the outcome of economic growth, but also a precondition of overall development and even of democratic life. The unevenness in telecommunications expansion becomes an increasing obstacle to communication between developed and developing countries. Similarly, the rates of several services which have not yet fallen commensurately to costs, hamper their use by poorer consumers. Here is an area of communication which needs to be reconsidered in many countries, particularly in view of its social, economic and cultural significance.

5. Group and Local Media

A next step in the organization of social communication is at the level of groups or local communities. To achieve group cohesion, to mobilize local resources, and to solve problems affecting smaller or larger groups, communication is necessary, and various means are utilized. Communication at this level is increasing in both developing and developed countries. Frequently, local communication is assisted by the mass media, which have used the flexibility of modern technology to give small or remote communities new facilities, such as radio stations which are financed by a central organization and managed locally. But communities and individuals have also taken the initiative in creating their own means of communication. These means cover a wide range of media from local and wall newspapers, mimeographed leaflets, photos, posters and dazibaos, local radios and itinerant loudspeakers, to pamphlets, slides, tape recorders, exhibitions, experimentations, local fairs, film and music festivals, puppet shows, itinerant information vans, street theatre and an endless list of similar devices and means. They are often used for social purposes, as a support to local development schemes for hygienic and health campaigns, for religious and political actions, as well as in relation to all initiatives where conscious involvement of local populations is felt necessary. Among promoters of such types of information means and group media are public authorities, development officers, professionals such as agronomists and barefoot doctors, teachers and local political activists, priests and artisans.

More emphasis should be placed on these media and local activities for four main reasons: one, because they may be overshadowed and pushed into the background by the big media; two, because mass media have been expected to accomplish tasks and goals for which they are not fitted; three, because in many countries the neglect of a certain balance between big and small led to unnecessary wastage of scarce resources, by using inappropriate means for diverse audiences; four, because by establishing links between them broader horizontal communication could be developed.

Signs of such a shift of emphasis can be related to the changes taking place in overall development strategies, which are turning away from the top-down models of recent decades and concentrating on greater participation of communities in expressing their very existence and their own particular needs and formulating plans and organizing action to meet them. This change has a broad impact on the use of media to support development action, not the least of which is establishing or expanding the use of local media. Thus communication, in quite different ways, becomes an indispensable component of development efforts and of social life in every locality. In this sense, developmental media activities are not, in any way, a "threat" to freer information flows, but on the contrary, one of the conditions of democracy, since a more active participation in development choices and activities is part of a democratic way of life. At the same time, this does not mean that the role of large-audience media is going to decline, or that countries and communities have to choose between them. For different purposes, different means — thus a combination of group media and mass media is probably the appropriate answer.[1]

In many developing countries significant experiences and initiatives have been carried on with different, but not negligible, results. Examples from Peru, Mexico, Tanzania, Senegal, Philippines, India,[2] Botswana,[3] Thailand, China,[4] Mali,[5] and several other countries are quite extensively known.

These examples serve to illustrate the essentials of group media: they are all media functioning in a group process, defined on a sociological, rather than a technological basis. They can be traditional or the most advanced mass media, but they act to facilitate self-expression, persuasion, dialogue and discussion of group situations.

---

(1) A quote from a well-known expert in these issues may be relevant: "As the focus of the development programme turns toward local activity, there will be more and more incentive for a developing country to concern itself with local rather than large-audience media. Such a country will not have to *choose* between big and little media, for it needs both, but it will have to display wisdom and foresight in balancing big against little, national radio against local radio, wall and mimeograph newspapers against national newspapers, and the like. Most such countries already have some big media, and they are not about to throw them down the drain. Indeed, such media will continue to have important uses. The essential questions are (1) how best to use them, when development strategy turns toward localities? (2) what priority should now be assigned to maintaining and strengthening the system of large media as against the demands of local communication?" (Wilbur Schramm, *Mass Media and National Development-1979*, CIC Document No. 42).

(2) Since the inception of All India Radio (AIR) more than 40 years ago, folk media have been integrated into its rural broadcasting in the form of daily programmes narrated by traditional characters who convey the typical life and folklore of the rural area of a particular station.

(3) Reports from Botswana point out how the performing arts — drama, puppetry, dance, music — are used in live local performances and through radio as part of a two-way communication process in which performance is the catalyst for discussion about matters of local concern among community groups which had been alienated by more organized, exhoratory approaches to adult education and development projects.

Very often local groups use modern communication means (radio or television, new printing techniques, even microprocessors and video-tapes) adapting them to the needs of their environments and to the variety of local conditions[6]

In developed countries, too, there is an increasing awareness of the need for media of this kind, especially by minorities, special interest groups, and community or political activities. People in industrialised countries find themselves grappling with environmental problems, pollution, ecological issues, energy crises, unemployment, adaptation to technical change, and similar issues. They feel a need to express themselves without delay and with such means as are at their disposal.

Group media, sometimes called little media, have place in the whole arsenal of communication means, vehicles and techniques. They cannot and should not be confused either with point-to-point or with mass communication. Group media have their proper place — and it is with that in mind that they should be planned, financed and used.

6. The Mass Media

Since the invention of the printing-press and in more recent times of a multitude of communication forms including telegraph, telephone, telex, camera and film, phonograph, radio and television, the world has been truly transformed. Messages of all kinds are continuously transmitted to a vast number of recipients. The advent of the mass media and their presence in our daily life has been one of the major features of the contemporary world.

Quantitatively, the expansion of communication in recent decades has been steady

---

(4) In China popular media, small media, local information means have always been used by many people and all over the country, both before and particularly after the Revolution. For example, the folk songs, the revolutionary serial pictures, and the well known Chinese opera played not only a cultural, but also an informational and social role. However, the most cited example is the use of dazibaos, meaning posters in big letters or bold characters, used for conveying all sorts of messages. It may be interesting to quote an explanation given by a Chinese interpreter interviewed by a French writer: "We needed tens of thousands of square kilometers in the papers to air our problems and then, also in writing, to let our readers have their say. The answer can differ from province to province, from city to city, even from street to street. Only when we gather all these responses, shall we be able to develop a reliable picture of what the nation is thinking. In addition, the people desired to be in control. They wanted to find their voice; they do not want to be regimented." (From: *Popular Media in China,* Edited by Godwin Chu, An East-West Center Book, 1978).

(5) A typical example is the development in recent years of rural newspapers in Africa. Since 1972, more than 30 have been established (with the assistance of Unesco and bilateral co-operation agencies). Usually published as monthlies, these papers have circulations ranging from 500 to 45,000 and have proved effective agents in promoting local endeavours. The more wide-reaching ones provide horizontal communication links among sub-regional localities and some provide a channel for bottom to top communication, as in Mali where the Bambara-language monthly "Kibaru" provides a source of news for an entire day's programming every week on the national radio devoted to news and opinions from the rural areas.

(6) An interesting example is from Bolivia where local radio stations are operated from the mining centres. Some twenty such broadcasting operations, run by the miners' unions, provide an outlet for expressing their opinions, illuminating their problems and proposing corrective action. Despite intermittent official pressures against their operations, these group media continue to function as an important voice of public opinion. In Mexico, the Institute for Community Development started a multi-media experiment using group media operations for development activity in the barrios of Guadalajara as a bi-weekly bulletin featuring social, political and economic aspects of life for rural migrants in urban centres; neighbourhood festivals featuring locally-produced musical performances, poetry readings and discussion groups; popular theatre groups; a film club and community production of audio-visual materials.

MANY VOICES, ONE WORLD

and uninterrupted, in keeping with demographic, educational, social and political trends. It is certainly difficult to estimate the outcome of this rapid growth in information and entertainment, coupled with the efforts of an ever-growing audience to assimilate it. The following figures may indicate the scale of the expansion:

Increase 1950–1975	Percentage
Press (Number of copies, daily newspapers)	+ 77
Radio (Number of receivers)	+ 417
TV (Number of receivers)	+3235
Books (Number of titles per year)	+ 111

Unesco Statistical Yearbook, 1977

Most striking of all is the size of the audience that the media now reach around the world. The number of people untouched by the mass media has dramatically decreased in only 25 years. At the present rate of progress, almost everyone everywhere will be in the audience in a matter of decades.

Media audience increase 1960–1975	Percentage
Total world population	+ 33
Daily newspapers (circulation per thousand inhabitants)	+ 5
Radio receivers (number per thousand inhabitants)	+ 95
Television receivers (number per thousand inhabitants)	+185
Book titles (published annually per million inhabitants)	+ 30

Unesco Statistical Yearbook, 1977

The geographical extension is even more significant in that it means the mass media are no longer an exclusive prerogative of urban populations. Their expansion in practically all countries and to wide rural areas brings within their reach not only regional centres and national capitals, but remote corners of the world as well. This wider coverage has produced another major change in the nature of the messages transmitted, particularly in radio and the press. Rural newspapers and, more importantly because of their wider dissemination, radio programmes are produced in local languages. Where geographical isolation once cut off hundreds of millions from most distant events, they are now fast becoming members of the national — even global — community. This, plus the astonishingly rapid spread of television in developed countries, and its steadily growing influence in the Third World, has brought with it diverse social — in the broadest sense of the term — changes which have yet to be fully explored and assessed.

The expansion of various sectors of communication, and more particularly of mass media, increases the importance and stimulates the expansion of agencies which supply and circulate news to newspapers and broadcasters, and to other specialised consumers, the public in general getting news in an indirect way. Press agencies are the major and sometimes only source of information to these media, especially for news of foreign countries. More than 100 countries now have their own national news agency, a considerable increase over the past 10 years.

DISTRIBUTION OF NATIONAL NEWS AGENCIES

Africa	Arab World	Asia	Europe	Latin America	North America	Oceania
26	18	19	28	11	3	2

Among the news agencies there are five — Agence France-Presse (France), Associated Press (USA), Reuters (UK), Tass (USSR) and United Press International (USA) — which have a particularly wide international role due to the size and technological strength of their systems of collecting news and distributing it in many languages all over the world. Each has offices in more than a hundred countries, and employs thousands of full-time staff and part-time correspondents. They collect hundreds of thousands of words a day and, domestic distribution included, transmit millions of words. Each issues news twenty-four hours a day to thousands of national agencies, subscribing newspapers, radio and television organizations in over a hundred countries. All have regular services, usually daily, in Arabic, English, French, German, Portuguese, Russian and Spanish; some also provide their service in other languages.

Many other countries in all regions of the world have national news agencies of growing importance and a number of them maintain, individually or jointly, their own offices or correspondents abroad to collect or distribute news. Most national agencies have a network of correspondents in the country, while for external news they subscribe to or have exchange arrangements with two or more of the world agencies to receive foreign news and provide domestic news; many also subscribe to the services provided by smaller national agencies, either from neighbouring countries or from those with whom close ties exist. However, in a number of countries news services are not yet agencies in a proper sense, but more offices for collection and distribution of official information and a sort of gatekeeper for external news.

The total daily circulation of newspapers throughout the world is more than 400 million copies,[1] an increase of 20 per cent over the past ten years. Circulation per thousand inhabitants has increased even more on a world average: from 104 to 130. The total number of dailies is around 8,000. At the country level, the highest daily newspaper circulation (per 1,000 inhabitants) is in Sweden and Japan (nearly 600). Regionally, the highest circulation (per 1,000 inhabitants) is in the USSR (396) and the largest number of dailies is in North America (1,935). The lowest circulation is in Africa, with 14 copies per 1,000 inhabitants. Many local newspapers offer their readers little in the way of reporting in depth, foreign news, or the exchange of opinion. The small size of such papers is often cited as the reason, but some papers with only four or six pages manage quite successfully to keep their readers well-informed.

Available figures show that although circulation has grown constantly, the world-wide total of daily newspapers has remained about the same for years. This figure has remained static mainly because of mergers, the death of small local papers, and competition from radio and television, factors operating largely in North America and Western Europe.

The role of newspapers in circulating news is decreasing as broadcasting, particularly by television in developed countries, has stepped up its reporting and enhanced its appeal as a news source. But newspapers play an increasingly valuable

---

(1) Sources: *Unesco Statistical Yearbook* (1977) and *World Communications* (Unesco, 1975). Data cited here do not include China, the Democratic People's Republic of Korea and the Socialist Republic of Vietnam. Latest data for China reported that in 1966 there were 1,908 dailies; circulation figures for 1,455 newspapers around 1960 were 20 million copies or about 27 copies per 1,000 persons.

role in explaining, interpreting and commenting upon events in society, especially when broad debates on major social objectives or world affairs are taking place that require expanded analysis as opposed to straightforward reporting. When this is so, certain beliefs about the function of the press have to be revised,[1] and the need to specify the various functions of journalists reinforced.

The periodical press is such a diverse field that it is impossible to generalize about its structure, content or even to estimate accurately its size, and thereby its influence.[2] Magnitude aside, it is obvious the periodical press serves multiple audiences with an almost infinite variety of content. There are signs in many countries that the periodical press influence and appeal become a counter-weight and a corrective to the uniformity of mass messages.

Books are, as they have been in the past, an irreplaceable storehouse of knowledge and of cultural values. This century has seen a great and still accelerating increase in book production, which can be ascribed to the growth in the absolute number of literates, advances in education, the arrival of paperbacks, improvements in production and distribution techniques, and the spread of libraries and travelling libraries even to remote places. Between 1955 and 1975, world book production more than doubled, taking the number of titles published annually, and tripled in the number of copies printed. Eight billion books, and 590,000 new titles, now come from the presses every year. However, a high increase in book prices, largely due to paper cost, has impeded their necessary growth. The scene is also one of marked imbalance and dependence. Books are very unevenly distributed, both inside and among countries. Developing countries, with 70 per cent of the world's population, produce 20 per cent of the books published, and many of these are printed by subsidiaries of firms centred in developed countries. Imported books, sometimes unsuitable in various ways, have to be used in schools, and national literature is poorly represented in bookshops and libraries because of the inadequacy of publishing resources.

In all regions of the world, radio is the most ubiquitous of the mass media. Transmission capacity has more than tripled in the last quarter century. In 1950, some 50 countries in the world had no broadcasting facilities; 23 of these were in Africa. Around 1960, the number of countries with no radio transmitters had shrunk to 12, seven of which were in Africa. Around 1973, a world survey of 187 countries and territories showed only three of them with no transmitting facilities: Bhutan, Liechtenstein and San Marino. There are an estimated one billion receivers in the world, i.e. an average of approximately one for every four persons on earth. The

---

(1) The idea that reporters and newspapers have no further obligation than to present the news and the facts has often been challenged. In many Third World and socialist countries, leading authorities and journalists see the role of media as contributing to the solution of social, political and economic problems and needs. Many journalists understand their role in an analogous way in western developed countries. It may be relevant to quote here the voice of John Hughes, editor of The Christian Science Monitor and president of the American Society of Newpaper Editors, who said of their role: "Newspapers have responsibility to prepare their readers for social change . . . editors have a responsibility to produce newspapers that are more relevant to society's needs; that have more depth. . ."

(2) Statistics covering periodicals are grossly inadequate; data and estimates vary widely. The International Federation of the Periodical Press states that in 1975 there were approximately 410,000 periodical titles in existence. For the same year, reporting data from 137 countries, the Unesco Statistical Yearbook gives a figure of 123,000. The reliability of either figure is tenuous if one accepts estimates (Mountbatten-Stammer) made in the 1960s of only scientific and technical periodicals, which place that single category around the 100,000 level.

proliferation of receivers around the world is an important indication of the long arm of radio, and developing countries have made particular use of this medium in the last two decades.

In developing countries, radio is the only medium that can really be labelled "mass", where a large proportion of the population can be reached by radio broadcasts and possess the means to receive them.

Estimated Number of Radio Receivers in use					
Continent	Year	Total number (million)	Continent	Year	Total number (million)
Africa	circa 1960	4		circa 1960	22
	1970	16	Asia	1970	58
	1976	30		1976	113
America, North	circa 1960	184		circa 1960	136
	1970	326	Europe	1970	233
	1976	454		1976	284
America, South	circa 1960	14		circa 1960	3
	1970	31	Oceania	1970	8
	1976	58		1976	14

Source: Unesco Statistics on radio and television 1960–1976, Office of Statistics, Publication No. 23

No other medium now has the potential to reach so many people so efficiently for information, educational, cultural and entertainment purposes. Radio can be used easily and economically to reach outlying regions and for communication in the many vernacular - often unwritten — languages existing in developing countries. Almost all countries have a certain capacity to produce radio programmes in line with their political needs, cultural patterns and basic values. Radio is perhaps today the least transnationalized communication medium both in terms of ownership and programme flows. Despite these advantages, radio is to an extent limited as an international medium of communication because of language and technical barriers, except in the field of music where it promotes a universal language. Music needs no interpreter, and radio has achieved a great deal in preserving, encouraging and popularizing the music of various countries, especially folk-music. For example, the Asia-Pacific Broadcasting Union has built up a major collection of folk-music recordings which are exchanged among broadcasting systems affiliated to the Union. The rise of television as a communication medium is obviously more striking since it started from a zero base only a few decades ago. Its phenomenal development has been not only in the proliferation of receiving sets but also in the quality of its output. Television has multiplied the amount of visual information and entertainment available to the public to a vast degree and has introduced new dramatic sensations which involve the viewer in far flung events. Television, more than any other medium, epitomizes the advances made in communication in the last 25 years.

The age of television dawned in 1936 when France and the United Kingdom began regular transmission of programmes. By 1950, five countries had a regular TV service and by 1955 the number was 17. This figure had increased fourfold by 1960. A decade later, more than 100 countries were transmitting television programmes and, today, television services exist around the world in a total of 138 countries. The number of television receivers, reaching a formidable 400 million throughout the world, is proof of the immeasurable impact this invention has had on the lives of millions and on the spread of information. The most recent available figures show that between 1960 and 1976 the number of countries with more than one million television receivers increased from 13 to 34. At least nine nations have more than 10 million receivers and, in most developed countries, the number of sets approaches the number of households.

However, in developing countries it is the possession of a minority, sometimes a tiny minority, and in certain countries the programme content reveals that it is there primarily to serve the local elite and the expatriate community. Despite its phenomenal growth, television reaches in some 40 countries less than 10 per cent of household units, and in more than half of the countries, less than half of the households have TV receivers, By contrast with radio, the cost of a television set is beyond the income of the average family; community sets, for example in village halls, have only partially mitigated this limitation. Also, its limited range means that it is available chiefly to city-dwellers and reaches only a fraction of the rural population. Again by contrast with radio, the production of television programmes is an expensive business, and poor countries naturally have other priorities. The screens are therefore filled for many hours with imported programmes, made originally for audiences in the developed countries; in most developing nations, these imports account for over half of transmission time. It is in the field of television, more than any other, that anxieties arise about cultural domination and threats to cultural identity.

All sorts of technological innovations have accompanied or had their roots in the explosion of mass media, which opened the doors to larger audiences, expanded sources and resources for information and entertainment and supported important cultural and social changes. While it is obvious that mass media have widespread positive effects, the phenomenon of their growth is of such importance that much more research is necessary, not only in developing but in developed countries, since the expansion of mass media and their orientation cannot be guided only by political decisions or available resources. Fundamental research in all countries should provide the framework for future development of communication.

7. Satellites

The growth of planetary satellite communication has been spectacular, as shown in these two tables:

GROWTH OF THE INTELSAT SATELLITE SYSTEM

Year	Countries with antennas	Leased Half-Circuits
1965	5	150
1970	30	4,259
1975	71	13,369
1979	114	n.a.

Source: Intelsat Annual Report, 1979

GROWTH OF THE INTERSPUTNIK SATELLITE SYSTEM

Year	Countries with Earth-based stations	Satellites Type
1973	3	"Molnia"-2
1975	6	and "Molnia"-3
1979	9	"Stationar"
1980	12	"Stationar"

Source: Document provided from the Intersputnik, 1979

In the short time that satellites have been showering the planet with messages (since 1957 up to end 1979, around 2,100 satellites were launched) they have become an integral part of so many circuits — news agencies and the press, radio and television broadcasting, telephone and telecommunication links,[1] business, banking, commerce, agriculture, mining, aviation, navigation, meteorology, entertainment — that already their innumerable effects are directly and indirectly influencing the daily lives of the majority of human beings.[2]

More than 33 communication satellite systems of national, regional or international scope are now functioning or are under construction in the world. A score more are on the drawing board. They can be divided into four categories by use:

(a) International satellite systems. Intelsat and Intersputnik are the only systems of this type existing today. The Intelsat system provides direct satellite communication for more than 100 member countries operating over the three oceans. Although primarily a domestic system, Intersputnik is also used by socialist and some other countries.

(b) Domestic and regional satellite systems. The USSR's Molnia and Ecran, Canada's Anik, Indonesia's Palapa and the USA's Westar, Comstar and RCA are operational examples. The West European, Arab and Nordic country regions are likely to be the next to possess operational systems.

(c) Marine and aeronautical satellite systems. Examples of these mobile communication satellites include the Marisat system for ships at sea, Aerosat (in the planning stage) for commercial aircraft use, and the European Space Agency's Marecs (a marine satellite spin-off).

(d) Military satellite systems.

The European Communications Satellite System is to be operational by the mid-1980s, and a number of European satellite projects are already functioning. Major satellite systems now aloft include the Franco-German Symphonie experimental system, with Symphonie I and II launched in late 1974 and mid-1975, the Italian Sirio system, and the regional OTS system for inter-country telephone communications among European and North African countries. An experimental Japanese communications satellite was launched by NASA in April 1978 to test the possibility of sending television programmes direct to individual television sets.[3] Deployment of one or more domestic communications satellite systems is currently planned after assessment of the performance of three experimental communications satellite systems to be introduced in the next two years. Other potential regional communications satellite systems are the projected African Satellite System and the Andean Satellite System. Other national projects, in various stages of development, include those initiated by Algeria, Australia, Chile, China, Colombia, France, India,

(1) One example: In the past decade, the telephone capacity of international satellite communications has jumped from 150 to more than 10,000 circuits; the latest generation of satellite used for transmitting telephone messages can handle 6,000 calls simultaneously. In 1978, about 70 per cent of the 1 billion international calls were handled by satellite.

(2) This is apart from the military use of satellites — more than two-thirds of those now in orbit — which affects the whole world.

(3) NHK, the Japan Broadcasting Corporation, had long been working on a direct satellite transmission system that would provide quality reception on individual receivers of super high frequencies, which must be used in satellite transmissions but had heretofore been too weak to be received by home television sets. However, using a special converter and impact antenna, the experience to date has achieved very satisfactory technical standards.

Indonesia, Iran, Libya, Malaysia, Mauritania, Nigeria, Norway, Oman, Peru, Philippines, Saudi Arabia, Spain, Sudan, Thailand, Uganda, the United Kingdom, Venezuela and Zaire. More than 120 countries possess earth stations linked to satellites for transmission and reception.

With their amazing capacity, rapid increase in number and, most important, their combined use with television and computers, communication satellites have opened vast new areas of activity and their potential is enormous. Not only their potential, but the number of countries interested in using satellites for internal and international communication, leads us to stress the need for wider discussion and speedier solution of a wide range of questions of a legal, financial, economic, sociological, psychological, cultural and political nature.

8. Computers

Last but not least among contemporary developments, informatics has advanced at a speed not anticipated even by those working in the field. The pulsed transmission of information (coded binary, or digital, information) has progressively extended the scope of the computer systems initially installed in centralized services of large organizations. This was first effected by earth links (co-axial cables and radio links) and later by satellite linkages around the earth. This evolution has taken different forms: multiple terminals making possible various forms of teleprocessing (star-shaped configurations); an increasing interlinkage of computers (data transmission); or various data-processing service networks (data bases,[1] customized data-processing, storage and filing). Thus computer networks and/or systems have entered the sphere of communication. However, three basic functions constantly recur, and are now becoming increasingly "distributed": storage (memory), arithmetical and logical operational units (processing), peripheral input/output units (access). It is the latter which make communication between the user and the computer system possible. Constant improvements are being made in cost, performance, reliability and the size of computer hardware, as well as in the diversification of the capacities and the ways in which they may be used. Indeed, self-contained mini-systems are becoming increasingly numerous.

Computers are now capable of performing one billion operations a second, or a million times more than the pioneer computer of 1944. The size of processing and storage units has shrunk by a factor of about 10,000 while the speed of these units (measured in the number of instructions or calculations processed per second) has increased by approximately 50,000. According to experts' predictions, these trends are expected to continue at least into the early 1980s. Electronic circuits can be

---

(1) A distinction must be drawn between "data bases" and "data banks". It is now possible to establish and operate magnetic memories capable of representing billions of words, each of which is accessible in the computer system. These stocks of information are termed "data bases" in the case of bibliographical references concerning actual documents located elsewhere which must then be retrieved and read in order to secure the information desired. What in fact is involved is the automation, generally via "transnational" channels, of scientific and technical or similar documentation. The term "data bank" tends to be reserved not for such indirect information but rather for direct information through immediate reading of computerized "data". Once access to the computer system is secured it is possible to call up instantly on one's terminal or computer numerical values, statistical series, descriptive attributes, etc. Interest in these data banks is growing particularly since their computerization makes them amenable to all subsequent forms of processing (sorting, amalgamation of files, statistical calculations). However, their rapid development is limited by three factors: the cost of data capture and validation; the costs of up-dating; lastly, the preservation of various secrets.

manufactured as a unit known as a microcircuit on the surface of a silicon chip five millimetres in diameter. The number of components that a chip can carry has increased in recent years from ten to 64,000; manufacturers foresee a rise to a million by 1985. A wafer-thin element measuring 10 by 15 centimetres can store more information than the telephone directory of a large city. The speed of transmission from a computer or data-bank to a terminal has similarly increased, thanks first to the analogue system — meaning the use of signals in a form analogous to the relevant information — and then to the digital binary system; the latter translates all information into numerical form, and is called binary because it uses only two symbols instead of the usual ten numbers. Information in words is transmitted in this binary form and decoded on arrival, so quickly that the process is almost instantaneous. By the use of repeaters, signals can be transmitted over great distances with little or no loss in quality. Several thousand signals, interleaved and then automatically separated, can be carried at the same time.

The cost of electronic processing and storage units has fallen dramatically over the past 25 years; e.g. the cost per computation has fallen 180 times. A computer which

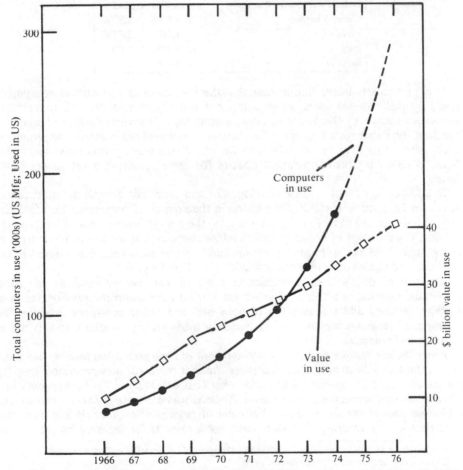

* Source: *High and Low Politics: Information Resources for the 80s*, Oettinger, Berman, Read; Pallinger Publishing Co., Cambridge, 1977.

might have cost a million dollars in the early days can now be acquired for $300. The cost of performing one million calculations fell within a decade from ten dollars to two cents, and the cost of a component carried on a silicon chip from ten dollars to less than one-fifth of a cent. Informatics, once the privilege of wealthy corporations and major government departments, is thus brought within the reach of the small business, the neighbourhood school, and even the home.

The reduction in data processing costs is well illustrated by the chart on the preceding page, comparing the rise in the number of computers used and their value in the United States over the ten-year period 1966–1976.

Industrialized countries are steadily increasing their investments in computer development which is growing in fact faster than indicated below because the costs of computers have decreased so sharply over the years. This table shows investment in computers (as percentage of GNP) for a few developed countries.[1]

	1970	1979
USA	2.11%	3.2%
Federal Republic of Germany	1.34%	2.45%
United Kingdom	1.55%	2.83%
France	1.18%	2.65%
Italy	0.77%	1.5%
Benelux	1.15%	2.3%

It is particularly interesting to note that the volume of investments in computers, made by their various users, when compared with the total of telecommunications investments made by the postal services, is quite high. In several developed countries the data show that resources spent for these two purposes are gradually approaching each other. This may be an indication for other countries, particularly developing ones, in rethinking their investment policies for communication development in the future.

In addition to overall political development and economic growth the most recent advances have led to a massive expansion in the volume of communication facilities and activity, thanks to three developments: (a) the growth, extension and increasingly efficient organization of communication infrastructures; (b) the use of new forms of energy and machines to produce, transmit and receive messages; (c) changes in the methods and signals used in communication (i.e. digital signals).

The use of digital data transmission methods can be regarded as the most important advance, in a technical sense, for it means the complete transformation of storage, retrieval and transmission of both oral and visual messages produced by "computer" language which itself has recently made an exponential leap forward in practice and potential.

From the continuous and steady development of communication means, two main conclusions may be drawn: one, that these changes represent an irreversible trend in the development of communication; two, that basically there is interdependence and not competition between different media. Nations which choose to concentrate on one technique should not do so to the detriment or neglect of another. While it is often said that we are entering "the electronic age", there is for instance no sign of the

---

(1) Source: *A four-year programme for the Development of Informatics in the Community*, Commission of European Communities, 1976.

demise of the print media. Newspapers, magazines and books will continue for decades to be major sources of information, knowledge and pleasure; efforts should be made to ensure their continuity, to increase their quantity and to improve their quality. Radio and television also need further expansion and larger investment, above all in developing countries. The same is true of the newest innovations in technology; all nations need to plan for at least their gradual introduction. Developing nations in particular should make their plans as a matter of urgency, in order to share in the advantages of new technologies and adapt them to their special needs and conditions.

Chapter 2
Expanding Infrastructures

The preceding pages represented an attempt to illustrate the continuous development and expansion of communication means. The second major trend is related to the creation and diversification of infrastructures for the collection, transmission and dissemination of various messages.

1. From Libraries to Data Banks

Problems related to the collection and storage of information concern all societies today. Not only is the quantity of information enormous, but a continuous supply of relevant information is required by individuals and organizations, by the media and agencies, by schools and institutions of learning, by governments and by firms in the course of their daily work. Considerable progress has been made toward the industrialisation of data collection, storage and retrieval, but it appears that understanding of the needs and creation of adequate facilities still fall short of what is desirable.

Libraries and documentation centres are probably the oldest and most common sources of classified, stored knowledge and information. Nevertheless, there are no satisfactory analytical surveys or statistics on the number of libraries in the world today; international statistics are obtained periodically from a large number of countries, but the data supplied vary so widely concerning the different categories of libraries (national, university, school, special) that no meaningful summation can be made. Recent data from 131 countries show that there are national libraries in 116 of them. These central points of a country's library system, vital for the provision of national bibliographical services and maintenance of archives, are most unevenly developed around the world. One indicator is their volume holdings which total some 160 million. Of this number, more than a quarter are in the national libraries of the USSR and the USA (126 and 19.6 million respectively) and another 50 million of the total are in ten countries of Europe[1]. The uneven expansion of libraries and their services is indicative, particularly since it shows the low priority given to book collection in many countries.[2]

Originally, librarians were simply custodians. But libraries have gradually become

---

(1) *Source: Unesco Statistical Yearbook,* 1977.

(2) A few random examples of the magnitude of library services are indicative: in Gambia there are 139 libraries, of which more than 90 per cent are in schools; Nigeria reports 182, but this does not include school libraries; Mexico has more than 2,400 libraries, Panama 140, Peru 347 and Brazil — not including school libraries — 3,518; Iraq reports 4,415 of which only 56 are outside of school; Malaysia 576; Thailand 890. *Source:* ibid.

service centres for the general or specialised public. Public libraries now have a central role in the social, educational and cultural life of many communities, providing more than facilities for reading and study; larger and more specialized libraries became indispensable reference centres for students and researchers; documentation centres specialised for particular areas (science, trade, the arts, etc.) grow in importance. It is difficult to say that all countries have created an appropriate infastructure for the supply and storage of indispensable data. This is why there is often a dearth of necessary information before political and economic decisions are made; this is also why in negotiations between developing and developed countries, or between buyers and supplying companies on the world markets, the former are handicapped by the absence, or at least by slowness in provision of data for such negotiations. This is one of the areas where more efficient supply and flow of information becomes a prerequisite to reduce dependency in international economic relations.

Both social and technological changes are in many places challenging some of the traditional roles of the library, no longer the sole important source of collected information, and causing transformations in library organization and services. This is particularly the case as new electronic computerized technologies come more and more into use. For these fledgling systems to fit eventually into the international networks now fast being extended, many developed and developing countries will have to organize national systems that can achieve the necessary input-output links to existing national or international networks. Multiplication of such networks is a significant part of the changing library scene in most developed countries.[1] But even the most advanced countries are discovering many difficulties in adapting to new technological possibilities for information collection, storage and dissemination. A particular drawback is that the procedure and methods of the traditional library are often outmoded.

For current purposes of collection and supply of news to a growing number of official and private, primary or secondary consumers, news agencies play a leading part. Along with the growth, in size and number, of straightforward news and photo agencies, there has been a similar growth in agencies collecting and disseminating news in specialised areas such as business and commercial data, stock quotations, tourist information, weather and sports reports and so on. In some countries, newspapers can subscribe to agencies providing a background service on current events, sometimes supplying complete articles which combine comment with "hard" news, and often run by professional groups within the field. The rapid growth in demand for visual news led to a new type of agency specializing in videotape and film for television. While they do not yet match the scale of the long-established agencies, the potential effects of these new agencies on the exchange of views, particularly

(1) It might be of interest to mention a report by the National Commission on Libraries and Information outlining a major programme for development of information services in the United States: (a) a top-level agency in the Federal Government should be designated or created to develop, guide and lead the nation's effort to coordinate its library and information services; (b) bibliographic services that cover wide segments of the printed or non-printed literature and that serve extensive groups of users with the means to identify and obtain it, must be designated and supported as national information utilities; (c) national telecommunication linkage of information service facilities including computers must be extended and subsidized to provide nationwide access to national resource library collections and to national information utility services from any inhabited location that has telephone service; (d) existing state and regional library and information programmes can become the building blocks of a national programme; the partnership of Federal-state-local services must be developed to make the best [use] of resources.

between nations, are significant.[1]

There have also been spectacular technical developments in recent years in the collection, editing and transmission of quantities of news at an increasing pace. But, in general, only the world agencies and a few large national agencies possess the facilities to utilize these developments. By using the cathode ray, it is now possible to write, correct and edit for immediate automatic transmission. Computerized systems are in use for the storage, retrieval, editing and transmission of news and commercial data. The capacity, range, speed and quality of transmission of news, messages, photos and facsimiles have all been increased. Improved and extended cable systems, telephone and teleprinter services and radio circuits within and between countries and continents are now supplemented and, in some places, have been replaced by transmission via satellites. Technically, news and reports in verbal and visual form can be transmitted simultaneously through the different satellite systems to earth stations throughout the world which, in turn, can pass on the messages instantaneously by land-based systems to the home offices of news agencies, newspapers and broadcasting stations.

The capacity of the human memory is today being infinitely multiplied by amassing information in computerized data banks. Storing exhaustive collections of facts, easily up-dated if necessary, coherently organized and instantly available, data banks are becoming increasingly indispensable for the efficient operation of large-scale information based activities for a wide variety of users (public bodies, news agencies and information media, business and industrial firms, universities, libraries, researchers, etc.) and their use is spreading rapidly.[2] Nevertheless, their utility is limited due to the often narrow criteria for the selection of data being put into data banks or other systems for news storage. The usefulness of these modern and powerful devices for data processing depends not only on whom they serve, but also on the plurality and diversity of data collected and stored.

Where previously only scattered data sources existed, centralized systems can now offer the distant user easy access to stored and classified data in fields as diverse as administration, science, technology, economic and social affairs. Typical centralized systems currently in operation are those used in banking, weather forecasting, medical diagnosis and airline reservations. Linked to telecommunications and advanced audio-visual technology, data banks make it possible to answer all types of questions, according to the data that has been fed in, ranging from information on a particular

---

(1) Major ones are VISNEWS (London), UPITN (United Press International Television News, London), CBS (Columbia Broadcasting System, New York), ABC (American Broadcasting Company, New York). These groups have operations similar to press news agencies, with central offices and film crews and correspondents abroad; news clips were normally flown from the field to the home office for editing, but now satellite transmission is taking over.

(2) Many large multinational firms already operate or participate in international data networks for their own internal use: Cybernet, Mark III, Satellite Business Systems, etc. Specialized networks such as SITA for the airlines, in which 200 companies participate, and SWIFT, an electronic bank transfer system linking 500 American and European banks are other examples of private international networks open to subscribers. In Canada DATAPAC is used as a public network and in Japan, NTT is planning to start operating a national public data network; KDD, the Japanese international carrier is bringing its VENUS system into operation. In Europe, national telecommunication services already offer — or soon will — public data networks: in France, the PTT has set up TRANSPAC; in the United Kingdom the Post Office operates the EPSS system; in the Federal Republic of Germany, the Bundespost is establishing the EDS network; the public data network for the Nordic countries, which will link Denmark, Finland, Norway and Sweden, will be fully operational in 1980; the Telecommunications Administrations of the nine member countries of the European Community are setting up EURONET, a polyvalent, linked data network.

situation at a given moment (such as road conditions), to a selection of information on a specific subject (current plays), topical information, (stock prices), and so on.[1]

If within twenty years — or even less — not only the mass media but a large number of decision-making bodies, businesses and households are linked to central data banks, there will obviously be a radical transformation in the ways and speed that information is circulated and put to use. The same is going to happen with the expansion of data banks for scientific, technical, cultural and business information. In other words, all these informatic networks with their quantities of information and data are bringing about a new mode of communication. It does not seem premature to start preparatory work in all countries for new opportunities such as these, even if they have to be on a limited scale for quite some time. However, since the distribution and development of many of these most recent technological advances in the multiplication of information sources and services are mainly concentrated in a few areas around the world, the equitable distribution of their potential benefits is a major subject of international concern. There can be no doubt that these data exchanges cross political frontiers. This, however, is not a wholly new phenomenon; previous services were already highly concentrated and confined to certain points in the world. International study — not limited to industrialised countries alone — of the flow of data across frontiers, leading to proposals for action, would help in bringing about a recognition of its importance and its implications, and thus facilitate a more equitable development.

2. Amplification of Telephone Services

In developed countries, the telephone has particularly fostered an extension of interpersonal togetherness. The telephone contributed to the development of the urban metropolis; neither skyscrapers nor the so-called satellite-towns would have been built without the telephone. Modern industrial manufacturing, processing and commercial operations, spread widely over countries and continents, could not function as they do without telephone inter-connections between their numerous units. In short, industrialized economies would experience great difficulties if continually expanding telephone services were not available. It also made a special impact in rural areas and the sprawling suburbs, the growth of which was undoubtedly spurred by the availability of quick, easy communication over extra-community distances.

In many countries that have expanded their telephone services, concentration has too often focused on development in and between urban centres, overlooking the great need for and advantages to be gained from links between villages, and between rural outposts and the provincial centres. A single community phone connecting local teachers and health workers to larger administrative centres, farmers with central markets, local leaders with district officers, etc, would certainly bring important and beneficial change to village life. Nevertheless, there are many more countries which

---

(1) One such established network is "Prestel" in the United Kingdom, a service run by the British Post Office. It is different from data banks mentioned earlier for two reasons: (i) its data are not specialized but cover multiple subjects; (ii) it is a computer-based information retrieval system that uses the ordinary citizen's TV set with his telephone line linked to it. The user dials a number to get certain information (for example a railway timetable) displayed on his TV set. What is offered are displays of any of the 100,000 pages of text which various information providers have placed in the memory of the system's computer. Technically, Prestel could also be used to send messages from one subscriber to the TV set of another subscriber via the Presel computer, though that service is not yet offered.

have not expanded sufficiently, or have ignored the need for telephone services. They do not belong solely to the group of least developed countries; there are examples even at higher levels of development, such as in socialist countries.

Since the origin of the telephone, distance has been a major element in fixing tariffs. With the utilization of satellites, it can no longer be a factor. The same applies when "new telephone services" are introduced (telecopy, visual data supply, etc.) where rates no longer depend on the distance the messages are transmitted. In the future there will be a progressive revision of bases for rate setting, which will lead to still further increase in the use of this means of communication.

The use of satellites for telephone connections and the possibility of video telephone add still further dimensions. Telephone links via satellite have expanded capacity for international communication and will undoubtedly be augmented as demand grows incessantly. Many companies and telecommunications authorities around the world are active in the video-phone research and development, attempting to foresee its future potential. A video telephone, by adding a visual image to voice communication, can stimulate face-to-face personal communication and be used to view textual and graphical material as well. Video telephones may also be used as computer terminals and provide a video display of computer-controlled information. However, at present it seems unlikely that video-telephone will be widely used, since there are technical limitations to providing all telephone subscribers with the facility. But it may be supplied to a certain number of telephones, either for specialized purposes or in institutions for collective use.

Given the obvious importance of the telephone, many countries appear to have erred in neglecting to build adequate telephone networks. Unlike the rising costs of some postal services, the decreasing costs for some newer technologies, such as the telephone and electronic data transmittal, will undoubtedly force changes in telecommunication strategies. International and national development assistance institutions will have to consider upgrading the low priority which has hitherto been given to telecommunications projects. Hence, policy decisions on the development and financing of communication services are today a priority for all governments, professional communicators, and the public at large.

3. Vehicles for Specialised Messages

A special role is played by periodical journals. In some countries they are numerous and flourishing; in many others, although limited in size, their impact is growing. Broadly speaking, the periodical press can be divided into two main categories — general interest publications intended for mass circulation and those addressed to specific audiences. In recent years the former have been more and more hampered by financial difficulties because the larger the circulation, the greater the percentage of the cost that goes into printing and distribution; a middle level of circulation has proved more viable. Hence, while many mass circulation periodicals have failed in the past 20 years, special interest periodicals addressed to particular audiences are generally flourishing. They often represent a channel for more than the simple transfer of information, providing a forum for debate, for the publicizing of ideas and discoveries, and for the exchange of experiences. They may also seek to influence the decision-makers or to promote creativity in many fields such as politics, literature and the arts, business and commerce, natural and life sciences, technology, communications, etc. An important category of periodicals is that serving cultural and entertainment interests, satisfying the artistic and literary needs of various groups of readers. A noteworthy trend is the growing number of "underground" periodicals circulating in many countries, particularly in the Americas and Europe. Usually printed in small quantities and "anti-establishment" in content, their protests against selected social, economic or political patterns sometimes have an influence quite out of proportion to the size of their actual reading audience.

Diversified extension of the media is also exemplified by the use of shortwave radio by many countries for external broadcasting to reach audiences, more particularly in neighbouring countries and around the world if feasible. Some of these stations are even located on territories of foreign countries with possibilities of reaching distant audiences. In the past quarter of a century, such broadcasting has increased five-fold; in 1950 there were 385 short-wave broadcast transmitters in the world, today there are more than 1,500, and their total power has increased proportionately.

In most of the countries with such services, direct external broadcasting is for the most part financed by the State or State-established corporations. There are varied, usually combined, reasons for Governments to undertake external shortwave services. The first is to maintain contacts with their nationals overseas, to provide news from home and maintain cultural affinities. The second is to provide up-to-date, factual reporting on national and international events as a service to those who might not have access to what the transmitter considers objective news. The third is to portray internationally an image of the country's socio/economic/cultural life that will foster listener interest and understanding. Another is to spread abroad a country's national policies and views on current events and global affairs. Finally, unfortunately, some external broadcasting has been used for blatant propaganda and attacks against other nations.[1] This, of course, raises problems concerning principles of national sovereignty and non-interference in a country's internal affairs.

The USSR and the USA have the highest number of hours of external broadcasting, estimated at 2,010 and 1,813 hours per week respectively in 1978. The People's Republic of China follows closely with more than 1,400 hours, and the Federal Republic of Germany, the United Kingdom, Democratic People's Republic of Korea, Albania and Egypt, each having more than 500 hours. In all, 26 countries broadcast each more than 100 hours per week,[2] and over eighty countries are engaged in international broadcasting today.

It is, of course, difficult to estimate or pattern the audience for this multitude of international transmissions. The number of radio sets in the world capable of receiving shortwave transmissions is estimated to be between 200 and 300 million. The audience is obviously increased when medium-wave transmission is taken into account[3].

---

(1) In a study perpared for the Commission by B. Bumpus the following motives for maintaining international broadcasting services are listed: promoting the national interest; national prestige; keeping in touch with nationals abroad; promoting understanding between nations; disseminating news with accuracy and objectivity; spreading a particular creed or doctrine; attempting to influence the internal affairs of another country; fostering the national culture, including the teaching of the national language; and reserving a place in the broadcasting spectrum against a future need. *International Broadcasting,* CIC Document No. 60

(2) *Source: International Broadcasting,* by B. Bumpus, op. cit.

(3) Some sample surveys carried out by the BBC in recent years show regular reception of their programmes by various segments of the potential adult audience ranging up to 30% in a few countries depending on the type of broadcast (national language service, World Service or language-training broadcasts) and the audience sample (urban, rural, etc.). In numbers, the BBC estimates the regular adult audience listening to BBC external broadcasts once a week or more to be of the order of 75 million persons, while the total adult audience which includes people listening less often, is around 130 million.

To the Commission's knowledge, there has never been a complete public review of the myriad implications, both positive and negative, of international broadcasting. Pending the undertaking and outcome of such a study, we would propose as a minimum that countries refrain from using external broadcasting for purposes contrary to the principles of the United Nations and of the Unesco Declaration on the mass media.

4. Broadcasting and Broadbands

The growth of electronic communication has been spurred by the ever increasing number of transmission channels being utilized. When radio was invented in the first decade of this century, the wave lengths used were what we now call long wave, able to travel over great distances. Gradually medium waves were brought into use, reaching only over a country or region. To expand transmission capacities even further, broadcasters adopted higher and higher frequencies (short wave, VHF, UHF) for both national and international broadcasting.

The number of countries making significant use of ultra high frequency broadcasting (UHF) is constantly growing. In 1960, only 16 countries had a total transmitting power of more than 30 kilowatts. Around 1972, there were 35 such countries; now practically all developed countries and almost two-thirds of countries with a medium income level have at least such UHF transmitting power.

Still other recent technological advances offer more chances for electronic communication, without the interference problem that bedevils air-wave broadcasting. These new carriers are the broadband vehicles such as coaxial cables and optical fibres. The last, which is only beginning to come into use, promises with its enormous band width, to be a major communications carrier, both for long distances and in links to individual homes. Operational installations are increasing rapidly around the world.[1]

Although the capacity of the radio spectrum is not unlimited, a more rational use, including the eventual employment of single sideband broadcasting, co-axial cables and optical fibres will provide new channels to meet ever-increasing demands of both private and public communication.

5. Cinema and Television Combine

The term cinema is customarily used to encompass all the paraphernalia surrounding the mass medium of popular films, from the production apparatus, its output and viewing places, to all the industrial, artistic and socio-cultural activities relating to it. Cinema is one of the major technologies for mass entertainment as well as for disseminating information and various messages on a broad scale, alongside the press, radio and television. Yet the data about and forecasts for the cinema industry are ambiguous if not contradictory.

Today, world production of feature-length films totals some 3,000 every year. In 1977, the last year for which detailed figures are available, India was the world's top

---

(1) Despite its recent establishment, the optical fibre field is already a major industry. One study estimates that the 1978 world market totalled 68 million dollars, of which 30 million was in the telephone business alone. Projections indicate that by the middle of the 1980s, the global market will top one billion dollars. Optical fibre systems have been launched in Canada and Great Britain; fibres stretch under the streets of Chicago, Las Vegas and Tokyo and are being installed in Berlin and Brussels; Japan has sold India a network to be set up in Bombay.

producer (557), followed by Japan (337), France (222) and Italy (165), while the USA and the USSR lag somewhat behind in film production. All in all, eleven Asian countries produce more than half the world's feature-length entertainment films. Twenty-one European countries and the USSR produce about a third. The rest are produced by some twenty countries, notably the USA, Mexico, Egypt and Brazil.[1] What is interesting about all these figures is that North America and Europe do not lead in film production as they do overwhelmingly in other media.

The cinema is a complex aesthetic, psychological and social phenomenon. Films are "documents", comprising pictures and story, accompanied by words and music; they are thus highly complex and multi-dimensional productions. Throughout its development and much earlier than the emergence of other non-specialized media, film has played a multi-faceted role, providing information, drama, music and so on, either singly or in varying combinations.

Its history began with newsreels, and even today, the cinema still plays an important informative role in some countries, despite the fact that newsreels and documentaries have disappeared from the cinema screen in countries where television is ubiquitous. Thousands of documentary, educational and training films are produced every year, and not only in countries making feature films. They are made for television, for educational programmes — both in and out of school — and widely presented to other specialized audiences in cultural centres, lecture halls and in commerce and industry. In contrast, the vast majority of feature-length films, intended for a mass audience, are dramatized fiction — serious, comic, tragic, fanciful — designed primarily for entertainment, with high, medium or low cultural value, yet sometimes carrying a "message". Finally, the wider use of 8mm and 16mm film, especially super-8, is of particular utility not only for local and group communication activities, but for professionals as well.

The number of cinemas and patterns of cinema attendance vary widely around the world. In Asia as a whole (for the period 1965–1977) the number of cinemas was on the increase up to 1973 when a down-trend started. For attendance the pattern was similar up to 1971 and the downtrend has been more marked since. Wide disparities affect the region in this respect. Only 11 of the 41 Asian countries registered an increase in the number of cinemas during the period, but the massive increase of the number of cinemas in India alone more than made up for the decrease shown in 30 other countries of the region. Cinema attendance in India went up 23 per cent from 1966 to 1975, but for Asia as a whole there has been a decrease of 5 per cent, due mostly to the dramatic drop in Japan from 373 million in 1965 to 165 million in 1977. In the USSR, the number of cinemas and halls in which films are regularly shown has increased by 50 per cent over the past decade and spectators by 30 per cent.[2] In much of the rest of the world except for Africa, the number of cinema-goers seems to have more or less stabilized at a much lower level than ten years ago. In any case, there are still some — though ever fewer — countries where the cinema continues to be a major medium and primary source of entertainment.

This does not, however, mean that films as such are playing a lesser role. On the contrary, the dramatic decline in cinema attendance in Western industrialized countries (about 27 per cent in EEC countries over a period of 20 years) was compensated by the rapid expansion of television, which screens a huge number of films in all countries. In other words, while there has been a notable decrease in most western countries in the number of persons attending films in public cinemas, they are

(1) *Source: Unesco Statistical Yearbook,* 1977.
(2) *Source:* Unesco Office of Statistics.

nevertheless seen by much larger audiences through television[1]. Also the links between the two media are growing as more and more producers are making films especially intended for the television audience[2], and the growing video cassette industry will provide still more films for television and home presentation.

Thus the newer medium is giving new life to the older one, and films remain a major resource for information, education, entertainment and culture. Both media, which had and still have in many countries separate life and competitive attitudes, might benefit from a comprehensive development policy and coordinated activities and resources. In addition, interaction between the two media could help to improve understanding between different cultures if television broadcasters in industrialized countries would show more films produced in developing countries.

6. Entertainment and Leisure

As the cinema rose to the pinnacle of the show business world and became the first medium for really mass entertainment, other media sought to encroach upon and expand this mass market — publishing, radio, recordings and television. The magnitude of the combined products of these media means that the role of communication in entertainment and leisure time activities — although often intertwined with one or other of the functions of communication reviewed up to now — demands particular attention because of its vital cultural impact and widespread economic ramifications.

Three major trends can be identified here: (1) the immense growth of entertainment facilities worldwide, with the involvement of practically all the media in some form of entertainment; (2) technological inventions which permit more "do-it-yourself communications" in which many people play an active part not as spectators but as actors in their own entertainment; and (3) the growth of a huge industry providing an immense dissemination of cultural and artistic achievements and performances, as well as facilities for entertainment and industrialized cultural products connected with it.

It is almost impossible to illustrate this trend by reliable world-wide figures and statistical data. But there is no doubt that cultural, entertainment and leisure-time activities are constantly increasing and diversifying and thus becoming more important.

Print media, including newspapers, respond in large measure to readers' expectations for culture and entertainment. The same is even more true for broadcasting where radio was the first mass entertainer on a world scale and where

---

(1) By way of illustration, a recent study in France shows cinema attendance to have dropped from 411 million in 1957 to 180 million today. Over the same period, the number of television sets has risen from 440,000 to 16 million. It is estimated that there is a cumulative audience of almost four billion television viewers who watch the five hundred films screened annually. On the basis of this report, the French Conseil Economique et Social has expressed the view that "what appears to be new about the film industry crisis, about which there is so much talk today, is that it is one of adapting to the demands and requirements born of various forms of competition which are themselves bound up with a change in the patterns of supply and demand of leisure and cultural activities of the general public." Hence, if there is a crisis in the film industry, there is certainly not a crisis in the audio-visual media in general. In simpler and more direct terms it has been stated that the cinema is such a sick industry because the French have never before seen so many films. (See *Les Perspectives des Industries Francaises du Cinéma,* Conseil Economique et Social, May 1979).
(2) At the Annual International Market of Television Programmes in Cannes (France), more than 1,500 feature-length films were offered to assembled representatives and broadcasting rights were purchased for half of them.

television, for those who can afford it, is probably the most efficient and attractive medium. Evidence in a number of countries shows that more people spend more of their leisure time seeking entertainment, diversion, relaxation or escape by looking at the television screen than through all other media combined.

It is the gramophone record, also thought at one time to be destined to obsolescence, that has achieved the greatest upturn in popularity. The introduction of long-playing records, and more recently of tape cassettes, immensely increased its audience. Pop, folk and classical music all shared in the expansion. Today, about two billion records or tapes are sold every year, with North America and Europe accounting for nearly 85 per cent of the total.

To all these leisure activities and products one must add photography and amateur film-making. In several countries, the rate of increased expenditure in these fields is already higher than that for the growth rate of other culture and leisure items.

In our times, 'the leisure industry' has become big business. It covers the production of equipment such as television and radio sets, hi-fi equipment, record-players and tape recorders, camera and cine-camera for amateur use, musical instruments, the provision of software, including books, magazines and records, and the organization of concerts, festivals, sporting events, travel and tourism. The enterprises concerned make the decisions about what is produced; in practice, there is considerable variety of choice and often a response to the tastes of the customer. Enterprises thus involved are also heavily engaged in the infrastructure of communication, in the new science of informatics with its computers and development, so that they have a large influence over the future as well as the present.

Technological advances continuously contribute to the outpouring of entertainment tools: pocket-size radios, portable colour TV sets, hi-fi equipment, instantly-developing individual cameras, audio-visual cassettes and discs, satellites for transmitting entertainment, cultural and sporting events. A few figures on production of certain items serve to illustrate the growth and magnitude of the industry.

WORLD COMMODITY PRODUCTION

Item	1965[1]	1970[1]	1976[1]
Photographic film (thousand sq.m)	190,882	212,411	244,769
Television receivers (thousand units)	29,975	45,815	49,164
Radio receivers (thousand units)	72,847	107,840	122,534
Transistors (million units)	2,504	7,739	14,895
Sound recorders (thousand units)	7,275	22,914	47,637
Sound reproducers (thousand units)	16,736	20,713	19,147
Gramophone records (thousand units)	447,000	667,040	963,338

(1) *Sources. United Nations Yearbook of Industrial Statistics* (1974 and 1976)

This growth in the entertainment/leisure industry is most striking in developed countries. However, there is already a growing reach into the urban areas and among the upper-middle classes of developing countries, and it will probably continue to spread. An international market, influenced particularly by a few countries and a few transnational companies, has been created, where not only manufactured goods, but cultural and light entertainment programmes, aesthetic values, ethical norms, foreign models and so on are being circulated.

This whole field has many important considerations for the development of communication and of society, among which the following are significant: (a) it is obvious that almost all communication media and facilities will play an increasing role in the areas of culture and entertainment; (b) the growing number of consumers, with the possible exception of newspaper readers, expect the media to supply pleasure, relaxation, culture and distraction rather than information; (c) if these two trends develop, it will be desirable to encourage others which favour the use of leisure-time to meet the real needs, spontaneously expressed, of individuals and communities, rather than to allow an exaggerated control merely by commercial interests.

7. Extension Towards New Areas

In recent times, informatics has become an integral part of communications, first to control switching and routing functions and later to provide store and forward functions in digital communications. Computers, at first in isolation and later linked up with telecommunications and the mass media, began their career in a few limited fields, before gradually reaching almost all other areas and thereby extending the range of roles played by informatics in the communication process.

This range is extremely wide, extending from government administration to company management; it embraces marketing, banking, insurance, education, home data-processing, etc. Data-processing has innumerable applications in the fields of science, technology and education, in particular in agriculture, medicine, meteorology, hydrology, elaboration of mathematical models, automation of industrial processes and so on. Directly applied to the information system, informatics gradually improves the work of news agencies, newspapers and broadcasting, improving the efficiency of the collection, processing, storage and use of news and data.[1]

Such a new area automatically increases the impact of a few countries on developing parts of the world. The technologically advanced countries not only give birth to inventions, but they are the suppliers of goods and the providers of necessary skills. Data communications circuits — or network information services (NIS)[2] — using the existing telephone switching networks, telex networks and leased circuits, developed in the early 1970s in the United States, European countries and Japan. More recently planning and implementation of public digital data networks such as Datapac in Canada, Transpac in France, Integrierte Fernschreib und Datamnetz in the Federal Republic of Germany and Northern European Data Network for the Scandinavian countries have rapidly developed. In Japan there were

---

(1) Some particular applications may be noted: (a) electronic tele-typesetting enables newspapers to be printed by remote control; (b) electronically operated office machines memorize texts typed on them and retype them automatically at will; (c) electronic mail provides instantaneous point-to-point transmission of letters; (d) computer-assisted learning enables students to learn at their own pace, to simulate experiments, and to receive instruction adapted to their particular learning situation.

(2) "NIS is a data processing service connecting the terminal equipment on the user's side with the central computer of the provider through a data transmission network." (*Report on Present State of Communications in Japan, Fiscal 1978,* which is also the source of data cited here).

2,949 data communications circuits in 1977, an increase of 34 per cent over the previous year; 2,689 of them are privately operated over circuits provided by the domestic public telecommunications service (NTT). Japan also has 62 international link-ups, 60 of which are privately operated. In monetary terms, the scale of sales of NIS was $3,000 million in 1980, accounting for an estimated one-third of the entire computer industry. The Western European market for NIS — $410 million in 1975 — is expected to increase to $1,360 million in 1980. At present 66 per cent of this market is in England, the Federal Republic of Germany, France and Sweden; US companies account for a 60 per cent share of the total European market.

Special mention must also be made of remote sensing because of its broad potential and international implications. Technological advances in remote sensor systems in recent years, coupled with the desire for greater information on the earth, its oceans, and atmosphere, have led to the development and increasing use of a new generation of remote sensor systems operating in the microwave region of the frequency spectrum. These new systems, called passive microwave sensors, are capable of providing information previously unobtainable with basic imaging techniques such as photography, television or multispectral imaging used in past remote observations.

Microwave applications are numerous, and the information acquired from the microwave passive sensor data can be used for improving and protecting earth and water resources; planning, preserving and utilizing land resources; protecting and monitoring the environment. More specifically, the data obtained can be used for predicting the weather and long-term climatology changes; for detecting, quantifying and monitoring water and atmospheric pollution; for understanding the earth, ocean and atmospheric dynamics. Typical applications are assessing world-wide agricultural conditions and crop forecasting, making inventories of forest types and timber volume, studying soil erosion, planning land use, surveying water resources, predicting typhoons and hurricanes and weather and climatic conditions and a host of other applications providing valuable data to international, national and local agencies, to governments, public and private institutions.

A major concern in this area is linked with the sovereignty of countries surveyed. Technical facilities are so powerful that important data about a developing country may now be better known in some foreign capitals than by the national government. Another major concern is to assure that data derived from remote sensing is not kept unnecessarily secret but is available to countries concerned and, in particular, to the developing world which must have the technical facilities and trained personnel to treat and assess the data accumulated. At present, the developing nations are virtually completely dependent on the few countries utilizing advanced remote sensing capacity and lack the resources of evaluating and utilizing the potential of this source of information. It is another field that requires broad international co-operation if the development of mankind is to benefit fully from this new technological tool.

All these sophisticated developments have contributed massively to the growth in the scope and impact of communication. The diversification and multiplication of methods of gathering, processing and transmitting knowledge — including knowledge hitherto inaccessible — will have increasing effects on daily life. But it would be shortsighted to see these changes as merely technological; just as politics and economics influence technological choices, so technology has political and economic consequences. The new techniques are aspects of change and agents of change. However confident any society may be of having grasped the historical and contemporary essentials of communciation problems, it may well discover in the next decade, or at furthest in the next century, that other technological advances have produced unforeseen effects, uncertainties, and imponderables. But as technology advances, the essential consideration at every stage should be that its progress is put at the service of better understanding between peoples and the furtherance of democratization within countries and not be used to reinforce vested interests of established powers.

Chapter 3

Integration:
Changing Patterns

In their early stages of development, different communication media operated more or less in isolation from each other. Each had its own objectives to satisfy the needs, real or assumed, of its particular audience for information, entertainment and culture. Gradually however, we are witnessing the blurring of frontiers between different forms of communication. Numerous connections and relationships have been established between them, while at the same time they are aiming at more diversified audiences.

1. Combination of Traditional and Modern

Where traditional communication is still predominant, the role of parents, peers or village leaders is vital in initiating the young into the community and preparing them for active integration in the life of the group. Even where modern media have penetrated isolated areas, the older forms maintain their validity, particularly when used to influence attitudes, instigate action and promote change. Extensive experience shows that traditional forms of communication can be effective in dispelling the superstitions, archaic perceptions and unscientific attitudes that people have inherited as part of tradition, and which are difficult to modify if the benefits of change are hard to demonstrate. Practitioners of the traditional media use a subtle form of persuasion by presenting the required message in locally popular artistic forms. This cannot be rivalled by any other means of communication. Examples abound where song, drama, dance groups and the like are used to promote campaigns against social evils (such as alcoholism, burdensome dowries, discrimination against women, archaic taboos) or for advances in farming, health, nutrition and family welfare, agricultural reforms, national integration and similar national goals. There are many countries around the world which illustrate not only the essential importance of traditional media for illuminating contemporary subjects and concerns and promoting political and social aims, but also emphasize their inter-mix with the more modern means of communication.[1] It should, however, be mentioned that while

---

(1) For instance in India, realizing the value of interpersonal communication in the context of developmental publicity, the Directorate of Field Publicity was set up in 1953. It reaches into the hinterlands — sometimes with mobile vans, but often by foot marches manually transporting equipment — with more than 200 field units which organize community film shows, photo exhibitions, song and drama programmes, group discussions and debates. Similarly, the Song and Drama Division of the Ministry of Information and Broadcasting established in 1954 has become the biggest live entertainment organization in the country. The Division has its own 41 departmental drama troupes. Besides, it utilises the services of private registered parties which are specifically trained to disseminate messages through folk art forms like drama, composite programmes, folk

combined use of traditional folk forms, interpersonal communication and modern media, carefully organized and blended, leads to interesting socio-cultural experiences and results, adverse examples, may also be cited which show detrimental influences particularly when some preconditions and particularities of each environment have not been respected.

Traditional ways of communication tend to predominate in remote rural areas. In African and Asian village societies, for instance, daily events and cultural developments are presented through stories, songs and dances. However, they also serve a purpose in urban areas, since these old methods have not disappeared from city centres and live on to influence radio, television and film production. And people in the towns of the Third World, often belonging to a first generation of settlers in urban conditions, retain their traditions and their fondness for remembered styles in song, dance and story. In urban areas of industrialized countries throughout the world, vestiges of traditional communication survive as a component of educational, cultural and entertainment activities. The performing arts, particularly popular theatre, thrive in all societies and preserve the traces of traditional communication; listening to music, watching shows, sport and travelling are universally popular, and vary in the manner in which they are pursued only because of disparities in economic resources, facilities, personal income levels and social status, cultural traditions and so on. However, the disruptive impact of the technological revolution is changing the socio-cultural landscape both in urban and rural environments.

Therefore, there are basic questions about the links between modern and traditional media from the viewpoint of their mutual influence or reciprocal and complementary support. The main challenge both to policy makers and communication practitioners, is to find a formula to preserve the relationship between traditional and modern forms of communication without damaging the traditional ways nor obstructing the necessary march towards modernity.[1] *Moreover, use of traditional modes in modern mass media productions should be extended.*

2. Links between Interpersonal and Mediated Communication

The importance of interpersonal communication is evident, for example, in critical or exceptional situations or during periods of major political or social change: election campaigns, agrarian reforms, religious upheavals, national emergencies during wars,

---

recitals, puppet shows, ballets, religious discourses, etc. There are thousands of registered troupes in India which give innumerable performances every year. As media, they are alive and responsive to new ideas. Though they have a limited approach, they have the advantage of catering to homogeneous groups. Its effectiveness is, therefore, superior to that of the modern media. (Reference: *Towards a National Policy on Communication in Support of Development: The Indian Case* by G. N. S. Raghawan and V. S. Gopalakrishnan, CIC Document No. 43).

(1) Attention may be drawn to the call from the African economist and sociologist, Sine Babacar: "The umbilical cord that formed an intrinsic link between the traditional media of communication and the socio-cultural foundations of the developing countries is today being loosened and broken. The vital concern now is to cut our losses while there is still time through a policy of systematic collection of the products of oral tradition but also and above all to dovetail coherently the *use and promotion of traditional means of communication* and the rational mystery of new technologies"; as well as to this word from India "Today, the communicator in India has the 'technical know-how' of getting maximum returns from traditional arts in terms of positive communication, with minimum effort. The experience has given a new awareness of the great potentialities of the indigenous media for the much needed persuasive communication". (H. K. Ranganath, *Not a Thing of the Past; Functional and cultural status of the traditional media in India.* CIC Document, No. 92).

counter-culture experiments in community living or group protest, campaigns against social evils and so on. Similar examples are events in the political and social life of many developing countries such as the long march of the Gandhian movement in India, the liberation movements in Africa, the successive mass political campaigns in China and the overthrow of the monarchy in Iran. Interpersonal communication has also been emphasized in the programmes for political and cultural integration conducted in Peru, Tanzania and many other countries. In some socialist countries the importance of interpersonal communication is stressed by simultaneous development of different ways for working community-level information (wall sheets, residential groups, workers' unions, farmers' brigades). In all these cases there has been a close relationship between interpersonal and mediated communication, with the media's impact influenced, strengthened or modified by the pervasive action of interpersonal communication.

Such examples suggest that policy makers should understand the importance of interpersonal communication when carrying out their essential (if sometimes abused) function of promoting changes in attitudes and influencing public opinion. Interpersonal communication, both spontaneous and organized, has played and will continue to play a far more important part than is normally recognized. From an instrumental and methodological standpoint, there are obviously relevant lessons to be drawn. Social scientists have observed in many instances that mass media can effectively change people's perceptions, but interpersonal communication is more likely to be effective when the goal is attitudinal change. In other words, policy makers and planners should bear in mind that if communication is to remain on a human scale it must take its cue from both the present and the past. They must aim to achieve the most fruitful and least alienating combination of the virtues of direct contact between persons and the advantages of mass media and new technology.

Thus, policy issues relating to communication also have to take into account the extent to which interpersonal communication is to be utilized, organized and integrated with other parts of the system. If overall communication power is to be used to help promote social, cultural and political action, decisions must be taken on how to structure the links between different communication channels and actors, and to provide the mechanism for feedback and the ties between interpersonal networks and the media. This last point is essential, for most research and practice has shown that if use of the mass media to achieve social objectives is to have any impact at all, interpersonal communication is vital as a support to the dissemination of the message from the media.

3. Extension of Visual Expression

Visual communication is a basic form of expression which this century has seen dramatically vitalized by the invention of moving images carried by the cinema or television screen. Nevertheless, despite the instant appeal of such images, the older static picture has lost none of its importance, as the frequent and widespread use of wall sheets, posters, hoardings, illustrations and comic strips and "picture novels" testifies.

Take the poster, for instance: either handwritten or printed, often illustrated, a traditional example of a simple means of communication between the producer of goods or ideas and the potential consumer. It fulfils a multiple function: advertising, informing, exhorting, persuading. Posters have also been a favoured communication medium at particular moments in history, such as the First World War, the Mexican revolution, the October revolution in the USSR, the student movements in the 1960s, and during various periods of change in China. In a large number of countries (like Brazil, Switzerland, Finland, Hungary, Sweden, Italy — to mention only a few noted for their excellence in graphic design) posters have a recognized impact for particular social purposes (promoting solidarity, children's welfare, energy saving, etc).

Modern comic strips (they have certainly ceased to be solely or predominantly 'comic', although the old name is still used) are soaring in popularity in many countries today, perhaps not only due to their entertainment value but because their contents have diversified to include material with sociological undertones and because production techniques have ensured a more attractive appearance. The most celebrated are syndicated in thousands of newspapers or published as comic books reaching a world-wide audience of millions. Others may be disseminated to smaller audiences, but nevertheless often attain high quality, aesthetic value and socio-political influence. Certainly their public appeal cannot be discounted, for they offer a concise and easily understood story, using originality of illustration, rapid narration and dexterity in exploiting the full potential of the format. Comprehension of their messages is accelerated by the clarity of narrative to an extent that they are sometimes almost universal in impact. Once dismissed as banal or even harmful, today they are often praised for their semantic, artistic or instructional qualities, or their satirical exposure of modern life and human foibles. However, they are also open to criticism. The fact that they are often syndicated throughout the world means that they may conflict, in some countries, with cherished moral or cultural values. Also, some comic strips give a falsified account of history, have racist or militarist overtones, or encourage a fascination with violence which has anti-social effects.

4. Cooperative Efforts for News Circulation

Another significant trend towards closer cooperation and even integration of efforts is in the field of news circulation. No so long ago, news was exchanged between countries and between news agencies on the basis of mutual political familiarity and recognition of common cultural and linguistic ties. Today the situation has changed because the necessity "to hear and be heard" has created an increased demand for wider contacts and exchange of news between various national news agencies and between countries. More countries now demand to play a role in world affairs and the lack of facilities in many of them for putting their message across to the international community is a matter for concern.

Another important reason for greater cooperation between national news agencies is the economic, social and industrial growth of the developing world as a whole, which, combined with the technological progress of industrialized nations, plays a vital part in breaking down barriers to the exchange of news and information.

Well-established, large agencies have at their disposal a wide network of communication facilities which, with their long experience of collecting, processing and distributing news, makes the transmission and reception of their services a matter of daily routine. But the transmission of news items from the smaller national news agencies to the larger agencies and the flow of news between national agencies — particularly mutual exchange between developing countries — present continuing problems.

Initiatives to overcome these difficulties take different forms. Regional or sub-regional news agencies are already under way. The thirteen English-speaking countries in the Caribbean, with organizational and planning help from the United

Nations Development Programme (UNDP) and Unesco, began the operation of CANA — the Caribbean News Agency — in 1975, in conjunction with Reuters. It became an independent regional agency in 1976 and now comprises seventeen media institutions, some public, some private. An African news agency (PANA) is being organized and the Organization of African Unity decided to locate it in Dakar. Asian news agencies are also preparing the ground for a continental network for news exchange. A feasibility study has been made for a feature agency in Latin America. The oil-producing countries are envisaging the creation of a joint news agency, particularly for the dissemination of relevant news regarding energy problems and prospects in the world.

An interesting recent development has been greater regional cooperation among the agencies of developing countries. This collaboration among news services has been built upon political and economic affinities and joint interests. Also, limited technical facilities and financial constraints have been a stimulus to greater cooperation in news exchange, in common use of carriers, joint appointment of foreign correspondents, mutual assistance in journalists' training and arrangements for diffusion via satellite.

In 1975, the non-aligned countries organized a pool of national news agencies. Within a year the number of pool members was 26; by 1978 it had grown to about 50. The pool is conceived as a vehicle for improved knowledge and mutual understanding among the non-aligned nations, designed among other things to strengthen bilateral and multilateral cooperation among them. It represents a concrete effort to reduce the dependence of non-aligned and other developing countries upon the major international news agencies. The pool operates through regional centres such as Tanjug, the Yugoslav agency, the Tunisian agency TAP, the Moroccan agency MAP, INA in Iraq, Prensa Latina in Cuba and the Press Trust of India. It also cooperates with the Inter Press Service, a cooperative enterprise founded in 1964, in providing news services to Latin America and other developing regions. During the first three years of its existence the pool's contribution to the volume of news exchange between the non-aligned countries has increased five-fold and now amounts to more than 40,000 words per day. The pool has also contributed to improving telecommunication facilities, including satellites, lowering transmission rates, and increasing training facilities for news agency journalists and assistance to establishment of agencies in countries without such services.

In some instances, cooperation focuses mainly on the content of the news flow; in others the emphasis is on improving utilization of technical facilities; elsewhere it represents a contribution to political ties, or it can be a supplement to a self-defence mechanism. Despite obvious obstacles, of a political and technical nature which such cooperation has to meet and eventually overcome, the regional structures may increase the sources of information, as much as they can help in enriching and diversifying the interpretation of events.

It is important here to underline that, contrary to what was feared and sometimes alleged about the growing number of and exchange between smaller national agencies, the use of the services of the large national news agencies (i.e. the international news agencies) by the national news agencies is also increasing. The reasons for this are several: the quality and variety of services offered by large agencies; the fact that they are equipped to supply news from all parts of the world; the technical limitations of many news agencies in small and developing countries; the increasingly felt need for comparing news from different sources; the growing capacity in developing countries to make appropriate critical selection of news coming from abroad.

Along with these infrastructures for news collection and circulation, there are regional associations of news agencies (in Europe, Africa, Arab States, Asia) whose long existence has proved useful in prompting development of agency operations as well as cooperation in such areas as training programmes, pressure for more advantageous transmission rates and so on.

In addition, regional broadcasting unions, for radio and television, operate in Africa, America, the Arab States, Asia and Europe.[1] In general, the most important broadcasting unions have similar aims, including the promotion of professional cooperation in all fields of common interest, in particular with regard to programme, technical and legal matters. These unions such as Eurovision and Intervision have set up structures for news and programme exchange; similar systems exist for the Arab countries and in Asia. With the advent of communications satellites, programme exchanges and transmissions became possible at the inter-continental level. Some of the regional unions pay particular attention to intra- and inter-regional programme exchange, as well as technical cooperation in training, production, scheduling arrangements, etc. For example, international hook-ups linked 105 broadcasters to televise the 1976 Olympic Games from Montreal to reach an estimated 1.4 billion persons. This world-wide interest in sport is further exemplified by the EBU report of programmes transmitted by Eurovision in 1978, showing that sporting events make up more than 85 per cent of the total. However, the exchange of news is receiving increasing attention; the members of the ABU, for instance, set up a television exchange system in 1976, for sharing of news features and in 1978 Singapore, Indonesia and Malaysia began exchanging news on film. In addition, 45 minutes of news per day is available from Eurovision to ABU members and future plans call for a single satellite reception centre for redistribution in the region.

We see as a positive trend the growth of news agencies, the inter-agency cooperation and the expansion of regional activities, especially in broadcasting. This growth helps to fill existing gaps in the total news supply picture around the world, but its further development depends on the establishment of national agencies and other communication infrastructures where they do not yet exist and improving the capacities of the weaker ones. Such a trend should be supported by all those concerned, in developed as well as in developing countries.

5. Diverse Messages to Diverse Publics

Much progress can be recorded in new techniques and facilities which make for greater diversification and individualization of messages. This helps to overcome the stifling uniformity that afflicts much of mass communication and precludes variety of choice. However, uniformity and lack of options are not only technical problems; their solution does not lie only in technicians' hands. They are basically political problems, sometimes related to ambitions for "social engineering", by those who feel responsible for shaping societies and human minds. While some solutions which will permit contents to be diversified and adapted to various environments may come

---

(1) Arab States Broadcasting Union (ASBU), Asian Pacific Broadcasting Union (ABU), Caribbean Broadcasting Union (CBU), European Broadcasting Union (EBU), which includes a large number of companies from other parts of the world, Inter-American Association of Broadcasters (AIR), Ibero-American Television Organization (OTI), International Radio and Television Organization (OIRT), North American National Broadcasters Association (NANBA), Union of National Radio and Television Broadcasters of Africa (URTNA).

from scientists and technologists, their implementation, or non-implementation, will often depend on political decisions.

In the print media, two modern technologies are being used that help small-edition publications to survive in the mass market and allow for editions that can be tailored more directly as to the needs and interests of the diverse groups that compose the "mass".

Electrostatic copying has enabled some publishers to provide printing on demand. Rather than storing thousands of unsold books in warehouses, they run off copies as orders come in. In such a publishing operation, no book need ever be out of print. Computer printing exists in many forms ranging from the automated composition now being widely introduced in newspapers to the individual printout that responds to an information retrieval enquiry. Newspapers and magazines that have introduced computer composition can produce editions with varying content for different markets. The flexibility of this new technology also permits the economical introduction of text variations. In particular, the advent of the computer in newspapers is part of a total transformation of the industry. In the 1970s computers were introduced for composing purposes and the first electronic terminal for use by journalists and editors came on the market in 1973.[1]

It may not be long before output from a visual display terminal could be tailored to particular readers: since most of today's news is now available in computers that are fed by news services, it would be possible, in principle, for a subscriber to dispense completely with a standard newspaper and have individual access to the news by a retrieval system. The user would provide the computer with a series of key words on which to search the stored news, and be provided with his own "newspaper" containing only the items he is interested in. However, while such possibilities cannot be ruled out, technical problems exclude their early realization and the whole idea is open to question.

Manufacturers are making their equipment ever more "intelligent". With the arrival of the portable, remote, feed-in, "stand alone" unit, the newspaper becomes a network of micro-computers with a wide repertory of skills. All indicators point to a further acceleration of automation in the newspaper industry, fostering greater diversification of service to subscribers.

Limitations to diversification imposed on electronic media are obviously greater. And the ways to overcome these obstacles and problems to be solved are even more difficult. The extent to which broadcasting over the air can serve a variety of national

---

(1) The introduction of computer typesetting is a good example of the necessity to evaluate carefully both the potential sociological and economic impacts of new technologies before their adoption. In many instances, typesetters have vigorously resisted this labour-saving technical advance (which, indeed, has proved cost-effective in a large number of installations) and halted production of newspapers for long periods by protest strikes. However, hasty introduction without prior meticulous matching of technical possibilities with production needs can lead to serious problems, as for those of the London *Daily Mirror*: ". . . from November 1978, the *Daily Mirror* began to convert from hot metal to computer setting, planning to complete the changeover by May this year. The result was an escalating disaster. Pages could not be finished in time, resulting in delays in the critical printing and distribution processes, and consequent subsequent loss of sales. Worse, instead of losing staff, the problems of running two separate systems meant that the *Mirror* had to employ more, not less, staff — and all at the substantial wage rates, now in excess of £200 per week, which had been negotiated as a quid pro quo for the loss of jobs. By the end of April, the *Mirror* knew they were heading for financial disaster unless something was done to curb the losses caused by the computer system problems. Additional production costs had soared to over £5 million in 1978/79 and the coming year was looking twice as bad." (*New Scientist*, 28 June 1979).

and local groups of people, as well as special audiences simultaneously, is limited by the small number of channels available.

Another recent development in countries with heretofore rigidly centralized broadcasting systems has been the establishment of or clamour for diversified local broadcasting. This trend, particularly evident in Western Europe[1] evolves from myriad, often contradictory, economic social and political factors: commercial interest; professed needs of geographical or community groups; demands for broader access to and participation in pluralistic broadcasting structures; activism on the part of political and minority groups and so on.

There is much variation in the results. Some of the new broadcasting organisations are a reflection of local and even parochial interests, others of an ideological background. Some, however, try to establish ties to groups in the community — educational and cultural circles, religious denominations, labour interests, business and industrial concerns. Many stations adhere to professional broadcasting of the traditional type, but some make a real change through widespread participation in programming and audience assistance in production.

"Citizens' band" radio, which is beginning to develop in many countries, is a trend revealing the same desire for more diversified and individualized broadcasting.[2] The system enables individuals to operate short-range transmitter-receivers (10–20 kilometres) for broadcasting to others possessing similar equipment. Governed by various regulations as to licences, range, fees and conditions of use, such individual radio is increasingly used by public bodies, organized community groups, business firms and above all by ordinary citizens for interpersonal communication. Various forms of Citizens' band radio operate in over 25 countries, mostly in Northern America and Europe. This system, which is relatively inexpensive, might be useful in some regions without the necessary telecommunications infrastructures.

Cable television is a communications system which employs coaxial cable and other sophisticated electronic equipment to deliver a range of programming and information services to various receivers. Although cable is not new, since rudimentary systems were operating in the late 1940s, advancing technology, changing regulatory policies, and improved marketing and services have combined to stimulate development in recent years. Many people look to the development of cable television as an answer to the need for more diversified content. In several countries, it has already been extensively exploited and it now offers the possibility of a virtually unlimited number of channels for a multiplicity of users and purposes. In the United States, for example, nearly 4,000 cable systems serve 14 million subscribers, or one out of every five American homes. Cable television is likely to be serving more than 30 per cent of the population by the early to mid-1980s. Several other countries,

---

(1) In various forms, initiatives for increased local broadcasting are being considered or undertaken in such countries as Italy, France, the Federal Republic of Germany, Spain, Sweden and the United Kingdom. Italy is a particularly striking example where in 1971 illegal private cable television set in motion hundreds of independent operations which led to a 1974 court decision that the State monopoly was unconstitutional. Today, more than 500 independent television stations and more than 2,000 local radio stations are on the air.

(2) Comment by **Mr. S. Losev:** "With all the due respect for 'citizens' band' radio, I don't think it is true to qualify it as a trend for widespread participation and still less as a trend revealing the same desire for more diversified and decentralized broadcasting, since it is not a means of broadcasting, but of interpersonal communication. It is not of any use for the countries which just started developing their own communication system, since they will certainly rather start with setting up a national radio station and with supplying its citizens with necessary transistors to receive these broadcasts. Thus, this paragraph does not correspond to real interests of developing mass communications systems in developing countries."

particularly the United Kingdom, Netherlands, Canada, Belgium and Japan, are expanding facilities for cable operations; below are a few examples of their size.

CABLE TELEVISION

	Number of cabled receivers (in thousands)	% of all receivers	Local independent programmes
USA (1)	19,397	17.1%	Yes
Canada (2)	3,144	48.5% of households	Yes
Belgium (4)	1,674	approx. 60%	Some experiments
UK (3)	2,000 in 1974 4,000 today (est.)	20% (est.)	Experimental
Switzerland (3)	445	25%	No
Austria (3)	50	2.5%	Projects in view
Denmark (3)	730	50%	Some experiments

Sources: (1) Statistical Abstracts of the United States 1979.
(2) Canadian Cultural Centre, Paris.
(3) Council of Europe, 1977
(4) Belgian Embassy, Paris

Cable began as a means of improving reception of local television signals by delivering them to the home through a community antenna and cable. Very soon its capacity to carry a variety of programmes to the viewers, or to satisfy requirements for different content, became of prominent interest. These functions are still its basic selling points, but the enormous information-carrying capacity of coaxial cable also means that many additional services could be delivered by cable. The key to cable television's potential is its wide-band, multi-channel capacity (new systems typically have 30 or 40 channels) and its potential for two-way communications. Extra capacity has also allowed some systems to make channels available for public access, educational purposes and other local programming.

Cable television offers TV viewers a variety of choices and to many of them a possibility to select programmes according to their needs (individual or local), tastes and preferences. However, as with any new technology, the introduction of cable television has profound effects on the existing broadcasting situation. Capital investment in cable hardware may constitute, at least for the forseeable future, more of a privilege of the affluent urban dweller than a realistic option for more than three quarters of the world's population. In addition, since one of the most obvious advantages of cable is the provision of channel choice, this advantage is of little use unless there are a number of stations with a variety of programme material available to fill those channels. In most countries of the world, the use of cable would require opting for one of two unsatisfactory alternatives to utilize this channel choice: having to rely on foreign stations for programming, or leaving valuable channel capacity unused or under-utilized. Some countries that have introduced cable television note its detrimental effect on "cultural sovereignty". Cultural sovereignty or national cohesiveness is difficult to maintain when multiple choice cable channels are available, particularly in countries with limited programme-producing capability, which must resort to showing foreign programmes or foreign stations to fill cable channels.

The promise of cable television (multiple channels, multiple choices for the viewer) may well have been oversold in its early development period. Although the technology lends itself to a wide choice of programmes that can serve individual and minority needs, it also tends to splinter the national audience into many mini-audiences, which is not in all circumstances viewed as beneficial. Moreover the cost of providing separate programme material for three dozen or more channels all at once is beyond the means of many such enterprises.

One of the most favoured aspects of cable television is the availability of channels for educational and community access programming. In some countries where cable has been introduced, the regulatory authorities have made it a prerequisite that cable system operators, whether public or private, provide a community or public access channel which citizens of the community can use for local interest programming. There were high expectations that community access channels would enrich community life by fostering communication among individuals and community groups; provide a new forum for neighbourhood dialogue and artistic expression; revolutionize the communication patterns of service organizations, consumer groups and political parties. In effect, cable television's provision of the community access channel was hailed as the technology that would personalize the electronic media and create a sense of community in urban settings, which had been depersonalized by the advances of other technologies. The success of cable television has varied from place to place. Where the cable system operator, public or private, is bearing the brunt of expense for studio time and hardware, much depends on the enthusiasm and experience of that operator. Most public access stations have been learn-on-the-job propositions, and because they are community access channels, most of the programme personnel are unpaid volunteers, whose time and experience, if not intelligence and enthusiasm, may be limited. Many community access channel television products have broken new ground and the public access station has been the scene of many novel experiments, some of which have caused professional broadcasters to admit to surprise and admiration. But the community access channels are subject to the audience fragmentation aspect of cable television and their programmes must compete with, and usually suffer in comparison with, the large range of professional television fare that is available via the cable system.

Thus, despite the impressive technological gains in broadband communications, such as coaxial cable and optical fibres, it is not at all clear that many countries are in a position to implement them simply because they have been invented. The advantages and disadvantages of these innovations indicate that not all remote, widely dispersed rural communities are necessarily well served by these relatively new means of transmission and reception. Furthermore, the cost of laying miles of cable or glass fibres underground in congested urban settings is increasing, not decreasing as in the case of satellite communications.

However, the trend towards opening up ever more facilities for specialized audiences and individual needs must be maintained. An area in which diversification of programmes and their content is particularly important is education. Learning needs and instructional aims vary so widely that educational technology can have a positive impact only if it broadens its capacity to transmit a wide range of messages. The Instructional Television Fixed Service, which is one of several such schemes operating in the USA, is a multi-channel system through which special programmes are transmitted to various schools and other receiving points. Teletext[1], currently

(1) Teletext is a generic term for information retrieval services which make use of a home television receiver and existing television broadcast and cable transmission systems allowing individual users to obtain information on demand from a central computerised service or data bank; Viewdata systems provide the same services via the telephone.

used in Great Britain, is another example of specialization. The BBC has developed the CEEFAX system and the IBA a programme entitled ORACLE, and where the Post Office operates the PRESTEL system. Similar experiments are under way in Canada, France (Antiope, Videotex), Federal Republic of Germany, Japan and the United States, and are being considered in other countries. These services — sometimes distributed by cable — and technologies offer viewers a large number of new uses for their television receivers: electronic newspapers, library services or mail and banking services, to name just a few. The introduction of these additional options for use of the viewer's video terminal leads to new forms of individualized reception, rather than being aimed at a mass audience; in certain circumstances, this may entail a risk of audience fragmentation. In short, the cable system well illustrates an axiom of communication development: technological innovations must be carefully fitted to specific environmental and societal conditions.

Generally speaking, the use of communication technologies for instructional, educational and learning purposes has always been related to the question of small and large audiences, to collective and individual needs and facilities. The advantage of applying the mass media to education are threefold. The potential size of the audience may be enormous; the quality and effectiveness of the message may be superior to that of classroom teaching; and the vividness of the technique may transcend normal educational processes by illustrating abstract concepts through animation or dramatization. The same factors underlie the growing use of the media for adult education and non-formal education, notably in mass literacy programmes and community development schemes. In view of the multiplicity of available media (films, records, audio-visual presentations, radio, television, video-cassettes, video-recording, portable television, computers, microprocessors), the number of educational levels involved (literacy, adult education, rural development, education at pre-school, primary and secondary stages, technical training, professional training, university and post-graduate education), the flexibility in application (continuous, regular, or occasional), and the variety of context (use for groups, with or without a teacher, and use in self-instruction), the possible combinations in the whole process of education are indeed multifarious.

There are four basic models for using modern technologies to reach educational goals: (1) using an existing communication system as it stands to impart information of educational value to its normal audience, e.g. parents' education in Sweden, family planning in Pakistan, BBC literacy programme in the United Kingdom; (2) calling upon an existing communication system to introduce certain new components into an educational system, including non-formal education, with a view to making more or less major changes in the presentation and circulation of information within that system, and hence in the functions fulfilled by it, e.g. El Salvador middle-level reform, technical training in Thailand, Radio Sutatenza in Colombia; (3) using a communication system to perform all instructional functions of a traditional educational system by simulating its normal teaching process, e.g. Tele Scola, Portugal, or Tele Segundaria, Mexico; (4) setting up a new system, defining entirely new functions, leading to the remodelling of structures and to new educational processes, e.g. SITE in India, PLATO, USA, or primary education in the Ivory Coast. The results of these developments have varied widely and most have yet to be fully evaluated to derive the optimum benefits from past experiences.

Recent developments in the miniaturization of computers made possible by micro-processors open broad new possibilities for computer-use in education. Until very recently, high cost and huge size had limited their use principally to large systems and to such purposes as administration, operational and university research, automatic documentation, school time-tabling, assessment of student performance and so on. Now cheap ($200–$300), capacious, dependable mini-computers linked to magnetoscopes, television screens and telephones make it feasible to have an "electronic blackboard", to individualize various forms of programmed learning and multiply teaching resources and learning processes. Many educators look to the new equipment to facilitate at all levels introduction to training in logic and manipulation of formal languages; and they may permit totally new forms of memorization, imaginative creation and social communication to be developed.[1]

To this, one should add an increasingly widespread element in education — equipping people to make use of communication. Some of those involved in this field concentrate on the absorption of information as a product; some on encouraging creative use of communication; others on teaching non-professionals to express themselves in printed or audio-visual media, or in the use of light equipment such as cameras, micro-computers and techniques of reproduction. A similar development is the widespread use of newspapers as a subject of study in schools, which enables young people to make judgments, to perceive intentions, and to distinguish what is true from what is invented (whether or not a semiological approach is adopted). In certain cases, the content of a film or a television programme is used as a point of reference in teaching.

The disadvantages of the mass media when used for educational purposes in many ways mirror their advantages. Massive coverage, with programmes reaching a whole school population, can result in a standardized product, not focused on or fitting into a specific learning situation. This points to the requirement for close collaboration between programme producers and classroom users in the preparation of instructional materials, so as to avoid certain snags due for example to the difficulty of varying the pace of direct transmissions or to lack of flexibility in programming. Much work still remains to be done in order to develop educational media by capitalizing on their great strengths and minimizing their weaknesses. In this connection, there can be no doubt that combined use of video recording and direct transmission would make it possible to circumvent many drawbacks pointed out by educators. In addition, if more attention to the use of media were provided in teacher training institutions and through in-service courses, educators would be more receptive to their potential and to their introduction into the classroom.

Another new opportunity for broadcasters to provide services for the special needs of smaller audiences is the FM radio multiplexing technique whereby two or more separate signals of information are transmitted on a single broadcast channel. Radio stations may broadcast programmes intended for a general audience while at the same time delivering, through a special decoder, programmes intended for limited audiences. There are hundreds of radio stations using this technique today to meet particular needs, such as information services for those who cannot cope with printed information and further education programmes for practising professional groups. In this way, public radio can extend individual services to limited audiences without

---

(1) However, widespread introduction of new devices may be several years in the offing, as many caution against rapid acquisition until the wide variety of equipment now being produced — offering different capacities and capabilities almost from one day to the next — has been thoroughly tested. "Development of micro-computers in the next five years will provide capabilities that are now available in only large systems ... no large scale investment should be made until the situation has stabilized." (*Final Report*, Unesco European regional experts meeting on use of computers in education, Budapest, March 1979).

diminishing regular broadcasting operations.

Diversified two-way communication has expanded in another area with the recent development of teleconferencing[1] in countries like Australia, Canada, Japan, Sweden, United Kingdom and the United States. Teleconferencing can be seen as an innovation in its own right generating a variety of new uses and possibilities for group inter-action over distances. As the use of satellites opens up the capacity for broadband connections on a grand scale, so the manifold applications on the horizon seem almost limitless.[2]

All these techniques are interesting in several respects: (a) they show that by imaginative use of communication equipment it can be made to serve other purposes than that for which it was initially designed; (b) they demonstrate not only the utility of such equipment in developed countries for sophisticated uses, but also its potential for developing and rural regions; (c) in this perspective, many can be combined quite simply with existing electronic networks, and hence require no additional transmission infrastructures; (d) they should not be dismissed out of hand by developing countries, since there appears to be no really considerable barrier (technical, financial or even social) to their introduction as a means to increase the volume and diversity of messages or to broaden the audience; (e) they appear, at least on the technical level, to offer considerable potential for diversifying messages and further democratizing communication. However, realizing or rejecting this potential depends, of course, on the economic, social and political choices that must be made.

6. Combination of New Technologies

Two technological breakthroughs of the mid-1970s, telematics and micro-informatics, open up a whole new world of applications in the era of mass diffusion of information. But they also open up something even more novel — the era of informatization of communication. Micro-computers, as we have seen, had already made an impact in highly developed countries, but they now offer opportunities to developing countries too. The other trend, the merging of computing and telecommunication (the interlinking of computers by telecommunication, or telematics) also offers huge possibilities. Until quite recently, there was relatively little connection between them; any use of one technology by the other was mainly incidental. The present trend is leading to closer connections between computing technology and data communication facilities, constituting the converging complex of

---

(1) A catalogue of teleconferencing systems has identified many different video, audio and computer conferencing systems intended specifically for small group communication. Particularly interesting is computer conferencing for group communication. This can involve a wide range of print-based communication activities. Users type their messages to other "conference participants" on standard computer terminals, usually linked by telephone to a computer network and in return receive printed messages at their terminals. Participants can come in at their own convenience, see what has happened since they were last present, make whatever responses are appropriate and leave. Between sessions, they may check their libraries, draft responses, reflect on solutions and use computer conferences when they choose. The medium operates solely through the written word.

(2) Two examples may be cited: one, an educational communications experiment which was initiated by the University of Hawaii. This has produced a satellite complex known as PEACESAT, which links ten terminals throughout the South Pacific in a multilateral network. The PEACESAT network possesses capabilities for telecommunications (telephone and telegraph), voice (radio), and data transmission (including facsimile). Another one, in Alaska, where a two-way traffic of messages between physicians in medical centres and village health aides has been established via satellite to facilitate the rapid transmission of instruction and information about medical matters.

technologies called informatics.[1]

Since the advent of the digital computer, there are few human activities which are not in some way connected with, influenced by or involved directly in electronic data processing. This has produced what is called the "information explosion", enormously increasing the quality of data which can be stored, processed, analysed and transmitted. The links between computers and telecommunication systems have given an additional dimension and an even more global significance to mankind's ability to handle and use data. This phenomenon is increasingly found in all countries, including many technologically less developed.

Although all data storing and processing has influenced many fields, its utilization in scientific work is particularly significant. Since access to the store of scientific and technical information and data presents a particular difficulty for developing countries, if only for its staggering quantity,[2] they are especially interested in international and regional information systems. Initiatives to establish integrated information networks at the national and international levels, in many cases involving computerized data banks, are flourishing. Cooperative efforts within the United Nations system (IOB, IATFIS), and the UNISIST programme of Unesco, are helping provide a framework for effective world-wide access to information; they include fully operational networks, such as the International Information System for the Agricultural Sciences and Technology (AGRIS) and the International Nuclear Information System (INIS), and planned and developing systems in many fields, including development sciences (DEVSIS) and science and technology policy information (SPINES).

The accelerating rate of production of scientific and technological information (STI), its fast rate of obsolescence, its highly technical nature (resulting from ever greater specialization) and its dispersal (due to the interdisciplinary nature and internationalization of science and technology) make it imperative to strengthen and coordinate the STI systems required for the promotion of activities in these sectors. To this end, it is vital to overcome obstacles of all kinds which hinder universal access to national, regional and world sources.

In connection with these networks, the employment of satellites and particularly of large-scale satellite systems merits attention. The "inter-satellite" links will furnish

---

(1) This trend was summed up as follows by D. F. Parkhill: "Technologically, the direction in which I believe we are likely to move with increasing speed during the next few years is towards integrated systems of information processing and communications hardware and software in which the boundaries between what is communications and what is processing blur and become for all practical purposes indistinguishable. The services provided by such systems will then become a complex and constantly shifting mixture of different forms of information handling, some of which we today associate with telecommunications, others with data processing, and many more which defy simple categorization and only become possible in a merged system. Many of the services remain to be invented, but any minimum list would certainly include conventional person-to-person and store-and-forward forms of communication; information storage and retrieval; voice, video and computerized conferencing; information manipulation, processing and augmentation; information distribution, control and management; man-to-machine and machine-to-machine communications and information display" (*Communication technologies of the 1980s — The future of computer communications,* CIC Document No. 81)

(2) According to certain estimates made by international bodies, in the fields of science and technology alone in the early 1970s some two million scientific writings were issued each year; in other words, six thousand to seven thousand articles, reports, research papers, etc. per working day. Another estimate claims that the number of technical journals published throughout the world today exceeds 100,000. The stock of technical information already accumulated, has been calculated at ten trillion (10^{13}) alphanumerical characters representing the quantity of scientific and technical knowledge recorded in all forms from the birth of science to the mid-1960s. (Source OECD).

very high capacity communication facilities directly between satellite platforms without the need to transmit down to earth and back up to the other satellite. Countries will not have to invest in separate domestic satellites. In the near future, they will use the high capacity, multipurpose satellites of international systems like Intelsat or Intersputnik for domestic applications, such as linking rural areas to the national communication system, and at the same time meet their global communication needs. In this area cooperation, coordination and integration will be necessary, so that fewer satellites will be needed to provide countries with access to global communication, as the geo-stationary space is limited.

Thus, technological innovations open up vast new possibilities. However, a word of caution is necessary: they are not instant miracles, but tools to be introduced and used only after careful consideration is given to all possible resulting ramifications. Each has particular potential, yet none is an isolated means; they are parts of a total system, which should be planned and shaped bearing in mind the integration of all its parts. Technological innovations can often have negative effects, both economic and social, and may distort directions and priorities for overall development activities. However inviting, introduction of some new technologies should be seriously considered, and perhaps delayed, in certain development situations. It must also be remembered that introduction of new technologies is often easier than subsequent provision of software required for their optimum utilization. This requires the attention of each national community and all its elements — governmental and non-governmental, public and private. Caution is further advised because of the fact that the control of the production and utilization of these information processing and telecommunication systems is at present mainly in the hands of industrialized countries and, in some instances, of a few transnational companies. The implications of this situation for worldwide social and economic development — and, in particular, the installation of a New International Economic Order — require the attention of the international community as a whole.

Chapter 4
Concentration

In the course of its development, communication has been affected by many changes: a greater variety of expression, an extension of its scope, a multiplicity of media and a diversification of its means. Overall, these developments emphasize how communication has been transformed from a singular yet complex social phenomenon into a vast new industry, bringing with it even broader, more variegated implications.

1. The Communication Industry

Communication, once carried on by small enterprises which lived in an atmosphere of craft rather than industrial production, is today an important industry which bulks large in the economy of any nation, in terms of plant, employment and requirements for capital. This holds true in countries with market or centrally-planned economies, and whether the economy as a whole is a big or a small one.

The organization of communication on an industrial scale, with ample resources, did lead to the widespread and rapid provision of more abundant information, to diversified and popularized cultural activities and to broader participation in social development by a population better informed and more alert to changing realities than ever before. But it can also happen that access to information is unbalanced and unequal, both between city and countryside and between one nation and another; that the information flow is one-way culturally biased and poor in content, and that it relates to alien concerns and alien realities. These ill-effects too can fairly be laid at the door of industrialization, when conducted without suitable responsibility and democratic oversight.

There are significant differences regarding the industrialization of communication, but the basic trend is a general one. As a result continuous and ever more substantial capital investment is called for in the different fields of communication. Two consequences of the increasing scale of this capital investment are increasingly prominent: first, the number of people utilizing the media must rise if the process is to be economical (in terms of the cost of serving a single person or sending a single message), and, second, control of financing and equipment tends to pass into the hands of large-scale enterprises, which are able to pool the capital needed.

The most common components of the communication "industry" can be found, to a lesser or greater extent, in most countries: various print media enterprises; radio and television companies; news and feature agencies; advertising and public relations firms; syndicates and independent companies producing and distributing print, visual and recorded material for print and broadcasting conglomerates; public or private information offices, data banks, software producers; manufacturers of technological equipment and so on.

It is conventional to divide communication structurally into two main branches: production on the one hand, and distribution on the other, of information, opinion and entertainment. In practice, the division has never been absolute and overlap[1] and unified control is now often much greater than in the past. But the distinction has its relevance because many countries, when developing their communication systems, have given priority to distribution at the expense of production. Hence, they have found themselves dependent on investment from abroad in the infrastructure, on news compiled by outside organizations, on entertainment also created far away, and in general on sources of production over which they have no influence.

Although most countries now have national news agencies, they often have meagre resources — material, technical or staff — so that their supply of news must be supplemented by outside material. For this reason, among others, the mass media in such countries still depend mainly on news selected and transmitted by larger outside agencies. Entertainment schedules on radio and TV are also heavily laden with imports from abroad and the advertising field is often influenced, if not controlled, by branches of international companies. In many instances this pattern leads to large-scale foreign intervention, heavy external investment and unhealthy competition in the development of the material-producing branch of the communication industry. It may also sometimes cause the creation of national and international monopolies in one or more of its components. Such centralization often tends to create a certain amount of standardization in media products. Thus, equal attention should be given to the first branch — the production services — so that countries can be less dependent on foreign imports to supply their communication network and in a position to build a stronger base for preserving cultural identity.

The development of the communication industry has various implications: on the structure of the national economy as a whole; on resources for economic growth; on employment patterns and opportunities and so on. This is important, because it is on these grounds that communication issues and information services in many countries are now a field for planners and those concerned with economic policies. Such a trend needs to be strengthened. But the industrialization of communication has another important consequence: the so-called 'information explosion'.[2] Although this is far from being a universal phenomenon, it is obvious that most countries will experience it sooner or later. It is, thus, certainly not premature to draw attention to possible interpretations of that 'explosion'. From the theoretical, forward-looking viewpoint, the following factors may be highlighted: (a) rapid access to more abundant information; (b) broader participation in social development through the fostering of a greater awareness of reality; (c) balanced, pluralistic interaction in the cultural field of a kind that fosters democratization; (d) consciousness of a common destiny in the development of a global society. However, analysed from a sociological point of view, the same phenomenon may have quite different aspects; (e) access to information is unbalanced and unequal, both within individual countries and in the international community; (f) the information flow is often one-way, culturally

(1) As an example, the distributors (newspapers, radio and TV stations, etc.) produce some of their own material, but they receive a great part of it from other sources and that portion is generally increasing.

(2) An example of this phenomenon is illustrated by a Japanese study which assessed population growth in relation to the volume of information supplied from 1970–75. During that period, the population increased by only 7 per cent, while the volume of information produced (covering 34

unbalanced and repetitive in content; (g) news saturation occurs primarily in urban and semi-urban centres, leaving the majority of people untouched by the major issues and events of their time; (h) news transmitted by transnational agencies frequently relates to realities which are divorced from the problems and requirements of the national culture and national development.

The "communication industry" also includes what has come to be called the "cultural industry", meaning that it reproduces or transmits cultural products or cultural and artistic works by industrial techniques. At the beginning of this century, public access to cultural creations was generally limited to the bookshop or library, museums, theatres and concert halls. Today, cultural productions — books, films or recordings, television programmes — often reach a multi-million audience.[1] Such massive dissemination, built up mainly in the last three decades, points to a vast democratization and popularization of culture, certain products of which until then had been largely the province of the intelligentsia and the wealthy. This is a trend, positive and commendable by itself. Yet some claim that this has debased culture or diminished cultural values. Although there may be a basis for certain criticism, it is surely more important to stress the positive effects, both cultural and social, and to encourage private and public efforts in promoting the diffusion of artistic and cultural works.

In addition to enlarging the cultural audience, the industrialization of production and marketing of cultural creations has provided more work and better earnings for a large number of creative and performing artists, writers, professionals and

---

categories of communication — information supplied through different carriers, ranging from mail, telephone, and data to TV, schools and books) increased almost 70 per cent. The figures show also that the information volume increased more rapidly than real-term GNP.

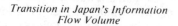

*Transition in Japan's Information
Flow Volume*

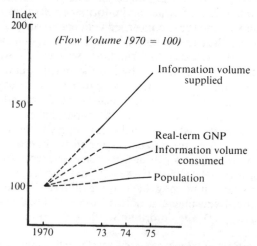

(*Source: Report on Present State of Communication in Japan, 1977*, Ministry of Posts and Telecommunications, published by The Look Japan, Ltd.).

(1) For instance, a 1978 performance by the Berlin Philharmonic Orchestra of Beethoven's Ninth Symphony was seen and heard by 120 million persons; the BBC production of Galsworthy's novel *The Forsyte Saga* has been shown to huge television audiences in 57 countries.

technicians.[1] Another broad benefit results from the expansion of international cultural exchanges which the industries promote; the films of Bergman, Fellini or Satyajit Ray are appreciated around the globe; the books of Mishima, Borges and Gunter Grass are international best-sellers; Picasso reproductions and Ravi Shankar recordings can be seen or heard in virtually every capital in the world. However, the large investments required by cultural industries, their methods of production and marketing and the very magnitude of their operations raise general problems concerning cultural development policies, content and quality of the mass product and effects on consumers which require serious reflection and, more particularly, further research.

Thus, the production branch of the communication industry — notably publishers, news agencies, data-suppliers, film and recording producers, and advertising agencies — is vital to the progress of the industry as a whole. Mass production has its dubious aspects, but it would be unfair to say that industrialization is on balance harmful to communication. Without it, the level of communication would undoubtedly be lower. It can nevertheless, create a cultural environment affected by undesirable external influences, or marked by uniformity and stereotyping. In many countries, innovation is precluded by the force of inertia, or else by a dogmatic interpretation of the interests and tastes of the public. Creative individuals, and spokesmen for the audience, must have more say in cultural policy if it is to be genuinely democratic.

The communication industry is closely connected with other branches of industry. The first of these are the printing and newsprint-producing industries and the electronics industry, which provides the media with the photo-setting machines, the radio and television broadcasting equipment, the radio and television sets, and other devices and equipment without which modern mass media cannot function. It also has links with other branches of the industrial complex, such as computer manufacturing, chemicals, transport and many others.

So managerial circles in various industrial branches have increasing influence on the media and their functioning. In any case, the many inter-lockings between the media and other industries have fostered rapid mutual growth, which has most often required a very high level of investment and, at the same time, produced equally high profits. The huge size and spread of these components and their growth rate within the overall industrial complex has had a number of divergent effects on the social, economic and political development of every country.

We are interested in these issues for three main reasons: first, the industrialization of communication calls for much greater attention from policy makers, planners and media practitioners; second, the imbalance and lack of correlation between different branches of the communication industry is still a major cause of dependence in the communication field; third, since the communication industry is not and cannot be like any other industry, it deserves particular scrutiny, which has not yet been universally recognized.

2. Pluralism in Ownership and Control

The phenomenon of industrialization is closely linked to media ownership[2] which in

(1) Eg. in 1976, in France alone, the record industry produced $60 million in revenue for composers and performers.

(2) Any attempt to draw up profiles or models of ownership, control, management and financing of the mass media is difficult and must be circumspect. This is due to several reasons:

today's world is itself of a pluralistic, diversified nature. Pluralism in ownership has two different origins. On one side, the structures of ownership and control of the media have gone through considerable transformation since the Second World War owing to a) technological advances, b) concentration of production and marketing, c) the capacity for a global span of communications across the world. On the other, both ownership and control patterns depend closely on the overall political system in each country. For all these reasons the ownership patterns vary widely and their co-existence is part of the world picture of communication models in our time.[1]

In the majority of countries around the world, newspaper publishing is a private, commercial operation. This holds true for dailies and periodical papers, except for ten African and eight Asian countries, Cuba and the countries of Eastern Europe. However, in almost all countries there are private but non-commercial newspapers owned and managed by political parties, non-governmental organizations, etc. In socialist countries, newspapers are either owned and published by political and official bodies or else by such associations as trade unions, youth organizations, factories, collective farms, sports associations, higher education establishments and so on.

While newspapers which are commercial enterprises expect to sustain themselves by sales and advertising, they are not always viable on this traditional basis. Capital and profits from other media and from business in general are often injected into the newspaper industry. In many cases, the financing, or at least the deficits are covered by governments or political bodies. Assistance from the State has taken various forms, including tax concessions not enjoyed by other industries, reduced postal and telephone rates, guaranteed Government advertising, and subsidies to the price of newsprint. Although the press is suspicious of Government involvement in its affairs, a desire to preserve variety by keeping the weaker papers alive has led to consideration of various schemes.[2] Direct grants to papers in need are made in seven European nations.

---

1. The delineation of a single model or even several typical patterns is obviously fruitless, since neither would be adequate to represent accurately the gamut of systems governing the ownership, control and operation of the mass media around the world.

2. The difficulty of presenting an infinite variety of models in this field to give an international, or even a national, picture which reflects reality is further compounded by incomplete, vague or conflicting data.

3. Moreover, the various national constitutional, legislative or statutory provisions governing mass media under consideration often differ widely from actual practice.

4. In the majority of systems there is more than one single formula for each of the aspects: split ownership, pluralistic control, tiered management and multiple-source financing are common.

5. Finally, to blur the picture even more, structural and operational patterns of the media are undergoing major revisions in many countries due to inter-related social, political and economic developments.

(1) In the words of one Commission member: "Our world contains a bewildering variety of working models for the ownership and control of communication systems. These range in their diversity from systems in which the state owns and controls all channels of communication to those in which the state is debarred by the Constitution from interfering in the flow of information, with an infinite variety of alternative models filling the spectrum between the two extremes. It is not the task of this Commission to confer its blessing upon any particular model" (*Communication for an interdependent, pluralistic world,* by **Mr. Elie Abel,** CIC Document No. 33).

(2) A few examples: in the United States, the newspaper industry is pressing the Government for some kind of tax-relief formula that will provide an incentive for retaining ownership of local newspapers outside of chains.

Since the advertising revenue in the larger dailies in the Federal Republic of Germany fell by about

Smaller newspapers and some parts of the "quality" or "specialized" press have experienced difficulties from a contraction of operations and size, which has led to limitations on the variety of information sources. This has induced many governments to examine the possibility of subsidies to help keep newspapers alive or to establish new ones, in monopoly circulation areas and to promote plurality and variety in general. The chart below summarizes various forms being considered or employed in 13 European countries:

Type of Subsidy	France	Germany	Italy	Sweden	Norway	Denmark	Finland	Holland	Belgium	Switzerland	Austria	Ireland	Britain
VAT concessions	√	√	√	√	√	√	√	√	√	√	√		√
Other tax concessions	√		√						√				
Direct grants	√		√	√	√			√	√		√		
Low interest loans		√	√	√	√	√		√					
Postal concessions	√	√	√	√	√	√	√	√	√	√	√		√
Telephone and telegraph concessions	√	√	√	√	√	√	√	√	√	√	√		
Rail concessions	√								√	√			
Transport subsidies		√					√				√		
Government advertising		√				√	√	√		√			
Training and research grants				√	√			√				√	
Newsagency subsidies	√		√	√	√								
Subsidies to political party organisations					√	√			√				
Subsidies for joint distribution					√	√							
Subsidies for joint production				√									

Source: Anthony Smith, "Subsidies and the Press in Europe," *Political and Economic Planning,* Vol. 43, No. 569, London, 1977.

Structural patterns in the periodical press industry follow that of the press in general. In socialist countries, the magazines are published or produced by public bodies and numerous social/cultural/economic groups. In the Western industrialized countries, particularly the United States, major consumer magazines are essentially privately owned and a vital element in the marketing structure.

---

50 per cent from 1974 to 1976, the government looked into the creation of a loan fund for ailing newspapers to be administered by a press foundation. Various financing schemes for the fund have been put forth, including tax rebates and publishers' contributions, but the proposal is still under consideration.

In the United Kingdom, three post-war Commissions on the press have studied the problem of concentrated ownership and closures, but no suggestions concerning subsidies or loan arrangements have yet been accepted.

In Sweden, however, the Government has established a varied assistance programme, including production grants, low-cost loans, and various subventions.

Whether the book publishing industry is in the public or private sector depends as with other media primarily on the political and economic system of the country. In many countries, publishing is essentially a private enterprise activity, but most also have extensive government publishing operations (e.g. Government Printing Office in the USA; Her Majesty's Stationery Office in the UK). Mergers between publishing houses, the grouping of several houses under an 'umbrella' of finance and distribution, and financial control by interests outside the publishing sphere have been increasingly common developments in recent times. In socialist countries, publishing is part of the State-owned economy. Most developing countries have adopted a mixed system with the State taking an extensive share, partly because of the absence of adequately equipped private entrepreneurs, partly because of the preponderant importance of educational books which comprise over 80% of the publishing output of the developing part of the world.

Radio and television present a different and more complex pattern of ownership. Early in the development of radio, it was widely recognized that the persuasive power of the new medium posed unprecedented questions and that the ownership pattern of the press should not necessarily be followed; moreover, the small number of wavelengths then available raised the danger that the first in the field might establish a monopoly. For these reasons, governments were more concerned with broadcasting operations than with other mass media and to a greater or lesser degree, the radio and television services of all countries became subject to some State involvement. Many countries have established publicly-controlled broadcasting corporations and the idea of an autonomous but socially responsible broadcasting authority was adopted in several European countries, in Canada and Australia, in Japan, and later in some countries in Africa. The degree to which the authority really makes free policy decisions and gives equal access to divergent opinions, or on the contrary relays the views of the Government, of course varies according to political circumstances.

When a broadcasting system is organized in the form of a public service, it may operate independently, under the overall authority of government or parliament which has defined the basic legal statutes, charters and regulations. In most instances, the transmission facilities are owned and operated by the state (e.g. PTT administrations), but there are exceptions where the broadcasting organizations own and operate the distribution facilities.

Where broadcasting is organized as a government service, the state owns and controls the system, with many variations in the division between central authority and day-to-day management responsibility. This system has been established in the socialist countries, where broadcasting activities are generally the responsibility of a state committee or divided between central and provincial authorities. In Africa, all the national systems are government owned and operated, with the nominal exception of four countries (Ghana, Malawi, Mauritius, Nigeria) where public corporations are formally independent of government authority in day-to-day operations. In the Asia-Pacific region, the pattern is somewhat different. For example, in Japan, Australia, and the Republic of Korea, in addition to the public corporations (NHK, Japan; ABC, Australia, KBS, Republic of Korea) there are a number of privately-owned commercial broadcasting services. Government-operated organizations in many other Asian countries accept paid publicity and several also have private commercial competition.

Private commercial broadcasting predominates in the USA and most of Latin America. The State serves as the regulatory authority, issuing licences and maintaining varying degrees of operational control. In the USA, the Federal Communications Commission enforces certain general rules and has the power, rarely used, to cancel or not renew the licence of a station.

We see, therefore, a spectrum of ownership patterns ranging from private enterprise in the American style, through the autonomous State corporation common in Europe, to Government ownership which is the system in the socialist world and in most nations of Africa and part of Asia. But the distinctions have become less sharp; privately-owned radio and television exist alongside the public organizations in such countries as Britain, Japan, Australia, Canada and Finland. In the USA, the Public Broadcasting network, financed mainly by public funds (provided partly by the Federal Government and partly by the various States or cities), has grown from serving a small minority to commanding a substantial audience. Latin America has some government-operated stations, and some religious and educational broadcasting, as well as the commercial network. The advent of cable television is likely to bring about further variations in ownership and control.

The financing of broadcasting services has traditionally been from three major sources: state subsidies, licence fees and advertising. The present economic condition of the broadcasting industry is forcing a revision of previous patterns almost everywhere. Notably, government or public subsidies are growing and being diversified, so that licence fees, where they exist, are proportionately playing a diminishing share, while advertising revenue is becoming an increasingly large resource for broadcasting support. The increasing costs of broadcasting operations will soon force most systems to seek new and/or diversified sources of financing. Generally speaking, the combination of economic and technical developments will demand wider public participation in solving the problems raised.

Finally, the feature film industry is basically a private commercial enterprise, except in socialist countries and a few other parts of the world. However, public authorities are finding it increasingly in their interest to have some involvement in the film industry. Certain areas of film production and content are being stimulated by the introduction of awards and grants. In recent years, some governments, mainly in Western Europe and in Canada, have begun to subsidize commercial producers for both cultural and economic reasons.[1]

The world picture of communication, particularly of ownership, financing and management patterns, shows a wide variety of practices and decidedly pluralistic image. A diversity of systems has been adopted by different countries and they operate simultaneously with varied results. The Commission does not favour any particular one of the existing operations over another or recommend any standardization of ownership practices or models. But we are receptive to proposals, and even inclined to suggest serious consideration of measures, which should lead, in any of the existing public or private systems, to avoiding abuses and distortions by improving autonomy of the media on the one hand and social accountability on the other.

(1) For instance, in the Federal Republic of Germany, a public institute, the Filmförderungsanstalt (Film Advancement Institute) was created in 1971 in West Berlin for the subsidizing of native German films. The institute guarantees help to producers for the production of native films or international co-productions to theatre-owners, and to agencies which carry out both domestic and foreign advertising for films. This is all funded by a special fee levied on all commercial screenings in the Federal Republic and West Berlin. In addition there are further federal *Länder* and community measures to assist the film industry.

3. Concentration and Monopolies

Concentration of ownership in fewer and fewer hands is causing anxiety in many countries today. Industrialization has tended to stimulate a concentration in the communication sector through the formation of oligopolies and monopolies in the gathering, storing and disseminating of information. This concentration operates in three directions: (a) the horizontal and vertical integration of enterprises connected with information and entertainment; (b) the involvement of enterprises operating in different branches with the media expansion (hotel and restaurant chains, airline companies, automobile manufacturers, mining companies, etc. are now involved in the press, film production or even the theatre); (c) the merging and intermeshing of various information industries into large-scale multi-media conglomerates.

Although there are sometimes political reasons and pressure for concentration in main areas of communication industries the principal stimulus comes from conditions in national and world markets of profit rates, capital flows and technical developments. Vertical integration is enforced by the development of new technologies as, for example, in the computer industry, where some companies not only do research and development and manufacture and sell the machines, but operate and maintain the entire system and supply the software. Concentration is indeed the result of several factors as illustrated by the newspaper industry: (a) basic trends in the market economies; (b) trends towards standardization of information products, messages and contents as needed by some public authorities; (c) economic pressure stemming from technological changes in publishing and distribution patterns; (d) pressures resulting from competition for circulation and advertising revenue; (e) competition between rival media; (f) uniformity of "cultural products" in general; (g) lack of economic and social need for some newspapers; (h) rising production costs and decreasing advertising revenues; (i) planned consolidation of newspapers; (j) administrative arrangements, financial incentives and tax policies discouraging independent enterprises; (k) managerial shortcomings; (l) inflation and general recession; (m) lack of new initiatives, both private and public, as well as of new financial resources.

Concentration is a world-wide phenomenon, which can occur in any kind of economic system, but its extent and its patterns vary widely in different countries. When brought about by private interests, it is more pronounced in developed countries; but concentration caused by public authority is a feature of both developed and developing countries. As the amount of capital investment required in the communication industry rises, the control of financing and the provision of equipment tends to pass into the hands of large-scale enterprises since only they are able to raise the capital needed. Obviously, where ownership, operation and control of the media and communication industries are unified in central government organs, without democratic control by the public or people's representatives, concentration approaches the ultimate.

In industrialized countries concentration occurs in numerous directions: (a) extension of media ownership, through partnerships between owners of different mass media organizations and the rise of multi-sector conglomerates; (b) increase in size of individual enterprises in several areas (news production, cultural products, software production, manufacturing of communication equipment); (c) growth of newspaper chains:[1] (d) concentration not only of daily newspapers, but of various

(1) Since 1945, the number of newspaper groups — ranging in size from two to 80 dailies under the same ownership — has grown from 60 to 165 in the United States. These groups own more than 60

journals (dailies, weeklies, monthlies specialized papers, entertainment publications, etc.) by a single publishing house; (e) mergers between newspapers and distribution companies; (f) control of the press by various industries or banks; (g) mergers of the press and other media;[1] (h) growth in the relative importance of some media operations since a decreasing percentage of firms share an increasing proportion of the total circulation[2] etc.

Many people are concerned by the phenomenon of concentration,[3] which in their view constitutes an extremely serious threat to the existence of a free and pluralistic press as well as to journalists' opportunities for employment.[4] Press concentration

---

per cent of the 1812 daily newspapers. This trend to growth of chains continues; in 1978, of the 53 daily newspapers that changed ownership, 47 went into groups. In the UK, by 1963 there were 51 cities with competing newspaper firms, only 43 by 1968, 37 by 1973. Fifty years before, the number had been over 500. Twelve Western European countries now have fewer daily newspapers than a decade ago, with precipitous drops in Belgium, Denmark, Switzerland (−30%) and France (−20%). Circulation patterns also point to concentration of news sources, as in the United Kingdom where nine out of 111 newspapers account for 60 per cent of the daily circulation. In the Federal Republic of Germany the number of copies sold has increased, while the number of independent newspapers (editorial units) decreased from 225 in 1960 to 134 in 1973. In Japan, three large Tokyo-based newspapers dominate the scene: with their satellite papers in five other cities, they have between them, a daily circulation of almost 27 million, which represents 50 per cent of the total circulation of all daily newspapers published in Japan. In some countries, the monopoly newspaper has passed from being an exception to the rule. (Sources: *The Mass Media: Aspen Institute Guide to Communication Industry Trends.* Praeger Publishers, 1978; *Editor and Publisher*, January 6, 1979, *Unesco Statistical Yearbook*, 1977).
This is also clearly illustrated in the following table showing the trend of over half a century in the USA:

Year	No. of Dailies	No. of Chains	No. of Chain-owned Dailies
1923	2036	31	153
1930	1942	55	311
1935	1950	59	329
1940	1878	60	319
1945	1749	76	368
1953	1785	95	485
1960	1763	109	552
1966	1754	156	794
1971	1749	157	879
1976	1765	168	1061

Source: C. H. Sterling and T. R. Haight: The Mass Media: *Aspen Institute Guide to Communication Industry Trends,* Table 221-A (Praeger, 1978).

(1) In the USA, groups and individual newspaper and magazine publishers also own some 650 radio and some 190 television stations. There are about sixty communities where newspapers own television stations transmitting in the same area and 200 where newspapers own radio stations.

(2) By the beginning of the seventies the top five firms in the respective sectors in the United Kingdom accounted for 71% of daily newspaper circulation, 74% of the homes with commercial television, 78% of the admissions to cinemas, 70% of paperback sales and 65% of record sales. (Source: *Mass Communication and Society*, edited by Curran, Gurevitch and Woollacott; Edward Arnold in association with the Open University Press, London, 1977).

(3) A typical example is that of a spokesman for a group of publishers protesting against the acquisition of a local newspaper by a large communications conglomerate in the United States who stated "(This sale) radically altered competitive balance and raised questions on how it will affect the diversity of editorial opinion. We are concerned about freedom of information and how the First Amendment (to the United States Constitution) is being served by this type of concentration of power ..." *Editor and Publisher*, August 11, 1979.

(4) At its twelfth congress in March 1974, the International Federation of Journalists adopted a resolution on press concentrations which urged governments to take legislative and other measures

has been viewed as harmful and dangerous to the readers, the journalists, and the owners of smaller units alike. The falling number of dailies diminishes the variety of views in the press, narrows the choice open to readers, limits the range of opinion and the field of debate, promotes conformity and the acceptance of the values of a dominant minority and thus can be a serious threat to the intellectual pluralism that is vital to democracy. Where the same companies produce multiple-audience publications, say, dailies for general consumption, women's magazines, children's periodicals, economic weeklies, large circulation evening papers, photo-magazines, comic-strips, etc. press concentration is yet further increased.

Concentration of ownership is also promoted by the growing integration of the whole communications industry, in which informatics, the press, radio and television, the cinema and live popular entertainment — sharing the same technology and thus dependent on heavy capital resources — can become units in one gigantic machine. Large corporations, through subsidiaries which are not always easily identified, acquire interests which pave the way to the emergence of a new oligopoly. Indeed, this unification at the level of financing and equipment can present dangers of centralization and uniformity under public as well as private ownership. In some countries it has proved necessary to take new rigorous measures to prevent a concentration of power through the acquisition of press, radio and television enterprises by consortia, particularly because there are signs of monopolistic mechanisms which are difficult to identify with the means presently available under anti-trust laws.

Others feel that the phenomenon of concentration in the industrialized countries should not be presented in a simplistic way or in a totally negative light. It should be considered in terms of the total volume of information available in a given society; indeed cases may be quoted where newspaper mergers lead to the dissemination of more abundant, and more diversified, information. There is also much truth in the argument that the number of newspapers is by no means necessarily equivalent to diversity of opinion. Those favouring the view that press concentration is beneficial to the public also claim that it leads to more efficiency through rationalization of organization, management and production and by placing central resources at the disposal of smaller units, all of which leads to providing more information to more consumers. They believe that modernization of the press may lead to increased sales, and that press concentration may permit newspapers to obtain information more rapidly and from wider sources.

4. Transnationalization

At the international level, communication patterns closely follow other sectors of economic life, in which the general expansion of transnational companies in the most vital fields is one of the significant recent trends affecting the world market, trade, employment, and even the stability and independence of some countries.

The phenomenon known as "transnationalization" or "transnationality" has affected practically the whole field of communication. Indeed, one can speak of a transnational communication phenomenon. Just as in other sectors of the transnational economy, it is possible to identify in the industrial and financial operations of mass communication, centres which control production and services

---

designed to foster the existing diversity of newspapers and to adopt all measures which rank the mission to inform above the interests of newspaper owners.

and the peripheral markets to which they are addressed.

Film companies are a long-standing example of the transnational process. In the early days when films were silent, they nevertheless "spoke" an international "language" of image, story and action: it was possible for Charlie Chaplin to be as familiar a figure in Russia or France as in the English-speaking world, Later, in the heyday of big Hollywood productions, films depended for their appeal on spectacle on the grand scale — battles, shipwrecks, burning cities — while the stars, celebrated for their personal beauty rather than their acting ability, might be of almost any nationality. Economically, a film of this kind earned its costs in the major American market but made its extra profits by world-wide distribution even years later. (It is still possible to see a revival of *Gone With the Wind,* made in 1939, in Lahore or Lagos.) The major studios in this era were businesses on a considerable scale, well-organized and heavily capitalised, and often financially linked with film distribution.

Since the advent of television, which has taken over the dominant place of the cinema in mass entertainment (at least in developed countries) there has been a change in the structure of the film industry. In the US, the process of concentration was reversed, and the production centres were obliged to give up their distribution interests under anti-trust legislation. The independent producer came to the fore. A producer, wishing to make a certain film, raises money from banks and other sources outside the industry, perhaps in several countries which will constitute the eventual market. Since control is now in the hands of the film-maker, and the film is not an item in the production line of a company, the result has been a general improvement in artistic quality and originality. However, it has increased the transnational character of the film-making process. If a film has an Italian director, a British script-writer, American actors, and a location in Yugoslavia, and if its audience is intended to be cosmopolitan, it is hard to establish its national character. Co-production between national producing centres adds to the intricacies.

In the final analysis, a film is marketed as a commodity. This generalization should not obscure the fact that — with films as with books — there are various markets because there are various audiences, some of a minority nature and some on a mass scale. But there is a flow from countries which are rich in financial resources and production experience to countries which merely supply an audience. The volume of film production in this or that country is not the dominant factor in distribution; thus, the USA is far from being the largest producing country but is the principal exporter of films (followed by Italy, France, Britain, India and the USSR). The domestic product still has the largest slice of the market in many countries, if only for reasons of language. But imported films, made with greater resources and sophistication and popular among national elites, have a disproportionate influence on cultural patterns.

Publishing was the first mass medium to develop an export trade, with European book publishers opening up markets and, later, subsidiaries in former colonies. However, for book publishers, export was a minor sideline until fairly recently but has undergone rapid expansion, so that it is now essential to the profitability of certain major firms. This is especially the case with books in the English language, so widely distributed in Asia and Africa as well as in Europe. American book exports are valued at $300 million and British book exports — which represent 40 per cent of sales — at $250 million. Educational, scientific and technical books predominate in these exports, and educational advances in developing countries have been a major factor in the boom. To the statistics of export, one must add the considerable volume of books produced by publishers which are subsidiaries of firms in developed countries, such as Macmillan/India, Longman/Africa, Orient/Longman, and the

Hachette group with investments in various publishing houses in French-speaking Africa. As an example of concentration of ownership, it may be mentioned that one financial "umbrella" covers the firm of Longman and its overseas subsidiaries, the leading paperback firm of Penguin Books, several British newspapers, and the US publishing house of Viking Books. Those publishers who are strongly involved in the educational field have also become producers of films, video-cassettes and other material, drawing on the resources of informatics and new technologies, while the need for capital has led them to establish links with newspapers, magazines and television. This expansion in markets and products has fostered the growth of publishing as an international industry and the growth of multinational media operations generally. Thus, the industry is characterized both by horizontal and vertical integration as well as transnational investments. Investment has been supplied by such large corporations as ITT, CBS, RCA; an Italian publishing group is owned by the car firm FIAT, and Paramount Pictures (USA) has a 20 per cent share in a publishing house. There are also joint ventures, such as the investment in video by six leading European publishing firms.

The example of certain big news agencies is another illustration of how activities of national companies (or cooperative undertakings) become transnationalized in character, and the case of radio and television presents a different phenomenon in the transnational structure of communication. First radio and then television emerged as national enterprises. Along with their expansion, the need arose for greatly increased production of programmes for transmission. This fostered the transnational expansion of the record industry (in the case of radio) and of "canned" television programmes. So television has a strongly transnational face, especially in the sphere of popular entertainment which constitutes a large part of its output. Situation comedies and long-running series, originally made for a national (in most cases American) audience, reach the screen with dubbing or sub-titles in various languages. In many countries, the volume of imported material is so great — given the popularity and influence of television — as to raise serious issues of cultural dependence. Britain and Canada are two countries which have made a certain proportion of nationally-produced material mandatory on the screen, but for less developed nations the home-produced material is often a poor second to imports in their daily programming. In fact, a few international television operations are providing most countries with news and entertainment programmes. Here, transnational television corporations act as producing branches of national information industries and make national mass media extremely dependent on foreign component-producing industries. Problems are also presented by the amounts of news, film and documentary programmes offered by a few transnational film agencies. The version of world events transmitted to developing countries, and, conversely, the picture of life in developing countries shown to viewers in Europe or North America may be distorted or culturally biased, and in any case lacks the variety that could be supplied only by a diversity of sources.

The transnational corporations have created models of productive efficiency with high-capacity technologies. The high rate of their profits stimulates further investment in communication industries. These are companies with high capital intensity and high research and design costs. In the electronics production industry, particularly, most of the firms who manufacture equipment for the production, transmission and reception of radio and television are based in the industrialized countries, are typically transnational and characterized by vertical integration. Fifteen transnational corporations, controlling in different ways the largest part of operations in international communication, are located in five countries:

Rank	Corporation	Sales (in million $)	Employees
1	IBM (USA)	14,436	288,647
2	General Electric (USA)	13,399	375,000
3	ITT (USA)	11,367	376,000
4	Philips (Netherlands)	10,746	397,000
5	Siemens (FRG)	7,759	296,000
6	Western Electric (USA)	6,590	152,677
7	GTE (USA)	5,948	187,170
8	Westinghouse (USA)	5,862	166,048
9	AEG-Telefunken (FRG)	5,187	162,100
10	North American Rockwell (USA)	4,943	122,789
11	RCA (USA)	4,789	113,000
12	Matsushita (Japan)	4,677	82,869
13	LTV (USA)	4,312	60,400
14	XEROX (USA)	4,094	93,532
15	CGE (France)	4,072	131,000

Quoted by Cees Hamelink, *The Corporate Village* (Rome: IDOC Europe Dossier 4, 1977)

One of the most lucrative sectors of the communication industry is advertising, with national and transnational ramifications and channels. Although the colossal size and ever-growing extent of advertising firms in the United States creates the impression that it is primarily an American phenomenon, it has become an enormous world-wide activity. Annual expenditure on advertising is now reckoned at $64 billion a year. More than half of this is spent in the USA, but several other countries — Britain, France, Federal Republic of Germany, Japan, Canada — account for over one billion dollars each.[1] The dependence of the mass media on advertising is also growing. Few newspapers in the world of private enterprise could survive without it. As for radio and television, advertising provides virtually the sole revenue for the privately-owned broadcasting companies which are dominant in the US and in Latin America and is an important source of financing in various other countries.[2]

---

(1) From 1960 to 1971 the number of US advertising agencies with overseas operations increased from 59 to 260. Per capita advertising expenditure in 1974 still put the United States far ahead of other industrialized market economies, (US, $126.32; Switzerland, $114.49; Canada, $76.06; Denmark, $69.67; Netherlands, $56.75; Federal Republic of Germany, $40.70; France, $37.75; Japan, $37.95). But the gap is narrowing. Japan, for example, has catapulted its advertising outlay from $483 million in 1970, to $4.1 billion in 1975, a more than eightfold increase without taking price change into account.
(2) The press is still the medium which gets the largest share of advertising. Nevertheless, the example of broadcasting shows that advertising represents a constantly growing source for financing in all parts of the world. Advertising revenues of radio and television broadcasters in the United States total almost 10 billion dollars (about 20% of all expenses for advertising). In Western Europe most broadcasting stations depend more or less on advertising. (There are exceptions: the BBC depends solely on licence fees; Switzerland permits advertising on TV, not on radio, etc.). In Latin America, advertising overwhelmingly supports the radio and TV services, to such an extent that in certain countries advertising accounts for more than 40 per cent of the airtime. For some broadcasting stations in the USA and Latin America advertising revenues contribute almost 100% of their total budgets. Developing countries are also using advertising as a support for broadcast financing. Around the world, in 71 out of 91 developing countries, broadcasting services gained some part of their revenue from advertising. (According to E. Katz and G. Wedell, *Broadcasting in the Third World,* Harvard University Press, 1977). Another study of broadcasting financing in 43 English-speaking countries showed only four (Australia, Botswana, Gambia and the U.K.) with no

Advertising undoubtedly has positive features. It is used to promote desirable social aims, like savings and investment, family planning, purchases of fertilizer to improve agricultural output, etc. It provides the consumer with information about possible patterns of expenditure (in clothing and other personal needs, in house purchase or rental, in travel and holidays, to take obvious examples) and equips him to make choices; this could not be done, or would be done in a much more limited way, without advertising. Small-scale "classified" advertising — which, in the aggregate, fills almost as much space in some newspapers as "display" advertising by major companies — is a useful form of communication about the employment market, between local small businesses and their customers, and between individuals with various needs. Finally, since the advertising revenue of a newspaper or a broadcaster comes from multiple sources, it fosters economic health and independence, enabling the enterprise to defy pressure from any single economic interest or from political authorities.

Nevertheless, what distinguishes advertising from the editorial content of newspapers and from radio or television programmes is that its avowed purpose is that of persuasion; a balanced debate in advertising is a contradiction in terms. Because advertising is overwhelmingly directed toward the selling of goods and services which can be valued in monetary terms, it tends to promote attitudes and life-styles which extol acquisition and consumption at the expense of other values. A particular material possession is elevated to a social norm, so that people without it are made to feel deprived or eccentric. The resources of commercial advertising can greatly exceed those at the disposal of individuals or groups in disagreement with the selling campaign, even of the public authorities; thus, the advertising budgets of tobacco companies dwarf the sums spent by governments on warning consumers of the health dangers of smoking. Various controls and safeguards exist in most countries, such as codes of conduct for advertisers, legislation to ensure accuracy in factual statements, and acceptance policies[1] by radio and television authorities which bar some forms of advertising (thus, tobacco advertising in several countries is permissible by poster and in the press but not over the air). These controls modify, but do not eliminate, the overall effects of advertising.

Small countries, and developing countries especially, face a special problem.

---

commercial revenue to help finance the public broadcasting services. In a similar study of 31 French-speaking countries, only seven (Belgium, Burundi, Comores, Guinea, Haiti, Upper Volta, Madagascar) were found with no broadcast advertising. (Study made by the Canadian Broadcasting Corporation, 1976). Other countries, such as Tunisia, also broadcast no advertising. Even a number of publicly-owned broadcasting authorities, e.g. in western European nations and in Canada, carry advertising and are at least partially dependent on it. There is also advertising in several socialist countries. Indeed, the only developed countries with no advertising on television or radio are Belgium, Denmark, Norway and Sweden.

(1) Comment by **Ms. B. Zimmerman:** "Many broadcasting organizations have commercial acceptance policies. The objective of these policies is to ensure that advertising scheduled on broadcast facilities is presented with integrity and good taste, and is appropriate to the national culture. Many such policies require material to be truthful, non-political, non-controversial, and be suitable for broadcast in word, tone and for viewing in the intimacy of the home. These policies often limit the number of minutes per clock hour of commercial messages, as well as the frequency of scheduling of messages. Some broadcasting organizations consider certain types of products and services inappropriate for broadcast advertising and do not allow such commercial material. Advertising in or adjacent to programmes for children may be prohibited. Often certain types of programmes, due to their very nature, are not allowed to be sponsored or interrupted for commercials, e.g. news broadcasts, public affairs and consumer information programmes, ceremonial broadcasts, etc."

Control of advertising is vested to a considerable extent in a few big agencies, of which four (three American and one Japanese) engage in expenditure of more than one billion dollars a year each. These agencies are transnational corporations; they produce advertising, either directly or through subsidiaries, for newspapers, radio and television in many countries throughout the world. Hence, some developing countries depend for the financing and indeed the existence of their broadcasting systems, not merely on advertising, but on imported advertising. In this situation, codes of conduct in advertising become more difficult to enforce. Therefore, advertising is seen by many as a threat to the cultural identity and self-realization of many developing countries: it brings to many people alien ethical values; it may deviate consumer demands in developing countries to areas which can inhibit development priorities; it affects and can often deform ways of life and life-styles. Moreover, the threat to withdraw advertising — by private interests or by a government — can jeopardize press freedom.

We can sum up by stating that in the communication industry there is a relatively small number of predominant corporations which integrate all aspects of production and distribution, which are based in the leading developed countries and which have become transnational in their operations. Concentration of resources and infrastructures is not only a growing trend, but also a worrying phenomenon which may adversely affect the freedom and democratization of communication. Concentration and transnationalization are the consequences, perhaps inevitable, of the interdependence of various technologies and various media, the high costs of research and development, and the ability of the most powerful firms to penetrate any market. The trends have their counterparts in many industries; but communication is not an industry like any other. Transnational corporations have a special responsibility in today's world for, given that societies are heavily dependent upon them for the provision of information, they are part of the structure that fosters the development of economic and social models, as well as a uniformity in consumer behaviour unsuitable to many local environments. Transnational media have a major influence on ideas and opinion, on values and life-styles, and therefore on change for better or worse in different societies. The owners or managers have a unique kind of responsibility, which society has a right to insist they assume. Public awareness of the structures of ownership is a necessary starting-point. But we are inclined to draw two conclusions for communication policies in developed and developing countries to help safeguard internal democracy and strengthen national independence; one, that some restrictions on the process of resource concentration may be in the public interest; second, that some norms, guidelines or codes of conduct for transnational corporations' activities in the field of communication might well be developed to help ensure their operations do not neglect or are not detrimental to the national objectives and socio-cultural values of host countries. In this connection, the UN Commission on transnational corporations should pay particular attention to the communication, information and cultural implication of their activities.

Chapter 5

Interaction:
Participants

It is now necessary to examine the roles that are played — or could be played, or should be played — by those who are active in communication processes: individuals, social groups, private interests, public authorities, transnational corporations, and international organizations.

Who has priority among the participants is a matter of opinion. Pride of place is sometimes given to individuals and private bodies and interests, sometimes to official institutions and the representatives of society, sometimes to professional communicators. The relative importance and degree of involvement of each of these agents varies according to national characteristics, traditions and historical experiences. Their standing also reflects the social and cultural features, or needs and constraints, of each system established to provide for the exchange of messages. But only if all these numerous protagonists are involved can the many problems in the world of communication be solved.

1. Individuals

As soon as communication moves outside personal relationships and becomes a socially organised process, the individual has a two-fold role: he communicates on his own account, and he is the recipient of communication. Far too often, the latter is stressed and the former ignored. Worse still, the individual is often not even treated as the recipient of information relevant to needs, but as a mere consumer of a product whose content is none of his business. Thus, the messages of information and persuasion are transmitted from the educated to the uneducated, from the organizers of collective action to participants at a lower level, from producers of commodities to consumers. Where this occurs, the motives may well have a large admixture of goodwill, generosity, integrity and idealism; the teacher and the preacher have been rightly honoured in all ages. The assumption that the traffic should be in one direction often stems, almost without deliberate purpose, from the structure of society, from the nature of established channels of information, from the balance of knowledge and experience, from traditions of passivity and acceptance. Yet it is an assumption that should be challenged. Such dangerous terms as "social engineering" indicate the extremes to which one may be led when human beings are regarded as malleable material, to be manipulated at will. And this manipulation can be rendered more formidable by the resources of modern mass communication. It is more necessary than ever to bear in mind that communication at its best is an exchange, to which each can make a contribution.

As a healthy reaction, a high value should be attached to the many examples of "alternative communication", which operates horizontally instead of vertically and enables individuals to assume an active role in the communication process. Obstacles are numerous, but the imagination of people — particularly many organized social groups, the young and marginal segments — show that print media, local radio, amateur films, citizens' band radio, cable television, even small computers and so on, may become tools for liberating people's initiatives.

Fundamental to this issue is the question of individual rights in the field of communication. Notably, the rights of the individual include:

(a) The right to know; to be given, and to seek out in such ways as he may choose, the information that he desires, expecially when it affects his life and work and the decisions he may have to take, on his own account or as a member of the community. Whenever information is deliberately withheld, or when false or distorted information is spread, this right is infringed.

(b) The right to impart: to give to others the truth as he sees it about his living conditions, his aspirations, his needs and grievances. Whenever he is silenced by intimidation or punishment, or denied access to the channels of communication, this right is infringed.

(c) The right to discuss; communication should be an open-ended process of response, reflection and debate. This right secures genuine agreement on collective action, and enables the individual to influence decisions made by those in authority.[1]

To these basic rights, we should add the right to privacy. The individual often needs to be protected from intrusion into his personal life, an intrusion against which he may be defenceless when it is backed by the power of modern technology. The development of data banks, in which a virtually infinite number of facts can be collated, has given this question a special importance. Obviously the filing of census and similar information is a social necessity. But there is cause for concern when (a) the filing of intimately personal information infringes the individual's right to privacy; (b) information is filed without the knowledge of the person concerned; (c) as a consequence of this, he has no chance to challenge information, which may be inaccurate or based on mere allegations; (d) trivial information, for instance about a minor legal infraction is retained beyond its justifiable relevance; (e) information is transferred from one data-bank to another, for instance from health or social welfare records to police records.

Another growing trend, closely related to the individual's role is the provision of opportunities for individuals to influence the public authorities, the media agencies and media professionals to that they take account of individual and collective

---

(1) In the Universal Declaration of Human Rights (adopted by the UN on 10 December 1948) the following articles are relevant to these rights:

Article 19. Everyone has the right to freedom of opinion and expression; this right includes freedom to hold opinions without interference, and to seek, receive and impart information and ideas through any media and regardless of frontiers.

Article 18. Everyone has the right to freedom of thought, conscience and religion.

Article 12. No one shall be subjected to arbitrary interference with his privacy, family, home or correspondence, nor to attacks upon his honour and reputation. Everyone has the right to the protection of the law against such interference or attacks.

Article 13. (1) Everyone has the right to freedom of movement and residence within the borders of each state.

Article 20. (1) Everyone has the right to freedom of peaceful assembly and association. (2) No one may be compelled to belong to an association.

interests, or even afford people direct access to media and direct responsibility in their management and utilization. Regrettably, it is true to say that sometimes the management of media and communication systems is conducted in a hierarchical, authoritarian way, whether they are in private or public ownership.[1] However, some modern communication techniques, while they can be used to reinforce the power of those in authority, can also extend the individual's right to tell and to discuss as well as to know. Phone-ins on the radio, for instance, are a speedier and more informal adaptation of the "Letters to the Editor" page in a newspaper. Interviews on television provide another opportunity. The mass media themselves are affected by these developments, which make an inroad on the one-way style of communication; many newspapers and broadcasting stations reshape their policies on the basis of surveys of the public's preferences. Many experiments are being carried out, using various media, for a two-way exchange of messages between the public and media professionals — sometimes, a real dialogue between them or between readers/listeners themselves.

2. Groups and Voluntary Organizations

On another level of interaction, the role and activities of groups, voluntary organizations and non-governmental institutions united by common interests, opinions and purposes, are important in involving individuals in collective affairs, one of the specific aims of socialization. Clearly, these groups have a great capacity to influence social decisions. Some of them — organized social groupings, such as political parties and trade unions, churches or religious communities, women's and youth organizations, professional associations — have a permanent existence. They are mirrored on a local scale by community associations, tenants' leagues, youth clubs, and indeed "gangs" whose activities are not always nefarious. Others are formed to pursue a specific objective. It may be to achieve reforms, to change the law in one direction or another, to protect the environment, or to defend freedom of communication itself. Pressure groups are now a recognised feature of society, to which political leaders pay heed in all but the most dictatorial countries.

As these groups generate and promote alternative ideas, they provide a forum for debate on current issues independent of political or governmental channels. They demand publicity for minority viewpoints and for the discussion of problems that had hitherto been ignored by the mass media. Not infrequently they make a break-through, and their cumulative pressure has brought about some changes in the habits and procedures of the mass media. But in general the media fail to provide adequate time or space, or else adequate freedom from editorial interpretation, so the groups create their own avenues of expression. Established organizations normally have their regular journals, sometimes even their own book publishing houses. Newer groups start weekly papers, circulate leaflets from house to house, and hold street-corner

(1) Comment by **Ms. B. Zimmerman:** "While the internal structure of broadcasting organizations may be heirarchical in appearance, the Report neglects to note that the actions of broadcast managements in free societies are subject to constraints from a number of sources: via the scrutiny and criticism of regulatory agencies, the press, the public, politicians, governments, staff and performers unions, authors' societies, foreign embassies, press/media councils, competing broadcasters, special interest groups, etc. Public accountability comes also through audience research and, in the case of many public broadcasting organizations, through advisory or programme councils, whose officers are often elected from independent bodies to advise on education, religious, agricultural or other specialized programme areas. Therefore, the structure may be pyramidal but many factors mitigate against "autocracy"."

meetings. During the 1960s, an upsurge and proliferation of the "underground" or "alternative" press in western countries not only gave a voice to novel attitudes and ideas, but also developed a style of journalism with a freshness of tone, a frankness, and a readiness to echo spoken language that had been missing in the "big" press. Communication as a whole, especially among the younger generation, was the richer. It also happens that a minority paper is started first, and a movement or group is formed as a consequence, so that communication generates a broadening of the democratic process. In other words, their communication needs have led such groups to set up their own machinery, the full potential of which the mass media have failed to grasp. Interaction between these two forms of communication appears vital to the media's democratization and to promoting access to and diversified participation in them.

Society is enriched, not weakened, by the growing number of all sorts of groups formed on the basis of common interests and opinions. By various means, public authorities can assist these groups which by their very nature must be protected from any interference or control. On the other hand, to be effective, such groups must maintain a democratic structure. When these conditions are fulfilled they are able to make an important contribution to communication and, by that, to social progress.

3. Communities

The community is in fact an aggregation of groups which vary in social class, economic status, often in political or religious affiliation and also in outlook and opinion. Any community, large or small, is held together by a nexus of communications.

Communication links are vital for the promotion and development of a national entity. In any social set-up exchange of information is necessary for persuading citizens to accept the rules of social and political life, if possible to join in pursuing agreed goals, or at the minimum to live together in peace. But if communication power is used to repress and silence minorities, or to conceal divergences that actually exist, the effect must be to alienate a section of the citizens and thus to weaken the national community. The role of communication is just as important at the level of the smaller community — the village, neighbourhood, centre of employment or "living environment". There is an increasing trend toward seeking solutions for social problems (including development, public health and sanitation, adult literacy, the status and needs of women, care of children) in a flexible and decentralized way, through community organisations and through producers' or consumers' co-operatives. This creates a need for continuous and many-sided communication — a need that often outruns the communication resources that exist in a local framework. The creation of the required facilities cannot be the sole responsibility of local initiative; governments, as well as larger non-governmental and private bodies, are expected to make their contributions.

Naturally, the ways in which a society meets its communication needs, and shapes both the strategy and the content of communication, vary extensively from one country to another. The governing principles — and still more the actual practice — may be more or less democratic, more or less tailored to the interests of dominant groups. Seldom is the communication network imaginative enough to allow a full expression of all the interests of the people. Whatever the social or political system, communities and individuals need more facilities and rights to develop communication to its full potential.

Mass communication is by definition directed at large groups of people, but it is their reaction as individuals and as amorphous or organized groups, as well as in communities and environments, which determines the impetus, focus, content and impact of the established communication policies and practices. Again, the development of such a reaction is vital for the democratization of communication and to increased participation in and access to societies' myriad communication activities. This is an issue, it seems to us, which often fails to receive the attention it deserves.

4. Institutions

Institutionalized communication, using all the means at the disposal of governments, corporations, political and labour groups, non-governmental organizations, etc., has become a most potent force today, and is developing at an increasing rate. It undoubtedly reflects the trend towards hyper-organization in the private sector, and, to a large extent, the growth of state machinery as a whole, a trend emerging in varying degrees throughout the world. It also reflects the increasing role which the public authorities and institutions in general are playing in all countries in seeking to solve socio-economic problems and fostering the growth and development of society. Simultaneously, it constitutes a recognition that those who direct activities designed to promote social well-being have to inform the people concerned to be sure of enlisting their support; in other words, establish a favourable public opinion.

It goes without saying that the situation varies considerably from country to country, both in the concern of the authorities about public opinion and in the opportunities for public opinion to exert its strength. However, no nation or government anywhere can now afford to overlook it. There are a growing number and variety of bodies dealing with different aspects of public opinion and information: political parties, ministries of information; services to inform people about their rights and duties; networks of village-level workers in developing countries; and a variety of national and local associations, such as workers' and farmers' groups, all of which spread information on public matters with a view to formulating attitudes and motivating action.

Related to the process of forming and influencing public opinion is another activity somewhat loosely called public relations, which over the past few decades has grown into a multi-billion dollar communications industry. Its operations are varied and not clearly defined; in earlier days public relations companies were not even fully accepted, due to scepticism about malpractices in so-called public relations activities. Public relations is a fast-growing activity whose personnel is largely drawn from among journalists. Government departments, industrial and commercial enterprises, trade and professional associations and labour unions all employ public relations staffs, whose function is to supply relevant information to the media and to the public. In practice, public relations is also used to convey a favourable picture of the organization concerned, to reply to criticisms, and sometimes to ensure that inconvenient items of information are not disclosed. These departments or services are also channels for reactions from the public, providing "feed-back" to the organizations concerned. Useful and indeed necessary in the complex world of communication, public relations activities also raise ethical questions because of the selective character of the information transmitted.

Public relations in turn shades into lobbying. The aim of lobbying is to secure advantageous conditions for an industry, for an economic interest such as farming, for consumer groups, etc., in particular by ensuring that certain laws are passed and others are not passed. Its pressure is exerted on public opinion, but more intensively on government agencies and on the members of legislatures. It may also play an important communication role by helping to clarify complex technical operations or legal problems related to pending legislation. It is clearly desirable that lobbyists should be identified in relation to the interest they serve, instead of masquerading as impartial experts, and accordingly they are obliged (in the USA, notably) to register themselves. The US register now shows a total of 15,000 lobbyists, and it is estimated that they spend one billion dollars a year to influence decision-makers in Washington, plus another billion to persuade the general public.[1] It should be noted, however, that lobbies of citizens and consumers sometimes achieve victories over those of industrial interests. A classic case was the success of the campaign in the USA to impose higher safety standards in car manufacture.

A wide range of communication activities carried on by various organizations has become indispensable and increasingly influential throughout the world. But, necessary though it is, institutionalised communication has its dangers. It can be used to manipulate opinion, to give information an official aspect, to create a monopoly in the sources of information, and to abuse the principles of 'secrecy' or 'security' by concealing facts. Far too many people in positions of power and influence consider that information is an asset in their hands, not a right for all who need it. The uses made of institutional communication depend on the purposes assigned to it — whether to channel opinion in a single direction or to develop critical attitudes; whether to strengthen the narrow interests of an elite or to promote general involvement in collective issues and decisions; whether to subdue the ruled to the will of the rulers or to create opportunities for participation; whether to humanize or to bureaucratize social relationships. Communication practices are not ends in themselves; they are always part of a larger whole.

5. Professionals

In a world which scientific and technological upheavals have radically transformed, those involved in mass communication and informatics are mainly professionals whose task it is to collect, formulate, store, retrieve and disseminate the different messages and to devise and operate the means and technologies required for transmitting them. Professionals in communication are obviously of key importance, an importance that grows as communication itself becomes more all-pervasive, and it is not suprising that their numbers are constantly on the increase, their qualifications are becoming differentiated and their functions increasingly specialized and diversified.

These professionals now include a wide variety of specialists required for news collection and dissemination, for data storage and selection through the modern media and new communication infrastructures with their increasingly complicated technologies and varying content. The qualifications necessary to carry out the numerous job categories in the ever-expanding communication world are constantly multiplying. In almost all branches of the economy, not just the media as such, the numbers employed in the storage, processing and utilization of information are increasing constantly in all countries and have become truly enormous in the developed countries.

Journalists working for press, radio and television, as well as producers and

(1) Source: *Time* Magazine, August 7, 1978.

directors, are obviously of key importance, since they decide the form and content of information reaching the public. The growing complexity of the task, even of straightforward news reporting, has created demands for new levels of professional skill and background knowledge. It has also resulted, especially in television, in great team effort, combining the skills of reporters, cameramen, sound technicians, editors and so on. Though there is still a strong tradition of learning on the job, standards of professional training and general education have risen over the years and continue to rise. Special attention needs to be paid (and has been paid by the best publishers and broadcasters) to the equipment needed by foreign correspondents, who should have as much knowledge as possible of the language, social structure, traditions and culture of the country which they must portray to a distant audience. But this kind of problem does not present itself purely on an international level. Most journalists have an urban upbringing, a limitation in a country with a mainly rural population; they often come from a social class in which familiarity with popular attitudes and ways of thinking is not common, particularly in developing societies. While professional journalists must always carry the main burden of supplying information and comment, their work is often supplemented by contributions from people active in specific spheres; politicians write articles on politics, sportsmen on sport, doctors on health problems, lawyers on the law, creative writers on literature and the arts. Freelance journalists, or part-time correspondents and "stringers" abroad, often have an expertise drawn from other activities and experiences. This broadening of human resources has surely been to the benefit of the content of journalism.

Present-day expectations in communication produce an apparent paradox. Demands for knowledge at a higher level, combined with the sophistication of the technologies involved, create a need for ever-greater professional skill, for more professionals in communication activities. But other demands — for democratization, for freedom of expression throughout society, for communication as an exchange instead of vertical dissemination, for decentralization to localities and communities — generate a desire for "do-it-yourself" communication in which the non-professional takes an active share. These demands, however hard it may be to reconcile them in practice, are in fact not in opposition to each other.

6. National and Transnational Companies

Privately-owned organisations in the communication field wield a power in setting patterns, forming attitudes and motivating behaviour which is comparable to that of government, and sometimes — because of the financial resources committed — even greater.[1] This power is exercised in various ways: (a) ownership of media and other communication means, or investment in telecommunication channels; (b) production of software and distribution of various kinds of programmes and contents; (c) advertising and marketing; (d) various indirect ways of influencing the production of messages.

Private ownership is particularly prevalent in the daily and periodical press, in television (in the US and Latin America), cinema and book production and to a lesser degree in radio and press agencies. In many cases, private financing is the sole source

---

(1) Of the 100 largest economic units in the world, 50 are Nation-States and 50 are multinational companies (Calculated on the basis of World Bank Reports and figures published in business trade papers). In 1977, for instance, the gross revenues of American Telephone & Telegraph Company were more than 36 billion dollars; this was greater than the GNP of 118 of the 145 Member States of the United Nations.

of financing, in others it is supplemented by funds from public bodies or from licence fees. In every case, the institutional model usually takes one of the following forms: ordinary business enterprise, enterprise enjoying a special status, public corporation model, co-operative model, trusts or mixed public/private companies. Strong views are held about the advantages of private ownership in the mass media.[1]

Private media companies in industrialized countries are characterized by: expansion; concentration or integration, both horizontal and vertical; links between the manufacturing and information industries; the vital role of advertising; creation of large multi-purpose corporations; concentration of distribution. Although these features are more prominent in Western European, North American and certain Pacific area countries, many developing countries are witnessing similar phenomena.

National governments have found it necessary to intervene and apply corrective measures which limit the power of such private companies. But that power is not confined to the national level. The huge size and virtual independence of transnational corporations has become, in the last twenty years, a qualitatively new phenomenon in communication.[2] Two significant trends may be recorded: (a) while the outright ownership of media institutions by transnational corporations in the developing countries is declining, these corporations are exerting their influence more and more through programme sales, technology, professional models, marketing patterns, flow of entertainment material, etc., with the result that the importance of these issues has superseded that of outright ownership; (b) with the growing number of joint ventures between international capital and local capital, both private and public, foreign influence has become in many cases more forceful and more acceptable.

To sum up, private enterprise is heavily involved in all areas of communication and in many ways. In our pluralistic world, private ownership/control patterns in communication exist on all continents. Nevertheless, there are essential differences between industries producing everyday consumer goods (food, clothing, etc) and those producing information and cultural items. The same commercial logic should not guide both types of enterprises. Circulation of messages cannot be dissociated from ethical and social norms, spiritual and cultural values. This is why we are concerned, along with public opinion in many countries and international public opinion in general, with issues relating to communication ownership/

---

(1) This concept of radio as a "private activity of public interest" is what has made of it the unsurpassed vehicle for free thought and what has conferred to it the characteristics of variety, popularity, flexibility, and wealth of orientation. The price of such advantages is the constant striving on the part of radio-broadcasters to achieve an increasing perfection in their installations and programs, and an increasingly keen awareness of the tremendous duties and responsibilities contracted with their hearers." (From the booklet "*Doctrine of Private Radio Broadcasting of the Americas*", published by Inter-American Association of Broadcasters, 1978).

(2) The *World Economic Survey 1971* stated, with reference to the multinational corporations, that "while these corporations are frequently effective agents for the transfer of technology as well as capital to developing countries, their role is sometimes viewed with awe, since their size and power surpass the host country's entire economy. The international community has yet to formulate a positive policy and establish effective machinery for dealing with the issues raised by the activities of these corporations. The deliberations of the United Nations on this subject reflect the preoccupations and currents of thought of the times. The United Nations Economic and Social Council, in unanimously adopting resolution 1721 (LIII) in July 1972, formally and explicitly recognized the importance of multinational corporations as a subject for comprehensive study and possible action by the world organization. The social consequences of the activities of multinational corporations was the theme of a resolution adopted by the International Labour Conference in 1971. The General Conference of Unesco (1974) requested the Director General to convene a group of experts "in order to report on the impact, of transnational corporations in the fields of education, science, culture, communication environment and development."

operation/control structures and their consequences, on both national and transnational levels.

7. The State

The State, finally, plays a growing role in orienting, controlling, organising and dispensing communication activities. In short, the State deals either with conditions for communication in a country (which is its main prerogative) or with the delivery of messages and contents (which is necessary in particular circumstances, but may also lead to restrictions). So, government responsibilities are, on one side, discharged through: (a) legislation regulating rights and responsibilities in various fields of communication; (b) the inclusion of resources for communication in overall planning; (c) regulation of conditions governing media ownership and communication activities; (d) attribution of facilities (e.g. distribution of frequencies) for telecommunications; (e) control of communication channels and carriers; (f) direct public ownership of media and other means of communication and, on the other side, through (g) direct involvement in various communication activities by creating national, regional and local public bodies; (h) measures aiming to prevent the spread of distorted views and the abuse of communication practices; (i) limitation of imported contents and messages, etc.

For the trend towards a continuously increasing involvement by public authorities in all fields of communication, three major reasons are usually cited: (a) ideological and political, since increased governmental responsibilities in other fields of public life are bound to embrace communication, or at least some aspects of it; (b) economic and financial, since the mounting costs of communication often require public investments (in many developing countries the choice is not between privately-owned and publicly-owned media, but between publicly-owned media or no media at all); (c) moral, since the impact of information, culture, education and entertainment on the nation as a whole calls for the attention of the authorities. However, State power in communication may be limited by the restraint of authorities themselves, by citizens' action, and by economic constraints.

State authorities undeniably have responsibilities in the field of communication, whether in centrally planned or market economies, and whether in developed or developing countries. This is a generally accepted practice and prerogative. But direct governmental control of the mass media is a more controversial issue. It may avoid the dangers which can arise from commercialism, consumerism, and the profit motive; yet government-controlled media have too often demonstrated a poor record in satisfying popular needs for adequate information and wider access to diversified sources. The principle has an obvious theoretical justification, since governments are supposedly representative of the will of the people, but experience shows that it may have many flaws.

There are outstanding examples of public media enterprises which have maintained autonomy from government control and of governmentally-operated systems which show respect for a plurality of opinions. However, there are also too many examples of governmental or quasi-public operations which abuse their monopoly, thwart any deviation from centrally-posed value systems, stifle diverse opinions and restrict respect for individual interests. The replacement of private oligopolies by public monopolies has resulted in many cases in restricted information flow and in the imposition of a single set of norms. Official involvement and ownership has also meant a larger measure of officialization of news flows. In some countries, public concern about information and communication has led to rigid rules, to censorship and discrimination, to drastic measures to limit the scope of communication and communicators, and even to the stifling of the basic human right to a free exchange of ideas.

Control over communication content is not easy to harmonize with respect for individual rights, notably the right to dissent and debate. Some of the governments most eager to enjoy this control are those which represent narrow ruling elites or which gained power by armed force. Even governments which have democratic title-deeds, and are genuinely devoted to the welfare of the people, are inclined at times to prevent the speading of information and opinions that they consider harmful. A look at the record of governments that have straight control of communication contents is not encouraging. It is hard to resist the conclusion that no government, however wise, ought to be the sole judge of what the people need to know, and still less of what the people should be allowed to say.

Government involvement in communication is a fact of life, a part of world reality. Public involvement takes many forms — from direct governmental intervention and ownership, through activities of non-governmental bodies, to users' participation — such diversity depends on the sovereign decision of each country. We consider nevertheless that there is particular value in experiences which support public involvement to prevent the monopolization of communication; which foster a fair balance between different parties involved in the process of communication; which harmonize public involvement, respect autonomy of the media and promote plurality of opinions. In this way, communication facilities may serve not just some but all people, not just those in power but society as a whole.

8. International Bodies

This description of the various participants in the communication process would not be complete without some reference to the role played by numerous international and regional organizations, both intergovernmental and non-governmental. First, the United Nations and Unesco, which since their founding have provided central forums for key debates on vital communication issues, from the definition of human rights in the field of information to the promotion of a new world communication order. While the UN General Assembly has undertaken some tasks of coordinating and harmonizing communication and information activities of concern to the UN system as a whole, Unesco was initially given specific responsibilities in the sphere of mass communications; these were subsequently extended to more general aspects of communications development, particularly as regards normative action and operational activities. In regard to more technical communication issues, two members of the UN system play a vital role in the worldwide organization of communications: the International Telecommunications Union provides a forum for international agreements on regulations in this area, while the Universal Postal Union is responsible for regulating the international mail services. Other intergovernmental organizations, such as the Food and Agriculture Organization of the United Nations (FAO), the International Labour Organization (ILO), the United Nations Industrial Development Organization (UNIDO), the World Intellectual Property Organization (WIPO), the World Meteorological Organization (WMO), etc., necessarily deal, within their respective fields of competence, with different issues relating to the supply of information and the use of communication networks for specific purposes. All the specialized agencies, as well as the United Nations Development Programme, the World Bank and the regional banks, support development assistance programmes in various communication fields. However, the relatively limited scope of such international cooperation has prompted recent calls for broader action and increased resources, as well as for consideration of new procedures for the planning, coordination and operation of development aid.

In addition to dealing with communication issues, international and regional organizations, and particularly those belonging to the United Nations system, have extensive public information activities of their own. While the main goal of the UN information network[1] is to promote the international aims and policies of the United Nations system as agreed by its members, the question arises whether the means at its disposal (technical, operational and financial) are adequate to attain the objectives assigned and whether UN organizations should not be given wider responsibility for alerting public opinion to global problems and activities affecting all mankind.

Along with an increasing concern of governments, the intergovernmental organizations necessarily came to deal with an ever greater range of communication issues and objectives. The growing world-wide interest in communication matters also spurred the process of cooperation among international and regional associations representing the different media (broadcasting, press, etc.) and professional groups (journalists, publishers, editors, film producers, etc.). Since there is unanimous agreement that increased cooperation is necessary in order to alleviate the many communication problems faced in all countries by the media and by the professionals concerned, there can be little doubt that the influence and activities of all these professional organizations and associations will become ever more important in the coming years.

---

(1) The network of the United Nations Office of Public Information comprises sections for radio and visual services, press and publications, external relations, all at UN headquarters, as well as 59 UN Information Centres in countries all over the world — and the recently established Centre for Economic and Social Information. In addition, the UN Specialized Agencies have similar public information operations.

Chapter 6
Disparities

Although the development of communication facilities is continuous and global, still discrepancies and disparities are among its basic characteristics. The way that communication facilities have grown conceals many discrepancies all over the world: between linguistic or ethnic majorities and minorities, between prosperous and poor population groups, between individual countries and between geographical regions. Numerous facts and figures demonstrate this truth.[1]

1. Within Countries

The figures cited in earlier chapters indicate a steady growth of the chief communication channels and media throughout the world. But a closer analysis teaches a less comforting lesson. In many countries this growth is failing to keep pace with the increase in population, so that the provision for under-privileged groups and regions (people in remote rural areas, linguistic minorities, nomadic groups, and the poor in general) is on the decline. Elsewhere, social inequalities are worsening because of the absence of desirable political decisions, administrative inefficiency, and lack of economic resources. The disparity of treatment between men and women also remains very wide, and women's needs in print or broadcast material are inadequately met.

Disparities in communication resources and facilities exist in all countries, both developing and developed. Overall national data to demonstrate imbalances and discrepancies are, however, very fragmentary, but simple observation and deduction from certain available data are enough to prove the point. It is well known that more expensive media, like television receivers, are in many countries concentrated in towns. There are developing countries where TV transmitters cover only the main cities and the immediate surroundings. Hundreds of thousands of villages have not a single telephone, the existing networks being for urban populations. In quite a few developing countries, more than nine-tenths of the daily press is regularly sold only in towns so circulation of the print media is confined to a small percentage of the population. Illiteracy obviously excludes many, as does the limited production and distribution of newspapers, periodicals and books. These basic drawbacks are compounded in many countries by the number of languages used by different

---

(1) However, global statistics mask a number of facts: first, production in the communication industry in many areas is growing more slowly than the overall population; second, communication data are very scanty and unreliable for a majority of countries in the world; and third, summaries of data do not sufficiently reflect the dramatic discrepancies that exist within countries themselves or between developed and developing countries, or between developing countries.

population groups, but for which it would be economically impossible to provide print material.

The broadcast media reflect similar inequalities. In many countries, again, the large number of languages used makes it difficult to produce programmes for all linguistic groups hence depriving some from sharing in this popular source of information and entertainment. As has been noted, possession of a television set in a large number of developing countries is a privilege of urban elites. But even if programmes reach outside the main population centres, the audience is often culturally disadvantaged as their content may be completely alien to the spectator's background. A recent study of broadcasting in 91 developing countries[1] showed that the proportion of imported television programmes ranged from 30 to 75 per cent, and averaged about 55 per cent, of all programmes broadcast, and even national broadcasting disfavours rural populations in many countries. A survey[2] of radio programmes in an Asian country pointed out that from a sample over a one-month period 87 per cent of the news dealt with events in the capital city.

In other areas, too, the wide imbalance between urban and rural populations is noted almost everywhere in developing countries; of particular significance is the spread of scientific and technological information (STI). Field surveys in five countries — India, Sri Lanka, Malaysia, Tanzania and Costa Rica — prepared for a Unesco meeting on STI services to the rural sector all showed that while technical information may be available in specialized centres, it is too often not disseminated to villagers in timely or appropriate form; existing information on new technological developments such as cheap, durable construction materials, effective methods to destroy agricultural pests, hygienic practices to prevent intestinal diseases or nutritional ways to counteract certain causes of blindness simply does not reach those in need.

Even at middle levels of development, disparities persist; the case of Brazil illustrates the point. Four hundred and forty of the 991 newspapers in the country are published in only two out of twenty-two States — Rio de Janeiro and Sao Paulo. The same is true for periodicals, with those States possessing 512 out of a country-wide total of 700. Out of 944 radio stations, 750 are in two regions, the South and Southeast. Persons in these regions have 83.2 per cent of the television sets in the country. Radio broadcasting for ethnic minorities accounts for 0.46 per cent of total programming time.[3]

As stated earlier, developed countries are not without communication disparities. There are five countries in Europe that only have ten or less telephones per 100 inhabitants. In Australia, 180 aboriginal communities lack telephone service, 105 have no radio service. In the USA, less than three per cent of the cities — covering only 13 per cent of the population — have more than one daily newspaper.[4] In general, for developed countries, stratification — by sex, age, education, income level, nationality or race, employment, geography — produces groups which are relatively "communication poor".

(1) *Broadcasting in the Third World*, Elihu Katz and George Wedell, the Macmillan Press Ltd., London, 1978.
(2) *Communication planning for Afghanistan*, Unesco, Paris, 1978.
(3) *Communication Policies in Brazil*, The Unesco Press, 1975.
(4) Sources: 1977 *Statistical Yearbook*, United Nations; *National Communications Satellite System Report*, Australian Government Publishing Service, Canberra, 1978; *The Mass Media: Aspen Institute Guide to Communication Industry Trends*, Sterling and Haight, Praeger Publishers, New York, 1978.

2. Regional Disparities

If one wants to know how well or how badly the human race is served in terms of its communication needs, statistics which show world averages are not very revealing. A more realistic picture emerges when they are broken down into the continents or regions, as in the tables below.

Area	Percentage distribution of daily newspapers (circulation)	Percentage distribution of radio receivers	Percentage distribution of book titles published	Percentage population
Africa (excluding Arab States)	1.0	1.9	1.4	9.9
Northern America	16.2	44.9	15.4	7.5
Latin America	5.6	8.8	5.2	10.5
Asia (excluding Arab States)	21.8	11.2	16.4	43.8
Arab States	0.7	1.9	1.0	4.5
Europe	28.2	16.5	45.6	4.5
Oceania	1.7	1.5	0.8	8.1
USSR	24.8	13.3	14.2	8.1

Source: *Unesco Statistical Yearbook*, 1977.
Not including China, Democratic People's Republic of Korea and the Socialist Republic of Vietnam.

Area	Consumption of printing and writing paper per 1,000 inhabitants kg per year	Cinema seating capacity per 1,000 inhabitants	Circulation of dailies per 1,000 inhabitants
Africa (excluding Arab States)	900	4.0	13
Northern America	66,900	52.0	281
Latin America	4,300	22.0	70
Asia (excluding Arab States)	2,600	8.6	65
Arab States	1,500	7.4	20
Europe	23,200	39.0	243
Oceania	11,000	30.0	305
USSR	4,900	98.0	396
World Average	9,000	25.0	130

Source: Ibid.

Note: It should be noted that in this Chapter both terms, Northern America and North America, have been used, according to the adopted Unesco groupings. The former includes only: Bermuda, Canada, Greenland, St. Pierre and Miquelon, and the United States of America. This grouping has been used when the similarity in developmental levels was more important. The second term, North America, covers a wider geographical grouping of countries with varying levels of development, including: Antigua, Bahamas, Barbados, Belize, Bermuda, British Virgin Islands, Canada, Cayman Islands, Costa Rica, Cuba, Dominica, Dominican Republic, El Salvador, Greenland, Grenada, Guadeloupe, Guatemala, Haiti, Honduras, Jamaica, Martinique, Mexico, Montserrat, Netherlands Antilles, Nicaragua, Panama, Panama Canal Zone, Puerto Rico, St. Kitts-Nevis and Anguilla, St.

Over most of the world, the growth fails to keep pace with growth of population. In particular, growth in books and newspapers fails to keep pace with the expansion of the literate and educated public. Therefore, the discrepancies between different regions will continue to widen, if the rate of growth of communication facilities does not increase considerably and without delay.

A country-by-country analysis would reveal further discrepancies, since a well-equipped country may be included in a poor region. Argentina in relation to Latin America is one example, but the most striking is Japan in relation to Asia:

Population			Number of telephones		Telephone calls	
in millions	%		in thousands	%	in millions	%
111	5	Japan	48,646	89	45,985	73
2,184	95	Asia without Japan	6,280	11	16,738	27
2,295	100	Asia[1]	54,926	100	62,723	100

Population			Daily press (circulation) 1976		Radio receivers 1976		Television receivers 1976	
in millions	%		in thousands	%	in thousands	%	in thousands	%
111	5	Japan	57,820	66	59,650	46	26,827	63
2,184	95	Asia without Japan	29,766	34	69,764	54	15,651	37
2,295		Asia[1]	87,586	100	129,414	100	42,788	100

Sources: Unesco Office of Statistics; *World Radio and TV Handbook,* 1979; ITU, 1978; H. Bourges *Décoloniser l'information,* Edit. Cana, Paris, 1978; Data from Centre de documentation sur la Chine contemporaine, Paris.

With 5 per cent of Asia's population, Japan has 66 per cent of the press circulation, 46 per cent of the radio receivers, 63 per cent of the television sets, and 89 per cent of the telephones.

The developing world (Asia, Africa and Latin America) has threequarters of the world's population but only half of the number of all newspapers and only a quarter of their total circulation. Circulation averages at one copy of a newspaper for every three people in Northern America, but only one copy for ninety people in Africa and one for fifteen people in Asia. Although India has 835 different newspapers, they circulate almost entirely in towns and cities; circulation stands at 16 copies for 1,000 of the population. Eight African countries or territories and three Arab states have no daily newspaper at all; thirteen other African countries have only one newspaper

---

Lucia, St. Pierre and Miquelon, St. Vincent, Trinidad and Tobago, Turks and Caicos Islands, United States of America, United States Virgin Islands. The term Latin America has been used for the rest of America, except countries in Northern America.

(1) Countries included in the total of Asia are the following: Afghanistan, Bahrein, Bangladesh, Bhutan, Brunei, Burma, China, Cyprus, Democratic Kampuchea, Hong Kong, India, Indonesia, Iran, Iraq, Israel, Japan, Jordan, Republic of Korea, Kuwait, Laos, Lebanon, Macao, Malaysia, Maldives, Mongolia, Nepal, Pakistan, Philippines, Qatar, Saudi Arabia, Singapore, Sri Lanka, Syria, Thailand, Turkey, Vietnam, Yemen A.R., Yemen P.D.R.

each. In many developing countries, provincial or small-town papers are published only once or twice a week, and papers scarcely circulate at all in rural areas.

Radio is of vital importance to developing countries because of this low penetration of newspapers into rural areas and, of course, because of illiteracy on a mass scale. Yet in the sphere of radio and television the discrepancies are just as glaring, as we see from these graphs:

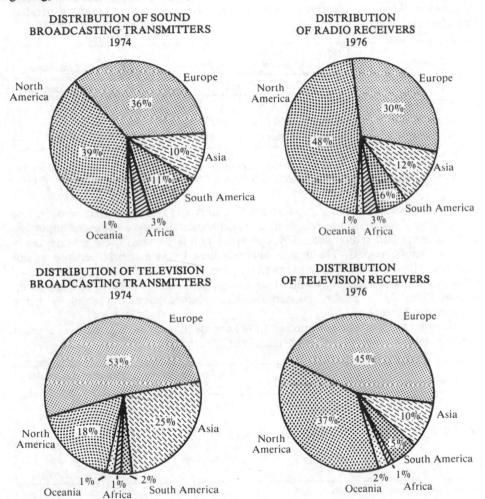

DISTRIBUTION OF SOUND
BROADCASTING TRANSMITTERS
1974

North America — Europe 36% — 39% — 10% Asia — 11% — South America — 1% Oceania — 3% Africa

DISTRIBUTION
OF RADIO RECEIVERS
1976

North America — Europe 30% — 48% — 12% Asia — 6% — South America — 1% Oceania — 3% Africa

DISTRIBUTION OF TELEVISION
BROADCASTING TRANSMITTERS
1974

Europe 53% — North America 18% — 25% Asia — 1% Oceania — 1% Africa — 2% South America

DISTRIBUTION
OF TELEVISION RECEIVERS
1976

Europe 45% — North America 37% — 10% Asia — 5% — South America — 2% Oceania — 1% Africa

Source: Statistics on Radio and Television, 1960–76, Unesco Office of Statistics, Paris, 1978.

3. Disparities between Developed and Developing Countries

Despite these disturbing figures, the most striking picture comes from direct comparisons between developed and developing countries, indicating the relationship between economic development and the level of communication infrastructures and activities.

Interesting conclusions are provided by comparing various groups of countries. In the following table, Group A consists of countries with a gross national product per capita of less than $400. Group B consists of countries with GNP per capita between $400 and $2,500; it also includes the oil-exporting states which have a high GNP but whose general development puts them in this middle bracket. Group C consists of developed countries — all of Western Europe except Portugal; USSR, German Democratic Republic, Czechoslovakia, Poland; USA, Canada, Japan, Australia, New Zealand, Israel.

Countries	Daily Press	Radio Receivers	TV Receivers	Telephone *	Cinema Attendance
	per 1,000 inhabitants				per inhabitant
A. With low GNP	19.2	56.0	5.4	1.3	2.7
B. With middle GNP	19.0	57.2	22.5	15.1	1.1
C. Developed	328.0	741.0	338.0	352.0	7.4

* Data about telephones do not include China

Sources: Unesco Statistical Yearbook, 1977; World Bank Atlas (for population figures); World Radio and TV Handbook 1979; World Communications, Unesco, 1977, Statistical Abstracts, USA, 1978, IPC Report, April 1979, Vol. 4; Internal Report, INA, etc.

It will be observed that the gap between Group A and Group B, while considerable in the fields of television and telephone communication, is only slight in the important fields of press and radio. The really enormous gap is between these groups, taken together, and Group C. The gap is widening year by year, firstly because wealth breeds wealth and the capacity to invest is a crucial factor, and secondly because of differences in population growth. It is a gap that could be narrowed, let alone bridged, only by a mighty cooperative effort far in excess of anything being attempted at present.

Television is a somewhat special case because it can be regarded as a mass medium only in countries above a certain level of development.

Countries	Number of countries	Number of countries with television	Number of countries with colour TV
A. With low GNP	45	28	3 (6% of countries)
B. With middle GNP	56	56	33 (59% of countries)
C. Developed	27	27	24 (89% of countries)

Source: World Radio and TV Handbook, 1979

Poorer countries either have no television, or have a television audience confined to urban centres, generally to higher socio-economic classes of the population. Almost half of the developing countries possess only one TV studio. In Latin America all countries except two have television, in Asia three-quarters of the countries have it, and in Africa, only 60 per cent of the countries have a television service. It is worth remarking that there is an element of deliberate choice; some countries have decided that television would be an unjustified expenditure in relation to other needs, and still more have made this decision concerning colour television.

Very high frequency radio is a medium possessed very unevenly by countries in the same three groups:

Countries	Number of countries	Number of countries with ultra-short waves	% out of the same group of countries
With low GNP	44	11	25
With middle GNP	49	29	59
Developed	27	25	93

Source: World Radio and TV Handbook, 1979

The limiting factor was not always financial stringency, but in some cases a choice of priority. Among the countries which do have VHF, there are huge discrepancies in transmitting power. VHF power in kilowatts ranges from 0.25 in Burma, 5 in Mozambique and 61 in Zaire, to 1,198 in Poland, 1,823 in Canada and 1,935 in Britain.

The use of the telephone, as might be expected, varies widely. Here are some figures from seven countries which have not much in common except a large geographical area:

Country	Number of telephones (per 1000 inhabitants)	Number of telephone calls annually (per 1,000 inhabitants)
USA	744	1,020,953
Japan	424	401,241
FRG	373	264,944
USSR	75	3,701
Brazil	35	2,731
China	4.5	565
Zaire	2	14

Source: ITU, 1977

As noted earlier, countries do not always expand their telephone networks in strict relationship to their economic capacities. Decisions on investment, and social habits in the actual use of the telephone, also play a part. It is interesting to compare four differing countries and to show a relationship between GNP and telephone communication, taking Brazil as a base, with a datum figure of 100:

	Brazil	USSR	F R Germany	Zaire
GNP per inhabitant	100	215	577	10
Number of Telephones per inhabitant	100	214	1,065	5
Telephone Calls per inhabitant	100	135	9,701	0.5

Source: ITU, 1977

The higher the level of technology, the greater the disparity; it is greater in television than in radio, greater in informatics than in television. Available data indicate that developed nations possess over 95 per cent of the world's computer capacity, measured by the value of equipment. Disparity in this sphere is increasing rather than diminishing, because each new step forward in sophisticated technology accentuates the advantages of a small number of countries.

POPULATION, GNP AND COMPUTERIZATION IN 1977

	Industrialized Countries		Developing Countries (including China)	
	Nb or value	%	Nb or value	%
Population (in millions)	1,075	25%	2,925	75%
GNP (in billions)	4,760	80%	1,200	20%
Value of operating computers (in billions)	82	95%	4.4	5%

Sources: Population and GNP, Maurice Guernier (Club of Rome)
          Computerization, P.A.C. (Paris) 1977

Computers are the core unit in data communication systems. Their installation around the world, on a monetary basis, is shown in the chart below:

INSTALLATION OF COMPUTERS IN THE WORLD
(monetary basis)

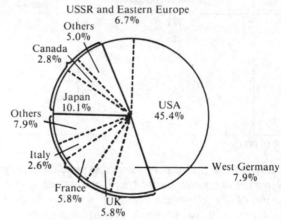

Note: IDC Survey as of the end of
1976 (total amount: $82.189 billion)

Source: Report on Present State of Communications in Japan, The Look Japan, Ltd. 1978

The principal industrially advanced countries account for 87.1 per cent of the total.

Obviously, the development of communication depends largely on investments which various countries put into telecommunications infrastructures and equipment. From this point of view, developing countries labour under great difficulties.

While the relative figures have improved a little faster in developing than in developed countries over the decade, a very different picture emerges when the investment is shown in absolute terms. Developed countries were able to invest $16,60 per head of population in 1968 and improve this to $54,40 in 1977. For the developing countries, the figures were $1,60 in 1968 and $6,70 in 1977. At this rate of progress, they will be disadvantaged for a very long time to come.

Or, looking at telecommunications investments in relation to gross domestic product, another sampling shows similar imbalance; with an investment ratio almost three times that of the less developed countries and an enormously higher GDP, the richer countries obviously invest billions of dollars more in this sector.

INVESTMENTS IN TELECOMMUNICATION INFRASTRUCTURES

	in $ per inhabitant	% out ot total investments	in $ per inhabitant	% out of total investments
	1968		1977	
Developed Countries (except socialist countries and FRG)	16.6	3.5	54.4	3.9
Developing Countries (a sample, representing 8% of the total)	1.6	1.8	6.7	2.0

Source: ITU, 1977.

AVERAGE TELECOMMUNICATIONS INVESTMENT PER ANNUM
AS A PERCENTAGE OF TOTAL GDP[1]

More developed countries		Less developed countries	
United States	0.83	Venezuela	0.51
Canada	1.07	Upper Volta	0.27
Federal Republic of Germany	0.82	Burma	0.23
United Kingdom	1.23	Chad	0.05
France	0.68	Kenya	0.30
Italy	0.82	Malaysia	0.34
Japan	1.05	Pakistan	0.32
Australia	1.09	Thailand	0.30
Switzerland	1.13	Singapore	0.53
Sweden	0.47	India	0.17
Belgium	0.60	Fiji	0.62
Spain	1.06	Costa Rica	0.60
average	0.90	average	0.35

In most cases, developing countries are still not in a position to meet vital needs. However, both developed and developing countries will probably be obliged to devote to communication a larger slice of their total investment in the next decade.

But infrastructure, naturally, is only the provision of opportunity. If the individual is to take advantage of the opportunity, the price is decisive, best measured in terms of labour-hours. Buying a newspaper for a year costs 22 labour-hours in the USA, 45 in France, 43 in China, and 150 in Brazil. A radio costs between 5 and 12 labour-hours in the USA, 30 in France, 207 in Brazil and up to 357 in China. A colour television set costs 87 labour-hours in the USA, 300 in France, and 1,520 in Brazil, where even the figure for a black-and-white set is 491 labour-hours; in China a black-and-white set requires 750 hours. The cost of a postage stamp in the same four countries is 3 minutes, 6 minutes, 14 minutes and 16 minutes respectively. Persons in developed countries are much better off, since for them the cost of various facilities, calculated in working hours, is several times lower than in developing countries.

(1) Figures relate mainly to the period 1965 through 1975/76 and are estimates based on data taken from the *ITU Yearbooks of Common Carrier Telecommunication Statistics* and on data contained in World Bank reports and files.

4. Towards Less Inequality

Developing countries are making strenuous efforts to expand their various media. Their rate of growth, of course, is higher than in the industrialized world, but the extremely high level of development reached by the latter maintains their superior position. The starting levels for growth in the developing world were so low that despite their advances, inequality persists.

Comparative data about broadcasting development over the last two decades indicate major trends in several areas:

ESTIMATED NUMBER OF TELEVISION RECEIVERS IN USE (1960–76) (in thousands)

Year	Africa	America, North	America, South	Asia	Europe	Oceania	Total
1960	122	60,781	2,110	7,064	20,973	1,125	92,177
1965	562	77,822	5,511	19,330	74,352	2,395	179,972
1970	1,206	96,541	12,571	27,427	125,255	3,479	266,479
1976	2,756	142,700	20,300	39,400	174,200	5,733	385,089

TOTAL NUMBER OF RADIO RECEIVERS FOR THE YEARS 1960–1976 (in thousands)

Year	Africa	America, North	America, South	Asia	Europe	Oceania	Total
1960	4,000	184,000	14,000	22,000	136,000	3,000	363,000
1965	10,000	265,000	21,000	42,000	184,000	3,000	525,000
1970	16,000	326,000	31,000	58,000	233,000	8,000	672,000
1976	30,000	454,000	58,000	113,000	284,000	14,000	953,000

Source: ITU, 1977

The number of radio receivers in Africa increased more than seven times, and that of television receivers more than twenty times; in Asia the respective figures are more than five times higher than sixteen years before; in Latin America four times more for radio receivers and almost ten times more for television sets. Nevertheless, radio broadcasting virtually saturates the population in developed countries, with more than one receiver for every single person, while in Africa there is one radio set for every 18 inhabitants; in Asia, one for 13. Breaking down the global figure of television receivers by regions data shows that there is one receiver for every two persons in North America and one for every four in Europe and USSR, one for 12 in Latin America, one for 40 in the Arab States and Asia, and one set for every 500 persons in Africa.

There is also a wide discrepancy in the quality of communication products — both hardware and software — exported by the developed countries on the one hand and by the developing countries on the other. Exports from developing countries are substantial only in radio sets (largely from a few centres such as Taiwan, Hong Kong, Singapore) and in films (here it is often a case of export from one developing country to another). The relevant figures are shown on the next page.

Developing countries today emphasize another concern: some critics complain that developed countries utilize 90 per cent of the radio spectrum and of satellite orbiting space, which should be resources open to all mankind. Assignment of radio frequencies inevitably bears a relationship to the number and power of transmitting stations, of which developed countries have a preponderance, but it must also be related to the social and cultural needs of all nations.

CULTURAL COMMODITIES EXPORT
(in percentage of world total)

Commodity	Export from Developed Countries			Export from Developing Countries		
	1971	1974	1976	1971	1974	1976
Printed matter	94.70	92.85	93.6	5.30	7.15	6.4
Printed books	93.40	91.51	—	6.60	8.49	—
Television receivers	94.88	94.78	—	5.12	5.22	—
Radio receivers	87.16	78.22	—	12.84	21.78	—
Sound recorders	98.12	94.70	92.9	1.88	5.30	7.1
Photo, cinema supplies	98.74	98.32	97.1	1.26	1.68	2.9
Developed cinema film	79.55	76.73	79.4	20.45	23.27	20.6

Source: UN Yearbook of International Trade Statistics, 1975 and 1977

5. Beyond Quantitative Disparities

In the search for answers to the problem of inequality, and especially the difficulties faced by developing countries, a primary or even exclusive emphasis is sometimes placed on technical assistance for the development of communication infrastructures, on material and financial assistance, and on transfer of technology. However, assistance of this kind, however necessary, cannot by itself lead to a new communication order that will intrinsically improve on the existing one. Other inputs, other transformations are necessary as well.

There have always been those who see the introduction of new or improved communication means as the answer to all problems in communication, even as the key to changing the world. At the beginning of this century, the chief engineer of the American Telegraph and Telephone Company, in predicting the advent of international telephony, forecast that it would herald in world peace.[1]

In our day, some may make idealistic forecasts and see similar possibilities stemming from omniscient technological devices, or from communication satellites shaping an "instant world", a global community where everyone knows and respects other ideologies, other cultures, other races. The efficacy of the media's contribution to promoting noble ends was also an underlying supposition supporting the adoption by consensus at Unesco's 1978 General Conference of the "Declaration on fundamental principles concerning the contribution of the mass media to strengthening peace and international understanding, the promotion of human rights and to countering racialism, apartheid and incitement to war". While the Declaration acknowledges the fact that developing countries require "adequate conditions and resources enabling (the media) to gain strength and expand", the main thrust of the document forcefully emphasizes the importance of attitudinal changes, and the ethical and purposeful — not the material — development of the media which must take place so they may play their proper role in helping to promote change in the world and achieve the aspirations of all peoples. This is our stand too. The removal of

(1) "Some day we will build up a world telephone system making necessary to all people the use of a common language, or common understanding of languages, which will join all the people of the earth into one brotherhood . . . When by the aid of science and philosophy and religion, man has prepared himself to receive the message, we can all believe there will be heard, throughout the earth, a great voice coming out of the ether, which will proclaim, 'Peace on earth, good will towards men'."

quantitative imbalances, no matter how necessary, is far from being sufficient for the fundamental issues and grievances being raised by those who aim at freer and more balanced communication, between individuals, groups and nations, in the framework of a new, more just and more efficient world information and communication order. For the inequalities are not merely material: they relate also to broad questions of control, pressure and dependence.

If disparities in communication, both within nations and internationally, are to be reduced, this can be done only through far-reaching changes, both in national communication policies and in international cooperation. Larger investment and the provision of more equipment will not alone be sufficient. What is needed is change in attitudes, greater mutual understanding and responsiveness. The developing countries should also seek, not merely to deal with gaps that can be quantitatively measured, but also to achieve self-reliance in communication capacities and policies. This calls for the acceptance on all sides of a perspective of independence in decision-making, diversity between one society and another, and democratic participation.

Part III

Problems and Issues of Common Concern

In the preceding pages, we have endeavoured to outline the progress and dimensions of the many forms of communication present in the world about us. Thanks to the fast-increasing variety and efficiency of the media, and to the skill of communicators and journalists who are constantly becoming more numerous and better trained, the effects of communication are strongly positive and indeed impressive. One cannot fail to pay tribute to the scale of the achievement.

While communication has been improved and amplified within almost every nation, there has also been some improvement in the conditions of international exchange of information and in the balance and diversity of its content, which is at the core of the debate on problems of communication. Also, as the world debate has proceeded, there has been some advance in the dialogue and mutual understanding among the protagonists.

Unsolved problems, nevertheless, remain, and it is now our task to examine them, to consider the factors involved and the possible lines of development, and thus to move toward solutions. To place the emphasis on the difficulties, inconsistencies and imbalances still evident in the world of communication inevitably means presenting a picture in dark tones. But this is only a reflection of the truth that the complexity of the problems increases even while the instruments for solving them are being developed and perfected.

Chapter 1

Flaws in Communication Flows

Such concepts as "freedom of information", "free flow of information", "balanced flow of information" and "free access to the media" are the natural outgrowth of the basic principle of freedom of speech and opinion. If that freedom is an individual right, freedom of information has both individual and collective aspects, taking on a broader character by virtue of the diversification and extension of the means of mass communication. The transposition of freedom of expression to the realm of modern communication structures inevitably sets new questions and raises new problems.

1. Free Flow

The Universal Declaration of Human Rights states: "Everyone has the right to freedom of opinion and expression; this right includes freedom to *hold* opinions without interference and to *seek, receive* and *impart* information and ideas through any media and regardless of frontiers" (emphasis added). The whole post-war period has been a time of struggle for the implementation of this right.

Progress in that respect has certainly been achieved around the world. Nevertheless, in some countries it has been halting and intermittent and sometimes, even thwarted by retrogressive autocratic measures or increasing monopolistic trends. It must also be noted that if people have more possibilities to receive information, the same is not true for other main components implied in freedom of information. Two of them — the right "to seek" and "to impart" information — have been widely and frequently neglected. Over-emphasis on the "right to receive" information results mainly from the very nature of present day societies, reflected in media structures. This unilateral approach has distorted the issues, and in many instances, reduced the whole problem of free flow to defending the media from official restrictions.[1] In reality, such a limitation of the concept means that power centres in the communication world are trespassing on the full rights of the individual.

The range of obstacles to the free flow of information to the public is almost

---

(1) A similar concern, which is shared by many media research workers and policy makers, also features prominently in a Papal text, namely a Pastoral letter which states: ". . . In practice, *freedom of communication includes freedom of individuals and groups in seeking out, circulating and imparting news and freedom of access for all the media of social communication.* Freedom of communication which failed to take account in its exercise of the objective necessities of the right to information, would be designed more to satisfy the informer than to serve the public good".
(Pastoral Letter *Communion and Progress* on the media of social communication, prepared by special mandate of the Ecumenical Council, Vatican II, 1971).

infinite; their nature and gravity, number and frequency vary from one country to another, but it is revealing that they abound in all societies without exception. This is not to gain-say, however, that there are countries, indeed many, where the obstacles are aberrant, if not illegal. According to recent reports and analytical assessments these obstacles can be classified into two categories: (i) "evident" obstacles, curbs and pressures; (ii) "non-evident" obstacles and impediments.

Some barriers to freedom of information are easy to recognise. Among these are physical violence and intimidation; repressive legislation; censorship; blacklisting of journalists; banning of books; monopolies established by political action; bureaucratic obstructions; judicial obstructions such as closed hearings and contempt of court rules; parliamentary privileges; and restrictive professional practices. But the absence of these blatant obstacles does not always mean that full freedom of information exists. Other obstacles include economic and social constraints and pressures; de facto monopolies (public, private, or transnational); inadequate infrastructures; narrow definitions of what is news, what should be published, and what issues should be debated; and a shortage of professional training and experience. Obstacles of this kind, too, limit the citizen's right to be informed and should be eliminated. Still other obstacles can arise from entrenched cultural attitudes and taboos, and from an unquestioning reverence for authority, whether secular or religious.

Among the most evident and, certainly, the most invidious obstructions, is physical violence against journalists and newspapers: harassment, detention, torture, kidnapping, murder, bomb attacks. Such abhorrent acts — or threats to carry them out — have been so widespread in some places that they virtually paralyse journalistic operations. The victims do not represent any single political orientation; all ideological groupings have suffered. And some have suffered simply because they belong to a profession that some rulers deem to be "dangerous".

Many governments exercise rigid control of the media, over the diffusion of news and the licensing of those permitted to exercise the profession. The fact that such practices are based on codified laws does not preclude their impropriety, when they are not in conformity with international legal instruments, particularly in countries which have ratified those instruments.[1] There is also a host of legal constraints and administrative measures adopted by governments to control aspects of news collection and dissemination which can be more or less restrictive depending on their scope or method of application. Libel laws are undeniably necessary to protect the individual from damage to his reputation, but even in democratic countries these laws are much stricter in some legal systems than in others; the law of libel has been used to deprive the public of needed information, and to impose crippling financial penalties on minority publications. Similarly, while it is true that certain types of reporting before or during criminal proceedings may deprive the accused of a fair trial, legal practice in some countries carries the principle of contempt of court — with arbitrary punishment by the judge — to excess. Wholly unjustified is the practice in some countries of excluding reporters from trials of a sensitive political character. But probably the most serious restrictions of a legal character arise from such concepts as "official secrets", "classified information", and "security". The

---

(1) Of particular relevance is the International Covenant on Civil and Political Rights (UN, 1966) which states: "The exercise of the rights provided for in paragraph 2 of this article (right to freedom of expression) carries with it special duties and responsibilities. It may therefore be subject to certain restrictions, but these shall only be *such as are provided by law*. . ." However, even such justifiable laws should not permit executives and bureaucracies to interpret them at their will.

advance in open and informed debate that has followed the passage of Freedom of Information laws in the USA and Sweden surely shows that other countries are imposing unnecessary restrictions. While it will be agreed that the State has a right to withhold information affecting national defence from the public domain, such laws are abused when they are extended to cover information of a political character, information in the technical or industrial sphere, and — worst of all — expressions of opinion. Such vague wording as "forbidden areas", as "any matter relating to the security of the Republic", [1]can be open to very narrow or broad interpretations, the very indefiniteness of which often forces journalists and editors to apply self-censorship constrictions on their work.

Censorship is a widespread practice, sometimes limited to particular subjects (pornography, obscenity, violence, religious matters, delicate issues in international relations, foreign dignitaries, protection of the young, etc.) but often covering subjects potentially disturbing to the leading elite or groups in power. Prohibitive censorship may be based on laws[2], more often on discretionary powers or even abuses. Censorship exercises coercion in innumerable ways: (a) as prior censorship, where material is submitted to a censor for approval before it is reproduced and distributed; (b) as post-publishing, but pre-distribution censorship, whereby a newspaper or book is subject to review before it is released; (c) post-distribution censorship, where copies of material that has been disseminated are confiscated; (d) issuance of Government instructions on how stories about selected events and issues should be slanted; (e) lists of prohibited stories or subjects; (f) pre-dispatch review of foreign correspondents' cables; (g) banning, seizing or deleting imported publications, films and other imported items; (h) suspension or banning or seizure of publishing, printing or broadcasting facilities; (i) boycotts of individual authors or banning of particular manuscripts; (j) establishing an "Index" of prohibited publications; (k) expelling individuals from writers' or journalists' professional organizations thus depriving them of possibilities to publish. Obviously the very existence of these measures often leads to a large amount of self-censorship on the part of journalists and editors. In many instances all or some of the above measures are extended to the theatre, cinema, music, art, broadcast entertainment and other cultural fields.

Access to news sources, to people, places, documents and information in general — or even to a country — is a particularly thorny question. For it is through such administrative measures as granting of visas, restriction of journalists' movements, limitations on persons or offices as contacts for newsmen, withdrawal of accreditation or expulsion from the country that governments may heavily restrict the flow of news. There are also very often discrepancies between the treatment of national journalists and foreign correspondents.

All obstacles to and restrictions on the free flow of information are not set up by

---

(1) Regulations in force in Brazil read: "Authorisation for presentation, exhibition or radiophonic transmission will not be given when material (a) contains anything offensive to public decorum; (b) contains scenes of violence or is capable of encouraging criminal acts; (c) gives rise to, or induces, evil habits; (d) is capable of provoking incitement against the existing regime, public order, the authorities, or their agents; (e) might prejudice cordial relations with other countries; (f) is offensive to any community or religion; (g) in any way prejudices national dignity or interests; (h) brings the armed forces into disrepute." (*Index on Censorship*, July/August 1979).

(2) For example, most countries have censorship laws that come into play during periods of national emergency; these are not to be compared to indiscriminate or abusive legislation or censorship without legal sanction.

public authorities. They also arise in areas where there are private monopolies, concentration of media ownership and formation of conglomerates. When the public has only a single source of news, or where various sources have the same general orientation, it is the monopolist who is in a position to decide what facts will or will not be presented, what opinions will or will not be conveyed. Even if the owner of a monopoly does not abuse his power, no single outlet can present the amount and range of news that multiple sources make possible. Concentration of ownership can produce the same obstructions and tends to a standardisation of reporting, editing and presentation that is a limiting factor on the type of news that reaches the public. Moreover, the financial, commercial or industrial concerns that are involved in the corporate ownership may prevent the publication of facts that cast an unfavourable light on their activities.

This leads to the whole question of commercial influence on the press and broadcasting, particularly the impact advertisers, both private and governmental may have on news selection or their possible censorship role. Even if they do not actually attempt to influence directly editorial policies or news selection, advertisers sometimes pose threats to free journalism by forcing self-censorship on the media, when their financial position is determined by maintaining the good will of those providing advertising support. News content may also be diluted when the media, in order to maintain the mass readership or the broadcast ratings necessary to attract advertising, appeal to the lowest common denominator of public taste.

Some ethnic and linguistic minorities suffer from a restricted flow of information because the established channels do not supply it in a form that meets their needs and takes account of their cultural traditions. This may be the result of wilful discrimination (some languages are forbidden by dictatorial regimes), of over-centralisation, of domination of the media by majority groups, of neglect and indifference, or of a lack of suitable professional manpower. People living in remote areas are also likely to be under-informed, because of the inadequacy of communication facilities.

In recent years, industrial disputes have become rather frequent in the press of various countries, and have also occurred in radio or television.[1] A particular cause for conflict is the desire of managements to introduce new technological processes — notably computer setting, whereby journalists type their copy direct and it is set in print without being handled by the traditional compositor. Such changes threaten the jobs of workers in the printing industry, and the dispute revolves around "manning levels". The newspaper industry differs from many other industries in that its product is of no value when it is out of date; thus, even a cessation of work for a couple of hours, causing the loss of a newspaper edition, deprives thousands of readers of their daily information. While noting as an objective fact that industrial disputes are an interruption to the flow of information, we do not wish to be understood as denying the legitimate right of workers to improve their wages and conditions and to protect themselves from unemployment. A somewhat different

(1) Some illustrative examples. In the Federal Republic of Germany, in 1976, a subsidiary union called, for political reasons, a strike which was followed by a lock-out which affected 16,000 wage earners, representing 70% of the daily press work force. In March 1978, a strike followed by a lock-out, affected almost the entire press in FRG depriving readers of all news: less than one million dailies were distributed, as compared with a customary 19 million; 327 out of 350 newspapers ceased publication. In Great Britain, during the period extending from 1 November 1976 to 28 February 1978 alone, a series of wild-cat strikes prevented publication of some 54 million newspaper copies; The Times, the Sunday Times, and the associated literary and educational weeklies were suspended in 1978-9 for almost a year; and in 1979 the commercial television network was off the air for three months.

question arises when printing workers strike in protest against the content of what they are asked to print. At various times in history, this has been a justified contribution to the struggle for social justice and freedom; but it is not hard to imagine circumstances in which such action could imperil diversity of expression.

Extremely serious on an international scale has been the effect of high costs of important materials or facilities. High transmission rates in news sent by cable and telex restrict transmission by countries whose media must keep to limited budgets.[1] Paper is a material consumed in vast quantities whose price in recent years has spiralled out of proportion to the general world-wide inflation. The problem is most often publicised in terms of newsprint, but it is having a more lasting effect in limiting the production of school textbooks, and indeed books of all kinds, in developing countries, and in preventing or delaying the modernisation of textbooks in desired directions. As for newsprint, its price on world markets rose from a datum figure of 100 in 1970 to 329 in May 1977, and has continued to rise since. A sad by-product of this situation has been the introduction of a covert form of censorship, as some governments limit the import of newsprint, distribute it by official allocation schemes, and use these schemes to discriminate against the opposition newspapers.

Obstacles to freedom and distortions of democracy are dangerous symptoms in every society. It is sometimes argued that such criticisms constitute an interference in the legal or political affairs of nations, or in the natural processes of private enterprises, but such abuses of State power or monopolistic practices are still serious impediments to the free flow of information. Certainly, there is a margin in almost all systems to improve the existing situation and decrease restrictive measures to a minimum. There are ways, means and forces in each society to overcome and eliminate restrictions on the freedom of information. What is basically needed is the political will.

It is generally conceded that the concept of "free flow", has, in practice, increased the advantages of those who possess greater communication resources. On the international scene, more powerful countries and bigger organisations for the provision of information (data banks, computerised sources for specialised information, news agencies, film distributors, etc.) have in some instances a preponderant position, which can produce adverse economic, social and even political effects. Thus, it is claimed that the "free flow" doctrine has often been used as an economic and/or ideological tool by the communication rich to the detriment of those less well endowed. Awareness of the flaws in the "free flow" ideology has widely increased, particularly in the last decade. Critics of "free flow" have deepened their insights and sharpened their remarks. But it is necessary to make a clear distinction between those who aim to restrict freedom of information and those who oppose the present "free flow" situation in order to achieve more universal freedom of information. A similar distinction must be made between those who defend "free flow", but in no way seek to monopolize information flows, and those determined to maintain and extend monopolistic positions and the "status quo" in international communication and use the free flow doctrine to blunt developing countries criticisms. Despite many disputes about the validity of such criticisms it seems irrefutable that "free flow" between the strong and the weak, the haves and the have-

---

(1) The present commercial rates, including the press bulletin service tariffs where available, are beyond the financial capacity of the average news agency in a developing country. There have been many calls for concessional tariffs, low rate dedicated circuits, multilateral cuts in cable costs and so on, but to date there have been few generalized reductions mainly because required political decisions have yet to be taken.

nots has had undesirable consequences for the latter, and hence at the international level for the developing countries.[1]

The critics from the developing countries have found, by experience that the theory of "free flow" is invalidated by the overwhelming preponderance of information circulated from a small number of industrialized countries into the huge areas of the developing world. In order to be really free, information flows have to be two-way, not simply in one direction. The concentration of news agencies, telecommunication facilities, mass media, data resources, manufacturers of communication equipment in a small number of highly developed countries does, in fact, preclude any chance of a free flow between equals, a democratic exchange among free partners. A dependency situation still exists in a large part of the world, and there is a growing determination to transform dependence into independence as harmoniously as possible. The developing countries also resent the fact that, because of their limited resources and means to collect and disseminate information, they have to depend on the large international agencies for information about each other. The news flows are neither free nor balanced. This solid base of criticism is the foundation of the present call for a new world communication order.

Thus, the confrontation about "free flow" and freedom of information has come to be a key issue in the international debate on communication. Some encouraging concrete initiatives have already taken place or are being promoted: (a) arrangements between news agencies and broadcasting organisations in developing or non-aligned countries for wider dissemination of news from and about them; (b) increased

---

(1) Recognition of existing imbalances in information flows between unequal partners is no longer a controversial issue. From various viewpoints and sources, the fact is admitted; the following are typical statements: (1) by *Le Monde Diplomatique* "the sharing out of this power (information) which is monopolized in national societies by the dominant classes and elites or the established powers, and at the international level by governments and private transnational corporations — a few news agencies and publishing companies or telecommunication and data processing industries in industrialised countries — which ensure a one-way flow of information to the developing countries." (January 1979, Paris); (2) by the President of the Republic of Finland: "The freedom of the strong led them to success, while the weak lost their foothold despite their alleged freedom. Such was the result, whatever those who advocated a juster policy for society and for mankind may say". (Urho Kekkonen, 1976); (3) by the Twentieth Century Fund Task Force: "The Task Force believes that there is a serious imbalance in the flow of information between the developing and the developed nations. . ." (*Report on the International Flow of News*, 1978); (4) by the General Manager of Reuters ". . . The aspirations of those countries that feel they are badly reported, too little reported, that they have too little possibility of being known to the rest of the world. . . are entirely legitimate, many of the complaints that are made are well founded, and it is the duty of all of us to help fulfil these aspirations. That I would accept and affirm entirely." (Gerald Long, June 1979); (5) by a meeting of communication specialists held almost ten years back "We believe that at the present time what is known as the "free flow of information" is in fact often a "one-way" flow, rather than a genuine exchange of information. . ." (*Final Report*, Unesco meeting, Montreal, 1969); (6) by the Ministers of Information of the Non-Aligned Countries: "The present global information flows are marked by a serious inadequacy and imbalance. The means of communicating information are concentrated in a few countries. The great majority of countries are reduced to being passive recipients of information which is disseminated from a few centres. In a situation where the means of information are dominated and monopolised by a few, freedom of information really comes to mean the freedom of these few to propagate information in the manner of their choosing and the virtual denial to the rest of the right to inform and be informed objectively and accurately." (Declaration, New Delhi, July 1976); (7) by a member of the CIC "The most thoughtful of journalists and students of communication processes are fully aware of the historic dependencies, disparities and imbalances that handicap the developing nations. They acknowledge that the present patterns of information flow, running heavily in one direction, must be altered for the benefit of all nations, developed and developing alike." (**Mr. Elie Abel,** *Communication for an Interdependent Pluralistic World,* CIC Document No. 33)

interest by some major newspapers and news agencies in industrialised countries to collect and publish news and reports on socio-economic issues from developing countries; (c) suggestions for the creation of resource centres (for exchange of news, television programmes, films etc.) in Africa and Asia; (d) the growing regional cooperation among news agencies and broadcasters and programmes for establishing regional news agencies; (e) the agreement between sixteen important newspapers in different parts of the developed and developing world, to produce a common quarterly newspaper supplement featuring views regarding the new international economic order, the second issue of which appeared in September 1979;[1] (f) increasing efforts by international and professional organizations and media of industrialized nations to augment technical and educational co-operation for communications development; (g) the inter-governmental conference being planned for 1980, in Paris, to organize and co-ordinate bilateral and international assistance in the field of communications; (h) inter-professional meetings and seminars on such topics as implementation of and links between the new economic and communication orders.

However, the most important result of the whole debate is the wider recognition of the implicit flaws in the "free flow" concept, as well as of the fact, that in the present-day world preconditions have to be created for the implementation of a real free flow of information, if a generous principle is not to continue as an advantage for the few and a detriment for many on both national and international levels. A large gathering of media people from all parts of the world, convened by our Commission in Stockholm (April 1978) was able to state in its general report "that the areas of agreement and mutual understanding are constantly increasing ... There was no dissenting voice as to the existence of imbalance in the flow of news and information in the world today".

Despite all these hopeful developments there are warning signs that show how difficult it will be to transform, generalize and put into practice the free flow of information. Under its present guise, some governments, transnationals, media and organized pressure groups have on occasion tried to undermine internal stability in other countries, violating their sovereignty and disturbing national development. Still, there are also instances where national sovereignty has been invoked to justify restrictions on news collection and dissemination which amount to basic infringements on the free exercise of human rights. Elsewhere, under the cloak of seemingly progressive measures to correct journalistic malpractice, media activities and journalists have been placed under the exclusive control of the state apparatus, constricting the national and international flow of news. The concept of free flow of information should never be used either as licence for subversive action or as an excuse for repression of individual and collective rights and liberties.

Another important aspect of information flows is the near monopoly of the industrialized countries in such areas as: scientific and technical information; data related to industrial, commercial, banking and trading operations; information on natural resources or climatic conditions obtained by satellite and so on. Much information of this type is guarded by governments, large research centres or national and transnational corporations which, for various reasons, may restrict its

(1) The following newspapers from all regions of the world issue a joint quarterly supplement: Asahi Shimbun (Japan), Dawn (Pakistan), Excelsior (Mexico), Frankfurter Rundschau (Federal Republic of Germany), Indian Express, Jornal do Brasil, Magyar Nemzet (Hungary), Le Monde (France), El Moujahid (Algeria), El Pais (Spain), Politica (Yugoslavia), Die Presse (Austria), Le Soleil (Senegal), La Stampa (Italy), Zycie Warszawi (Poland), Development Forum (United Nations).

release and dissemination.[1] The uneven geographical distribution of data banks and the practically monopolistic use of a large amount of computerised information by a limited number of privileged consumers, is at the origin of demands from developing countries for a freer flow of scientific, technical and commercial data. The inferior position of developing countries in this regard has serious consequences for their development plans, deprives them of vital data in many important areas, and often hampers their negotiating situation when dealing with foreign governments or transnational corporations. This is an example of how obstacles to the free flow of information can be particularly detrimental to the developing world.

Many paradoxes emerge in debates about the free flow of information. For example, in conferences to discuss international cooperation in the field of informatics or data networks, representatives from some countries which are staunch defenders of the free flow of news often show surprising reticence about opening up flows to share scientific and technological information, stating that bilateral rather than international exchange arrangements are usually more suitable. Or, again, concerning transborder flows in general, it is said their countries can do little about broadening access to data because their governments have no control over the private corporations or institutions that possess it. (This is the reverse side of the argument that governments have a sovereign right to control what information goes in or out of a country.) Thus, much valuable commercial data — patent and new product information, market analyses, commodity price and supply projections, financial and monetary movements, industrial research findings etc. — are often available to only a favoured few. On the other hand, some of the most vigorous proponents of a broader information flow from developing to developed countries restrict out-going and incoming information and limit its internal circulation. In short, one finds some of the strongest supporters of unfettered news flow not as equally concerned about limited access to technological, commercial and even scientific data, while others, who complain about this situation, have few compunctions about hindering the free flow of news.

Freedom of information is of major concern to everyone; a generous aspiration which, however, as a doctrine has sometimes been misapplied and narrowly interpreted and for which all necessary conditions for its genuine implementation on both the national and world level have yet to be created. These aspects have drawn our particular attention and we feel they may be equally salient for all others interested in communications development and democratization. Hence, we do not feel that frank recognition of an imbalance in information flows is a threat to freedom of information. On the contrary, if the causes of the imbalance disappear, many arguments for restricting the free flow of information will also disappear. If the disparities within and between countries in communications resources and facilities decrease, the inherent risks of free flow for developing countries will largely wither away and a freer exchange of messages and ideas can be established. But this does not prevent us from insisting that many derogatory and arbitrary restrictions to the freer flow of information should be eliminated straight away. There are no justifiable reasons or excuses for violations of freedom and democracy.

---

(1) Comment by **Mr. E. Abel:** "No evidence in support of this doubtful proposition has been placed before the Commission."

2. One-way Flow

The implementation of the free flow principle resulted, for reasons explained earlier, in an imbalance often called a one-way flow. This flow (data, messages, media programmes, cultural products) is directed predominantly from bigger to smaller countries, from those with power and technological means towards those less advanced, from the developed to the developing world and, on the national level, from the power centre downwards.

The one-way direction of news derives from historical, cultural and linguistic patterns. Even in a single geographical region like Europe some more powerful countries still dominate the news scene and cultural and artistic exchange. Many small countries, in spite of their economic strength and cultural level, are largely, except on particular occasions, neglected by many information media. Important events and valuable achievements (scientific, economic, cultural) are often unknown, only because they happen in smaller countries or areas which do not attract world attention. More prominently, the one-way direction is based on links from former colonial periods and surviving economic ties, as well as on cultural and language influences. Historical links between former colonial powers and their one-time possessions produce a selection, both of editorial decision and interest among readers; Zimbabwe is a major topic in the British press, while the French press devotes far more space to the Central African Republic. The process can work the other way too, causing the Indian reader to be much better informed about political developments in Britain than in France or Germany. Links between developing countries themselves, hardly established at all, are still the follow-up of the former colonial period: media in Kenya show more interest in Tanzania than Zaire; or in Niger more to the neighbouring French-speaking countries than Nigeria. The one-way pattern is also evident in the Americas, where the predominant position of the United States in the economic and political life of the region is reflected in the importance given to news about the United States in Latin American media. Thus, media everywhere are far from the ideal of treating all news according to its intrinsic importance.

Hence, news flows tend towards a north-south direction and inhibit development of exchanges between developing countries themselves. While there is a flood of news on the east-west axis between North America and Europe, as well as, although on a lower level, between socialist and western countries, the much lesser, one-way flow between north and south can hardly be called an exchange due to the excessive imbalance. There are, obviously, various reasons, both inside developing countries and on the international scene, which prevent media from counteracting the blanketing effect of the one-way flow.

The existing infrastructures, and the consequent role of those who work in international communication, have as a corollary this imbalance in the circulation of information. The controversy about the imbalance first sharpened over the question of international news flows and the predominance of the major transnational agencies in the collection and dissemination of news. Their massive world-wide operations give them a near monopoly in the international dissemination of news; thus the world receives some 80 per cent of its news through London, Paris and New York. The imbalance in the circulation of news is above all else the difference between the quantity of news dispatched by the industrialized world towards countries in the developing world and the amount of news flowing in the opposite direction. It is extremely difficult to establish composite or average figures on news flows since empirical studies so far undertaken have been limited in scope and time or both, but it may be said that the major agencies only devote somewhere between 10 and 30 per cent of their news to the totality of the developing world. Still, a large amount of compiled but fragmented data is now available illustrating striking imbalances as far as the Asian, African and Latin American areas are concerned.[1]

While one-way flow is determined largely by the structure of communication on a world-wide scale, it has other causes within both developed and developing countries. In developed countries small-town and regional newspapers tend to be highly parochial in their interests. Much the same applies in radio and television, other than on nation-wide networks. "Popular", as contrasted with "quality", newspapers give their readers very little news from abroad unless it is sensational or tied to celebrated personalities. Hence, there is considerable need for reform in the publishing side of the media, particularly in the role played by editors. The entire responsibility for one-way flow should not be placed on the distributing organisations such as the news agencies. A one-way direction in news flows is evident in the content of messages, in the choice of subjects, in the intrinsic value judgments implied in the presentation and selection of news, in the implicit rather than explicit themes, in the choice of books for translation, of music and plays for broadcasting. At the same time, it is worth remarking that much of the responsibility for this selection rests with publishers and editors in the developing countries. It is also true that the best radio stations and television producers, best-equipped documentation centres and computerised data sources, as well as most responsible newspapers in developed countries have taken serious cognizance of the problem in recent years and made efforts to remedy the imbalance, which can be said to be diminishing steadily, although not so fast as could be wished. The debate about this is itself having a positive impact.

Within developing countries, communication facilities are often inadequate or even rudimentary because of the lack of material and professional resources. Newspapers are small, and internal networks for news collection and dissemination are extremely limited; they are poor sources of news for the outside world and ineffective

---

(1) A few examples illustrate these points: "... AP sends out on its general world wire service to Asia from New York an average of 90,000 words daily. In return Asia files 19,000 words to New York for worldwide distribution. UPI's general news wire out of New York to Asia totals some 100,000 words and the file from all points in Asia to New York varies between 40,000 to 45,000 daily ... AFP's service from Paris to Asia is 30,000 strong. In addition some 8,000 words are collected in Asia and distributed within the region to Asian clients. The same 8,000 word file is sent back to Paris for incorporation into other world services of AFP... The flow of news is uneven in that a lot more is sent from London or New York to Asia than the other way around. Although the feed from the West is supposed to contain news of the rest of the world it is heavily weighted in favour of news from North America and West Europe. UPITN sends about 150 TV new stories per month from the West to Asia, whereas its output from Asia averages about 20 a month. In the case of Visnews about 200 stories are sent from London to Asia every month as against 20 from Asia and another 10 from Japan." (From V. G. Kulkarni, Hong Kong representative of the Press Foundation of Asia, at a meeting in Sri Lanka, 1977). One illustration from Latin America is similarly indicative: "A study carried out in Venezuela in 1977 revealed that on one particular day the country received 1,360 new items from external sources, 20.44% of which (278 items) came from North America, while it exported through the 10 agency correspondents 71 items, of which only 20 through North American agencies (UPI: 16; AP: 4). In other words, for every 100 news items from the USA received in Venezuela, the country dispatches seven, via AP/UPI. The same study rated the imbalance of domestic as compared with international news at 5 to 100. (Quoted by Luis Anibal Gomez: *Imbalance in the field of communication (II) — Latin America and the Caribbean*, CIC Document, No.55).

distributors of incoming news. In many places, national news agencies and newspapers and broadcasters, lacking their own correspondents, depend entirely on international agencies for foreign news,[1] just as they often depend mainly on governmental sources for national news. In some developing countries, international agencies are obliged to distribute news only through governments or government controlled agencies, rather than direct to newspapers, which causes inefficiency and delay and is in some cases a method of censorship.[2] Therefore, every effort must be made to establish new and to improve existing media structures in developing countries — newspapers, broadcasting services, training facilities, and tele-communications. The extension of regional and multinational cooperation for that purpose is essential.

Imbalances exist in all media — press, broadcasting, films and television, book production etc. While it is true that revenues from exports to developing countries by companies in the industrialized world are marginal in comparison to those received from other developed countries, the effect of the one-way flow is more visible and audible in the developing world — in the air, on the screens, at newspaper kiosks. bookshops — because their media output is disproportionately small. These facts are readily admitted by practically all concerned and need no further elaboration here. So less research and evidence is necessary to substantiate the quantitative imbalance than that required to refine and deepen its qualitative analysis in order to have a clearer perception of the substantive, cultural, social and political aspects of the one-way flow.

All of this is not sufficient to remedy the present situation without corrective action in the developed countries as well. Such initiatives as the News Agency Pool of Non-Aligned Countries and the Inter Press Service have been limited to an extent in some industrialized countries by a lack of response and utilization of their news and broadcasting services. Incoming news from many developing countries does not always readily flow into the media in the industrialized world. Hence, more developing country news sources are necessary. But, as important, is the necessity for more receptive attitudes on the part of editors in the press rooms of newspapers and broadcasting stations in the rest of the world, since they use only a small portion of foreign news which they now receive from different agencies, both from developed and developing countries.[3]

(1) Comment by **Ms. B. Zimmerman:** This is unusual for television broadcasters who derive a great deal of news from exchanges between the regional broadcasting unions. Also, some major broadcasting organizations have their own foreign correspondents in various parts of the world.

(2) *Sales to non-aligned countries by three international agencies*

	Number of countries	AP		UPI		Reuter	
		Direct	Via Govt.	Direct	Via Govt.	Direct	Via Govt.
Arab region	18	5	4	5	8	7	10
Africa	41	2	3	1	–	5	27
Asia	14	2	4	1	3	3	6
Americas	9	8	–	7	–	5	2
Europe	3	2	1	1	1	2	1
TOTAL	85	19	12	15	12	22	46

(3) Comment by **Mr. E. Abel:** "Gatekeepers generally, whether in the print or electronic media, select comparatively little foreign news for publication, regardless of its source. To suggest that their

Seen from a particular standpoint, the imbalance in the information flows has some origin in the developing countries themselves. The polarisation inside many developing societies between elites and large masses, or between well-off minorities and under-privileged majorities narrows the size of communication activities in general and decreases both supply and demand in the "information market". Such a social dichotomy also limits chances for a freer circulation of information, as it enlarges the restrictive powers of leading political forces in many countries. In addition to that, very limited communication infrastructures and scarce financial and professional resources are also causes for insufficient out-flow of various news, messages, and cultural products between developing countries and towards developed ones.[1]

But seen broadly, the one-way flow in communication is basically a reflection of the world's dominant political and economic structures, which tend to maintain or reinforce the dependence of poorer countries on the richer. A report on many spheres of industrial or trading relationships would present a similar picture. But we must stress again that communication is not an industry like any other. It intimately affects the psychological and social framework within which men and women lead their lives. Hence, the quantitative imbalance is also a qualitative imbalance — an influence on the mind which has been described as "conditioning" (although the process is not, in most cases, deliberate). Imbalance in news flows has been made the focus of international debate, but there is just as much imbalance in films, radio and television entertainment, book production, and indeed the whole range of cultural influences. While there are aspects of this imbalance in most parts of the world, its effect is most marked in developing countries because of the quality of messages and the difficulty of penetrating into big news markets, as well as because their general communication capability is weak.

In the sphere of information — which ought to mean not merely news and data but facts and reports necessary for interpretation and analysis conducive to intelligent understanding — the quantitative and qualitative effects of this imbalance are inextricably connected. They lead to dependence on one side, to domination on the other.[2] The grievances of the developing countries are on the one hand

---

lack of response to the Pool of the Non-Aligned is in any degree symptomatic is to dodge the issue. The overseas reports of all major international agencies, whether from developed or developing countries, must pass through the same turnstile and most items are denied admission. It would be hard to demonstrate that news from Norway or New Zealand gets more sympathetic attention from the gatekeepers of Europe and North America than does news from, say, Niger."

(1) In his address to the opening meeting of the first session of the CIC, **President Sean MacBride** said: "So many complaints and criticisms on the international sphere, justified or exaggerated, about monopolies and imbalances in communication, or about the role of transnational companies or the neglect of cultural identity and heredity, are certainly connected with what is often taking place inside various countries". (CIC Document No. 5). In a recent article on this general situation of imbalance, one author points to a similar conclusion: ". . .External factors and difficulties such as inadequate resources and the domination of western news agencies do not explain or justify the absence of a free press in the developing countries. The Third World must look inward and carry out a ruthless investigation into its policies and attitudes toward the press. A free press does not exist in most developing countries because national governments would not allow it to develop as an independent institution, a free and powerful agency of cultural expression." (Altaf Cauhar, "Free Flow of Information: Myths and Shibboleths", *Third World Quarterly,* July 1979).

(2) In the words of one Commission member: "Such hegemony and domination are evidenced in the marked indifference of the media in the developed countries, particularly in the West, to the problems, concerns and aspirations of the developing countries. They are founded on financial, industrial, cultural and technological power and result in most of the developing countries being relegated to the state of mere consumers of information sold as a commodity like any other." (*The New World Information Order,* **Mr. M. Masmoudi** CIC Document No. 31)

quantitative, arising from the evident fact that coverage of the developing areas in the media of the developed countries is inadequate; and on the other hand qualitative, in that the news actually published, sometimes gives a highly skewed picture of realities. There is a concentration on political affairs, generally presented in terms of crises, coups and violent conflicts, or at best the emergence of striking personalities and pronouncements by elites. Processes of development, affecting and enhancing the lives of millions of people, are neglected, or are described solely in their effects on the political scene rather than examined in their substance. It is true that, in recent years, there has been some lessening of this kind of superficiality, thanks to a growing awareness on the part of journalists from the industrialized countries of the importance of events and developments in the developing countries and a recognition that these should be more widely reported and faithfully depicted. One-way flows and qualitative distortions are not only a phenomenon in international reporting; they are also predominant within developing countries given the urban orientation of communication structures and bias which unavoidably follows.

For adequate presentation and interpretation of events from various parts of the world many preconditions are necessary; one of them being the increased role of journalists from developing countries: they must have expanding possibilities for the coverage and distribution of reports about their own countries; they should be in a position to counteract the bias sometimes contained in stories which only present western perceptions of distant realities; at the same time, they should have more opportunities to report and interpret international affairs from their particular vantage points.

The imbalance in news circulation, the one-way flow of messages and ideas, is a common concern of all countries. Professional communicators, politicians and the interested public in both developing and developed countries are seized with the problem. It has roots in both the north and the south; remedies must also be sought in both regions. And, because the problem is so basic, solutions to it cannot be delayed.

3. Vertical Flow

Ideally, communication is a continual exchange between equals, or at least between reciprocally responsive partners. In practice, this ideal has never been and probably cannot be entirely realised. The flow is vertical instead of horizontal and is mostly in one direction — from the top downwards. Inevitably, this has an effect on the style of work of communication professionals. They consider their task in terms of effectiveness, "getting the message across", translating information into simple terms, winning and holding attention. These skills are certainly necessary; a professional who fails to interest his audience is no professional. But this concept of communication tends to eclipse the equally important objective of encouraging access and participation for the public. The ordinary man or woman becomes excluded, accepting the idea that professional skill and equipment are prerequisites of communication. Meanwhile, improvements in technique are designed solely to place added resources at the disposal of the producer and sender of messages. Thus, the whole structure of communication is geared to the assumption of a vertical flow.[1]

_____

(1) Jean d'Arcy has stated the problem in these terms: "Over fifty years' experience of the mass media — press, film, radio, television — have conditioned us, both at the national and international levels, to a single kind of information flow, which we have come to accept as normal and indeed as the only possible kind: a vertical, one-way flow from the top downwards of non-diversified anonymous messages, produced by a few and addressed to all. This is not communication.

This overall picture is more or less true of all industrialised societies, but is modified in accordance with social and political conditions, and with traditions of independent thinking or — on the contrary — of subordination to authority. Where conditions favour genuine democracy, local initiative and self-reliance, there is scope for plurality of sources and horizontal flows of information, as well as for supplying information which people need in order to take decisions, solve problems, and pursue their own interests. Strictly vertical communication is typical of societies built on rigid social stratification, hierarchy and elitism. Highly centralised and tightly controlled information systems with top-down flows are admirably suited to societies which repress dissent and deviation from official policies, or to societies in which behaviour patterns are imposed. Such systems are often created and maintained by governments, which concentrate powerful means of communication in their hands and thus render open dialogue difficult or impossible. However, a similar concentration of resources and a similar top-down flow can be brought about by privately owned organisations, if these have a monopolistic or an overwhelmingly powerful position. There are many who consider that such use of big media is virtually endemic in all types of highly structured contemporary societies (mega-societies) and there is a growing concern that the very nature of mass media offers the minority who control them enormous power to spread downwards their chosen ideas and images to the majority of people.[1] Yet, the advance in modern electronic systems now also offers the possibility of localized, inexpensive, flexible and decentralized communication structures which facilitate broader public access and participation.

This uni-directional use of communication is intended, by those who control the levers, to produce an efficient and smoothly functioning society. This aim may be achieved, at least for a limited time, and more particularly when society can be insulated from outside influences. But it is likely, in the long run, to lead to social breakdown.[2] The power of the media is never unlimited, especially at the deeper

Confronted by this problem, however, our "mass media mentality" reacts only by stepping up the vertical flow, increasing everywhere the number of newspapers, radio and television receivers, and cinemas, especially in the developing countries, without recognizing that it is this very vertical nature of the flow which is at issue." (*The Right to Communicate,* CIC Document No. 36).

(1) This was underlined in a recent report on "education and the media"presented to the "States-General of Philosophy" (Paris, June 1979) with reference to several essential features of the media: "The mass media bring images of the world and discussions of ideas to an optimal public and this must be welcomed. Nor should it be forgotten that the media also provide the idea governing the selection and arrangement of images and the comments formulated thereon: not just any idea, but the idea or vision of the world of *the select few who have the political and economic privilege of disseminating ideas and images to the whole world, together with comments thereon.* . .(emphasis added). What is of momentous importance are the constraints inherent in the nature itself of the mass media, and which turn them into something other than mere vehicles, transforming them into mechanisms of thought. . .A form of communication without reciprocity, which should therefore be termed dissemination, since it involves neither feedback nor exchange. . .When we no longer have to provide answers for the reason that no questions are raised, then we are no longer "answerable" for what we report: this is known as irresponsibility. . ." (Rapporteur: Régis Debray, published in the 22nd June 1979 issue of the newspaper *Libération,* Paris).

(2) In the words of a Commission member. . . "The non-existence of a free flow of information, a one-way communication situation, monopolies of information or communications (whether by governments or private companies) cause a breakdown in the nerve system of the society which will produce cultural setbacks in the widest sense of the word. The same situation at the international level also causes similar breakdowns and setbacks among members of the international community. . .A disorder in the human nerve system disturbs and unbalances personality. The same thing happens to societies. A disorder and breakdown in the communication system will distort perceptions of reality both by governments or members and groups in society, or deprive them of

levels of human reaction. Communication based on free response and free exchange is not only more genuine and more humane, but is also a better safeguard of social harmony.

Vertical flow does, in advanced societies, produce a large volume of information. But usually the information is offered indiscriminately, is not addressed to distinct and separate audiences, and is not conceived in response to human needs and demands. This has led some observers to point to "information overload" — a phenomenon which can lead to mental confusion, alienation, or withdrawal into passivity.[1]

For a certain period of history, there was a general welcome for the lavish outpouring of information, as a contrast to the sparse trickles and the mass ignorance of the past. But now it is increasingly seen that people need to inform others as well as to receive information, to exchange messages, to engage in dialogue and interaction, to intervene in communication through access and participation. Hence, there is more and more agitation for change. Individuals, dissidents, reformers, consumer advocates, professional communications analysts, civic organisations and even some who now control the direction and sources of information are calling for new structures and new concepts to change the present flows of information. These include means and paths for flow from bottom to top. People are seeking new expanded ways to inform their governments of their opinions, needs and grievances. They are also searching for channels to make themselves communicatively interactive with the media on local and national levels. Further than just changing the vertical flow into a more equal exchange, the possibilities for extending horizontal flows are being pursued, between cultural and ethnic communities, between groups with similar social, professional, cultural or sports interest, between individuals in neighbourhoods or working environments.

The predominantly downward flow of communication is one of its major flaws. A trend towards broader horizontal exchanges would liberate many more voices for communication and open up diverse new sources. However, more freedom to communicate is not synonymous with everyone having the opportunity to say whatever he wishes to whomever he wishes, at any time and in any way. Obviously, each person will never have the possibility or the means to communicate with everyone. But increased participation by more people in communication activities should be accelerated to advance the trends towards democratization of the communication process and expansion of multidirectional information flows — up, down and across — from a multitude of sources. Full development of such trends will depend on the extent of popular demand and participation, as well as on public support and encouragement.

---

needed information to make national decisions and policies. . .Public opinion will wither and with it social control will cease to function. The government will have to rely more and more on information about society and its members from its own intelligence apparatus and eventually become captive of its own apparatus. . ." (**Mr. Mochtar Lubis,** *Interaction between Culture and Communication* CIC Document No. 76)

(1) "Information overload" provokes myriad observations; here are two typical examples: "Bombarded by ever-increasing rates of message transmission, man becomes fragmented and disorientated. Nothing seems real or permanent — everything is transient." (Benjamin Singer, quoted in *Instant World,* Ottawa, 1971). "On the one hand, the communication systems offer an increased output and a greater variety of choice; on the other, the psychological demands inherent in these choices require initiative and active effort. How can these demands be met, when the human nervous system responds to an excessive input by loss of initiative and loss of involvement?" (P. Hall, *Europe 2000,* Duckworth, London, 1977).

4. Market Dominance

Commercialization of the broad field of communication interchange and the specific area of information circulation has already been described. Today, over a large part of the world, many communication operations are commercial activities — the press, periodicals, books, films, recordings, data supply, telecommunications, a large portion of broadcasting. It is difficult to find many equivalents in business activities in market economies to the tremendous expansion in recent years of the mass media, the billion dollar revenues from sales of cultural and leisure products, the ever-rising advertising budgets, the interlinking between various media and between the media and other industries to form huge conglomerates. This naturally brings many problems in its wake, but one stands out more than all others, for it is concerned with the very nature of the communication message itself.

The content of communication — information or entertainment, or a mixture of the two — is treated as merchandise, marketed and sold in the same way as other commodities. As a number of observers have pointed out, this is a consequence of commercialization which is an economic reality.[1] The "social service" aspect of many communication media and vehicles has diminished, just as the quality of a large portion of information and messages has decreased their value as a "social good".

This is the inevitable result of "marketing", which conditions all producers' activities, and not necessarily due to their individual qualities and tastes. In a business enterprise, sales and profits are essential considerations in the minds of those who make decisions about the production of books, films, or television programmes in order to meet competition and ultimately survive. Still, many select information because they feel that it is genuinely needed, or in response to public interest, and promote entertainment chosen for reasons of artistic creativity and originality. A sense of responsibility, a desire for critical esteem, and factors of cultural taste all play their part. For radio and television systems which are public corporations, direct merchandising is minimal. For institutions such as national theatres and opera houses, the annual State subsidy is a greater financial factor than the sale of tickets. For small publishing houses and "fringe" theatres, catering to a minority public, costs are low and profits beyond the necessary basic return are not sought, so that cultural objectives are paramount.

Even so, commercial considerations are seldom absent from decisions which affect choices and priorities in communication. Some analysts assert that even the news has become a commercial product; at the least, its presentation is influenced by an implicit conception of the audience. In internal reporting, important developments in the countryside are pushed aside by unimportant, even trivial, news items concerning urban events and the activities of "personalities". Such distortions have a chain-reaction on international news flows. Significant events and issues, particularly when they come from parts of the world unfamiliar to the reader, are inadequately publicized. Public interest is certainly one justifiable reason for the selection of news,

---

(1) An author of several studies of the consumer society and consumerism has written: "Today, consumerism defines precisely that stage at which merchandise is directly produced as signs, as value/signs, and signs (culture) as merchandise. . .Nothing that is produced and exchanged today (objects, services, bodies, sex, culture, knowledge, etc.) is any longer either strictly decodable as a sign or strictly measurable as a commodity; everthing pertains to a general political economy whose determining factor is no longer either commodities or, to be sure, culture." (J. Baudrillard *Pour une critique de l'economie politique de signe,* Editions Gallimard, Paris, 1972).

but deference to the market lies behind many of the distortions that we have discussed.[1]

The same considerations apply to broadcasting, particularly television. It is agreed that many programmes are of low quality, and the mechanism producing such programmes is obvious: programmes with narrow audience appeal attract fewer viewers, and therefore less advertising. In a competitive situation, the television broadcaster is naturally unwilling — or simply cannot afford — to forego revenues, so he produces programmes which appeal to the widest possible audience[2] and which all too often lack content of the highest quality.[3] In such instances, the ratings — audience polls of viewers' preferences — decide in large measure what is shown on the screen.

This dual influence of audience and advertising has caused, according to some critics, a part of television to become anti-cultural — not just dominating culture, but, in essence, destroying it. We think this verdict is exaggerated, but it does reflect growing public concern about the quality level of much present-day commercialized production. The expansion of the media to virtual total coverage of the population, the industrialization of their operations and the formation of gigantic conglomerates results in a combined output of cultural messages and products which have created, to some degree, a "mass culture".

Information and entertainment can be offered in the market place; in the world in which we live it would be useless to cry out against this situation. Yet they are not merely commodities like any other commodities. Information is an immaterial good, a service with a high value to be reckoned on social and cultural rather than economic terms. They should be considered as "merit goods" (this term may be applied to goods, such as education and health services, which are so valuable to society that their provision should not be governed entirely by market forces). Moreover, information is a service that must exist before commodities in general can be produced and exchanged. These considerations ought to act as a corrective to the transformation of information into a simple commodity.

Recent advances in the field of informatics have also accelerated the emphasis on information as a commodity through the production and services offered by data

---

(1) Analysing this problem for a particular segment of the "information industry", the news agencies, participants in a meeting convened by ILET (Latin American Institute for Transnational Studies) concluded: "The agencies market their fact-gathering and reporting services, as well as their assessment of events. . ." By "commercialising" them, the agencies modify the nature and relative importance of events, which in fact do not "happen" for the public in general, unless and until they are selected for publication by the news sources. Thus the agency transforms a fact — whose specific dimensions and the manner in which it is to be understood are given by the context and circumstances relating to it — into a news item which, in order to *be* news, has to be presented in a "saleable" manner. Structurally implicit in the mercantile conception of news is the systematic discrimination against those facts which cannot be "sold" and which, according to this conception, are not "news" because they are not of interest to the dominant market. There is also a tendency to distort facts in order to match the focus to the forms in which they are most easily marketable. In this process, the social nature of the event and its intrinsic rationale, considered in terms of the historico-cultural context which produces it, are completely lost, and are replaced by a "decontextualized" message whose content is determined by the "logic" of the market. (*Informacion en el nuevo orden internacional*, 1977, page 39).

(2) "The competitive conditions (in television) give more and more reasons not to put on high quality shows." — said William Paley, Chairman, Columbia Broadcasting System, New York.

(3) Comment by **Ms. B. Zimmerman:** "This generalization is much too sweeping. Much programming done in the field of public broadcasting, even in competitive situations, is specifically planned for appeal to special interest, "minority" audiences, as part of the service provided by such broadcasting organizations."

processing, data transmission and data retrieval. Payment is charged for the bits of information treated, and the way this commodity is handled causes some problems. Important economic and policy issues are raised by the introduction of electronic treatment of information in such areas as postal services, banking and finance, insurance, education, publishing, libraries, legal services and many others. Electronic data treatment carried out in all these functions and services are strictly information operations, yet their traditional structures kept them clearly separated. As informatics takes over, these operations are carried out by almost identical infrastructures, still, neither the banker, book publisher, nor postal service manager considers him or herself in the same business. Analysts have singled out some of the questions posed by virtually identical information functions being undertaken by a variety of commercial operators. In particular, the expansion of informatics has forced researchers to examine not only its economic aspects but also the social consequences of this technological innovation.

Advertising, which is one of the faces of commercialism, must also be considered in its social context. Regarded as a market force, its main impact is in pressing certain selected needs at the expense of others, which may be more valid in terms both of real personal fulfilment and social progress. Regarded as a form of communication it has been criticized for playing on emotions, simplifying real human situations into stereotypes, exploiting anxieties, and employing techniques of intensive persuasion that amount to manipulation.[1] Many social critics have stated that advertising is essentially concerned with exalting the materialistic virtues of consumption by exploiting achievement drives and emulative anxieties, employing tactics of hidden manipulation, playing on emotions, maximizing appeal and minimizing information, trivializing, eliminating objective considerations, contriving illogical situations, and generally reducing men, women and children to the role of irrational consumer. Criticism expressed in such a way may be overstated but it cannot be entirely brushed aside.

It is surely true that advertising makes unsubtle and reductive use of such concepts as manliness, femininity, sexual attraction, and "happiness" interpreted in terms of material possessions. By doing so, it encourages people to jump to conclusions through association and identification rather than through reflection. Television advertising directed at children has caused particular concern.[2] It is reasonable to assume that the billions spent on advertising would not be laid out if they did not

---

(1) But its value for necessary consumers' information has also been emphasized: "Seen as a totality, advertising is the completely dominating source of consumer information in countries with a market economy. Even if each single advertisement normally gives the subjective view of the manufacturer — this is the nature of advertising — the totality of advertising provides the consumer with a number of alternatives from which he can choose depending upon his taste and purse. This means that advertising in many countries of the world is an important part of the communication forces. It is, however, important to note that much of the criticism of advertising is in reality a criticism of the media which carry it. In other words, advertising per se has become associated with the character of media which are, in fact, merely vehicles for it. This is specially the case for television advertising." (From comments sent to CIC by the International Union of Advertisers Associations).

(2) For example, in the Federal Republic of Germany, a national committee organized for the United Nations Year of the Child proposed a ban on all television advertising before 8.00 p.m. in order to protect children from becoming "victims of the consumer society". Also, testifying before U.S. Federal Trade Commission Hearings on proposed restrictions on TV advertising aimed at children, a child psychologist said that "young children may become skeptical of their parents, pre-school teachers, or any others who disparage sugared food products or a poorly made toy promoted artfully." "Mistrust results", he added, "when legitimate authority figures — such as parents — are

promise effective persuasion. Such persuasion, however, does little credit either to its originators or its recipients. Presented baldly, the idea that a car is worth buying because it has been seen being driven by a handsome young man with a smiling young woman by his side would appear totally irrational; the fact that this presentation does actually sell cars is a measure of the power of advertising. Bearing also in mind what may legitimately be attributed to other environmental factors as forces for influence and change, and what is known from social science in general, it would be unwise to assume that advertising has no long term effects or that such effects are wholly beneficial. At the same time, even those working in advertising would not deny that there is growing criticism of some obvious faults that are found in its practice.

In many societies, one of the main functions of advertising is linked to the dominant requirements of the market; to influence people to want and to buy increasing quantities of a wide range of products. The system depends on this for its survival. However, due to this multiplicity of its effects, there is a real need for an independent, comprehensive and systematic comparative enquiry into advertising in all its many aspects. Such an enquiry, which is long overdue, should ascertain both the direct and indirect, the intended and the unintended effects, and should provide the base for decisions that are found to be required and any new policies that may result from them.

Given the tremendous expansion of commercialized communication, with its multifarious — and often ambiguous — effects, perhaps new insights into the whole issue should be sought. Commercial interests and concerns in information, entertainment and culture, as organised today in many parts of the world, provide productive links with the audience as interpreters of its tastes and interests. Nevertheless questions arise: how may commercialism be integrated more closely with broad social and cultural goals and how may any extreme adverse effects be curtailed? New assessments of the particular conditions in each society may have to be carried out seeking answers to such questions as a basis for formulating new policies and installing new practices where found to be necessary. This is the thinking that underlies the protests voiced in many countries against the excesses of commercialism. Alike in the interests of the audience, of the responsible communicator, and of the creative writer or artists, any overwhelming dominance of the market needs to be curbed.

---

implicitly silenced or discredited, as they are if they pit their meager persuasion techniques against the might of television advertising directed at their young children."

Chapter 2

Dominance in Communication Contents

If individuals are to play their part as responsible citizens in the community at the local, national and even international level they must be adequately informed, possessing sufficient facts on which to base rational judgments and select courses of action. A full understanding of the events and issues which affect individuals can be attained only by the simultaneous supply of a variety, even controversial if necessary, of background data, information and facts.

There is ample evidence of advances in news collection and circulation all over the world. Improvement can be seen not only in the quantity of news that is circulated but also in its accuracy, relevance and timeliness. Today it is not only the educated elite but much wider groupings of people in most countries of the world who have more access to information. Yet, paradoxically, almost everywhere it is generally acknowledged that there are lacunae and distortions in information.

As shown by numerous surveys, the public at large is not well informed. Under certain circumstances, governments and many public or private bodies may also be ill-informed, uninformed or, more serious still, misinformed or misled. That there are inaccuracies and deficiencies in the circulation of news is undeniable, but the extent of these distortions is a highly controversial matter. It is for this reason that the Commission believes its attention should be concentrated less on the achievements already noted and more on the various aspects of the distortions to be found in the content of communication in general, particularly news, messages, data supply, cultural and leisure products etc.

1. Distortion of Contents

To evaluate whether news[1] is "distorted" or not, depends not only on the accuracy of particular information, but also on a definition of "news" and "news values". Several traditionally accepted definitions of what makes news indicate that the following qualities should be present; it must be circulated quickly after the event, be of wide interest, contain information which the reader or listener has not received before, represent a departure from the everyday pattern of life and contain

---

(1) The ongoing debate about news, particularly its accuracy and distortion, emphasizes so-called "hard" news, the data and facts collected and reported by news agencies and various media. But, the Commission is concerned with various contents; the benefits which people derive from communication are not obtained from the supply of news alone, however important that is, but accrue from all kinds of messages which the content conveys (soft news, commentaries, reports, articles, analytical surveys etc. via oral communication, print media, broadcasting, films, books, visuals, and so on).

information that is useful in reaching decisions. While each of these qualities clearly has its place in any definition of what constitutes news, many journalists, researchers, and politicians, particularly in the developing countries, no longer accept such a limited definition. They take the view that there are several more criteria which should govern the content of information, if it is to be of maximum relevance and use to those who receive it.

For them, emphasis should be on the need to place events and issues in a broader context thereby creating awareness and interest and to ensure their accurate presentation, as objectively as possible; on the fact that information can be used as a national resource and as an education tool, even when the messages conveyed are not overtly educational. They believe that news and messages essentially can never be neutral, that the criteria of what is news vary according to the needs of different countries and societies and that the definition of news depends ultimately on cultural perception. In developing countries, the concept of news appears to need expansion to take in not only "events" but entire "processes". For instance, hunger is a process while a hunger strike is an event; a flood is an event, a struggle to control floods is a process. They criticise the widely-held concept of news values for its excessive stress on the departure from the normal and lack of attention to positive news.[1] This concept may inflict on readers and listeners an endless hail of conflicts, catastrophes, crime, natural and man-made disasters, violence, political upheavals, social unrest and economic disorders.

The divergence between the different criteria of what makes news is probably not as wide as it first appears, and certainly they are not mutually exclusive. Most can agree, at least, that good news is as worthy and interesting as bad news, provided it is authentic and significant. If one accepts that communication plays an essential part in mobilizing the public's support and co-operation in any society's development, the communicator's role includes not only objective reporting of "hard" news but also commentaries offering analysis and instruction. In this way they could play a vital role in the worldwide struggle to promote human progress.[2]

Distortion of news, in the strict sense of the phrase, occurs when inaccuracies or

---

(1) One stated opinion was: "News is what is interesting, not necessarily what is important" (William Randolph Hearst). But a commentator on the Commission's *Interim Report* remarked: "So long as news is exclusively concerned with what is out of the ordinary, the ordinary becomes invisible to the media and to the audience. The trouble is that we have been culturally attuned to the theatre of news and we find non-theatre boring."

(2) The need to agree on a new understanding of "news values" has been highlighted on a number of occasions. At the International Seminar in Mexico City (1976) organized by ILET (Latin American Institute for Transnational Studies) the final report said: "the affirmation of the need for *another type of development*, concentrating on the satisfaction of human needs – endogenous and self-reliant development — should be accompanied by the emergence of a *new type of news* — reporting on social phenomena. Information is a social right, not an article of merchandise. Its aim must be to make people more aware, to give them full understanding of the economic and political situation of their problems on both the national and the international plane, and of their ability to participate in the decision-making process. Information is at once a social need and an essential factor for the full exercise of human rights. Information should be an instrument of liberation and also, in the industrialized countries, a means to the elimination of the prevailing ethnocentric prejudices."
In a recent dialogue with journalists, Mr. Brzezinski, Adviser to President Carter, also commented on the philosophy of news values: ". . . I'll be very curious to see what comes out of this luncheon. It is on the record. My guess is that there'll be more emphasis given to the one or two hard news items in it . . . such as who might be going to Vienna, or some response to a question, than to the basic theme that I tried to present to you . . . Now I hope I'll be wrong, but I suspect that I'll be right. That in turn has a lot to do with the philosophy of news in the United States. The American approach to news is to emphasize disparate facts. And the word "news" itself contains something. News, it has to

untruths replace authentic facts; or when a slanted interpretation is woven into the news report, for example through the use of pejorative adjectives and stereotypes. But there are various other ways in which the total picture of events and situations may be distorted. This occurs: (a) where events of no real importance are given prominence and when the superficial or the irrelevant are interwoven with facts of real significance; (b) when news is cobbled together from random facts and presented as a whole, or partial truths are assembled to form the appearance of a complete truth; (c) when facts are presented in such a way as to cause misinterpretation by implication, where the implicit conclusions drawn by the audience are favourable to particular interests; (d) when events are presented in a way that stirs unfounded or exaggerated doubts and fears with the aim of conditioning subsequent action by individuals or even whole communities and governments; (e) when silence is maintained on facts or events presumed to be of no interest to the public[1].

Some reasons for distortion in the presentation of news reflect the realities of the society in which the news is distributed. One reason is that many journalists, editors and broadcasters take their cue from public taste and interests. It cannot be denied that surveys reveal that many people show little interest in the major issues of the day – social, political or economic – unless they perceive themselves to be directly affected by them. Catering to the public interest is obviously a valid editorial criterion, yet is it not also reasonable to invest communicators with a certain responsibility to inform the public on matters that ought to concern them and not just appeal to their real or imagined interests?[2]

---

be new! You're all under pressure to produce news to beat your competitor. There's relatively less emphasis on interconnection of things . . . on dynamics . . . on historical forces. I tried to weave that into my own comments. I tried to give you a sense of how I feel . . . I think some of you will say it's academic, will say it's too theoretical and some of you who file on it may find your editors dropping it . . . It's very difficult to convey this kind of perspective in the context of an approach to reality which in America focuses very much on hard individual facts and is less interested in broad historical sweep . . ." (National Press Club, June 4, 1979).

(1) Since absolute objectivity does not exist, the accuracy of information is probably less a measurable quantity and more a question of judgement or viewpoint. It is the perception of the person responsible for deciding what is news, how to present and transmit it, that forms for the reader or listener the picture — bright, dim or disfigured — or realities, events and situations. It is difficult to illustrate this in a way which is acceptable to all, since interpretations vary. However, two examples may give some insight. One example from Africa. The 24th ordinary session of the Council of Ministers of the OAU, which was covered as usual by the western news agencies and also, to some extent, by Tass and the New China News Agency, decided to extend the mandate of the OAU Committee of Seven responsible for studying the effects of the petroleum embargo on the economies of non-petrol producing African countries, and to increase the membership of the Committee of Seven to twelve. The Ethiopian Herald, published in Addis Ababa, in its issue of 1 March 1975, informed its readers of this decision of the OAU Council of Ministers by printing an AFP dispatch with a Nairobi dateline, mentioning neither the enlargement of the Committee, nor its new mandate, which embraced the whole of the Arabo-African Cooperation. This concerns not only the press agencies but also the journalists of the Third World, who continue to rely exclusively on the services of the major international agencies for the information of their public, even when dealing with events taking place before their eyes. Another example regarding reports on recent events in Iran may be cited as a case in point. The *Columbia Journalism Review* said "by and large the American news media routinely have characterised the Iranian conflict as the work of turbaned religious zealots in league with opportunistic Marxists rather than – as they might have – the reaction of people outraged by a repressive regime. By doing so the press has helped to misinform American public opinion and narrowed the range of debate on this bellwether foreign policy crisis." (*Columbia Journalism Review*, January/February, 1979).

(2) This fact is widely, although not universally, recognized; the following words are worth repeating particularly since they come from a representative of a medium serving a huge audience:

There are many other reasons for inaccuracies or distortions in the news. Much as beauty lies in the beholder's eye, "news exists in the minds of men"[1] whose attitudes and perceptions often tend to be shaped by stereotyped or false information conveyed by educational texts, literature and other images to which children are exposed at an impressionable age. In some countries, communicators may lack access to information sources or the freedom to gather information may be impeded by government controls, bureaucratic intervention or other forms of official censorship. There may exist a vested interest in the misinterpretation of facts, or there may be a shortage of news channels available. A gatekeeping and selection process may influence news content, emphasis and presentation, while chauvinist attitudes and ethnocentricity in some professional communicators may warp their selection and interpretation of news from foreign environments. Some communicators may quite simply find it difficult to understand and interpret the circumstances and situations which occur in foreign countries. Among more technical reasons, restrictions on newspaper space and broadcasting time are further reasons for the poverty and distortion of content. Time restrictions on the broadcast media are particularly significant because in many countries they have come to the forefront in news presentation to the public. Limitations on the time at their disposal usually make it difficult for television and radio to give in-depth treatment or background analysis of the news items they broadcast. Although radio and television programming does allow slots for analysis and discussion, the vital function of commentary and evaluation tends to be left more to newspapers and periodicals.

News distortion should be seriously analysed by strict, methodological research. In a complex world where communication is expanding rapidly, it may be unavoidable but should be understood. Structural changes may be necessary to eliminate some of the causes of distortion. But for others, attitudinal changes may provide sufficient impetus. While the Commission is fully aware of the many difficulties facing journalists, editors and broadcasters in the collection, selection and distribution of the daily news, it is also of the opinion that, in many instances, a more heightened sense of journalistic responsibility might present a fuller, fairer and more accurate picture of the world to the public it serves.

2. Cultural Alienation

As communications have proliferated in recent decades and brought the external world to millions of people previously living in isolated communities, or who had but simple connections with the outside through conventional communication channels, so they have generated two major concerns that are widely aired: one, the development of mediated communication is a technical and social need, but may also be a threat to the quality and values of culture; two, the indiscriminate opening of doors to new experiences and impressions by the media sometimes alienates people from their own culture.

With the speed and impact of the media explosion, certain harmful effects have been observed. For many people, their conception of reality is obscured or distorted by messages conveyed by the media. The rapid increase in the volume of information

---

"journalism is more than a free competitive enterprise; in a democracy it is a great moral one . . . I stand by the overriding principal of providing the people with what they ought to know, rather than choosing only what some survey or instinct purports to tell us what the people might be interested in . . ." (Richard Salant, former President, CBS News).

(1) Wilbur Schramm

and entertainment has brought about a certain degree of homogenisation of different societies while, paradoxically, people can be more cut off from the society in which they live as a result of media penetration into their lives. The introduction of new media, particularly television into traditional societies has seldom failed to shake centuries-old customs, time-honoured cultural practices and simple life styles, social aspirations and economic patterns. Too often the benefits of modern communications – which disseminate unfamiliar, vivid, absorbing information and entertainment originating in urban centres and more often than not from foreign sources – have been accompanied by negative influences which can dramatically disturb established orders. At the extreme, modern media have trampled on traditions and distorted centuries-old socio-economic patterns. It must be acknowledged, however, that the process of modernization rarely takes place without some disrupting influence and effects. Moreover, in most societies some vestiges of the past are woefully and harmfully archaic, or even inimical to accepted present-day social philosophy and practice, thus should be changed to advance human progress. In any case, a powerful "cultural industry" has developed and expanded, with some very significant characteristics and divergent implications.[1] It is not only the media but the message that is important, and conditions must be created for national mass media and communications system to carry the cultural messages of the nation.

Industrialised societies are by no means immune to these dangers. In such societies, changes in the character and rhythm of work, urbanisation, and altered family relationships have already had drastic effects on the traditional way of life, and have made inter-personal communication, with its leisurely style, more difficult. The brash impact of the mass intensifies this process. In addition, since the same media with the same content are reaching millions of people (a peak television programme may be seen by well over half the population of a given country), a centralised influence is exerted on people in cities, suburbs and villages, people of different ideological or religious attachments, people of various ethnic backgrounds. Life-styles, habits and manners, tastes and preferences, even beliefs and opinions tend to become uniform, to the detriment of social variety and human individuality. The process can even cross national frontiers when nations get a considerable portion of their films and television programmes from abroad. These processes are not planned, yet they occur all around the world.

It has also been observed that so-called "crisis journalism", so frequently practised by the press and broadcasting, can have a disturbing effect on the rationality and tranquillity of a society. Individuals feel ill at ease or even threatened by the air of chaos, disaster and evil portrayed all around them. People may, generally speaking, react in one of two ways in such an atmosphere; they either turn in upon themselves,

---

(1) Some of its particular characteristics have been debated during a round table on the relationship between culture and communication organised by the International Commission (in Mexico, June 1979). On that occasion the following statement was made, as particularly, although not exclusively, relevant for Latin America: "The cultural industry is not a mere ideological apparatus, if we understand this to mean an apparatus, as described by Poulantzas, that does not create ideology but is limited to promoting and disseminating it. The cultural industry does in fact also create ideology. To defend its industrial character and to deny its commitments towards art and culture is in itself to adopt a clear and aggressive ideological position. Clearly, if the principle underlying the activities of the cultural industry is commercialization, all the productions of art, science, literature and culture in general which it mediates are necessarily affected . . . Clearly, too, the cultural industry plays a major role in moulding the mentalities of its consumers, exercises an increasingly marked influence upon the psychic economy. This is why I stated earlier that it is an ideological apparatus that can create ideology . . ." (Hugo Gutierrez Vega, *La industria cultural*).

obliterating from their minds as much as possible of the outside world and thus alienating themselves from their environment or they react irritably and impulsively, overlooking the real causes of society's problems and their own anger and frustrations.

Against this background, it is generally accepted that modern communications systems and the way they are used can pose a threat to cultural identity in most countries, if not all. However, it is necessary to think deeply and carefully (and more studies on the question would be desirable) about the concept of cultural identity. It has a nationally individual character; but – with few exceptions in history, and none in the modern world – it has also been formed by the assimilation of influences from outside. It is enriched not by a withdrawal into itself but by a willingness to share. Communicators, as well as educators, should be careful not to instil chauvinistic attitudes, harmful to international understanding, in a misguided enthusiasm for the protection of cultural identity.

Because communication is a part of culture as much as an influence upon it, the development of a national communication system can help to foster a thriving national culture. Mass media must be fully integrated in the whole communication system, which itself display the characteristics inherent in the nation and correlate traditional and modern communication means. Unlike critics who regard traditional methods as outdated and ineffectual, or see modern media only as "assassins" of traditional culture, the Commission is a strong advocate of enmeshing the two forms, where the two work in harmony. Solid evidence shows that not only is this possible but it is indispensable for ensuring the survival, spread and effectiveness of all media, both old and new, which any society has at its disposal.[1] It has the added advantage of mitigating the excesses of dominant vertical communication through the substantial benefits of inter-personal horizontal communication.

A major cultural issue in any communications policy is the choice and use of languages. Given the pre-eminence of language as the primary and most universal expression of culture, any act or set of circumstances that lead to the superiority of one or several languages over others, whether intentional or not, raises crucial issues. Particular attention should be paid to the development of national languages which in many places have been overtaken by former colonial languages as the favoured

---

(1) Three documents prepared by specialists in different parts of the world reached very similar conclusions:
"Indian experiments have established that it is possible to preserve the culture of a medium and yet make it an effective communication tool both as live performance and folk integrated mass media programmes. Such an achievement is possible only when there is a complete understanding and harmony among the champions and practitioners of both media ... The media experience has given a new awareness of the great potentialities of the indigenous media for the much needed persuasive communication." (H. K. Ranganath *Not a thing of the past,* CIC document No. 92). "The fact is that effective communication results not from utilizing one method alone but from the interaction of all the ways of communicating available in a society, on both the local and national scale. Therefore it can be said that communication and the dissemination of information are brought about by the interrelation of methods which embrace popular communication means, traditional communication, personal communication and the influence of opinion leaders. Such a process, which might be labelled a continuous cultural feeding cycle, would have the happy effects of closing the gaps between different standards of culture and the opposing attitude in society, while increasing social cohesion among the citizens of a society." (S. M. Hussein, *Main Forms of Traditional Communication: Egypt,* CIC documents, No. 93). "Communication must link up the man of today with the man of yesterday. Today, Africa is living through several epochs and experiencing the impact of several worlds ... In other words, the African continent, at the crossroads of traditional and modern communication, must find its second wind. (Massa Makar Diabaté, *Mains Forms of Traditional Communication: Africa,* CIC document No. 91).

instruments of communication. National languages require national dictionaries and terminologies rich enough in vocabulary for the expression of any concept in technology, science, education and culture. Recent developments in automated translation systems, which facilitate the exchange of technical, scientific and even cultural information, make the development of vocabularies and dictionaries particularly important. It is also important for an individual not to feel hampered by the limitations of his own language but enriched by the possibilities it offers for the expression of ideas, feelings and identity as a means of communicating with his compatriots. This is particularly so in developing countries, where the fragmentation or multiplicity of languages is not a "minority" problem, but a majority problem. Where numerous groups of the population are linguistically cut off from each other, cohesion in cultural, economic and political spheres is virtually impossible. Here language is no minor communication problem, but is central to the nation's viability. Unless the languages of a country's major population groups, at the very least, are used by the media, a valid and effective nationwide communication system cannot exist, since those whose languages are excluded are deprived of their right to participate in national affairs, culturally, politically and socially.[1] Different solutions to this problem may have different consequences, as the experiences of such countries as India, Belgium, Algeria, Guatemala, and Sri Lanka have shown, and they affect not only national culture but social cohesion as well. Such dangers, inherent in language selection, focus attention on a key issue for communication strategies and practices – a language policy.

3. External Influence

The problem of fostering endogenous cultures in the wake of intrusions from without is also a major issue. In many countries governments have established national policies intended to sustain and nurture their endogenous cultural activities. Where such policies exist, they may be either optimistic statements of intent or contain practical concrete instruments having sufficient scope and adequate resources and determination for them to be implemented. Even if they are well supported, it may still be debatable whether such cultural policies are strong enough to compete on equal terms with external influences as epitomized by the communication/ information/cultural force of transnational corporations. This anxiety is not exclusive to developing countries, for many in the developed world are equally sensitive to the potential danger of external influence.[2] In some instances, corrective measures have been originated. Some other countries have adopted the most direct form of

(1) "Language can easily reinforce the hegemony of a dominant elite, pushing minority elements into a position of subjection. Language is . . . a prime conveyor of culture. Hence, if we diminish the cultural standing of a language, we disorient its inheritors, and if we allow a language to die out, the result is an irreplaceable cultural loss". (Humphrey Tonkin "Equalizing Language", *Journal of Communication*, Spring 1979).

(2) "The concept of "cultural privacy" which is already receiving some attention will probably come to carry increasing weight over the next decade. This holds that cultures which may be intrinsically rich and satisfying but which are relatively weak in contemporary terms, can neither assimilate inexpensive foreign-produced media content, nor afford to produce material of equally commanding audience impact on their own. Under other names, the concept is familiar to Canadians." (*Instant World,* Information Canada, Ottawa, 1971). This familiarity prompted Canada to introduce guidelines requiring Canadian television and radio broadcasters to carry a certain percentage of Canadian originated program material in their broadcast schedules. Canada restricts cable television operators to importing three commercial U.S. television signals and one non-commercial

resistance to this potential danger with the application of strict censorship and border controls; in some cases these go so far as expulsion of all personnel, material and operations originating from foreign sources, thus in effect hermetically sealing the internal culture from outside influences. Such policies preclude the potential advantages of inter-cultural exchanges for fostering a rich, diverse cultural development. Other countries have regrettably adopted the extreme of authoritarian interference, in which the government or other bureaucratic bodies dictate cultural modes and expression and ensure the absence of some. In such a milieu, the possibility of a richly textured cultural progression is of course virtually eliminated, even though the controlled culture may perhaps produce manifestations of excellence.

An analysis of the cultural flows between countries shows how serious the imbalance is. The media in developing countries take a high percentage of their cultural and entertainment content from a few developed countries, and chiefly from a few large producers in those countries. The flow in the other direction is a mere trickle by comparison. But the problem cannot be stated purely in quantitative terms. The developed countries get the selected best of the culture (chiefly music and dance) from developing countries; the latter get a lot of what on any objective standard is the worst produced by the former. This unequal exchange is inevitably harmful to national culture in developing countries. Their writers, musicians, film-makers and other creative artists find themselves shouldered aside by imported products. Local imitations of imported culture and entertainment do not improve the situation; they too lead to the imposition of external values.

The connecting thread in this process is a commercial approach to culture, operating to the detriment of true values. Transnational companies[1] are playing an ever more active role in the world-wide provision of communication infrastructures, news circulation, cultural products, educational software, books, films, equipment and training. Although their role in extending facilities for cultural development and communication has been considerable, they also promote alien attitudes across cultural frontiers. Since similar cultures predominate in the countries where the transnationals have their roots, they transmit models and influences which are broadly alike. When these influences become dominant in very different cultures, the effect is to impose uniformity of taste, style and content.

U.S. signal. This very liberal restriction, combined with the fact that 75 per cent of all Canadian homes are served by cable television, means that Canadians spend only about one third of their television viewing time watching Canadian television programs. In children under the age of 12, it is estimated that only 17 per cent of the viewing time is spent watching Canadian programs. In order to bolster the Canadian periodical publishing industry, Canada has introduced measures regarding advertising that promote, via tax disincentives against advertising in foreign publications, the growth of the Canadian periodical publishing industry. Canada has introduced high tariffs on the importation of foreign television advertising film in a similar attempt to bolster the Canadian advertising film industry. Despite such measures the Canadian public continues to have a very high degree of access and exposure to foreign communication material.

(1) The term "transnationals" is used here in a broad sense: "an organization is "transnational" rather than "national" if it carries on significant centrally-directed operations in the territory of two or more nation states. Similarly, an organization will be called "international" rather than "national" only if the control of the organization is explicitly shared among representatives of two or more nationalities. And an organization is "multinational" rather than "national" only if people from two or more nationalities participate significantly in its operations." (Samuel P. Huntington, *Transnational Organizations in World Politics*). By these definitions, many organizations we have in mind are both transnationals and multinationals.

This is considered by some authors as "cultural invasion",[1] the type of intrusion that represents one of the major problems to be faced by everyone dealing with international communication issues. The socio-cultural tastes of foreign countries have been widely disseminated and are familiar to and often admired by many; people imitate them and they may become adopted norms of human behaviour in the countries exposed to them. But the imitations of alien cultures are not the same as the true development of a national culture, for they can in reality inhibit growth of national cultures by adapting to standardized international patterns of mass culture. Another negative factor is that creative artists in developing countries – authors, musicians, playwrights, script-writers, film-makers – often find it difficult to stand up to the competition of the industrialized products of the big conglomerates.

However, transnationals could not exert so much influence without the willing assistance of elites in developing countries. The responsibility is shared by external forces and by social and economic groups who have acquired a privileged position since the attainment of political independence. Without mutual support and understanding among those who have thus come to adopt a common outlook, cultural uniformity would not have spread to such an extent.[2]

Awareness of these dangers does not mean that national cultural development should proceed in isolation from other cultures. On the contrary, there are broad benefits from international exchanges between different cultures and value systems; but there is little cultural gain from an exaggerated influx of foreign commodities in a one-way communication flow.

The best answers to injurious foreign influence are not to be found in negative restrictions. Such influx is most irresistible when it flows into a relative vacuum. People can scarcely be blamed for welcoming even the most worthless and shallow forms of foreign entertainment (presented, let us remember, with much technical sophistication) if the indigenous cultural forms have been allowed to decay. To remain alive, genuinely popular, and attractive, these forms must be constantly renewed by fresh talent and fresh content. Writers and artists – both creative and interpretative – should be given full encouragement by the community and the appropriate State organisations, and allowed to give of their best in an atmosphere of liberty. This is the true safeguard of cultural identity.

4. Shared responsibilities

The subjects of imbalance and domination were among the most contentious in the early rounds of the world-wide debate on communications: On one side, the overwhelming amount of news and messages generated and disseminated by the developed world, conscious or unconscious distortions of the present-day realities and aspirations of developing countries, as well as their lack of resources which permitted little chance for their voices to be heard, were the major issues.

For others, the free flow of information was the primordial consideration

---

(1) Paulo Freire in his well-known book *Pedagogy of the Oppressed* writes: "Cultural invasion, which serves the ends of conquest and the preservation of oppression, always involves a parochial view of reality, a static perception of the world, and the imposition of one world view upon another. It implies the "superiority" of the invader and the "inferiority" of those who are invaded, as well as the imposition of values by the former, who possess the latter and are afraid of losing them." (*Pedagogy of the Oppressed*, Publ. Seaburg Press, page 159.)

(2) It must be noted that developing countries are not obliged to import these cultural products; they voluntarily do so because they are popular and relatively cheap. In television, for example, broadcasters fill their air time with imported programmes because they provide easily and inexpensively a finished product often impossible to match with local production.

fundamental to all communication, and to be protected from any threats by governmental interference or authoritarian regimes. Monopolistic tendencies or transnational operations in national and world communication were not responsible for existing inadequacies; it was merely up to developing countries to improve their capacities, and not restrict those of others.

Obviously, the world's communications problems are not so simplistic or categorically one-sided. True, a majority of countries are ill-equipped with communication resources compared to the industrialized world. But such imbalances are not only due to vestiges of the past, but also to present-day national and international realities; remedies must be found in joint actions by both developed and developing countries. It is also true that freedom of information is not sanctified the world over; it is not only threatened by defensive attitudes against cultural intrusion, but also by attempts to safeguard positions of privilege and power. It must also be admitted that transnational corporations play an ever more active role in communication and cultural activities, as their activities grow in the provision of communication infrastructures, news circulation, broadcasting programmes, software for educational purposes, book production, translations, visual aids, computers, cinema films, data banks, equipment, training and so on. While their contribution to the spread of facilities for cultural development and communication has been considerable, their activities nevertheless give rise to concern from a number of viewpoints. However, transnationals could not operate as they do without their acceptance by elites in many developing countries. Indeed, one can often find closer links between privileged groups in some countries and the purveyors of foreign models which they imitate than ties with the majority of their countrymen.[1] This shared similarity of needs and taste, familiar in many places and mutually supporting for host-country authorities and transnational operations, has eased the passage for cultural intrusions.

In pointing out all these problems related to flows in the exchange of information, messages and cultural products we are not seeking to make the media as such scapegoats for all the ills of society, as some people have done and still do. Nor do we see only in some societies causes of concern for all the ills of communication media and practices. At the present stage of knowledge about these issues, we cannot overlook any influential factor, particularly as they are generally overlapping and intermeshed, so that responsibility for many deficiencies in national and international communication systems must be shared.

---

(1) The similarity between privileged sectors in developing countries and larger population groups in industrialised countries has often been noted. "These sectors share a common culture and "way of life" which expresses itself through the same books, texts, films, television programmes, similar fashions, similar groups of organization of family and social life, similar style of decoration of homes, similar orientation to housing, building, furniture and urban design. Despite linguistic barriers, these sectors have a far greater capacity for communication among themselves than is possible between integrated and marginal persons of the same country who speak the same language." (Osvaldo Sunkel "Transnational Capitalism", *Journal of Peace Research*, 8/1971).

Chapter 3

Democratization of Communication

The flaws and obstacles which hamper the process of communication, and which were described in the last chapter, are proof of a lack of democratic relationships. It is the broad public, by definition, that has an interest in more, qualitatively better, and freer communication; and to ensure that the public makes its voice heard and gets its wishes satisfied means bringing the spirit of democracy into the world of communication. Because popular needs and desires are changed and enlarged as time passes, and because communication itself is going through an era of rapid change, any democratic relationship must be dynamic and evolutionary, not static. Democratization can be defined as the process whereby: (a) the individual becomes an active partner and not a mere object of communication; (b) the variety of messages exchanged increases; and (c) the extent and quality of social representation or participation in communication are augmented.

1. Barriers to Democratization

The nations of the world live under a variety of political systems, of which some are totally or predominantly undemocratic, while others are essentially democratic – although a state of ideal democracy is nowhere to be found. Ours is nevertheless a democratic age in the sense that virtually all political regimes claim to base their title-deeds on an implementation of the popular will; the idea that this is the sole legitimization of authority is thus accepted in principle. Similarly, the legitimization of communication is that it serves the people and is responsive to their needs. In moving toward democratization, this is what we have to build on.

It hardly needs saying that democratization faces many difficulties, obstacles and resistances. Some have already been discussed. Communication, necessarily, reflects the nature of the society in which it operates – a society that may well be inegalitarian and undemocratic. Thus, inequalities in wealth distribution inevitably create disparities between those who are well-served and those who are deprived in communication; a gap between a cultural elite and illiterate or semi-literate masses is a gap between the information-rich and the information-poor; and an undemocratic political system cannot fail to have adverse effects on communication. Yet, despite the logical connection between democracy in communication and democracy in society as a whole, the former is sometimes in the vanguard. There have been cases of a relatively free press – secured by popular agitation and the initiative of determined individuals – in countries that did have a democratic political system, as well as in countries with marked extremes of wealth and poverty.

An important political factor, which can co-exist with formally democratic institutions, is a rigid, centralised and bureaucratic system of administration. This tends to shape a communication system with the same defects. It is weighed down by inertia, resistant to innovation, hierarchical in its outlook, and unresponsive to the needs of the audience. The style of communication, and the use of the language also show signs of the dead hand of bureaucracy. In such a system, professionals develop a mandarin, self-enclosed set of standards. They imagine, because they adhere zealously to these standards, that their work is "highly professional". But genuine professionalism in communication is a skill in making information and ideas meaningful and interesting, using imagination and creativity, and taking full account of the quality of reception. These bureaucratic habits in communication are found in both developed and developing countries. In the latter, they are generally an effect of the gap between the cultural elite and the population at large, or of a structure in which bureaucratised communication is one branch of a generally bureaucratic administration.

Also, representation of the public in management and policy-making is often non-existent, inadequate or reduced to a formal mechanism which yields no effective results. In developing countries, this representation is not always achieved even if the will exists; the capacity to absorb popular resources is limited by a communication system still taking shape, and some central direction of communication is necessary to protect a – perhaps fragile or endangered – national identity. However, this is a problem that cannot be indefinitely ignored.

The modernisation of communication technologies makes popular control more vital, but also more difficult. The development of large scale information systems and data banks leads to amassing huge amounts of data of essential importance in social, scientific, economic and political spheres. Access to these information sources can obviously be restricted by those in control or it can be broadened to a wide audience of potential users. Pressure from the public must be exerted for democratic participation in decisions about diffusion of contents or information distribution and against concentration of control over communication.[1] Conversely, the public must be ever-watchful of official or private unwarranted accumulation and distribution of personal data about individuals. Other technological developments capable of limiting democratization are the various new information services made possible by systems linking computerized data banks with television terminals. In short, technological advances may become obstacles or threats to the democratization of communication; at the same time these new services can also lead to decentralized, more democratic structures.

There are other barriers to the democratization of communication which oblige us to place a renewed stress on the various freedoms – of information, expression, thought and belief – for it is limitations upon these that make it so difficult to advance the progress of democratization within communication systems. But one barrier that exists almost everywhere is the structure of vertical communication,[2] where the flow

---

(1) "It would seem to be a fundamental principle of public policy in a free society to strive to maximize participation and diversity and strongly oppose anything which could foster concentration of control. For it seems obvious that such control of the electronic media, whether by the state or by private interests, would represent a serious threat to the freedom of expression that is the lifeblood of a democratic community." (D. F. Parkhill, *Communication Technologies in the 1980's (I): The Future of Computer Communications*, CIC document No. 81.)

(2) Comment by **Ms. B. Zimmerman:** "Insofar as broadcasting is concerned, it is true that radio and television studios cannot be open to everyone at all times. Moreover, the public demands at least a minimum of quality in programmes and this necessitates a certain standard of talent and

runs from top to bottom, where the few talk to the many about the needs and problems of the many from the standpoint of the few.

For hundreds of millions of people, democratic communication can scarcely be a reality because of the inadequacy of communication channels, means and vehicles. From the individual's point of view, the non-existence of basic facilities for communication is a powerful constraint, since for many people the problem is not so much that the press is not free as that there is no press at all. The opportunities for communication are thus limited by the lack of infrastructures, lack of communications systems, and lack of production facilities (particularly the case in developing countries, but also true for social and cultural minorities in both industrialized and developing countries).

Diversity and choice in the content of communication are an obvious requirement in any democratic system, even though this is not the only requirement and even though it does not automatically ensure democratization. Every individual should be able to form his judgments on the basis of a full range of information and the presentation of a variety of opinions. For the communicator – whether professional or not — this pluralism is equally a necessary condition of democratic opportunities. As we have pointed out earlier, pluralism suffers through the concentration of power over communication, whether in the hands of State authority or of private interests. Since democracy implies the voicing of divergent opinions, even an inventive model of democratic control over a system speaking with a single voice can have nothing in common with real democratization.

The exclusion of disadvantaged groups from normal communication channels is a major issue. Their composition and size may vary from country to country, their problems may be more or less crucial, but they exist everywhere in the world: the poor, the handicapped, the geographically isolated; those subject to social, cultural or economic discrimination; national, ethnic, language and religious minorities; women, children and youth. Some of these groups in some places are denied such rudimentary rights to communicate as that of assembly or expression of opinion. Others, more numerous, are disfavoured by tradition or dominant social attitudes; this is particularly true for women, half of the human race.

Another barrier is erected between those who send and those who receive the messages in the communication process when people lack the knowledge for decoding or understanding messages. Among them are not only illiterates proper, who are unable to understand written language, or even those (still more numerous) who are unable to decode audiovisual messages or who decode them only imperfectly, but also all those individuals who do not feel at ease in the universe of symbols and who can be considered as semi-literate when it comes to understanding and interpreting these signs or appreciating their significance and being able to use them effectively. There is actually a new language of communications which must be learned and understood. All these points have to be taken into account when considering the concept of democratization of communication.

2. Breaks in the Barriers

In recent years an increasing number of initiatives have been launched to break

professional experience on the part of those who perform behind and in front of the microphones and cameras. Although radio and television have in most countries been set up in vertical organizations for purposes of economy and administration, the remedy is decentralization of the means and an increase in the number of local stations. Efforts in this direction are in progress in many countries."

down, or at least reduce, these barriers. Generally speaking, four approaches have emerged: (a) broader popular access to the media and the overall communication system, through assertion of the right to reply and criticise, various forms of feedback, and regular contact between communicators and the public[1]; (b) participation of non-professionals in producing and broadcasting programmes, which enables them to make active use of information sources, and is also an outlet for individual skill and sometimes for artistic creativity; (c) the development of "alternative" channels of communication, usually but not always on a local scale; (d) participation of the community and media users in management and decision-making (this is usually limited to local media). Self-management is the most radical form of participation since it presupposes an active role for many individuals, not only in the programmes and news flow, but also in the decision-making process on general issues.

Connected to active participation schemes and often running parallel to them, is a tendency observed in several industrialized countries to decentralize the mass media. This includes setting up regional or local radio stations, increasing the number of centres for programme production, introducing cable television and so on. A few examples are indicative of this growing trend. In France, a chain of film workshops has been established to provide an open communication channel for local people who wish to make short films on neighbourhood issues. "Mediatheques" have been established in Belgium for the distribution of video tapes and playback equipment. In the Federal Republic of Germany, a television station encourages the formation of community groups of persons with similar social concerns and problems by assisting them to make films about themselves which are then broadcast to stimulate formation of like groups in other communities. A different type of example is seen in Yugoslavia where, at the community and regional level, information centres are producing newspapers and radio programmes devoted mainly to local events and self-management issues. Radio and television centres publish the programming proposals, so that the broad public may discuss them and feed their reactions to the programming councils. It should also be mentioned that in several countries national minorities have at their disposal newspapers and radio and TV studios broadcasting in their own language. A flourishing example of minority group media is found in Australia where some sixty ethnic newspapers are published in 20 languages. Usually published monthly, they tend to contain little Australian news, but strive to maintain the cultural identities of the different groups and keep them informed with news from their countries of origin. In Saskatchewan, Canada, the provincial government decided to make cable television hardware a public utility and established guidelines for establishing a cable company and receiving access to the hardware. The guidelines stipulate, inter alia, that a cable company must be incorporated on a non-profit basis, provide for subscriber participation in corporate affairs, and indicate arrangements for participation of membership-based community organizations. Such illustrations could be duplicated from many other countries; they highlight the variety and vitality of group media in today's societies and show a trend that will

---

(1) Radio is usually considered as a typical means of message distribution of one-way communication. However, Bertold Brecht, almost fifty years ago, envisaged a different future: "Radio must be changed from a means of distribution to a means of communication. Radio would be the most wonderful means of communication imaginable in public life, a huge linked system — that is to say, it would be such if it were capable not only of transmitting but of receiving, of allowing the listener not only to hear but to speak, and did not isolate him but brought him into contact." (Bertold Brecht, *Theory of Radio* (1932), Gesammelte Werke, Band VIII, p. 129).

undoubtedly expand in the future.

In as much as decentralization allows the expression of local, regional and community interests and realities, it can be regarded as a means of furthering democratization. But decentralized media have often a tendency to imitate the workings of the centralized system, creating situations of local corporatism or mirroring the social hierarchy predominating in the area. When this happens, decentralization is not part of democratization and does not even lead towards it.

The past decade or two has seen the emergence of what has been called alternative communications[1] and counter-information. These terms, which began to be used in the 1960s, denote a widely varied set of undertakings whose common feature is opposition to institutionalized and official communication. One can find under this label local groups bent on breaking the monopoly of centralized and vertical communications systems, political parties or groups engaging in various forms of oppositional communication, dissidents, opponents to establishments, minorities expanding their communication capabilites, and groups engaged in new ecological experiments. The driving-force was not an absence of communications, but a reassessment and expansion of communications in the light of a new consciousness of their importance in society. This phenomenon is particularly noticeable in industrialized countries, but is also present in some developing countries, especially in Latin America. Although much alternative media practice is concerned with expressing political opposition, it has also been used to express the views of a wide variety of social and cultural minorities, of groups previously living in a communications ghetto. The tolerance shown by the authorities to such activities is usually inversely proportional to the sophistication of means used. Posters, flyers and loudspeakers are permitted more readily than the use of electronic mass media.

The stress on content as opposed to form and the urge to establish "horizontal communication" channels have led to experiments with an endless variety of means. Thus the traditional methods (flyers, pamphlets, posters, newspapers, news-sheets, meetings and festivals) have been supplemented, but not replaced, by more modern means and technologies (small gauge film, video, comics, telephone news). In industrialized countries, there is an increasing use of electronic mass media (FM radio, "pirate" or "green" radio stations, and even television) by various groups as "alternative tools".

Groups engaged in "alternative" communication belong to different categories. First, there are those representing radical opposition, of varying political or philosophical origin. Starting from the view that institutionalized communication is a mirror of a hierarchical society, counter-information sets out to challenge the influence of dominant information; it also seeks to establish channels which reflect and respond to the needs of those subjected to the flow of dominant information. Second, one finds community or local media movements, usually in the industrialized countries and particularly North America, which aim to decentralize communications so as to give an active role to information consumers. Third, trade

---

(1) Alternative communication is a process of social origin, whose content and significance are shaped by the dimensions acquired by the social praxis of the sectors under domination. No form of alternative communication is ever conducted on the basis of the one-way, individualistic, non-participatory flows which are a feature of institutionalized communication. An alternative communication process may originate in minority or individual initiatives; however, if it continues to be conducted on this scale — being stimulated and fuelled by broader social praxis — it will remain simply a marginal form of communication, corresponding to the "mini-praxis" of the community of the "initiates". (*Alternative experiences (II): Communication practices in Latin America*, Fernando Reyes Matta, CIC Document No. 68).

unions or other social groups with their particular communication networks. There are differences between these three categories but all are opposed to socially, culturally and politically hegemonic forms of communication. Also, most put the accent on content as opposed to form and on socially useful information as opposed to entertainment.

While these group activities are developing fast, there is also an increasing popularity for individualised communication making use of modern technology: two-way cable television, satellite reception antennae, 'ham' and 'citizens' band' radio, small gauge film, home video recorders and video tapes and discs, portable video cameras for home-made productions, electronic data transmission to the home and pay-TV. All these techniques open up new avenues of information and entertainment and permit those who were only recipients to now become participants or sometimes to have the illusion of being participants, in the communication process.

Certain problems, nevertheless, have emerged. Non-professional individuals and groups are confronted with technical and professional standards which they cannot match. In an effort to do so, they sometimes tend to copy the dominant models in communication rather than to tread fresh paths. Meanwhile, an opposite criticism has been heard: that individual ventures may lead to opting out from social life, or to a fragmentation of shared experience. On these questions, it is far too early to draw any firm conclusions.

Alternative communication has its greatest strength in interpersonal relationships, and thus has a capacity to defy or evade constraints by authority. As a social force, its importance is probably exaggerated by its more enthusiastic partisans. Measured quantitatively – by the content and regularity of transmission, or by the audience reached – it cannot compare with the mass media, and, indeed, that is not its purpose. Yet the radical departure from the dominant assumptions of vertical flow and the capacity it provides to develop horizontal networks, the achievement in strengthening the self-awareness of coherent groups, give it a significance out of all proportion to its quantitative scale.

Thus, in multifarious forms, individuals and groups are more and more participating directly in communication processes — with existing media, through official or institutionalized media, via alternative media — and finding new, effective outlets for creative expression. Democratization is a process rather than a static concept. Its further development is vital for the future, as failure to keep pace with social needs and technological advances can only mean that man will be subjected to increasingly dehumanized and alienating experiences.

3. Critical Awareness

Moves toward the democratization of communication do not come only from professionals willing to forge links with the audience, or even from outside groups setting up alternative channels. Another factor is the development of critical attitudes on the part of the audience toward what is offered to them, whether these are expressed through organized pressure groups or simply though spontaneous rejection of the fare provided by the mass media.

Action taken by numerous grass-roots groups – of citizens, workers, peasants, young people, women – has had a significant effect. In many instances these groups have been able to give strong expression to demands for access to and participation in the communications system. In many areas, citizens' groups have been formed to voice their concern to local and national authorities and to the broadcasters themselves. Tacit criticism is conveyed through the decline in viewing time registered in some countries, and by opinion surveys registering dissatisfaction with television programmes.[1] A striking example occurred in the Federal Republic of Germany where the Chancellor appealed for a six-day television week, an idea which a subsequent opinion poll showed was approved by a large majority of citizens.

To stimulate critical awareness and discernment is a major responsibility which the educator and communicator must shoulder together. The individual must learn to distinguish truth from falsehood, to separate opinion from fact, to take account of the subjectivity of the journalist, and to dissociate what is ephemeral, trivial, or specious from what is lasting, sound and valuable. Upon this also depends the ability of readers, listeners and viewers to maintain an attitude of constructive doubt by endeavouring to elicit from the mass of data and information reaching them that which merits consideration, withstands scrutiny and matches their own individual experience.

People need not only news which encourages and reassures them in their desires and expectations or confirms their set ideas, but also information which can validly lead them to alter, moderate or balance their judgements and opinions. The awakening and moulding of critical awareness constitutes a crucial aspect of democratization in the communication process.

4. The Right to Communicate

Communication, nowadays, is a matter of human rights. But it is increasingly interpreted as the right to communicate, going beyond the right to receive communication or to be given information. Communication is thus seen as a two way process, in which the partners — individual and collective — carry on a democratic and balanced dialogue. The idea of dialogue, in contrast to monologue, is at the heart of much contemporary thinking, which is leading towards a process of developing a new area of social rights.

The right to communicate[2] is an extension of the continuing advance towards liberty and democracy. In every age, man has fought to be free from dominating powers — political, economic, social, religious — that tried to curtail communication. Only through fervent, unflagging efforts did peoples achieve freedom of speech, of the press, of information. Today, the struggle still goes on for extending human rights in order to make the world of communications more democratic than it is today. But the present stage of the struggle introduces new aspects of the basic concept of freedom. The demands for a two-way flow, for free exchange, for access and participation, make a qualitatively new addition to the freedom successively attained in the past.[3]

---

(1) Recent figures of viewing time in France indicate a decline of 12 per cent. A March 1979 poll in the United States reported 53 per cent of the people watching less television than five years earlier. British satisfaction with BBC programmes dropped 27 points from 1960 to 1978 in a rating chart; 54 per cent of French viewers expressed their dissatisfaction in a 1979 poll.

(2) Comment by **Mr. S. Losev:** "The right to communicate is not an internationally accepted right on either national or international level. Therefore it should not be discussed at such length and in such a way in our report."

(3) One of the originators of the "right to communicate" idea, Jean d'Arcy, briefly described the successive stages which would lead to its recognition: "In the age of the agora and the forum, when communication was direct and interpersonal, there first emerged — a concept at the root of all human advancement and all civilization — freedom of opinion . . . The advent of printing, the first of the mass media, gave rise, through its very expansion and in defiance of royal or religious prerogatives to exercise control, to the corollary concept of freedom of expression . . . The nineteenth

Indeed, the idea of the right to communicate lifts the whole debate on "free flow" to a higher level, and gives promise to bringing it out of the deadlock to which it was confined for the last thirty years.

The concept of the "right to communicate" has yet to receive its final form and its full content. Far from being, as some apparently maintain, an already well-established principle from which logical consequences might, here and now, be drawn, it is still at the stage of being thought through in all its implications and gradually enriched. Once its potential applications have been explored, both in Unesco and in the numerous non-governmental organizations concerned, the international community will have to decide what intrinsic value such a concept possesses. It will be required to recognize — or not — the existence of a possible new human right, one to be added to, not substituted for, those that have already been declared. We quote, therefore, a formulation of this right, which shows the variety of its elements and the vision of its intentions: "Everyone has the right to communicate: the components of this comprehensive Human Right include but are not limited to the following specific communication rights: (a) a right to assemble, a right to discuss, a right to participate and related *association* rights; (b) a right to inquire, a right to be informed, a right to inform, and related *information* rights; and (c) a right to culture, a right to choose, a right to privacy, and related human *development* rights ... The achievement of a right to communicate would require that communication resources be available for the satisfaction of human communication needs".[1] We suggest that this approach promises to advance the democratization of communication on all levels — international, national, local, individual.

The call for democratization of communication has many connotations, many more than are usually considered. It obviously includes providing more and varied means to more people, but democratization cannot be simply reduced to its quantitative aspects, to additional facilities. It means broader access to existing media by the general public; but access is only a part of the democratization process. It also means broader possibilities for nations, political forces, cultural communities, economic entities, and social groups to interchange information on a more equal footing, without dominance over the weaker partners and without discrimination against any one. In other words, it implies a change of outlook. There is surely a necessity for more abundant information from a plurality of sources, but if the opportunity to reciprocate is not available, the communication process is not adequately democratic. Without a two-way flow between participants in the process, without the existence of multiple information sources permitting wider selection,

---

century, which saw the extraordinary development of the mass circulation press, was marked by constant struggles to win freedom of the press ... The successive advent of other mass media — film, radio, television — and the abusive recourse to all forms of propaganda on the eve of war were rapidly to demonstrate the need for and possibility of a more specific but more extensive right, namely, the right "to seek, receive and impart information and ideas through any media and regardless of frontiers" ... Today, a new step forward seems possible: recognition of man's right to communicate, deriving from our latest victories over time and space and from our increased awareness of the phenomenon of communication ... Today, it is clear to us that it encompasses all these freedoms but adds to them, both for individuals and societies, the concepts of access, participation, two-way information flow — all of which are vital, as we now sense for the harmonious development of man and mankind." (*The Right to Communicate* by Jean d'Arcy, CIC Document No. 36).

(1) As suggested in the paper: *An Emergent Communication Policy Science: Content, Rights, Problems and Methods,* by L. S. Harms, Department of Communication, University of Hawaii, Honolulu, USA.

without more opportunity for each individual to reach decisions based on a broad awareness of divergent facts and viewpoints, without increased participation by readers, viewers and listeners in the decision-making and programming activities of the media — true democratization will not become a reality.

Chapter 4

Images of the World

The crucial problems facing mankind today are closely intermeshed and the solution of one is very often governed by the solution of others. The protection of the environment, the rational use of natural, and particularly of non-renewable, resources, the energy crisis, employment, inflation, the struggle against the social ills still afflicting the majority of peoples, the gradual elimination of the injustices and inequalities that abound both within nations and between them, the defence of human rights, the struggle against the legacy of colonialism, the safeguarding of peace, disarmament — all these challenges, which are compounded with one another, can be met only by joining forces and showing a common determination.

To problems which assume an increasingly world-wide scale it is both necessary and urgent to find a global answer. Our ambition is not to seek solutions to the major issues over-shadowing the final decades of this century. More modestly, we aim to show that communication means and systems are not always making contributions they may be expected to do and to highlight the contributions which communication in general, and the media in particular, can and should make by encouraging critical awareness of these problems, or at least of some of them, and of their implications for men and women the world over.

In doing so, the Commission is conscious of being faithful to the spirit which animated Unesco's General Conference when it recognised, at its twentieth session, "the role that can and should be assigned to communication in awakening the conscience of, and sensitizing public opinion to, the major problems confronting the world and to their indivisible and global character, and in helping towards their solution" (General Resolution 4/0.1 on Culture and Communication), and when it affirmed, in the Declaration on the media, that "the strengthening of peace and international understanding, the promotion of human rights and the countering of racialism, apartheid and incitement to war demand a free flow and a wider and better balanced dissemination of information. To this end, the mass media have a leading contribution to make. This contribution will be the more effective to the extent that the information reflects the different aspects of the subject dealt with" (Article I).

1. War and Disarmament

Overcoming fear, toppling the barriers of distrust, fostering feelings of solidarity and amity, promoting knowledge of and respect for cultural values which are the reflection of the collective individuality of peoples — these are all tasks which have to be unceasingly pursued. The spirit of peace and the will to preserve peace must be tirelessly cultivated and consolidated. For the past thirty years, emphasis has been placed on all circumstances and in every forum on the need to build the defences of peace in the minds of men and women. How could the media shirk this vital aspect of their task, which is to enable men and women to understand and solve the inescapable problems of our age?[1]

No doubt everyone today feels concerned by the danger of war or of total destruction which threatens the world. Taking into consideration only the most common attitudes of the media and communicators, one may usefully identify five, not always absolutely hard-and-fast, categories.[2] In the first place are those who see it as their duty to inform, i.e. to report news "raw", and are not concerned, or do not consider it necessary to weigh the consequences which their work may have for the prospects of peace or war. In a second category are those who consider that their professional duties require them to maintain absolute neutrality, however big the issue at stake. Others take it for granted that the purpose and mission of the mass media is to promote social harmony and that they are consequently in the service of peace and opposed to all forms of violence. A fourth category is composed of those whose role is limited to supporting their respective government in all circumstances. Lastly, there are those who deem it advisable, given the very precariousness of peace, to prepare public opinion for all eventualities. A particular category might be formed of special correspondents who find themselves serving during a period of crises or international tension and who consequently have particularly important duties to discharge.

Whatever the different attitudes adopted, there can be no doubt that the media are in a position to foster — and have indeed done so on a number of occasions, in particular under the impetus of newspapers of high professional and moral standards — the emergence of a public vitally concerned by peace, alive to the importance of what is at stake, convinced of the urgent need to tackle the problem

---

(1) It may be useful to recall that this task is defined or specified in a large number of international instruments. Already in 1930, the League of Nations had considered the question of the press's potential contribution to the building of peace. In 1947, the United Nations General Assembly condemned, in its resolution 110/11, all forms of propaganda which jeopardized peace. Since then, the international community has on several occasions recalled that incitement to war and war-mongering are condemned by the United Nations Charter. Article 20 of the International Covenant on Civil and Political Rights of 19 December 1966, ratified by a large number of States, stipulates that: "(1) All war propaganda is prohibited by law; (2) The promotion of national, racial or religious hatred constituting an incitement to discrimination, hostility, or violence is prohibited by law." The Special Session on Disarmament held by the United Nations General Assembly (New York, May-July 1978) adopted certain resolutions and decisions which refer specifically to the media's contribution to the promotion of peace. In particular, it recognized that: "It is essential that not only Governments but also the peoples of the world recognize and understand the dangers in the present situation." To this end, "Member States should be encouraged to ensure a better flow of information with regard to the various aspects of disarmament to avoid dissemination of false and tendentious information concerning armaments, and to concentrate on the danger of escalation of the armaments race and on the need for general and complete disarmament under effective international control." The General Conference of Unesco, in resolution 11.1 adopted at its twentieth session, taking note of the work accomplished by the United Nations General Assembly at its recent Special Session, expressed its hope for the convening, at the earliest appropriate time, of a World Disarmament Conference, and invited Member States "to pay particular attention to the role which information, including the mass media, can play in generating a climate of confidence and understanding between nations and countries, as well as in increasing public awareness of ideas, objectives and action in the field of disarmament . . ."

(2) Comment by **Ms. B. Zimmerman**: "This classification, by oversimplifying the variety and mixture of concerns that are in the minds of the many people whose role it is to collect and disseminate news, seems to me to impede understanding of the complexities of day-to-day operation of the media in this sensitive and important subject area."

and not to leave it solely in the hands of governments.

Various studies have highlighted the interaction between public opinion and the media. Better still, they have shown that the mass media, and particularly television, can, if they wish, contribute more to determining view and position with regard to war than the traditional socializing institutions such as the church, the family, associations and clubs, or school. A positive example of this influence is the extraordinarily rapid awakening of concern for environmental problems and environmental pollution. Indeed, some have gone so far as to accuse the media in different countries under threat of acts of violence or terrorism of creating a climate of fear in order to trigger off a massive reflex demand for security. If the media thus have the power to spread fear, why should they not exercise this same power in order to free men from distrust and fear and to assert their unshakeable opposition to all forms of war and violence, and to all recourse to force in international relations?[1] It must however be acknowledged that responsibilities do not lie solely with the media, and that their efforts cannot do away with the need for a resolute determination on the part of governments to bring about general and complete disarmament. Government pressure, and the restrictions and regulations which governments may impose in certain cases, play an important role here: the national mood, and prevailing prejudices — from which it is difficult to remain free — must also be taken into account. The existence of powerful military lobbies, vested interests, the overt or covert links between certain information organs and the arms industries are also factors which hinder the media from playing the part expected of them.

The primary function of the media is always to inform the public of significant facts, however unpleasant or disturbing they may be. At times of tension, the news consists largely of military moves and statements by political leaders which give rise to anxiety. But it should not be impossible to reconcile full and truthful reporting with a presentation that reminds readers of the possibility — indeed, the necessity — of peaceful solutions to disputes. We live, alas, in an age stained by cruelty, torture, conflict and violence. These are not the natural human condition; they are scourges to be eradicated. We should never resign ourselves to endure passively what can be cured. Ordinary men and women in every country — and this includes a country depicted as "the enemy" — share a yearning to live out their lives in peace. That desire, if it is mobilized and expressed, can have an effect on the actions of governments. These statements may appear obvious, but if they appeared more consistently in the media, peace would be safer.

The arms race is a reality of our times, and measures of military escalation are news. But the striving for disarmament is also a reality, and moves to halt the arms race are news too. In a number of countries, the media's coverage of the Special Session on Disarmament of the UN General Assembly was disappointingly small.[2] It is always regrettable that people should be led to believe that disarmament is an

---

(1) Comment by **Ms. B. Zimmerman:** "The Report is accusing the media of exerting too much power, while at the same time advocating the exertion of power for other (valuable) purposes. In both cases, however, the situation is being viewed from the standpoint of "using" the media, which is an unacceptable concept."

(2) It may be instructive to quote an extract from a paper on this subject sent to the CIC: "Even such an illustrious event as the United Nations Special Session on Disarmament received scant treatment. Before the Session it was difficult to get it mentioned at all; I am reliably informed that the Government itself was "desperate" to obtain publicity for its own proposals. The huge Assembly for Disarmament and Peace obtained scarcely a mention, although 730 people attended it, and it was the biggest peace conference for years. At the same time a propaganda campaign developed in the press generally designed to pose a most serious Russian threat to the West, emphasising how our

idle dream, or that full employment and economic growth are impossible without the maintenance of the so-called defence industry. Indeed, serious studies have been made which refute this notion. In our view, it is incumbent on journalists, and on those who shape the policies of the mass media, to inform themselves thoroughly about these studies and bring the conclusions to the attention of the public. Regular meetings between communication professionals and researchers in this field, both within various nations and internationally might well be organized to exchange experiences and discuss problems related to the task of informing the public on disarmament issues. It is not inevitable that the world should spend vast sums — the total has been calculated at more than $1 billion every day — on weapons of destruction. The truth is that this represents a colossal waste of resources and of human talent that could be devoted to peaceful construction and progress.

Where a profit-making system prevails, armaments production is a lucrative business. Those who control it naturally exert as much influence as they can, both on public opinion and on political decision-makers, to keep the level of arms expenditure high. An enlightened and active public, aware of the margin in history between chance and necessity, can help to generate the political will and to ensure that it makes itself felt.[1] The military-industrial complex (to cite the phrase coined by President Eisenhower, who certainly knew what he was talking about) is a formidable reality. Even where the profit factor is absent, there are highly-placed officials, in and out of uniform, whose careers and personal interests depend on arms production. The

---

"defence" preparations were falling behind those of the Soviet Union, and how essential it was for us to spend more on "defence". What a good preparation for the Special Session! It could not have been more effective if deliberate!

During the Session itself, reports were thoroughly inadequate, at a later stage almost non-existent, and at one time were seriously (and deliberately) mixed up with reports of the NATO summit meeting. Thus James Callaghan's speeches to the NATO summit and the U.N. Special Session were reported together in *The Guardian,* as though they might be expected to have the same emphasis! . . .

How far is the British press a free press for those who desire peace and a world free from war?" (Rowland Dale, Secretary, Northern Friends Peace Board, Religious Society of Friends, United Kingdom).

(1) An expert meeting on the obstacles to disarmament and the ways of overcoming them took place at Unesco in April 1978. It suggested that "the recommendations relating to the press and the mass media be brought to the attention of the Commission in the hope that it may be in a position to conduct studies and give advice in these matters." The expert meeting urged that "the press and mass media should take the utmost care not to allow themselves to be used in the propagation of false or misleading information on strategic armament or other military matters." The expert meeting also hoped "that the press and media will focus more public attention on the escalating danger of the arms race and the need for general and complete disarmament."

More recently, **Mr. MacBride,** the President of the Commission, speaking about the problems of information and the building of peace, mentioned the following as being among the main factors in the way of disarmament:

"The absence of pressure from public opinion demanding with insistence the achievement of world disarmament and an immediate reduction in expenditure for military purposes.

The absence of an adequate public opinion in support of world disarmament is in part due to the failure of the media — electronic and written — to give priority to disarmament issues. Apart from the direct influence which they can, and do, exercise on governments, the military establishments wield a considerable amount of indirect influence by feeding material to the media so as to create fears in the minds of the people. This is done by exaggerating the dangers posed by a likely enemy. It is also done by exaggerating the military and armament potential of the other side. The only way of overcoming the pressures that are exerted on governments to increase military expenditure and armament is through public opinion. Public opinion has now become much more powerful than ever before and it is in a position to force governments to comply with its wishes." (Address delivered at the University of Peace, Brussels, 18 July 1979).

media should be vigilant in identifying these influences, and should never succumb to pressure from them.

The dangers of war are heightened by intolerance, national chauvinism, and a failure to understand varying points of view. This should never be forgotten by those who have responsibilities in the media. Above all national and political interests, there is the supreme interest of all humanity in peace.

2. Hunger and Poverty

It is impossible to continue indefinitely to make the best of a world in which 6 per cent of the population consume almost 40 per cent of basic commodities and in which the disparity in per capita income between the countries situated at either end of the development ladder is 1 to 200. In many countries, and in many fields, the intolerable gulf between the "haves" and the "have-nots" continues to widen because the richest nations continue to grow richer. All aspects of life can be seen in terms of the injustices and inequalities which it involves. For example, the resources of the oceans are being abusively or over-intensively exploited by a few nations, thereby infringing the equal right of all the others to enjoy their share of what constitutes a gift of nature to mankind as a whole and should be regarded as an element of our common heritage. The same is true of food production and distribution, the spread of technologies and industries, man's impact upon the environment, the structures of trade and the terms of trade, the utilization of raw materials, employment and labour.

The international media frequently provide striking reports of famines, floods, epidemics and other disasters suffered by developing countries, and thereby help to prompt governments and private organizations to launch relief and assistance schemes. However, the media should go beyond the state of promoting initial relief and reconstruction, they have to contribute to development and change as such; they also have to analyse the causes. Such a shift of interest towards what is now referred to as development journalism is also essential in the case of the national media of the developing countries themselves.

It is beyond the power of communication to solve these immense problems or to carry through the process of development. What communication can do is to focus attention, point out opportunities, attack indifferences or obstruction, and influence the climate of opinion. Communication thus plays a supporting and participatory role in development, but its contribution can be significant. This applies both to the mobilization of public opinion in developing countries and to the spread of greater understanding in the developed.

Sometimes the view is advanced that giving publicity to human suffering and deprivation leads to a reaction of helplessness. The record proves the contrary: reports on the Sahel drought in 1973–74, and more recently, on the plight of refugees from Vietnam and Cambodia, served to arouse the conscience of the public in more fortunate countries and led to active measures of assistance. But consciences should not be dormant from one emergency to the next. Planned development and measures to improve resources can forestall catastrophes. Sympathetic and well-informed reporting, both on problems and difficulties and on the active efforts that are being made in developing countries, can create a climate of hope and confidence and can generate effective support of these undertakings.

The developing world's policy-makers severely criticize the unconcern vis-à-vis the vital problems of their countries allegedly shown by the media of industrialized countries. The situation is indeed far from uniform in this respect; public opinion regarding development problems is more favourable and more progressive-minded in some industrialized countries than in others. Two cases in point are the Scandinavian countries and the Netherlands. It would be interesting to explore such differences and to discover their causes, which doubtless stem partly from specific cultural traditions and distinctive political features. The explanation may lie in the disparity between the individualistic approach generally adopted in many countries and the socio-ethical approach more deliberately pursued in a number of others.

Some express doubts regarding the impact and influence which the media can exert in this field. It must however be acknowledged that the way in which the public in the industrialized countries is informed about Third World problems is not very effective. The almost permanent spectacle of other people's suffering relayed by the media generates little more than indifference, which appears to be transmuted into a kind of progressive insensitivity, of habituation to the intolerable, which is clearly the very opposite of what is sought.[1] Nevertheless, it would be a grave mistake to abandon this task of informing and alerting public opinion — which has proved effective enough in the case of national problems. The extraordinary success of the television screening of serials on the African slave trade ("Roots") and on the extermination of the Jews in Hitler's Germany ("Holocaust") in several western countries gives food for thought in this respect and shows that much depends on the skills of creative artists.

Studies on the media's power to influence or modify attitudes and value systems suggest the need for prudence. Some feel that it is idle to consider how the media can help to modify attitudes and stereotypes until new structural relations in the societies under consideration — between the media managers and the aspirations of populations, between media owners and information policies — have been created. Communication, in the broadest sense, is an instrument of social change. Once a problem is recognised and understood, progress towards a solution can begin. However, the media should not be credited with unlimited power. Their contribution is to influence social norms, focus attention, demonstrate opportunities. Indeed, one of the things which they can do best is to help to build a climate for development, rather than to bring about changes directly. Their contribution can also influence attitudes. However, a distinction must be drawn between attitudes formed at the level of conscious affectivity, which can be influenced or changed, and attitudes rooted in the subconscious, which can only be strengthened or revealed, but hardly modified.

It should nevertheless be recognized that the changes which have occurred in the very concept of development should lead, and have already led, to a rethinking of the media's contribution. Development must arise from human growth, the people's confidence in its own strength, and social justice. If these premises are accepted, a development process should become progressively endogenous and self-sufficient by subordinating the dictates of capital or technology to the people's interests and by involving ordinary citizens as widely as possible in decision-making.[2]

---

(1) Mr. Robert Galley, France's Minister for Cooperation, has harshly criticized this state of mind, writing that "the western mass media portray Third World countries . . as "cadgers" when they seek our financial aid, responsible for making life expensive when the price of oil or coffee continues to soar, and for creating unemployment when they develop their own industries."

(2) A well-known supporter of communication's role in and for development, Wilbur Schramm, wrote in a paper prepared for the Commission: "Two development decades have failed to produce the improvements expected of them, particularly in the poorest countries and among rural people. This failure seems to be chargeable to strategy rather than tactics . . . A diffusion model of communication was most often combined with this (the paradigm of development, the so-called

This model of development requires a new understanding of the role of communication. The questions must arise from the grass roots; this suggests that more attention and support will be given to small media made and controlled locally. Horizontal communication, which permits give-and-take and face-to-face exchange, should take precedence over "top-down" communication, albeit with close ties continuing to be maintained between the two. This does not mean that the mass media will become unnecessary for development purposes. What it does mean is that imitation of models imported from the developed world should be avoided, and that the exponential development of ever more powerful media is not the only possible way forward.

In our interdependent world, the overcoming of poverty is in the interests of all countries, whether developed or developing. Communication, therefore, should pursue three aims; (a) to increase understanding of development problems; (b) to build up a spirit of solidarity in a common effort; (c) to enlarge the capacity of men and women to take charge of their own development.

3. A Gap both Old and New: the North-South Split

The gap between the North and South is a reflection and a legacy of the colonial past. The world today is still a world of dependence, a dependence which is political as well as economic and cultural. Dominance and oppression were more marked in the past; today, oppositions and confrontations are tending to become more prominent.

The facts which reflect this world-wide imbalance are well known. A minority possesses the major share of resources and income. Hundreds of millions of people are hungry while a few rich countries engage in large-scale consumption. The possessors of raw materials are only marginally involved in industrial production. The dependence of a majority on the minority is becoming ever more pronounced and entrenched. The gap between developed countries (mainly situated in the northern hemisphere) and developing countries (mostly in the southern hemisphere) is the crucial feature of the second half of our century.[1]

---

western model). Just as the economic benefits of industry were expected to diffuse down through the levels of society to the poor and the rural landless, so were new knowledge, innovations, and guidance in improving agriculture supposed to diffuse through the mass media to the inter-personal channels of society and ultimately to the villages and farmers, who would have the aid and guidance of whatever Third World version of a rural extension service was available. Neither diffusion model worked as well as expected, although both were built around the most potent technology in their fields — industry and mass media . . Planners and economists, stimulated both by what they saw around them and by such memorable books as Simon Kuznet's *Modern Economic Growth* (Kuznets, 1966) began to revise some of their thinking about development strategy, and call for a change." *Mass Media and National Development — 1979*, by W. Schramm, CIC Document No. 42).

(1) The United Nations Declaration on the Establishment of a New International Economic Order (May 1974) constitutes in this respect a document worthy of credence, as is attested by the sound work that went into its preparation, the difficulties of the negotiations which culminated in its adoption and the unanimous support which it finally won. Paragraph 1 of this Declaration notes that: "The remaining vestiges of alien and colonial domination, foreign occupation, racial discrimination, apartheid and neo-colonialism in all its forms continue to be among the greatest obstacles to the full emancipation and progress of the developing countries and all the peoples involved. The benefits of technological progress are not shared equitably by all members of the international community. The developing countries, which constitute 70 per cent of the world's population, account for only 30 per cent of the world's income. It has proved impossible to achieve an even and balanced development of the international community under the existing international economic order. The gap between the developed and the developing countries continues to widen in a system which was established at a time when most of the developing countries did not even exist as independent States and which perpetuates inequality."

This gap is of a double interest for any analysis of communication: on one side it generates imbalances and inequalities in the international communication system; on the other, the gap requires a proper reaction to this problem from the media themselves.

Faced by the reality of the opposition between the industrialized and developing countries, the media have adopted positions which differ from one country or situation to another. In Western countries many media simply reflect and bolster a self-interested public opinion concerned by short-term matters, and more or less indifferent to the great issue of inequality. Other media, generally among the most responsible, nevertheless make a worthy and determined effort in the opposite direction. Some, however, express concern and recognize responsibility, although their anxieties are aroused most often by effects felt at home, such as the energy crisis and galloping inflation. In the socialist countries, the analysis of the Third World's drastic situation leads them to identify and to blame specific historical factors; this analysis assigns almost the whole responsibility to the colonial powers. The question arises as to how these different approaches lead to any truly universal solidarity. In the developing countries, the media seldom have sufficiently powerful technical means, tools and the professional skills needed to make their voices properly heard. As a result, they are frequently powerless both to present what they regard as their legitimate demands and to react against what they consider to be misguided or unfair outside interpretations. It must also be recognized that they are not always ready to denounce with the necessary vigour the injustices and inequalities persisting in their own countries.

In the discussion of this problem, a manifest trend is noted to lay all blame at the other parties' door and to engage in self-justification.[1] It is too easy to ascribe all the causes of under-development to excessively rapid decolonization or to the colonial past alone. The causes do not lie solely in the advantages enjoyed by former metropolitan countries, nor in the low productivity of the former colonies. Nor, in many cases is the aid given by industrialized countries to the poorer countries so disinterested as it is claimed, for it is frequently tied up with factors involved in the political, military and economic strategies of the donors. A major effort has been made through official propaganda campaigns in various industrialized countries, aided and abetted by the media, to claim that the main — if not the sole — cause of inflation is the rise in the price of energy, and that unemployment has been triggered off by increasing competition on the part of the most dynamic developing countries — reflecting a new international division of labour — and, by and large, by the constraints and uncertainties of the world market.[2] These examples may help to bring communicators to show the utmost prudence and a full sense of their

(1) A recent study describes this trend through an analysis of the attitudes of the French press in the following terms: "a tendency to see the Third World through a distorting prism and to use news of this kind to justify preconceived notions . . . a tendency to disown all blame: on the right by ignoring Third World realities and by flatly rejecting grievances expressed against the West; on the left by distinguishing the French people, beyond reproach, from the Government, against whom all the charges are levelled; in the religious press, by giving maximum prominence to the work of Christians in the Third World in coping with problems of hunger and underdevelopment, without analysing the underlying, and essentially political, causes of this situation." (Hervé Bourges, *Décoloniser l'information,* Editions Cana, Paris 1978).

(2) It has become gradually clear that the description and explanation of the causes of the present economic crises is no easy task, and cannot be undertaken unilaterally. One example may be quoted concerning the manifest tendency of certain journalists to lay the blame for the unemployment afflicting many industrialized countries, in particular in Europe, on the shoulders of the Third

responsibilities when dealing with this crucial aspect of international relations, namely, the North-South gap. Above all — and this is a particularly thankless task — they must champion tomorrow's causes, even when these conflict with today's.

The new international economic order — which is the central issue at stake in North-South relations — involves complex concepts which are not easy to discuss in terms readily understandable to the general public, and concerning which no consensus has yet emerged. But this cannot justify the many misrepresentations in reporting on the subject. A lengthy catalogue could indeed be made of the circumstances in which the media, both of the industrialized and developing countries, have transmitted to their respective publics news that is incomplete, distorted or biased. Too much rhetoric on one side, too many prejudices on the other, too many blunt assertions and simplistic interpretations have served only to cloud a debate which is of great importance to the world economy. It is in any case understandable that developing countries are calling for more effective support by the media in helping to make their just demands more widely heard and better understood.

The disparity between North and South is not a mere matter of time-lag. Thus, it cannot be expected that the developing countries will "catch up" through being given financial and technical assistance by the developed. In reality, the disparities are becoming greater and more serious. This points to needs which go beyond the need for assistance: the elimination of unjust and oppressive structures, the revision of the present division of labour, the building of a new international economic order. Communication reflects the disparities which characterize the entire international scene, and therefore stands in need of equally far-reaching changes. These are the fundamental arguments for a new world communication order.

4. East-West Interface

In addition to issues which have produced confrontations between the North and South, there are certain conflicts of interest among industrialized nations. They may exist between large and small nations or between countries geographically close to each other, but more often they appear as a feature of relations between countries belonging to different socio-political systems. These relations are vitally important in the preservation of peace and the promotion of mutual understanding.

The cold war, which dominated the international scene for so many years, yielded in the 1970s to the conception of détente. This has not entirely prevented the recurrence of sharp disputes and antagonisms, in particular between the USA and the USSR. Still, the idea that there is a common interest in stability and peaceful co-existence was established, both for statesmen and in the thinking of millions of ordinary people.

The Conference on Security and Cooperation in Europe (the Final Act of which was signed in Helsinki in 1975) discussed the major issues from a military, political and economic standpoint, in the light of the development of inter-European and international cooperation. The message of Helsinki was clear: peace, cooperation and

World. Mr. McNamara, President of the World Bank, recently referred to the results of a study carried out in the Federal Republic of Germany in the manufacturing sector, covering the period 1962–1975, which shows that for 48 workers made redundant by technological advances, only one became unemployed as a result of increasing imports from developing countries.

international understanding. It is today for the journalists and professional communicators to spread the message.

Much has already been done to give life to the Helsinki agreement but there is a long way to go before its goals are attained. There may be differences of opinion in evaluating the achievements obtained to date and on the obstacles which obstruct the attainment of the agreed objectives. There can nevertheless be little doubt that communication can make a major contribution to the attainment of those goals.

Some sections of the media still tend to over-dramatize disagreements between East and West, with the result that tension becomes unnecessarily heightened. A stress on the alleged defects of the capitalist system on the one hand, or the socialist system on the other, obscures the obvious fact that these systems are solidly established and cannot be undermined by a war of words. Indeed, many economic publications play a constructive role in furthering economic cooperation between capitalist and socialist nations. Fascist or near-fascist ideas are voiced in some countries; if this cannot be helped, the media could well refrain from giving the impression that they are on a par with attitudes within the democratic spectrum. The question of reporting across ideological frontiers is of particular concern because full and accurate reporting can contribute significantly to mutual understanding. At present, the East disseminates more news about the West than vice versa, and there is a similar imbalance in films and television programmes. This imbalance may not be caused by deliberate discrimination, but it should nevertheless be remedied because it is the source of unnecessary ignorance and even of distorted impressions. To the extent that inadequate reporting is caused by restrictions on the free movement of journalists, or of facilities for gathering information, these too should be reduced to a minimum consistent with respect for law. Probably it will always happen that some accounts of life in the socialist world in the press of capitalist countries, and vice versa, will be regarded on the other side of the fence as superficial, as picking out the untypical, or as highlighting the darker side of reality. But if the exchange of information becomes more ample, misleading descriptions would be outweighed by those which are genuinely enlightening.

Communications can improve the East-West interface in two different ways. One relates to the contents of communication — the news, messages, ideas, images — while the other concerns cooperation between the media, institutions, cultural industries and professional associations common to all countries in the developed world. Both these aspects are dealt with in the Helsinki Final Act.

The crucial problem is probably that of the qualitative and quantitative imbalance in the exchange of information. As this imbalance recedes, mutual understanding and international communication will improve and the prospects for peace and security in Europe and the rest of the world will be enhanced. The first contribution to political détente that the communication media can make is accurate reporting about different countries. This would include wide coverage of the initiatives and agreements on international, multilateral and bilateral relations in Europe and outside it, in an effort to extend public knowledge and support for them. It would also provide a measure by which peoples could judge the success of efforts to achieve the goals of the agreements which have been undertaken. Broader public awareness would enhance mutual understanding between countries and greater tolerance for other ways of life, their advantages and drawbacks. Many people believe this improvement is already underway, and that the years that have passed since the Helsinki Conference have not been unproductive, despite the difficulties aired at the Belgrade Conference in 1977.

Some results have already been achieved in the exchange of oral, printed, filmed and broadcast information.[1] The media have made a major contribution in the last few years to extending cultural exchanges and activities. Programme exchanges are organized in particular between Eurovision and Intervision, as well as between the television broadcasting services of many European countries. The exchange of newspapers, periodicals and books has also increased, but their circulation remains limited. The fact that the public sometimes has difficulty in procuring these publications betrays a persistent lack of liberalism in mutual exchange.

Journalists' organizations have a special role to play in this area on both the national and international levels. Contacts and exchanges between journalists enrich their understanding of each other from which more thorough information about international affairs can be passed to the public. In Europe, journalists' associations hold regular meetings[2] where joint projects are worked out and cooperative activities undertaken, particularly in connexion with professional training and the improvement of mutual relations.

Higher standards in communication and improved international communication in Europe will not mean the dissolution of all ideological, political, social and cultural differences between the various European countries. On the contrary, they will give the people a better chance to understand each other's structures and conditions. While the expression of differences of all kinds is a permanent facet of a pluralistic world, such differences are not necessarily incompatible with the common struggle for peace and cooperation.

5. Violations of Human Rights

The Universal Declaration of Human Rights is an instrument whose historic significance and importance needs no stressing. It is today supplemented by an impressive array of texts, comprising in particular the International Covenant on Civil and Political Rights as well as some fifteen declarations — constituting what might be termed international law on human rights — as well as over 50 international treaties which represent the practical extension of the principles set forth in these declarations. Nevertheless, violations of human rights — sometimes

---

(1) Among the many suggestions agreed upon in the Final Act, particular attention has been given to the following: "the improvement of the dissemination, on their territory, of newspapers and printed publications, periodical and non-periodical, from the other participating states ... the improvement of access by the public to periodical and non-periodical publications imported ... an increase in the number of places where these publications are on sale ... increased cooperation amongst mass media organizations, including press agencies, as well as among publishing houses and organizations ... the exchange of both live and recorded radio and television programmes ... joint production and the broadcasting and distribution of such programmes ... meetings and contacts both between journalists' organizations and between journalists ... arrangements between periodical publications as well as between newspapers from the participating states for the purpose of exchanging and publishing articles ..." (Conference on Security and Cooperation in Europe, Final Act, Helsinki 1975).

(2) At one of the first meetings concerned with European security and cooperation (Brussels, May 1973) journalists from eighteen countries issued a press communiqué stating that: "...There was unanimous agreement on the need for providing the public with better news about the problems of European security and cooperation; on the all-important part to be played by journalists, and by the press, radio and television in this matter; and on the desirability of wider cooperation between journalists from countries with different political and social systems. To this end, the participants thought it would be useful to have more contacts, both bilateral and multilateral, between journalists, and to conclude cooperation agreements between national organizations of journalists".

insidious, quite often flagrant — are still numerous all over the world.

The problem of human rights claims special attention because it is affected in several respects by communication. Leaving aside the fact that information, as such, is a fundamental human right duly defined in several international instruments[1], information activities have to be analysed from the standpoint of their effective support or alleged non-support to other human rights. For it is largely through communication that men are able to learn about the rights which they have conquered, or which have been granted to them, as well as those which they have yet to win. In this connexion, the media can play a major role — always provided that they are willing and prepared to do so — in enlighting public opinion and in helping populations to take cognizance of their rights. Indeed, to enter into communication with others is in itself a means of feeling stronger and more aware, whereas isolation increases one's vulnerability and is a factor of uncertainty. The first task of the press and of the media in this field should therefore be to help to make human rights a living reality by ensuring that everyone enjoys the right to know what his rights are. Educators and communicators must jointly shoulder the responsibility of bringing human rights to everyone's knowledge, and teaching everyone to respect human rights and to cause them to be respected, both for one's own sake and for that of others.[2]

Being more fully aware of one's rights is not enough to ensure that they will not be violated. A second major responsibility of the media should be to lay bare and to denounce such violations. For it must be stressed that it is today less a matter of drafting new texts, in particular at the international level (although in certain cases it would be necessary to enact new laws at the national level) than of ensuring that existing texts are applied and respected. Those working in international mass communications should be eager to number themselves among the forces fighting to

---

(1) Of particular importance is the International Covenant on Civil and Political Rights, adopted by the United Nations on 16 December 1966, which states "1. Everyone shall have the right to hold opinions without interference. 2. Everyone shall have the right to freedom of expression; this right shall include freedom to seek, receive and impart information and ideas of all kinds, regardless of frontiers, either orally, in writing or in print, in the form of art, or through any other media of his choice. 3. The exercise of the rights provided for in paragraph 2 of this article carries with it special duties and responsibilities. It may therefore be subject to certain restrictions but these shall only be such as are provided by law and are necessary: (a) For respect of the rights or reputations of others; (b) For the protection of national security or of public order (ordre public), or of public health or morals." (Article 19 of the Covenant).

(2) Several international instruments are already keyed to this objective. For example, a recommendation adopted in 1974 by the General Conference of Unesco concerning Education for International Understanding, Cooperation and Peace and Education relating to Human Rights and Fundamental Freedoms states that "Member States should urge educators, in collaboration with pupils, parents, the organizations concerned and the community, to use methods which appeal to the creative imagination of children and adolescents and to their social activities and thereby to prepare them to exercise their rights and freedoms while recognizing and respecting the rights of others." Might it not be possible to conceive a corresponding recommendation keyed to the same objectives but referring to the specific methods of the media, with the term educator replaced by communicator and "children" by "adults"? It is indeed in this same spirit that the Declaration adopted by the General Conference at its twentieth session in 1978 proclaims that: "In countering aggressive war, racialism, apartheid and other violations of human rights which are inter alia spawned by prejudice and ignorance, the mass media, *by disseminating information on the aims, aspirations, cultures and needs of all peoples,* contribute to eliminate ignorance and misunderstanding between peoples, to make nationals of a country sensitive to the needs and desires of others, to ensure the respect of the rights and dignity of all nations, all peoples and all individuals . . ." (Declaration on fundamental principles concerning the contribution of the mass media to strengthening peace and international understanding, to the promotion of human rights and to countering racialism, apartheid and incitement to war).

promote human rights. Likewise, communciation systems must be founded upon a system of values which embraces respect for and defence of human rights, including the rights of every people to free and independent development. This entails the constant concern to safeguard human rights in their respective countries and to denounce all violations thereof in other countries. This second aspect is all the more important in that it is still all too common throughout the world for oppressed peoples to be deprived of the opportunity to make use of the media and to make their voices heard within their own countries. [1]

Indeed, the whole issue of human rights is intimately bound up with all the major problems facing mankind. Human rights are indivisible, but they are also inseparable from the major aspirations of our time. It is therefore vital to foster constantly an awareness of the links uniting human rights, development, peace, disarmament and many other issues. This broad vision ties in with the thinking of those who call for and urge the formulation of "third generation" human rights. If the principles proclaimed by the American Revolution (1776) and the French Revolution (1789) defined (with a few differences stemming from the fact that the former naturally stressed those principles designed to guarantee and strengthen national independence) the "first generation" human rights, namely, civil and political rights, the October Revolution (1917) gave rise to economic and social rights, which have been confirmed and enlarged by the different revolutionary movements occurring during the twentieth century and which constitute the "second generation" rights. What remains to be defined — as has already been proposed in certain international forums — are the "third generation" rights. These are conceived as being rights rooted in solidarity, and are seen as comprising for example the international right to development, the right to a healthy environment, the right to peace, the right of access to the common heritage of mankind — rights whose distinctive feature is that they all reflect a certain humane conception of life. It is surely highly desirable to include among them the right to communicate — a wide-ranging formula embracing the right of local communities and minorities of all kinds to make their voices heard and the right of peoples to reciprocity and exchange of information. [2]

However, it is possible for communicators themselves to contribute to the denial of human rights. This happens, for example, when the media transmit material which generally distorts or overlooks the rights of minorities or of entire social categories (for example women and young people). It also happens, not infrequently, when the media treat racial issues in a way that may foster discriminatory attitudes. The Declaration of Fundamental Principles states in this respect that "the mass media have an important contribution to make" in "countering racialism and apartheid". In the turbulent world in which we live, it is to be feared that the need to fulfil this responsibility is unfortunately unlikely to diminish for a long time to come. Journalists and editors everywhere have a duty to work out ways in which it can be

---

(1) In this respect, the Unesco Declaration recalls that "the mass media throughout the world, by reason of their role, contribute to promoting human rights, in particular by giving expression to oppressed peoples who struggle against colonialism, neocolonialism, foreign occupation and all forms of racial discrimination and oppression and *who are unable to make their voices heard within their own territories."* Ibid.

(2) It should be noted that some authors regard third generation rights as corresponding more to rights born of the relationship between informatics and freedom: the public's right of access to administrative documents, right to privacy, right of access to archives, the right to know and the right to correct, the right of remedy against the refusal to communicate or to correct. The aim is to remedy the fact that people all too frequently are not aware that they have the right to know, a fact which once again endows the media with extra responsibilities as well as increased potentialities.

exercised, both in long-term policy and in day-to-day practice.

It is important to place emphasis not only on the positive task of fostering understanding between nations, but also between ethnic, religious and social groups within nations. National and racial hatreds regrettably exist in many parts of the world, and little is achieved by a policy of brushing unpleasant facts under the carpet, even from the best of motives.

The principle to be respected as regards ethnic, cultural and religious difference is that each individual — Sinhalese or Tamil, Yoruba· or Ibo, Hindu or Moslem, Protestant or Catholic — is in the first place a human being, with the same needs and aspirations as other human beings; in the second place, each is a citizen, with a right to equal treatment under the law and to political self-expression. But members of a minority also have a right not to be pressured into assimilation or into conformity with the social customs, the language or the religion of the majority in the nation-state. The nation-state must understand that it gains in cultural richness by an acceptance of diversity.

The press and media in many countries have already played a notable part in mobilizing world opinion against apartheid, and in depicting the realities of life in Southern and particularly South Africa, where the political system is built on the denial of human rights to a majority of the population on a basis of racial discrimination. It remains true to the present time that this system is stabilised by heavy investment in South Africa by leading industrial nations and by a flourishing trade in imports and exports, including the import of vital materials such as oil. There is an ineradicable moral contradiction between this assistance and the professed ideals of nations which uphold democratic standards and verbally assert their repudiation of apartheid. The media should help to highlight this contradiction. International opinion, shaped to a considerable degree by the media, has ensured the isolation of South Africa in many political forums, as well as in sport and similar spheres, but not yet on the economic plane. Sustained pressure from the outside world must be an essential factor in putting an end to apartheid and introducing majority rule in South Africa.

The media have the power to promote public awareness and understanding of the culture, the social habits and traditions, the attitudes and hopes — and also the grievances — of each diverse group in the population. It would be useful for journalists to be trained in a way that enables them to play their part more effectively in this area. In the field of race relations, several international instruments have already sought to define the media's role. For example, it is incumbent upon them to divulge flagrant cases of discrimination in employment in courts of law or elsewhere, and to condemn the prejudices which underlie certain acts committed by the police. On the negative side, editors should be careful not to give sensational treatment to an isolated incident — a crime, a violent clash between persons of different ethnic or religious groups, the arrival of a group of immigrants or refugees — in a way that stimulates resentment or prejudice. But where hostility between communities is on such a scale as to present a real and serious problem, it is the task of the media to analyse its causes, to draw attention to the dangers, and to identify those who are fomenting it.[1]

---

(1) An appeal contained in the Declaration on race and racial prejudice, unanimously adopted by the General Conference of Unesco (1978) deserves to be quoted in this context: "The mass media and those who control or serve them, as well as all organized groups within national communities, are urged with due regard to the principles embodied in the Universal Declaration of Human Rights, particularly the principle of freedom of expression — to promote understanding, tolerance and

In matters of race and colour, attitudes of chauvinism and prejudice — or, on the other hand, attitudes of equality — develop at an early age. Parents and other members of the family, and also peer-groups in the school and the neighbourhood, are the major influences. But these attitudes can change, generally in response to changing social conditions. In former colonial countries that have gained independence, and likewise in the southern states of the USA, white people have come to regard black people as equals and value them as human beings to an extent that would have appeared impossible in an earlier generation. The media can play a significant part in promoting and accelerating such changes in attitude. Sympathetic and truthful reporting can portray the courage and self-sacrifice in struggles for racial equality, and explain why these struggles are justified. Books, films and television programmes can present members of formerly despised races as endowed with full human dignity and individuality, not as caricatures or cardboard stereotypes.

In various regions of the world, serious violations of human rights are often too readily based on such justifications as national sovereignty, executive privilege or reasons of state. Many people have frequently and successfully struggled against oppression and arbitrary actions carried out under the cloak of these justifications. These still, however, serve as a convenient alibi or implicit motive in many cases where, despite official denials, the exercise of human rights is virtually denied to certain categories of citizens. The media can make a major contribution here in clarifying the circumstances in which it may be legitimate — exceptionally — to invoke such justifications. Above all, they can be effective in helping to bring about, through their influence on public opinion, a recognition of the need for an active, responsible morality based on law, justice and respect for men and women.

6. Equal Rights for Women

Equal rights for women, and full participation for women in all spheres of social life, are "a necessity for the full and complete development of a country, the welfare of the world, and the cause of peace."[1] Yet, of all the violations of human rights, the most systematic, widespread and entrenched is the denial of equality to women. Despite some progress in recent years, there is no country in the world where women have achieved full equality. Although making up half or more than half of the population, they are treated as a minority group, disadvantaged and powerless. Often, the burdens of poverty, unemployment and educational backwardness weigh more heavily on women than on men. As an alarming example, two-thirds of the illiterates in the world are women, and the education given to girls as compared to boys tends to be inferior and is more often curtailed at an early age. Women need free access on equal terms to education, social participation and communication if they are to share rightfully in solving the problems of their societies. But this access is impeded by traditions, by prejudices based on social customs or sometimes on religion, by discriminatory laws in certain countries, and also by imposing on women a

---

friendship among individuals and groups and to contribute to the eradication of racism, racial discrimination and racial prejudice, in particular by refraining from presenting a stereotyped, partial, unilateral or tendentious picture of individuals and of various human groups.
Communication between racial and ethnic groups must be a reciprocal process, enabling them to express themselves and to be fully heard without let or hindrance. The mass media should therefore be freely receptive to ideas of individuals and groups which facilitate such communication."

(1) UN Declaration on the Elimination of Discrimination against Women.

disproportionate share of the responsibility for care of the home and work on the land.

Lack of education is a major barrier to choice of occupation. In developed countries, it is normal nowadays for women to enter the labour force (for example, 93 per cent of women in the USSR are employed outside the home). In the world as a whole, the 560 million women at work make up only one-third of the total labour force, and they are still, to a great extent, recruited for unskilled and subordinate jobs. Women thus hardly gain an opportunity to achieve economic independence, social security, and a proper consciousness of their own value. Even in several developed countries, the average earnings of women workers are only about 60 per cent of men's earnings. Access to certain professions (especially in the world of technology), to higher-paid jobs, and to senior management positions is generally far from equal. Moreover, in times of economic crisis women are the first to lose employment.

In recent years, women have become Prime Ministers in several countries. These are exceptional cases; in general, women are confined to a subordinate part in public life. In many countries, they are either excluded from public meetings or expected to stay silent while the men speak. The dominant figures in political parties and trade unions (even when these represent women workers) are men. Women now have the vote in most nations, but they find difficulty in being selected as candidates for election. They are in a small minority in legislatures and have only a token representation in Cabinets.

The world of communication reflects this inequality. Journalists dealing with serious issues and political events are seldom women, and few women become editors or hold directing positions. Evidence from other media tells the same story. In the USA, out of 3,000 film directors, only 23 are women (as measured by membership of the Directors' Guild). Although extensively employed as production and continuity assistants, women rarely have the responsibility for taking broad decisions.

In both developed and developing countries, public attitudes regarding the role of women in society are major determinants in deciding the status of women. In shaping these attitudes, the media exert a strong influence. The media seldom depict women as significantly involved in work, in the pursuance of careers, or in public life. A survey of Indian films (Pathak, 1977) found that, out of 46 women who appeared as characters, only twelve were in employment and nine of these were in traditionally female jobs. A study of fiction in Soviet magazines (Semonov, 1973) found that no information about their employment was given in the case of 48 per cent of the female characters: the job status of only 9 per cent of the men depicted went unidentified. Women are shown primarily as confined to the domestic sphere, or else as secretaries, assistants, and in similar roles ancillary to those of men. Even in domestic and personal situations, women appear as incapable of making decisions without masculine guidance.

In general, inadequate attention is paid in the media to issues of specific importance to women: to the activities of the women's movement, or to the social contribution made by independent and gifted women. Women appear, in magazine fiction and in television drama and comedy, as self-deprecating and dependent, irrational, superstitious and over-emotional. In advertising particularly, women are shown either as housewives whose interests are limited to domestic needs, or else as the sexually alluring background which makes consumer goods more attractive by association. This departure from reality is now widely recognized. In a recent inquiry, only 8 per cent of US and Canadian women agreed that the image of women presented in advertising was truthful. A number of studies conclude that the overall effect of the portrayal of women in the media is to reinforce, rather than to reduce, prejudices and stereotypes.[1] This distortion tends to justify and perpetuate existing inequalities.

Of course, the media are not the fundamental cause of the subordinate status of women, nor can it be remedied by the media alone. The causes are deeply rooted in social, economic and political structures, as well as in culturally determined attitudes, and solutions must be found in far-reaching changes. However, it is within the power of the media either to stimulate or to retard change to a significant degree.

Positive measures have already been taken in a number of countries. Legislation providing for equal opportunity in employment, and equal pay for equal work, has begun to affect the employment scene generally and also the media. Some organizations in the mass media are formulating new practices to eliminate sexist bias in language or images which degrade or deride women, or which perpetuate outdated stereotypes. Useful discussions and awareness sessions have influenced decision-makers in news and programming. Periodicals devoted to the cause of equality between the sexes, and feminist publishing houses, have proved viable and made an impact on the social atmosphere. All these initiatives can be extended and can lead to improvement in the image of women in the media.

The achievement of full equality for women is a matter of justice and of human rights; it is also necessary so that society can mobilize all its forces for social progress and especially for efforts of development. The world cannot afford to waste the great resources represented by the abilities and talents of women. This is the thought that should be constantly in the minds of those responsible for decisions in communication.

7. Interdependence and Cooperation

Many threats and perils — as varied as the uncertainty of food resources and the risk of famine, the proliferation of nuclear arms, cultural dominance, unemployment, the pollution of the atmosphere and the oceans — now face mankind. All these and many others besides have one feature in common: they can be averted only through resolute efforts and measures on the international level. "Governments today have become too big for the little problems and too small for the big problems."[2] Hence the rising level of world-wide independence. Doubtless it is difficult enough to master the unpredictable; what is quite impossible, however, is to do so alone.

---

(1) See CIC Document No. 59bis *The image reflected by mass media: Stereotypes (b) Images of women* by Margaret Gallagher: "Just as the media's potential for social change is culturally bounded, so must the roles which the media may be said to play in the socialization process be set within specific cultural contexts. The ways in which women are presented, misrepresented or unrepresented in mass media images reflect an interplay of social, cultural and ideological forces dominant in any given society at any given time. A review of documentation regarding the dominant images of women in the output of mass media throughout the world presents a picture remarkable for its overall consistency when compared from one country to another . . . The general finding that, from one culture to another even in those countries which rely less, or not at all, on imports — the media present a somewhat distorted picture of reality vis-à-vis the demographic characteristics of men and women, is of sufficient significance to indicate that media bias against women starts at home, even if it becomes reinforced and perhaps transformed by other, foreign, influences . . . Underlying practically all media images of women — though characterized somewhat differently from one country to another — is a dichotomous motif which defines women as good or bad, mother or whore, virgin or call-girl, even traditional or modern."

(2) Daniel Bell, *Toward the Year 2000:* Work in progress, Beacon Press, Boston, 1969.

The fragility of the eco-system may well have been responsible for arousing this awareness of the interdependence of problems. Today, the human race has no choice but to adapt itself to the natural conditions and resources of the planet. This adaptation will be painful, but it may well be fruitful also. While the origin of the change may be ecological, the change itself, whose beginnings we are now witnessing, will be mainly of an economic and social kind. It will entail enormous transformations in our attitudes and behaviour patterns. The new order is but the start of a vast but necessary process aimed at establishing a society that is both more just and ecologically viable.

If there is one thing that must generate solidarity among men and women, it is first and foremost the concern to ensure their survival. There is no choice but to come to an understanding with one another and, therefore, to communicate. Indeed, both from the technical and political points of view, communication in the broad sense of the term will be decisive in fostering the changes to come. Conscious of the seriousness of the problems now facing the peoples of the world, the mass media of all countries can play a more effective role in fostering an even closer unity of mankind. Interdependence requires a rapid flow of reliable information, transmitted via communication systems girdling the whole world.

A free flow of information both within nations and between them is vital for the forging of well-informed, democratic and self-reliant publics open to rational decisions. In ceaselessly striving to integrate the individual in the world at large, the media can contribute — albeit without in any way challenging the sovereignty of States or the patriotism of citizens — to the tricky task of developing a new sense of responsibility towards a higher and larger entity than the nation.

Too many people refuse to acknowledge, or are incapable for one reason or another of realizing, the truth of this world-wide interdependence. The information which they receive does not go beyond the limited range of local events and affairs.[1] Too many people are thereby deprived of information which would enable them to clarify their own aspirations and to see their own achievements in a larger setting. It is also the case that, whether deliberately or due to lack of understanding, the media sometimes distort the nature and importance of the increasingly complex relations of interdependence. If they wish to remain or to become a constructive factor in society, the media will have to be able to think ahead creatively. Taking account of national and local interests does not conflict with the need for communicators to become accustomed to thinking in terms of interdependence and to bear in mind the network of interlinks which increasingly underpin all decisions and all phenomena affecting human communities.

The information disseminated on the intergovernmental or international organizations dealing with major world problems is also not always satisfactory or comprehensive enough. Instances are many: reporting on various United Nations deliberations, North-South negotiations, Unesco's so-called politicization, ODEC's initiatives regarding energy prices, IMF interventions in the monetary market, etc.

---

(1) A number of surveys carried out in developing as well as in several highly developed countries show that a large percentage of citizens receive relatively little foreign or international news as compared with the volume of local and national news. Comparative analyses of newspaper content also reveal that coverage of major world issues and the affairs of other countries remains limited. This is particularly true of local media; however, the same surveys indicate that for a considerable proportion of people these media are the most regular source of information in many countries.

The same is true of the United Nations and the other organizations of the United Nations system, which are often maliciously attacked by certain media organizations that seem deliberately anxious to discredit them by decrying their lack of effectiveness or power (ignoring the fact that these are largely dependent on decisions — or disregard — by Member Governments) or by ridiculing their supposedly unwieldy procedures. Nevertheless, the world surely could not do without these organizations, whose problems stem largely from the lack of understanding and support on the part of the public and international opinion.

Accordingly, it appears necessary to equip the international community as such with its own tools of communication, or to strengthen them considerably.[1] For a world-wide organization such as the United Nations, the need is particularly vital, since a representative political institution can only operate effectively if its views, activities and problems are at least to some extent understood at all levels of the community which it serves and if it at the same time possesses the means of information needed to carry out its own activities.

Obviously, the task is an extremely complex one in the case of the United Nations system as a whole. Coordinating structures have been set up throughout the system, in particular in the form of a joint information committee which serves as the information arm of the UN Administrative Committee on Coordination. This information committee each year adopts a plan of action focused on a single theme for all the information programmes within the UN system. For example, the common theme for 1978–79 was: how can the establishment of a new international economic order contribute to meeting mankind's needs? Despite such efforts for coordination and concentration, much criticism has been levelled against the information services of the United Nations system.[2] Such criticism must be taken into account in organizing more substantial and more open briefings on the objectives, activities and

---

(1) According to Mr. Waldheim, the UN Secretary-General, "it is vital to use the new technologies and to seek new means in order to create a better understanding of, and wider support for, both the long-term objectives and the daily activities of our Organization". In an official document of the 30th session of the General Assembly, the Medium Term Plan, it is said that the problems related to the UN system's information work include among others: ". . . inadequate coverage of UN activities in the world's mass media . . . great variation in sophistication of the target audiences . . . need to counter biased reporting in some areas". The same document mentions as one of the medium-term principal objectives "to use a multimedia thematic approach to focus on major themes to which the UN is committed, such as international peace and security, disarmament, economic and social development, decolonisation, eradication of racial discrimination, human rights, equal rights for women, emergency relief, and others . . .". However, the broadcasting potential of the UN is quite restricted: broadcasting is done from Greenville, Tangier, Bethany, Delano, Dixon, Monrovia, Philippines; power of stations is limited, programme hours as well; however, programmes from the UN are broadcast by stations in more than 120 countries and territories; recorded radio programmes are distributed in several languages: Amharic, Arabic, Chinese, English, French, Greek, Hebrew, Indonesian, Japanese, Filipino, Portuguese, Russian, Spanish, Swahili, Turkish. Recently proposals have been made to cut down short-wave UN emissions.

(2) In the summary conclusions reached at a Seminar held in Uppsala, 1978, it was pointed out that a new information order ". . . involves the abandonment of the authoritarian centre-to-periphery modes of dissemination . . . Active information work means, to take a few examples, more meetings with journalists and other re-disseminators on a regional or sub-regional basis, more cooperation with international and national NGOs, more personal contacts with local organizations, such as trade unions, religious communities, academic institutions, etc . . ., and more continuous involvement with the existing national media in the different areas of the world, even those areas that suffer from political tension. It does not mean more pamphlets posted from the centre to the periphery and other types of one-way information flows" (Seminar on "The Basic Principles of UN Public Information Policy: Proposals for Reform and Problems of their Implementation" held at the Dag Hammarskjöld Centre, Uppsala, July 1978)

problems of the institutions which the international community has established. These should provide information whose presentation and dissemination would be more extensively discussed with journalists, non-governmental organizations and by and large with all those in a position to serve as a link between the international organizations and the general public in the different countries; as well as information that will be inspiring and thought-provoking rather than apologetic and defensive. The aim would be to develop new informational and educational activities focused on the major issues with which the international community is concerned. Greater effort must also be made to champion the universal causes to which the UN and its systems devote themselves.

The United Nations and its agencies, including Unesco, have established themselves over more than thirty years as a force for international understanding and the defence of peace. In that time, it has been increasingly recognized that peace depends on peoples as well as on governments. However, there is still no channel through which the UN can speak directly to the peoples of the world. Several nations maintain international services broadcasting to all parts of the world. Standards of veracity and reliability are in some cases high, but the voice is necessarily that of a single nation with its own attitudes and interpretations of world events. We consider that it would be valuable for the UN to explore again (for the matter has already been raised on several occasions before different authorities) the feasibility of setting up a more powerful world broadcasting service capable of conveying the outlook and serving the needs of peoples in all parts of the world, and of giving voice on crucial issues to international public opinion.

It is indeed difficult to accept that the international community does not possess its own media. But it is also vital for it to be able to enlist, rally and stimulate other media, and to cooperate with them. Otherwise, it will be impossible to create new values, new ideas or to give birth to a new ethic.

Chapter 5

The Public
and Public Opinion

Outside the sphere of interpersonal relations, a countless variety of messages is received by the public every day. But what and who is this public? And what is its response to the data, ideas, analyses, judgments and interpretations contained in these messages that both reflect and influence its behaviour and that is loosely called public opinion?

1. The Concept of the Public

Many definitions of the public and its opinion exist, reflecting the ideological and social differences found in a highly diversified world. We can, however, identify one common point: even within a single country, the public cannot be considered as an amorphous sum of the individuals who compose it. It is therefore necessary to speak not of the public but of publics. Similarly, public opinion is not simply the sum of individual opinions, but rather a continuing process of comparing and contrasting of opinions based on a wide range of knowledge and experience.

Both the public and public opinion are complex subjects, yet the notions these terms represent are often limited to inadequate generalities. On the one hand, there is sometimes a devaluation of the very idea of the public, whose existence itself may even be denied in some countries. On the other, the influence of the media on public opinion may be over-estimated, in some cases to such an extent that one might speak of a media-public, whose sole function is to swallow media-produced political stereotypes.

The public is indeed more than a mathematical total of individuals. It means a collectivity, which exists because individuals share certain experiences, certain memories and traditions, certain conditions of life. This collectivity, however, is not a uniform whole, even in quite a small community. Under observation, it reveals many variations based on distinctions of social class, economic interest, religious belief, political and ideological attachment, and so forth. It is because this aspect of the matter is sometimes ignored that the power of the mass media to influence the public is exaggerated. If the public were in fact devoid of attitudes and qualities of its own, it would be possible to impose on it any kind of belief, prejudice, or pattern of behaviour. The reality, however, is that the public tests and evaluates the messages offered to it by standards which it has inherited or adopted, and these standards govern its response of acceptance or rejection. This inter-action — the influence of the media and the public's response — is an essential factor in the functioning of communication.

The individuals composing the public are seen as a vast and anonymous target for the media, which transform them into atomized units lacking singularity. Frequently, political and social leaders, as well as those in charge of information, give the impression of addressing an homogeneous public, failing to distinguish between social and professional categories, and even in ignoring differences of age and sex.

While this assessment may at least be partially true for many countries and regions of the world, it cannot be applied to all. Far too simplistic, it does not take into account the different political and economic systems, and neglects the variety of publics existing within a single country: large and small publics, specialized publics, etc.

In no way, however, can the role of the public in the development of communication within and between nations be slighted. Indeed, its involvement in political decision-making and in general public affairs is of world-wide importance.

2. National Public Opinion

A collective phenomenon that has frequently eluded precise scientific analysis, public opinion is intimately linked with man's social nature. However, it is neither temporally changeless nor geographically monolithic.

Before the eighteenth century, in which the middle classes matured, there was little awareness of this phenomenon. For Hegel, public opinion meant public or social perception coupled with an evaluation of what was perceived. Voltaire glorified its power, while John Stuart Mill denounced its tyranny. Historically, this concept of public opinion has developed in step with the idea that the powers of government should be based on "the consent of the governed", and hence with the idea of democracy. Sometimes, the focus was on an enlightened opinion or on the role of the social and political avant-garde. Since the nineteenth century, however, there has generally been an increasing interest in the opinion of the "man in the street". And with good reason: retrospectively, we can see the importance of public opinion in many historical situations, as well as in more recent circumstances. Certain movements in the developing world have confirmed the power of popular judgment, giving examples of politically active publics capable of making both decisions and sacrifices. Public opinion has played an active role in anti-colonialist, anti-imperialist and anti-fascist struggles around the world and was active in the recent democratization of Spain, Greece and Portugal, and in the conflicts in Nicaragua. Events in Iran undoubtedly testify to the power of public opinion and provide valuable insight into the way it is forged and strengthened.

We might profitably define public opinion by what it is not. It is not innate, but is rooted in social and cultural structures. It is not simply the expression of the will of a people and, though it is closely linked with the public, it is not identical to it. Since it is not learned or imposed as a block by some recognized authority, it is not the same as an ideology. Finally, it is not equivalent to a body of knowledge, although it cannot exist without data and concepts generated by experience. Such data are used to judge whether the public approves or rejects a subject under consideration. For public opinion is considered to be that of people outside the decision-making process, external to the power centres, and differs from that of people who, because of their specific position, knowledge and skills, are responsible for decisions.

On the positive side, the plurality of opinions does not necessarily impede the forging of a single public opinion, which is a spontaneous and common resonance of events in men's minds, based on common interests and attitudes. For opinion is ultimately governed both by the mind's demands and the heart's reactions.

Obviously, public opinion is not simply a topic of theoretic or general interest. In many countries, public opinion is disregarded in an all too concrete fashion. Mass media (in particular the press and broadcasting) aid and abet this process. Under authoritarian rule, public opinion becomes a government instrument rather than an information source. Far too often, public opinion is artificially moulded and manipulated, so it can yield the frequently criticized passivity of the mass public, whose resulting immaturity, indifference to major issues and political incompetence can lead to a readiness to be governed by an elite or an oligarchy. The impact of television is such that it is not unreasonable to speak of veritable "telecracies", whose existence would seem to prove the impotence of dialogue as a system of communication. More likely, it is not the presence of these media but precisely the absence of dialogue that is responsible for the development of this situation. It should also be added that insufficient attention is given to those whose opinion is not of media interest, such as the "silent majority"; tacit opinion becomes a social force when large numbers of individuals who share viewpoints realize their common vision and promote their interests.

The mass-circulation press — including all forms of news dissemination — has long been referred to as the "fourth estate". Everyone today understands what is meant by the "power of the press" — its importance in the exposing of revolutionary ideas, in the denouncing of government abuses and social scandals, in the revealing of countless unlawful acts and injustices cannot be denied. Watergate and Vietnam are only the most recent examples of the press's ability to unearth facts, to forge opinion and to encourage the public to act. In 1974, Japan's Prime Minister was forced to resign after an aggressive press campaign against political corruption. Journalism can be an effective "counter-power" when government, economic and other established authorities attempt to restrict or distort information related to the public interest. Unfortunately, it is less effective than it is perhaps considered to be, since the reigning political and financial powers are unwilling to relinquish their privileges.

Finally, what is the correlation between public opinion and the mass media in societies in which the continual presence of these media is taken for granted? While this presence must surely stimulate thinking, bringing to its audience data from outside the individual's direct experience, many specialists consider that public opinion not only expect the media to uncover the problem, but to furnish the remedy as well. Democracy is not aided by such apathy for public involvement; discussion, judgment and participation are necessary for its survival.

Methods of testing public opinion, and of discovering what attitudes it favours or rejects at a given moment, are increasingly employed in many countries. This testifies to the importance attached to public opinion, often disregarded in the past. Governments and political parties test public opinion before deciding on their election programmes, or before deciding whether to hold an election or regarding new legislation, introduction of specific measures, etc. Another development, related to the formulation of public opinion on specific issues, is the innovation of holding referenda in some countries which formerly had no provision for this process.

The media, too, carry out regular surveys to inform themselves about their public or the audience, in order to determine tastes, but above all to assess the size of their audience. Such surveys, designed mostly to attract advertising, measure only the actual audience, and not a potential one. Elected governments are increasingly obliged to take account of the public's moods, especially during election campaigns and power struggles. Many different political systems recognize the importance of public opinion. In certain countries, specific mention of public opinion is included in constitutional texts, recognizing its potential for favouring democratization and participation. In others, as disparate as India, Italy and Peru, references to the role of public opinion promote its relevance on the political as well as the administrative plane. The Soviet Union's new constitution makes recognition of the importance of this role a necessary condition for developing social involvement. Elsewhere, public opinion is alluded to in legislative or regulatory texts, government directives and other official documents. In many other places, practical recognition itself reveals the importance public opinion has in the eyes of leaders and officials. Many countries are therefore highly interested in canvassing public opinion, utilizing general surveys, election pools, popularity ratings of political parties and leaders, and even market research and studies of consumer behaviour patterns. The most sophisticated scientific methods are used. Unfortunately, these modern methods have facilitated the manipulation of individuals, the swaying of public opinion, and the control of society in some countries. In many nations (the United States, Japan, France, Sweden, Federal Republic of Germany, Italy, and also more recently in India, Mexico, Yugoslavia, Hungary, etc.) polls are used to identify attitudes in the economic, political, cultural, commercial and other fields with increasing precision. Although potentially risky,[1] this practice should be adopted as widely as possible.

In this whole area, two contradictory phenomena can be noted: the growing importance of governments and, simultaneously, the strengthening of the role of public opinion. Although these two trends coexist, in many countries, if not in all of them, communication practices and contents have to be based on a much more rigorous analysis of the differences existing in the public and in public opinion. For it is doubtful that the further development of information systems could be achieved without a thorough knowledge of all the participants in communication processes.

3. World Public Opinion

Links between international politics and public opinions at the national level lead to consideration of world public opinion. But does this cosmopolitan community of national publics exist? If it exists, it must be admitted that it is still in the process of formation, and thus is fragile, heterogeneous, easily abused and still unable to be considered as an authentic power. Nevertheless, it is a question which merits attention here.

World public opinion is being gradually formed either around national problems common to a large number of countries (under-development, hunger and malnutrition, social inequalities, the energy crisis, youth problems) or around questions of international scope (co-operation for development, general disarmament, the establishment of a new economic order, decolonization, etc.). If "world public opinion" is still at its initial stage, it is possible all the same to identify certain issues around which it is taking concrete shape. World public opinion desires the preservation of peace through international agreement, and considers it the primary duty of governments to avert the horrors of a nuclear war. World public opinion is opposed to torture and inhuman treatment, and to the persecution of those holding minority beliefs (although there is no universal agreement as to which beliefs should be allowed to be openly expressed). World public opinion is opposed to

---

(1) The importance of polls does not mean that they are not often biased: questions are slanted; samples are too small or even false; public opinion polls are "constructed"; polls are taken "after the fact"; figures are invented; results are geared to "prove" pre-determined goals; data are often used without a full appreciation of their inherent uncertainty, and so on.

privilege or domination on the basis of race or colour. World public opinion wishes to see action taken more urgently to remedy the conditions of poverty, hunger, and backwardness which are the common problems of a majority of the human race. On each of these issues, there are of course people (even, in the aggregate, many people) who dissent from the general view; but they are increasingly conscious of being at odds with an attitude that has a collective, world character. Indeed, the problem is often not so much one of disagreement as it is of lip-service, casual or shallow awareness, indifference, lack of strong feeling.

Concerning all of these problems, the media have a moral and political responsibility to take account of public attitudes and opinions. If Pan African consciousness has not developed as expected, have media really done enough to stimulate solidarity throughout the continent? And if many western industrialized nations pay scant attention to developing world concerns, is not this due to some extent to the media? If signs of depoliticization are noted in some socialist countries, does this not imply that the media's contribution has failed?

The different forms of communication (oral, visual, interpersonal, mediated and even, more recently, "computerized") are used to diffuse information on international questions to every part of the world. Leaving aside questions of motive, it is clear that governments, newspapers, radio and TV commentators, reviews, private firms, political parties, trade unions and countless social organizations all use the media to present a specific viewpoint for which they hope to gain recognition. All governments have used, and still use, the media to help attain their objectives. It is difficult for the public to decide whether the viewpoint expressed reflects an objective attitude, or a narrow bias, masking ambition and partisan interests. Even sincere efforts at informing the public may generate instead a passive state, or lead to indoctrination. If, in the worst event, information sources are limited, and only one viewpoint expressed, the public is manipulated by propaganda. The media must attempt to present different viewpoints as objectively as possible in order for the public to form an independent opinion. "An ill-informed person is a subject, a well-informed person a citizen" as the saying goes.

It is hard to say whether it would be more accurate to speak of a world public opinion emerging through processes of its own, or of the convergence of national public opinions. What is important is that governments — even those by no means attached to democracy — are finding it necessary to pay attention not only to opinion within their own countries, but also to opinion as expressed in the world at large. There can, for instance, be no other reason for examples of amnesties, of the release of political prisoners whose names have become known around the world, and of proposals (whether genuine or deceptive) to soften the harshness of racial domination. Important, too, is the development of a common consciousness and common sympathies among women, among the younger generation, and among certain social categories, regardless of nationality. In all these ways, world public opinion is gradually becoming a reality.

4. Beyond the Concepts of the Public and of Public Opinion

Must modern communication continue to be seen as a one-way flow of information directed at the public? Might not this conventional relation of dissemination and reception be overthrown, thus transcending the present distribution of roles, in which the media give and the public takes, and forming a more equitable dialogue between peers?[1] Though utopian in implication, such a relationship is conceivable if greater prominence is given to the idea of citizen involvement. The aim is to create more democratic relationships by integrating the citizen into the decision-making processes of public affairs. Public opinion would then no longer be only opinion, but rather a consciousness transformed by knowledge of public affairs and the experience of social practices, and thereby uniquely qualified to judge.

What is needed is a rethinking of our communication systems and practices.[2] Is not a common goal to transcend one-way communication, which all too frequently leads to political indoctrination, unbridled consumerism and dictated social behaviour patterns? To reach it, people try to avoid the vertical power hierarchy of speaker-receiver and cease practices that "mobilize" citizens treated as objects.

There will always be a need for news from reliable and knowledgeable sources. But if this one-way flow were to cease being the dominant, indeed virtually unique pattern, and if it could be combined with horizontal forms of information distribution, then communication might become more humane and democratic and the public might shake off its passivity, becoming an active social force. The problems facing modern societies are increasingly complex; their solution calls for a citizenry possessing a high level of skill and understanding. If one wishes to achieve the provisions of the Universal Declaration of Human Rights and of the International Covenant on Civil and Political Rights that proclaim the citizen's right to take part in public affairs, it is vital to encourage transformation of the passive publics mastered by ruling forces and media into a true community, sharing a common system of values and rallied around unifying endeavours, indeed of publics which are much more than passive social spectators and witnesses of somebody else's performances.

---

(1) In this regard, it is instructive to note the opinions of two experts at the Cornell-CIAT International Symposium, Cornell University, Ithaca, New York in March 1974. Luis Ramiro Beltran, in *Rural Development and Social Communication; Relationships and Strategies,* said: "What often takes place under the label of communication is little more than a dominating monologue in the interest of the starter of the process. Feedback is not employed to provide an opportunity for genuine dialogue. The receiver of the messages is passive and subdued as he is hardly ever given proportionate opportunities to act concurrently also as a true and free emitter; his essential role is that of listening and obeying ... Such a vertical, assymetrical, and quasi-authoritarian social relationship constitutes ... an undemocratic instance of communication ... We must ... be able to build a new concept of communication — a humanized, non-elitist, democratic and non-mercantile model". Everett M. Rogers, in *Social Structures and Communication Strategies in Rural Development,* stated that "... the linear models imply an autocratic, one-sided view of human relationships" and rated the classical pattern a "passing paradigm".

(2) "In order to define a new communications policy, the new approach must be allied to a new ethic of communications ... This new ethic may arise from the repudiation alike of propaganda and cacophony ... The first stumbling-block of the communicative society is propaganda. This occurs, and cannot fail to occur in any human group, once a unilateral flow of information is released, and passively received ... The second stumbling-block is the fragmentation to which any unfettered proliferation of small communication units would necessarily lead ... In both these extreme cases, what is missing is dialogue: in the first case, as a result of the refusal of those who control the media to allow people to have their say; in the second, because the communicators — those who do make themselves heard — find very few interlocutors; because in the one case there is no feedback and, in the other, interaction is illusory. For purposes of social communication, there can be no other ideal than that of a clear and balanced dialogue between the transmitters and receivers of messages." (From a text prepared for the International Commission: *Communication: A Plea for a new Approach* by Francis Balle, CIC Document No. 40).

Part IV

The Institutional and Professional Framework

In the preceding pages, we have sought to describe the world of communication in all its complexity and diversity, highlighting the various forms of interaction between its practitioners as well as the contradictions, imbalances and discrepancies which all too frequently are a feature of its functions, structures and content. In the increasingly rapid evolution which we are at present witnessing, we must seek to determine the importance of the institutional factors of communication and the scale of human resources available.

These are clearly two instruments which will unfailingly be called upon to play a major, not to say decisive, role in improving communication systems and in establishing a more just, rational and effective order both at the national and international levels. A sound institutional framework is essential in order to make effective use of such tools as communication policies and information and communication development plans. The place, role, rights and responsibilities as well as the training of professionals constitute, together with norms of professional conduct, other dimensions of the context in which nations and the international community are striving, frequently with difficulty, to devise ways and means of tackling effectively the problems which face them.

Chapter 1

Communication Policies

Communication policies have long been a much-debated issue. The concept itself is the subject of considerable controversy and even polemic, and we are bound to recognize that there is still little unanimity concerning the importance and necessity of framing instruments of this kind, designed to give structure and consistency to overall action.

1. Relationship with Development Strategies

The desire for establishing rational and dynamic links between communication and overall development goals is, to be sure, at the core of all discussions on this subject. The concept of overall, integrated development has today won general acceptance, and it is in this perspective that efforts are being made to define the inter-links between development objectives and the various social activities (in particular education and communication) or to optimize the role which these activities might play in fostering overall development. Seen in that perspective, this is a world-wide problem, since no country is today without some general development goals or without an overall development perspective, although the ideological and economic methods and means of reaching the goals may be quite different.

However, the first question to answer is what type of development is being pursued. The model which brought the developed countries to their present position not only prevailed throughout the world for decades but was imitated by a large number of developing countries. In fact, setting aside their cultural development, certain countries achieved high national growth rates and substantial advances in material standards of living, as well as progress in educational, cultural, scientific and technological spheres; these countries may indeed be regarded, in these various respects, as developed. But they are developed to varying degrees and living standards may differ widely from one region to another even within the same country. This is the case in capitalist countries as well as in socialist ones. Material development in these countries has been, and continues to be, governed in some by more or less controlled market mechanisms and in others by State planning, which may be either authoritarian or take the form of guidance. However, the repercussions of such development on the general quality of life do not always appear to be foreseen and controlled. Indeed, it must be acknowledged that these repercussions are very difficult to perceive and control.

Most development patterns in the poorer countries, where the social and economic systems adopted also differ from one another, are of a similar kind, i.e. concentrated on progress in the material and economic spheres and, here again, little thought was ever given to the social repercussions of development strategies. While results achieved in development targets have been modest, most countries concentrated on establishing ever greater numbers of industries and infrastructures on the basis of imported models. Obviously, not all developing countries have reached the same material level and conditions differ within countries and from one region to another.

Thus development practices as such pose certain problems which appear to be common to all countries, particularly since general experience, both in developed and developing countries, has shown that the models which seemed capable of answering the needs of some countries, and which were subsequently imitated by others, have mainly failed to yield the expected results. The existing economic crisis, which affects a large number of Western countries, and which is much more than simply an energy crisis, reflects the many deadlocks, conflicts and illusions found in both the developed and developing world. Hence the fact that the question of development models and basic objectives has recently been subjected to re-examination by the international community.

The earlier post-war approach to development is now challenged: greater emphasis is placed on political and social reforms, focusing on such objectives as: human aspects of development linked to improvement of the quality of life; facilitating and increasing participation by the people in the decision-making process; and adoption of labour intensive and appropriate technologies, the equitable distribution of national income, etc.[1]

So, the basic problem is that of linking communication facilities and activities to other national objectives or, in other words, that of integrating communication development into overall development plans. Since communication is not an autonomous, separate sector, in this domain perhaps more than in others interdependence makes it essential to develop communication policies which are not limited to information, even less to mass media – they have to take into consideration all ways and means a society needs and can utilize for its overall development purposes. We must not lose sight of the fact that communication policies go hand in hand with those formulated in other fields, i.e. education, culture and science, and should be designed to supplement them. Communication should interrelate with these other sectors, so as to promote social, educational, scientific and other services. On the other hand, these policies should be limited to structural and material issues, and not be used to dictate content of communication or restrict expression of diverse opinions.

What is of paramount concern here are the consequences of new approaches to development for communication, its role and its systems. The development models of the past mainly utilized communications to disseminate information to make people

---

(1) A quotation from the report *What now? Another Development* (by the Dag Hammarskjöld Foundation, Uppsala, 1975) summarizes the basic new directions: "Development of every man and woman — of the whole man and woman — and not just the growth of things, which are merely means. Development geared to the satisfaction of needs beginning with the basic needs of the poor who constitute the world's majority; at the same time, development to ensure the humanization of man by the satisfaction of his needs for expression, creativity, conviviality, and for deciding his own destiny ... Another development requires transformation of socio-economic and political structures that have long been identified. They include such fundamental steps as agrarian reforms, urban reforms, reforms of the commercial and financial circuits, redistribution of wealth and means of production as well as the redesigning of political institutions through, inter alia, decentralization with a view to ensuring democratization of the political and economic decision-making power, promoting self-management and curbing the grip of bureaucracies. As history shows, few of these transformations can be achieved without changing the power structure itself."

aware of "benefits" to come from and "sacrifices" required for development and to instil a readiness to follow leaders. The imitation of a model of development based on the assumption that newly-created wealth will automatically percolate down and "irrigate" the whole society, included propagation of downward communication practices, sometimes over-simplified and assimilating the techniques of advertising. The results have been far from what was expected; today it is acknowledged that these theories in developing countries have produced greater benefits for the more advanced sectors of the community than to its more marginal sectors and that the gulf between rich and poor is not decreasing.

The crux of the matter then is to determine the implications of the new development approach to communication policies. What are the changes in communication patterns needed to reflect the change from a foreign to an endogenous development model? What type of communication practices and structures are needed to institute truly active involvement by the people in making global, overall development their own responsibility? What is the meaning of "another" communication order for "another" development?

It is self-evident that communication policies must also take account of demographic factors and of their consequences at different levels for development strategies. By the end of the century, it is reckoned that the world population will rise to over six billion, i.e. over two billion more than in 1975, of which the populations of the developing countries will represent over five billion.[1] Communication policies must provide for the development of resources needed to satisfy the requirements of the various population sectors: for example the elderly, whose numbers seem certain to increase (according to UN figures, the population aged 65 to 80 and over will have roughly doubled by the year 2000, as compared with what it was in 1970), as a result of the increase in life expectancy and the drop in the birth rates; or again, in the case of the young, whose age group[2] (generally taken to include those between 15 and 24) represents on average 7 to 10 per cent of the entire population and comprises students and young workers. Adding the number of all school-age children, aged six and over, which is increasing very considerably — above all in developing countries — it is not difficult to forecast the scale of certain needs, such as paper production for the manufacture of textbooks. These, and other such problems, are also part of communication policies which seek appropriate solutions for expansion of resources, infrastructures, facilities, equipment, etc.

With an eye to this new model of development which entails the people's involvement in the nation's affairs and which enables each citizen to affirm his or her personal and cultural identity, the essential objective of any communications policy, particularly for developing countries, must be to provide each nation with the infrastructures in general, with telecommunications and media in particular, best suited to its needs. It is of course true that economic, industrial and technical development is an important factor in raising the living standards of peoples and nations, and must therefore be pursued and reinforced. But here as elsewhere, since the main consideration is people, communication between men is fundamental to the qualitative improvement of human life and human societies. The fostering and democratization of such communication may help to bring about another form of development concerned with the quality of life rather than with the variety and quantity of consumer goods alone.

---

(1) Unesco Statistical Yearbook 1977
(2) *Thinking ahead.* Unesco, 1977

However, communications require different infrastructures. As the development of a nation proceeds, it becomes possible to create, extend or modernize this infrastructure. But this will not happen automatically; it depends on decisions which give communications necessary priority in development strategy. While it is true that communication by itself cannot bring about development, it is also true that inadequate communication renders development slower and more difficult, as well as impeding popular participation. Some governments in developing countries are conscious of this, but by no means all.

In this connexion, it should be stressed that the growing awareness on the part of populations of the need for such changes is extremely important. This awareness is indeed a powerful factor, enabling them to organize and prepare for change. To this end, communication cannot be the monopoly of the media, but must also occur through the intermediary of teachers, extension workers in health care, agriculture, etc., who have a vital role to play in progressively generating a climate of awareness and thereby eliminating the fears which the process of change sometimes arouses in people's minds.

For these various reasons, governments in most countries are concerned with national communication policies. Far from having already shaped global policies, some fragmentary measures — part of present-day or tomorrow's systems — are already being undertaken. Even countries that for reasons of principle hesitated to intervene in communication matters, now feel inclined to do so: because communication systems are increasingly complex; because new technological advances require more planning and oversight; because the expansion of international communication has to be supported by internal measures.

While the need for national communication policies may be more or less universal, it should be noted that their formulation and content differ very widely. They do not necessarily imply rigid, centralized planning, but may simply constitute a favourable framework for the coordination of activities, allowing flexibility and a wide choice of approaches. On the other hand, what they do call for is the allocation of public resources, decisions about general structures for communication activities, elimination of internal and external imbalances, and definition of priorities, which naturally vary from one country to another.

Some essential priorities will, however, recur in most countries. To secure a flow of messages and news which is not vertical, one-way, and produced by a few for the public at large, structural changes designed to facilitate a horizontal flow or exchange involving the active participation of both individuals and communities are needed. What is involved is more a matter of software than of hardware.

Due attention should be given to the fact that it is the concepts themselves that should be changed. One of the main aims of communication policies must be to correct and to adjust existing structures in order to meet the needs for broader flows and for democratization of communications.

In many countries, both developed and developing, various kinds of imbalance are to be found: between urban and rural communities, between the elite and the masses, between majority and minority groups of all kinds, etc. One of the main purposes in developing communications is to help constantly to reduce inequalities.

Moreover, in most countries — albeit at very different levels — a revolution is today occurring in communications technology which is throwing many existing institutions into disarray. Well thoughtout measures are needed in order to: (a) develop new technologies and encourage their use; (b) facilitate the extension of telecommunication networks; (c) identify and select the technical means best suited to the conditions and potentialities of each country; (d) foresee and neutralize certain potential disadvantages of technological development; (e) create training facilities in the use of new technologies, in management techniques, maintenance, utilisation of various equipment, etc.

It is generally recognized that both communications development and overall development are national problems, which every country has to solve by relying essentially on its own resources. Nevertheless, while the principle of "self-reliance" is of paramount importance, it must not be forgotten that communications on the national plane and communications at the international and regional levels are clearly interlinked. It is therefore essential not only to determine national communication policies designed to further overall development and to enlist public support, but also to incorporate in these policies measures to encourage cooperation and to step up exchanges at the sub-regional, regional and international levels.

The number of countries which frame national communication policies or which adopt general policy measures geared to the same objectives is constantly increasing. This is an essential trend and should be encouraged; however, these policies and measures should not lead to restrictions on cultural and information exchanges, but to decreasing barriers and inequalities inside and between different societies. The formulation of communication policies should: (a) serve to marshal national resources; (b) strengthen the coordination of existing or planned infrastructures; (c) facilitate rational choices with regard to means; (d) help to satisfy the needs of the most disadvantaged and to eliminate the most flagrant imbalances; [3] emphasize universal and continuing education; (f) help in strengthening cultural identity and national independence; (g) enable all countries and all cultures to play a more prominent role on the international scene.

2. The Institutional Framework

The formulation of communication policies is sometimes of a general constitutional nature, sometimes more detailed and specific, usually based on national legislation. Freedom of belief, of opinion, of speech, of expression, freedom of the press, freedom of information ... are expressions commonly used in Constitutions, together with guarantees of other freedoms in which communication is involved, such as the freedom of assembly and the freedom to hold processions and demonstrations, freedom of correspondence, freedom of travel, etc. In some countries, these freedoms may be made subordinate to certain duties or accompanied by guarantees of the material means necessary for their exercise. Once proclaimed, however they are often hemmed by certain restrictions, which may be minimal or may extend to various aspects of their exercise. It is sometimes a mistake to attach excessive importance to the provisions contained in countries' constitutions, since these solemn texts are frequently no more than formal declarations of intention or principles.

Laws and regulations adopted in application of the principles proclaimed in constitutions are many and varied, and draw on all branches of law: civil law, penal law, commercial law, fiscal law, labour law, and so on. Moreover, in many countries professional regulations adopted by the members of the professions themselves also form part of the legal framework; they may constitute a major source of communication law, and take essentially the form of codes of professional conduct and press or media councils.

As regards their legal context, different countries do not have the same problems or concerns. State intervention — whether by the executive or the legislature — takes different forms. The restrictions imposed upon the freedom of information vary both in the degree and the level at which they are applied. Existing regulations may apply to the establishment, ownership, organization and functioning of press, radio, television, cinema and theatrical enterprises, news agencies and advertising agencies and generally speaking all information enterprises.

This means that freedom of information is in practice not without limits; it is a political and professional ideal limited, as all others, by social contingencies. This emerges even more clearly when we consider the content of information, particularly regulations with respect to blasphemy, insult, slander, libel, State secrets, defence, and so on. Thus it cannot be said that the State is ever totally unconcerned in regulating communication at some level, and that it does not play a role, in some cases trifling, in others important, in this field.

There are, in the community of nations, fundamental differences of opinion as to what part the State should play in communication activities. Certain countries take the view that economic and social mechanisms should be allowed free play, and that freedom of information is essential to democracy. Some of these countries have provisions, in their written constitutions or customary law, virtually forbidding State intervention in the domain of information content and dissemination. In others, the State, often in the form of the executive, traditionally wields the main power, and is responsible for ensuring the predominance of the general interest over private interest, enlisting all the nation's activities, including information and communication, as a means to this end. There are of course, in both these groups, whichever of these two views of the role of the State they favour, wide differences and variations in regard to the models adopted. In many developing countries, particularly the least developed, intervention by the State is the predominant means of establishing communication infrastructures whether for reasons of ideology or because the private sector lacks the needed resources.

The legal framework should, in principle, safeguard and encourage pluralism, it should enable any individual to obtain information and opinion from various sources and to select freely between them. As pointed out earlier, this is the very principle that is most often violated. Whatever the laws or constitutions may say, it is infringed in practice by concentration of ownership in the press or by the establishment of monopolies, by law or in fact, in radio and television;[1] and in many countries it is

---

(1) As regards these monopolies, a tendency to challenge them is to be noted, to varying degrees, in certain countries. In France, for example, political circles and the public at large are beginning to discuss the desirability of relaxing the radio and television monopoly, and attempts are being made to set up local radio stations; some are calling increasingly for the introduction of pluralism. This has gone a stage farther in Italy, where the Constitutional Court decided to authorize transmitters covering a local area to operate. This has resulted in a considerable extension of local radio and television stations, which are thus excluded from the monopoly system. In the United Kingdom, the BBC and the IBA have for many years encouraged the proliferation of local radio stations. In the United States, where there is no legal monopoly on broadcasting, it may nevertheless be noted that the FCC encouraged the development of Citizens' Band radio by raising the number of frequency channels in 1975 from 23 to 40. It is at present exploring the possibility of raising this figure to 100. This means of communication is also encouraged in Sweden and Switzerland. Moreover, the desirability of recognizing the Canadian citizen's "right to communicate", and of mustering the means and resources needed to enable this right to be exercised, has been studied by the "Telecommission" in its report to the Government. Independently of the monopoly question, but in relation to the above-mentioned concept, the use of satellites to bring the telephone and television to the inhabitants of the Far North has been seen as an example of the application of this concept. Nevertheless, in respect of the monopoly system, there are still several governments in Europe which do not accept such policies and which continue to consider that telecommunications must remain the property of the State.

flatly denied by censorship or governmental control.

There are now some other issues, which concern not only the media, that are becoming ever more preoccupying. An important example is the protection of individual freedom and privacy, jeopardized as they are by the increasing use of informatics, as well as by the transborder flows of information that is electronically processed and stocked in data banks. The use of informatics is liable to impinge — through the centralization of information to which it may lead — upon the rights of individuals and raises the problem of the limits to be set upon this use. Regulation of access to data stored in computers, the control of computerized communications, the integrity of the data collected are but a few of the chief problems which call for legislation. Such matters as unlawful access to data concerning the private lives of citizens, unauthorized tampering with the data stored, the possibility for individuals to check information concerning them, to withdraw such information or to decide whether and how it is to be used are other aspects of the protection which may be accorded under certain conditions to individual privacy.

In order to prevent possible abuses committed through the use of data banks, whether private or public, in the collection, processing and dissemination of information of a private kind, several specific rules may be laid down. These govern in particular: the accuracy and continuous updating of the data collected; the need to prevent such data from being obtained by unfair or fraudulent means, and data concerning the intimate lives of individuals from being gathered or released; the conformity of the data with the motive for which they were collected; the establishment of time limits for the storing of certain categories of information; the obligation to secure special authorization for communicating the data stored to third parties; the correction of inaccurate data; the establishment of security systems in data banks to forbid access to all unauthorized persons. Other rules concern the conduct of the personnel operating the data banks, obliging them in particular to maintain professional secrecy; the limitation of right of access solely to duly authorized persons in the case of data which cannot be freely communicated to the public; the obligation to obtain the consent of the individual concerned in order to store personal data, except in cases clearly stipulated by law (national security, criminal proceedings, etc.), in particular data concerning political or religious views, race, ethnic origin which might lead to discrimination.

Use of data banks makes it desirable to establish in each country, rules governing not only the protection of individual privacy but also the safeguarding of social, commercial, public and private interests. States may therefore wish to possess machinery enabling them to protect their interests as well as those of society and of individuals and groups under their jurisdiction.

More generally, the growing use of informatics and data banks raises the question of whether such use is not likely to lead to a concentration of power within the hands of a technocracy. There is also concern that the use of these new technologies by governments and ministries may lead to a shift of power from the legislature to the executive, and more generally to a loss of control by citizens over public affairs. The number of countries with national legislation relating to these problems is increasing.[1] Until recently concern about data protection has been concentrated in

---

(1) Several countries, in particular in Europe and North America, have adopted laws governing these matters, and other countries are preparing to do so. A survey by the Intergovernmental Bureau for Informatics showed that at least 28 countries were planning to adopt protection/privacy laws and a total of 41 were investigating various controls to avoid negative social effects of computerization.

developed regions, where most of the data is collected and stored, but now a number of developing countries are also showing increased interest as their use of informatics grows, particularly their links with international networks, the international management of which might suitably be envisaged.

With regard to all these problems, it would be both impossible and undesirable to lay down any universally binding rules. More comparative research is necessary to increase the knowledge of the various solutions that have been attempted, and to consider which are the fairest and the most effective for the purpose of formulating realistic new policies based on the findings of such research. Beyond that, political, economic and social realities must be taken fully into account. No single communication system could be devised that could be introduced in developed and developing, or in capitalist and socialist countries. Certain fundamental principles, however, such as democratic control and its extension, remain valid throughout the world because they are grounded in universally recognized human rights. It is by using these principles as a yardstick that the situation in any given country can be judged to be generally satisfactory, and to give promise of the necessary reforms and adjustments; or to require extensive changes of one kind or another; or, as is sometimes regrettably the case, to be unsatisfactory in its essential character.

3. The Structural Framework

Independently of the political systems in force and to a great extent of the development level reached, the structures of communication are typified by the predominance of the media and technologies which make possible the organization of mass communications. It is therefore natural that such aspects should occupy a central place in communication policies and in the mustering of public and private resources in all countries. To be sure, this gives paramount importance to the top-down dissemination of information and can hamper trends towards democratization processes; at the same time, it opens the door to all kinds of ambiguities and creates serious risks of gigantism.

In our times, this type of organization is challenged by a philosophy which sees communication as the right of every individual. New technologies, now rapidly developing, provide ways of making this right a reality. Individuals and groups are (or soon will be) able to rely on media or resources of their own as well as on those of the mass media. Group media, amalgamating traditional means and the products of advanced technology, provide opportunities for local expression on a human scale likely to interest a wider range of individuals and to cater to a greater variety of interest. Thus such varied means — both modern and conventional — as cable television, local radio and television stations, local and rural press, factory newspapers, as well as data-processing applications may all serve to facilitate involvement in daily life by going beyond centralized distribution of news and information. This does not mean that only non-professionals can contribute to the goal of expanding expression on a human scale. The development of a core of trained communicators and a creative community is as vital to a communication infrastructure as the mechanical aspects of the system. Of course, all of this community need not be "professional" per se, but well-intentioned professionals may encourage non-professionals and help them in reaching standards necessary for efficiency in communication processes.

The development of the mass media and of advanced communications technologies must not be allowed to diminish the importance that traditional media and interpersonal communication continue to have in all societies. Undoubtedly, inter-relations do exist between modern and traditional media in many situations. Where their different components are compounded in such a way as to complement one another, interesting results are achieved. Thus, rather than supplant them, the electronic media are able, in particular through the audiences which they can reach, to support and supplement the traditional media.

Interpersonal and traditional communication should be safeguarded and encouraged, not only for their own sake, but also because they act as a corrective to certain tendencies. We refer to tendencies to limit communication activity to professionals, to emphasize information at the expense of discussion; to introduce technology simply because it is modern and impressive without considering its social utility. Communication policies will gain in scope and effectiveness if they take into account the value of interpersonal communication at all levels, as well as of group media and locally organized media.[1]

Communication policies are also necessary as a precondition for the reduction of the many disparities noted so often. The inequality and discrimination to which women are subjected throughout the world is a case in point. Their reduction must be based on organized societal effort, since inertia will push in the opposite direction: towards greater discrepancies between facilities for the well-to-do and those deprived, between cities and villages, between men and women. To this must be added the lack of opportunities in many countries for different minorities — national, ethnic, cultural, political, linguistic, religious — to make their voices heard. Deprived as they are in some cases, these minorities may resort to strong action and violence in order to express their views.

Some countries still have laws — or, more often, bureaucratic and administrative practices — which discriminate against women. These should be eliminated. Far more widely, however, the heart of the problem lies in mental assumptions attributing inferior capacities to women, long-standing attitudes to women either as solely a wife and mother or as a sex object. Change must be brought about through enlightenment and persuasion, in which the media have a vital part to play, and through education of the new generation — which requires attention, for example, to stereotypes in school textbooks and to educational curricula which assign separate courses to boys and girls. Reform is needed in attitudes of employers, of trade unions, of political parties, of officials and the police. A radical change in thinking, in a matter with such deep psychological and cultural roots, can be made only gradually through social change and new social attitudes; but the task should be taken up with a sense of urgency and pursued with determination. It would, however, be as vain to expect equality between the sexes to be conferred solely by men as to expect racial equality

---

(1) The OPID project (objectives, processes and indicators of development) sponsored by the United Nations University may serve as a useful reference in this context. It highlights the shortcomings of conventional theories of development, (which) implicitly (sometimes even explicitly) assume that all change in the direction of development is bound to be positive and desirable. It introduces the concept of "mis-development" as applied to "situations of social change in which unwanted 'effects' predominate: under-development, meaning that material needs are not fully satisfied; over-development, meaning that the satisfaction of material needs reaches the stage where it prevents non-material needs from being satisfied". The approach implies that countries in all regions of the world are potential candidates for mis-development. (Source: GAMMA/University of Montreal, *Activities Report* 1974–1978). It also implies that the optimum must be measured in terms of the quality of life, to which the satisfaction of material needs does no more than contribute. In relation to the mass media and advanced communication technologies, which are not ends but means, the fostering of interpersonal communication is in itself both a goal and a pre-eminent tool of development. The media as means could and should be an extension of interpersonal communication.

to be achieved without ethnic pressures. The actions taken by women's movements in recent years, often with great persistence and courage, have already secured important advances. They need to be continued and amplified.

Communication policies and development strategies, considered as essential means of solving the major problems of our time, should be designed first and foremost to ensure that the media of "information" become the media of "communication". Because communication presupposes access, participation and exchange, different media should be involved in the process of democratizing communication. It is here that the links between the democratization of communication and the democratization of development become apparent. For if communication policies are to be aimed at democratizing communication, and if, in addition, they must essentially be designed to be integrated into development programmes, then it is vital for those concerned to participate in the work of programming and decision-taking. There are many ways of achieving this, provided that the political will exists in the first place.

The difficulties in the way of democratization should not be ignored. The concepts of access, participation and equality are ideals, as yet only imperfectly achieved despite noteworthy progress in recent years. Powerful entrenched interests, whether in the controllers of the mass media or in governments, often raise barriers and there are dangers of political or economic manipulation.

To this must be added problems resulting from increasing transnationalization of communications. The transnationalization of the production, financing and marketing of communication is a factor which affects not only the media — publishing, broadcasting, cinema and advertising — but also data banks, informatics, telecommunications, the manufacture of electronic equipment and components, etc. This process has reached such proportions that transnationalization has become in many countries a factor largely, if not wholly, beyond the control of the policy-makers. However, countries have different attitudes in granting licences to transnational companies, and in some countries communication policies are so designed as to facilitate the elimination of discrepancies between national objectives and transnational operations.

Both in the developed and developing countries, communication policies can be defined and formulated only with the collaboration of all those entities which incarnate the active forces of the countries themselves. In order to ensure that such policies, and the plans deriving from them, are duly implemented, countries must rely first and foremost upon themselves. This is a point which cannot be too strongly stressed — one which in the first instance concerns the developing countries, well aware as they are of the need to reduce their dependence in matters of information and communication. Where they exist — and even if they have to be strengthened and increased — foreign aid schemes can make only a supplementary contribution to the policy of self-development and to endogenous efforts to mobilize national resources. This policy and these efforts must naturally be pursued by the developing countries in accordance with their specific situations, needs and local realities.

Chapter 2

Material Resources

Communication being a difficult phenomenon to define, it is equally difficult to identify all the material resources committed to it and all the infrastructures pertaining to it. In point of fact, a large proportion of a country's development resources and possibly all its material infrastructures might be involved, for in one way or another each serves the process of communication. This difficulty of identifying all the resources and infrastructures affecting communication makes it impossible to measure exactly its share in gross national products and in national development programmes, obliging us to limit consideration to only certain aspects of the question.

1. Infrastructures

Lack of basic information about existing infrastructures is one of the most serious problems affecting communication policy-making and planning. Unless a thorough review is made of these structures in each country, and unless precise knowledge is gained of the available equipment best suited to establishing new infrastructures corresponding to individual countries' needs, rational decisions cannot be taken for the medium or even for the short term.

In certain countries, in particular developing nations, even sufficient data concerning the mass media are lacking. Such lacunae make it difficult for policy-makers to choose between options or to quantify infrastructural requirements which, enormously costly, need to be known more exactly. Too many unknown factors are therefore entailed in the estimation of infrastructural needs, and too much improvisation and imitation of alien models and experiments is involved in the actual choices made. In any case, the cataloguing of global communication requirements and the identification of priorities have become key tasks, which must precede all efforts to formulate national communication policies.

Several developed countries have endeavoured in recent years to catalogue their overall communication needs, and to take stock of their capacities in order to frame global policies applying to the likely immediate future. The best known examples are those of Australia (with the *Telecom 2000* report), Canada (*Instant World* and its sequels), Sweden and Japan. A few developing countries (Afghanistan, Sierra Leone, Sri Lanka, Tanzania) have made similar attempts. Although these initiatives are interesting and instructive, any outcomes still remain to be evaluated. Nevertheless, such global approaches would seem the best course to pursue if countries wish to establish rational and comprehensive policies for communications development.

Another problem facing all countries is that of the selection and production of

213

equipment. Equipment for communication is capital intensive, and a highly specialized commodity. Only a handful of countries are original manufacturers. All the main developed countries have their own manufacturing capacity. Countries such as the Federal Republic of Germany, France, Italy, Japan, Netherlands, Spain and the USA are the principal producers of a full range of modern equipment. Of the socialist countries, Czechoslovakia, the German Democratic Republic and the Soviet Union are in the front rank. Many developing countries such as Algeria, Brazil, India, the Republic of Korea, Mexico, the Philippines and Singapore, as well as several others have begun, alone or together with foreign partners, generally under licence, to produce or to assemble communication equipment and machinery. The precarious nature of these undertakings is clearly highlighted by the fact that of the 60 nations making or ready to make transistors, few — though their number is now increasing — can produce the electronic chips which will make conventional transistors as out-dated as the vacuum tube. Many obstacles stand in the way of such undertakings. The dependence of several countries upon producers sometimes occupying a monopoly position is fairly evident.

Developing countries find it hard to compete, as those with the potential to become producers have not managed to standardize their production, and the smaller countries are at a disadvantage. In this area of industrial production, which is rapidly developing, measures are needed to ensure a better international division of labour and a fairer distribution of technological innovations.

Some producers in developed countries apparently feel that the right conditions do not yet exist for cooperation with a view to creating a production capacity in non-industrial countries. Developing countries, for their part, feel that they get no sympathy for their efforts to free themselves from dependence on a small number of production centres. It might be well to organize, under UNIDO's auspices, meetings between producers and customers, and particularly between existing and potential producers, to achieve a better understanding.

The need to develop infrastructures applies not only to the media in the accepted sense, but also to other sectors of communication such as data-processing, tele-informatics, data banks, etc. In deciding what kind of infrastructure should be developed, it is now necessary to bear in mind that equipment becomes more of a multi-purpose kind. In developed countries just as much as in those now building their infrastructure, the new breakthroughs in technology mean that the same equipment may serve newspapers, radio, television, teleprinting, tele-informatics and the telephone. Moreover, transmission technology makes increasing use of satellites for quite different purposes. Far-reaching innovations in infrastructure are inevitable. This is a sphere in which international technical cooperation should prove particularly fruitful.

This leads us to three conclusions: first, that the need for infrastructures has become a priority that no country can afford to ignore, particularly since lack of such infrastructures is one of the major obstacles to strengthening the independence of some countries vis-à-vis others; second, that it is vital to promote endogenous capacities in all countries for devising, producing and using new communication technologies, as well as programmes and their content; lastly, that developing countries should also foster the production of simple, cheap equipment which would be more within their reach and better suited to satisfying their immediate needs.

2. Technologies

It is also important, for the purpose of framing communication policies, to discern what the future trends of technological development entail. Technology in itself is seldom neutral; its use is even less so. In this connection, it is useful to know how decisions are taken concerning the main lines of emphasis of research and innovation, and who in particular decides to render the results of such research operational. It is clear that the general public exercises no control over such decisions, and that in the final instance it is not so much the market as the producers themselves that decide. Technological development demands careful scrutiny — as indeed do the social implications of new technologies; the crucial problem is to ascertain its aptness and potential effects in particular situations and to socialize the decision-making process in this domain. This leads to what may be called a dilemma regarding technological options. It may be wondered whether there is not a risk of increasing manipulation both at national and international levels and at political and economic levels, particularly in view of the volume of information produced, which often fails to correspond to actual needs. Thus, it would seem especially important to socialise so far as possible the decision-making process, (in other words, to associate multiple partners in decision-making not leaving it merely to technocrats or bureaucrats), whether in regard to defining priorities, employment policies or production and supply possibilities. The fact that governments, in industrialized and developing countries alike are frequently ill equipped to take decisions concerning new technologies deserves mention. Governments all too often tend to leave the matter in the hands of the technicians, giving them no directives in matters judged a priori to be too complex or too highly specialized.

The lack of standardization in the manufacture of equipment and materials is another problem arising between countries, even those belonging to the same region. The development of new technologies frequently gives rise to manufacturing disparities, sometimes to the disadvantage of investors and consumers alike. The lack of standardization between countries, particularly in the same region, is thus a major obstacle in the way of promoting greater regional cooperation; regional planning therefore becomes a priority. Efforts to promote more cooperation and a greater volume of trade and exchanges between countries may be bedevilled by the existence of markets supplying different types of the same equipment.

Radio, as the most wide-spread electronic medium, fortunately presents few problems thanks to standarization of recording tape formats, dry-cell sizes and agreed use of radio frequency spectra. The same is not true for television. The lack of standardization in this field has led to: (i) difficulties in exchanging programmes among countries and across regions; (ii) the complexity of making small gauge recorders and electronic news-gathering equipment compatible with heavy gauge studio equipment; (iii) the difficulty of adapting new technology within established television stations. When first developed, colour television added to the complexity of the problem. The existence of three basic frequency and line standards — NTSC; PAL; SECAM — slowed the pace of the adoption of colour TV in many countries. While conversion from one standard to the other is no longer a problem, it is costly and the results are not always of the same quality as the original. Where facilities for standards conversion are non-existent, programme exchange is rendered impossible. The present development of varying teletext and viewdata systems is retarding their introduction in some countries and may lead to competitive situations which force the consumer into a binding choice. The same is true for the varied systems of video-disc equipment now being widely marketed. At the level of videocassettes, especially the U-matic format, standards conversion has been easier and less costly through the recent introduction of multi-standard videoplayers.

But many countries, both developing and developed, now introducing new technologies, face a plethora of technical problems in selection of the right kind of equipment,[1] compatibility among different makes, and compatibility with the main studio equipment of the station.

The shortcomings which must be noted do not mean that, by and large, a considerable degree of standardization and adaptation has not been achieved in radio and television equipment. For example, there exist in Europe, as in other regions, transcoders enabling the necessary conversions to be made between the three colour television standards; bi-standard receivers cost about the same as monostandard receivers. It should be added that the measures taken by the International Organization for Standardization are aimed at reducing the shortcomings which still exist in this field.

Efforts made by developing countries to secure access to the most sophisticated technologies should not inhibit them from giving priority, whenever necessary, to alternative technologies, better suited to their particular needs, and from developing their own technological capacities to the full.

The nature and scale of the most modern technologies, and particularly the rate and extent of the sometimes abrupt changes which they may bring about, have in certain cases meant that they act as a factor of disruption and destabilization in developing countries. Simple, appropriate technology, making use of more readily adaptable facilities and methods and more capable of providing the type of immediate solutions aimed at, may often be a more valuable asset for developing countries than advanced technologies, whose cost may put them completely beyond reach and which may well prove to be unsuited to the purposes which they are expected to serve. In view of the rapid obsolescence of certain technologies, it is frequently in the best interests of developing countries to adopt low-cost, small-scale technologies rather than excessively sophisticated systems such as colour television.

Experience with these small-scale technologies indicates that there is no adequate understanding of their potential, and especially of the ways in which they can be adapted to specific purposes. Governments and other decision-making bodies are often unaware of the range of possible choices. Over-impressed by salesmanship from the dominant manufacturers, they fail to examine the relative merits of different classes of equipment.

Briefing and information campaigns concerning these "small" technologies are an essential pre-requisite, as they frequently do not receive the promotion lavished on the major innovations by the more prestigious technical publications. The populations concerned should be better informed of alternative options and existing possibilities. Government authorities, who sometimes have their sights set on the industrialized world's most modern technologies, should accept the idea that appropriate

---

(1) To give an illustration of difficulties coming from manufacturers, mention may be made of the use of one inch helical scan tape recorders. These are on the average one fourth the cost of the traditional two inch quad recorders and have a longer operational lifetime. The question of standards, however, is more critical. Two methods of head registration are current: non-segmented head and the segmented head — both incompatible. Two types of head wrap are used: alpha wrap and the omega wrap. And tape formats vary from one make to the other. Thus, while the trend is moving strongly towards one inch recorders — both for electronic field production and studio work — the pressures on manufacturers to come out with a solution has resulted in a variety of standards (for head registration, tape wrap, and tape format) many of which are not compatible.

technologies are not in all cases inferior technologies, and might often have high priority in developing countries, even if recourse to technologies comparable to those of developed countries continues to be necessary in many cases.

Here again, cooperation between the developing countries themselves is a must. Through joint projects involving appropriate technologies, it may be possible to overcome research and development and production obstacles which are too big to be surmounted individually.

Thus, the adoption of appropriate technologies and the need to define lines of development geared to actual needs are two particularly crucial problems in communication policies and planning. They are also bound up with the question of technology transfer. Like many other aspects of development strategies, technology transfer has had both beneficial and harmful consequences[1]. While intermediary technologies in many cases possess great advantages and should be given serious consideration by developing countries there are cases where the more sophisticated technology is the most appropriate[2]. In others on the contrary, lower cost technologies possess certain advantages[3].

On the basis of free choice and preferential treatment and in the light of criticism of inappropriate models, developing countries should, in our view, while focusing efforts on the use of alternative technologies take the necessary measure in order to preserve their national identity and to protect their cultural particularities, as well as to avoid the dangers of dependence.

3. Costs of Communications Projects

The need for the development of communications is pressing on all countries. Whether it be for a local functional literacy campaign or the launching of a satellite or the myriad possibilities for programmes and projects ranging in between — from the most basic to the most sophisticated — all nations require advances in communication facilities. But even assuming an optimum socio-political climate, even with clearly established communication goals and policies, given the present

---

(1) Although it is difficult to generalize about harmful effects, since they differ so considerably, the charges most frequently levelled are that such transfers (i) have consisted primarily in simple exportation of western technology, which reflects the economic and social conditions and practices of one part of the world only; (ii) have generally tended to be capital rather than labour-intensive; (iii) have created dependence upon foreign capital, foreign supply sources and foreign tastes and expectations; (iv) have been effected mostly by transnational corporations, which have maintained control over the technology; (v) have benefited elite sectors (newspapers, television, telephone) more than the masses; (vi) have contributed little to economic self-reliance and co-operation among developing countries; (vii) have fostered the rural exodus and increased migration.

(2) As an example, we may cite the use of computers in India for livestock insemination schemes, or the use of satellites for remote sensing of mining resources.

(3) This is true for example, of radio, the under-exploitation of which (as compared with television, a more costly medium) may not be justified in certain countries. A dilemma remains as regards the choice between black-and-white and colour television. Although the latter is more expensive, preference in certain countries is given from the start to the most advanced system, which is certain one day to predominate. Other countries favour black-and-white television, considering that colour television can be introduced at a later date. The choice between the two is sometimes less the result of a deliberate decision, being determined rather by the lack of spare parts for black-and-white television. If an adequate demand existed for black-and-white, it would seem possible to solve this problem. What is surely important is to make the right initial choice, in the light of clearly defined options and taking account of installation costs, the cost of equipment, televised films and the trends of technological development in general.

economic realities and trends of resource allocations, no country possesses sufficient funds for communication development. This has led to more detailed investigations of the costs involved for specific development projects; costs of telecommunications development, of press and broadcasting facilities, of training programmes, of various equipment items.

It is obviously impossible to give positively accurate data about cost of development projects or facilities and equipment items as these vary widely with the nature and scope of the projects, the types and size of different facilities and the vagaries of estimates. Different projects vary from a few thousand US dollars (where the modest amounts involved are not necessarily a sign of the importance of the project itself) to several billion US dollars (as in recently reported telecommunications schemes in the Middle East where the huge amounts expended are not always proof of optimum social or economic return although the projects' prestige value may be deemed important.)

Some examples of typical development projects in various fields give an idea of the costs involved and may be useful for general planning purposes but, obviously any individual project requires specific analysis. The joint Nordic-Unesco project for regional broadcasting development in Africa, which calls for $1,737,900 to cover the three years of the first phase of its operation, is primarily a training and research programme; the budget provides for experts, consultants, administrative services, equipment and production and in-country, sub-regional and international training. A UNDP-UNESCO-ITU three and one-half year project for the training of radio and television producers and engineers in Bangladesh calls for a UNDP contribution of 2.2 million dollars and the equivalent of $250,000 in local currency by the government; the budget covers an 18-member staff of local and international personnel, equipment, rental of premises, international personnel, equipment, rental of premises, international fellowships, etc. A 3-year Unesco funds-in-trust project financed by the Swedish International Development Authority for the development of Africa News Agencies will provide advisory services to strengthen existing agencies and personnel training activities; in addition to foreign experts and consultants the budget covers national and sub-regional training courses plus organization of management seminars and some equipment; cost, $2,181,200. Other project examples, from the Australian bilateral aid programme, are also typical of the range in variety and size of development activities: a project designed to provide maintenance and advisory facilities for the Aeronautical Fixed Telecommunications Network and other Indonesian aeronautical communications systems ($14,637,000); provision of a design for studios and transmitters for Radio Vila in the New Hebrides ($74,000) and a design study for a telecommunications network to link the main administrative and population centres there ($36,000); assistance to the Government of the Solomon Islands to establish a more effective broadcasting service, and undertaking a survey of the future development of broadcasting needs($381,000); the first phase of an extensive project to upgrade the telephone system on the island of Tongatapu ($680,000); upgrading the broadcasting facilities of Radio Bangladesh by supplying equipment and training as well as assisting with installation of the new equipment ($575,000).

Available cost data for satellite systems give an idea of the order of magnitude of investment requirements. For instance, in 1979, debate over a proposal to establish a domestic communication satellite in Australia produced contending cost estimates ranging from 100 to 400 million dollars. The TELESAT system in Canada required $75 million (CAN) capital for the space segment and $54 million (CAN) for the earth segment. Total investment for the RCA Alaska Communications system (ALASCOM) is reported to have exceeded $250 million. Capital costs for the American Telephone and Telegraph COMSTAR system totalled approximately 286 million dollars for the space and earth segments. For the proposed French-German broadcasting satellite, it is estimated that annual operating costs will be $35 million. In India, it was calculated that the SITE project satellite and ground station costs ($125 million) were four times less than would have been required for terrestrial transmission for the same geographical broadcast coverage. Incidental figures related to space communications: at present, it costs approximately $20,000 per kilo to launch a satellite and about $500 for a cylindrical antenna to receive direct satellite broadcasting in the home.

4. International Cooperation and Foreign Assistance

Financial assistance to developing countries has been one of the features of international relations between the industrialized world and these countries since their accession to national sovereignty. In recent years, not only the nature of this aid but the terms under which it is granted have been transformed. Aid, technical assistance, development programmes and cooperation successively followed each other as terms to define relations between the two groups of countries.

As regards the particular domain with which we are concerned, namely, international assistance for communications development, this is characterized by several distinctive features. Although it continues to be largely bilateral in form, such aid has been extended to include multilateral schemes, in particular as a result of the operations of international institutions established within the United Nations system and of regional financing institutions.

However, international assistance in general, tends to remain of ad hoc nature, sporadic and poorly integrated into overall development plans. Among the beneficiary countries where coordination should logically be secured in the first place, the lack of means and of overall development plans which is the consequence thereof — sometimes compounded by a lack of political will — are also responsible for the often disappointing results of the rather substantial cooperation efforts which have been undertaken to date.

Given its complex and multi-faceted nature, the communication sector is more directly affected by these deficiencies than other sectors. However, the essential factor is the limited resources made available in international cooperation efforts for the development of communication networks and media, and of telecommunications, as compared with funds allocated to other sectors or branches of development[1].

Some idea of the amount of funds available in the past from international sources and the size of certain projects is available from a brief review of the operations of some of the agencies involved. The World Bank Group[2] is the principle

(1) An OECD document on the world aid flow and its application to telecommunications mentions that, out of a total of $13 billion in public aid to development granted by Member States of this Organization in 1975, the total aid programmes devoted to communications amounted to a mere $175 million. In 1976, the total volume of financing provided by DAC member countries amounted to $14,168.6 million, of which $8,307.5 million represented grants, and $5,861.1 million represented loans. Overall figures for the share of aid to communication are not available, but there are no signs of any significant increase as compared with previous years. Aid provided by Comecon is far less substantial, the total volume of assistance emanating from countries with centralized planning systems amounting in 1977 to only $700 million.

(2) Source for all World Bank figures: *Telecommunication Journal* Vol. 46 IX/1979.

multilateral source of finance for telecommunications development. Through fiscal 1978, the Bank and the International Development Association (IDA) provided 1,685 million US dollars for this purpose in 75 loans and credits to 35 countries. This amounted to approximately 3 per cent of total Bank lending since 1960. Well over 85 per cent of the Bank Group's lending for telecommunications has been concentrated in the last ten years. The volume of lending increased from 2.9 million dollars in fiscal 1962 to 235.6 million in 1978 while the cost of related projects rose from 6.2 million to 1,233.1 million. The average size of telecommunications loans has been 22.5 million; the largest loan has been to India for 120 million and the smallest to Upper Volta for 0.8 million. The regional distribution of lending during the period 1962 to 1978 was quite uneven[1].

Through December 1977 the inter-American Development Bank had loaned $196.8 million for telecommunications projects, or only 1.6 per cent of its total loans to date ranking this sector next to last in sectors financed by the IDB[2]. Only recently has the IDB begun to finance rural telecommunications projects. In 1976, it loaned $29 million to Colombia toward the construction of public telephones in 2,200 rural communities. A loan of $12.2 million to Costa Rica in 1977 is for construction of 56 telephone exchanges and 1,300 public telephones located in rural communities. In 1978, Ecuador was loaned $9.6 million for construction of 128 telephone exchanges and 254 public telephones in rural communities[3].

In the period 1965–1976, ITU provided developing countries with technical assistance amounting to approximately US $ 108 million; 60 per cent of it during the last four years. The bulk of this amount (over $ 93 million) came from the United Nations Development Programme (UNDP); the rest of the assistance was supplied on a funds-in-trust basis, through associate experts or through ITU participation in various assistance projects sponsored by the United Nations. The annual value of the assistance provided by ITU to the developing countries increased from $3.36 million in 1965 to over $20.2 million in 1976. This increase was not however, uniform throughout the period under consideration.

Unesco's approved budget for 1979–80 for the Communication sector contains 1.17 million directly devoted to projects in developing countries as well as 1.67 million for projects financed by UNDP[4]. These UNDP and regular programme

---

(1) Tables 8/8.

| Summary of World Bank Group lending for telecommunications (1949-78) | | | | Regional distribution of World Bank Group lending for telecommunications (1962-78) | | | | |

Fiscal years	Number of loans	Amount (million US dollars)	Region	Number of countries	Number of loans	Amount of loans (million US dollars)	Total cost of projects (million US dollars)
1949–63	6	69.2	Africa	12	19	288.9[1]	819.6[1]
1964–68	11	161.4	Asia	16	33	972.7	4215.8
1969–73	27	707.8	Europe	1	1	40.0	95.0
1974–78	31	746.7	Latin America	6	18	359.2[2]	1077.3[2]
Totals	75	1685.1	Totals	35	71	1660.8	6207.7

[1]Two of these loans were to East African Posts and Telegraph, serving Kenya, Uganda and Tanzania.
[2]One loan of 11.2 million dollars to Jamaica was later cancelled at the request of the borrower.

(2) Gellerman, 1978; IDB News, 1977

(3) Source: The role of telecommunications in socio-economic development, Hudson, Goldschmidt, Parker, Hardy; Keewatin Publications, 1979

(4) UNDP financed projects executed by Unesco in the communication field, averaged some 3.4% of total UNDP allocations to Unesco over the three years 1976–1978 (at a very low gross level of

projects are aimed at development of policies, infrastructures, training, research, news exchanges, etc. in the field of communication. In addition, Unesco's current funds-in-trust programme totals 5.89 million dollars, with another 9 million foreseen shortly; contributors to this programme are the Nordic countries, Federal Republic of Germany, Netherlands, and Switzerland. The largest project (4 million dollars financed by the Nordic group) is for the regional development of training for press and broadcasting personnel in Africa. The other projects in 9 countries support various training and media development activities.

Total external contributions also include modest non-governmental assistance, particularly in the field of training, by professional organizations and substantial loans by suppliers from industrialized countries.

Aid for development of communications is still not regarded as a priority matter. Many funding institutions remain little inclined to support general communication projects, which are largely outside the priorities of organizations such as UNDP and the World Bank, and wholly outside those of the regional development banks and many institutions supplying bilateral assistance.

Several arguments are put forward to justify this situation: (a) the tangible results of communications projects are generally not evaluated, their yield is not measured and it is accordingly impossible to assess the real contribution made by communications to development; (b) the media tend to favour urban elites over the poorer rural populations, and their development accordingly does not benefit the population as a whole; (c) since developing countries have seldom formulated overall development policies for communication, they have been unable to catalogue their needs in this field or to establish priorities, thus making the choice of bilateral and multilateral aid options difficult; (d) policies for different media are rarely integrated and may even be mutually incompatible; (e) international agencies providing assistance do not possess a valid fund of experience, or even micro-experiments, in this field on which to draw; (f) the use of foreign technologies and imported models of infrastructures sometimes proves more beneficial to the countries providing the hardware, and sometimes even the software, than to those that receive or purchase them; (g) few countries have defined explicit communication policies; however, the policies implicitly followed, which are little more than a set of practices, do not provide an adequate framework for effective, structured cooperation, and the number of bodies or authorities with whom it would be necessary to collaborate generally remains too great; (h) lastly, military considerations relating to the policies or interests of political blocs may sometimes affect the development of structures in certain sensitive areas.

In recent years the importance of communications for development has been constantly stressed both at the political and technical levels, in many United Nations forums and above all in Unesco, from the General Conference to numerous expert meetings, as well as within regional intergovernmental organizations and among the non-aligned countries. Nevertheless, this recognition has not been reflected in assistance to communication projects and the situation outlined above has hardly changed as far as available resources are concerned. There has been no substantial progress. Often offers made have not been followed by tangible results. Neither the legislators nor the managers of development assistance have followed in the path mapped out by the policy-makers.

---

some $1.5 million in 1976). Even allowing for allocation to other UN agencies for specific communication projects, the total percentage of UNDP allocations is unlikely to reach 0.5% of their total resources.

Today, many developed States have stated their readiness to help the developing countries strengthen their communications infrastructure. However, at the bilateral level there has to date been more planning than concrete action leading to practical results; at the multilateral level progress is also slow. Multilateral agencies have not yet taken relevant decisions; there are no signs of a willingness to increase allocations to communication projects; the idea of an eventual special fund (with voluntary pledges or automatic contributions) still remains to be debated in decision-making forums. So the overall situation regarding both bilateral and multi-lateral resources and arrangements is far from satisfactory. However, it seems to us that, along with increased bilateral cooperation larger multilateral resources must be mobilized, equitably distributed and efficiently managed. Multilateral cooperation is not only an additional source for assistance to communications development, with a broad potential for accumulating and diffusing world-wide experience; it might also be forged into a corrective or palliative for some of communication's international deficiences and imbalances. It must, therefore, become more substantial, more effective and better coordinated.

In the light of the foregoing, we consider it necessary to highlight three trends, which should always evolve in conjunction and be mutually complementary:

    (a) the policy now beginning to emerge in certain developed countries whereby investments in communications and telecommunications are regarded as a priority target of bilateral assistance;

    (b) the encouraging, albeit still modest, indications of an increasing commitment on the part of multilateral agencies (international and regional) which have an essential role to play in correcting all imbalances is so sensitive an area;

    (c) cooperation, the pooling of experience, the organizing of mutual assistance and, in general, all joint undertakings and measures between the developing countries themselves.

Two observations may be added to these conclusions. First, international cooperation should not be limited to the conventional domain of the press, radio and television but should be extended to such new activities as the creation of new infrastructures, the strengthening of existing means, the establishment of new agencies, data banks, the development of informatics, satellite links, etc. Secondly, attention should be given to the potential distortions resulting from the massive introduction of new technologies into systems that remain fragile.

Chapter 3
Research Contributions

There is a continuously felt need for more analytic thinking about, and above all more comprehensive and critical inquiry into, communication phenomena and their relation to the way societies function. Greater interest is now attached to research covering the role, purposes and forms of communication and all the problems which it raises in the overall development of contemporary society. Indeed, it was such broad concern which led to the establishment of our Commission.

1. Main Trends in Communications Research

There have been several stages in the evolution of communications research. Until the thirties, little or none had been done on communications, with the exception of literary criticism, a few studies on propaganda and other surveys commissioned by the media to ascertain their impact upon the public and its tastes. Originally, such studies were designed as isolated projects focusing on specific problems. The approach was a simple and pragmatic one, geared to mass communication phenomena and the efficacy of this form of communication.

Subsequently, a large number of theoretical and practical models were used in the search for ways of improving advertising, organizing election campaigns, polling public opinion, supporting public relations activities and boosting newspaper circulation. Designed to enable individuals to adapt to the prevailing social norms, and to create media and messages capable of inducing the desired behaviour patterns, these models, inspired by psychological studies, were to help elucidate the factors motivating individuals considered principally as consumers of information and messages and to determine readers', listeners' and viewers' profiles. Frequently undertaken by the media themselves, such research was designed to supply them with the information which they needed for their programming, advertising and market surveys. Research of this kind is chiefly inspired by commercial, electoral or media considerations, and fails to take account of the inter-relationships between communication and many major problems affecting societies as a whole[1]. These

---

(1) This type of research developed above all in the USA, where the resources devoted to research are particularly substantial. In this country, mass communication research has gradually come to be a specialized academic field, developing, like other branches of the social sciences, primarily in response to the needs of a modern, industrial and urban society and expressed in certain types of empirical, quantitative and commercially focused studies. Past research was linked more closely with social psychology and professional and commercial considerations than with sociology as such. Relatively little attention was given to questions of power, organization and control, or to structural considerations, and few were the attempts to analyse the social significance of the media considered in their historical and modern contexts.

trends have marked the theoretical and methodological assumptions generally adopted and which still exist, in many countries.

However, a gradual change in the selection of research topics both on communication and its methodology began to take place after World War II. Research was little by little extended to new fields. The evolution occurred in several directions: (i) studies of innovation acceptance, particularly in the field of agriculture, pointing the way for new patterns of information distribution; (ii) the work of behavioural psychologists, helping to promote learning theories which have become important in the use of the media for educational purposes; (iii) a more scientific approach to communication theory, drawing upon laboratory techniques, advanced statistical methods and sophisticated sociological surveys.

In the 1960s, the focus shifted from the media's efficacy to studies of their actual effects, and to preliminary designs of new communication systems which could be integrated into various types of societies. In the first years of the decade, there was a dawning awareness of the fact that, in the developing countries, research was marked by models which in no way corresponded to the realities and needs of these countries. Imported theoretical and practical models had been used towards the end of the fifties and the early sixties in these countries in their own research programmes on the development and structures of communication. These models had inspired their past and present studies in these fields, studies which were generally carried out by specialists who either came from abroad or who had been trained abroad and who applied to communication problems in their countries ideological and cultural approaches which did not necessarily correspond to the concerns of the developing world.

Turning its back on the statistical approach, research theory and practice in recent years has undergone radical changes. This is partly due to critical evaluation of research concepts in developed countries by modern research specialists from these same countries; and partly as a result of experiments carried out in the developing countries, as well as by communications research developments in socialist countries. Despite the differences in background and interest, there is now a degree of consensus with regard to the inadequacies of the past and on the need for changes in approaches to communications research.

Many studies aim at establishing a closer link between communication and political questions or the broader aspects of social policy. For, if research is today governed by considerations and factors of a political nature, this is due first and foremost to the politicization of communication. Such research also takes into account international ramifications of communication problems and attempts critical, objective assessments of strategies, priorities, structures, imbalances, etc, as evidenced in the world's communication networks. Some research trends are developing from a re-evaluation of communication problems, but others derive from researchers drawing conclusions about communication issues from general problems found in different societies and economies and in international affairs.

2. Major Shortcomings

Communications research has until now been extensively undertaken in only a small number of industrialized countries. Developing countries have therefore been dependent on a small number of sources and restricted research approaches for findings which might or might not be applicable to their particular communication problems, and their own research capacities in this field are limited. Sufficient full-time research staff is lacking, as are specialist training facilities and adequate financing. The few researchers available for necessary national studies have usually been trained abroad and are often uncritical about research methodologies and priorities existing elsewhere. The historical circumstances in which research has developed in these countries have helped to create a dependency situation which is aggravated by the unsuitability of foreign research for their needs, with the theoretical and methodological models of developed countries continuing to serve as reference points for research and teaching.

Imbalances exist not only between countries but also between different fields covered by research. For example, while research on audience identification and measurement is important for effective use of the media, there are many other neglected aspects of communication which need research attention, such as the study of political, institutional, structural or technological alternatives of ownership models, of issues related to the power of the media and to the impact of powers on the media, the economics of alternative communication systems, of problems linked to access and participation or to manipulation of communication means, of the ways in which different people may use the media for education, information or entertainment, of the impact of both media and message, etc[1].

To be sure, research cannot tackle all problems at one and the same time in all places. Choices have to be made according to particular needs, priorities established for differing national or local circumstances. Certain studies may be more essential than others, particularly in relation to political and social ramifications of communication. A measure of balance and definition of crucial areas is, however; no less desirable in research than in the other fields of communication.

3. Trends and Needs

The tasks and goals previously assigned to communications research, the manner in which it was initiated, defined and organized, has been responsible for the fragmentary and imbalanced nature of the knowledge now available.

Current and future research should broaden its focus in order to deal with the truly fundamental problems of our time. It should not be content to serve to implement a given communications policy, or just to "support" the media establishment, in order to make an existing system or various parts thereof more effective, regardless of its validity or of the possible need to rethink certain dominant values or to suggest alternative means or ends. Research, instead of dealing with value-free micro-questions, must therefore endeavour to apply independent critical criteria and to explore the potential of new forms and new structures. However, the transformation or adaptation of structures, institutions and types of communications organization is not an end in itself. They may also prove to be quite inadequate. It is with a completely open and challenging mind that they must be investigated and judged, for it cannot be assumed that a given complex of structures is by itself necessarily and

(1) A strong concern about all these neglected areas was voiced by the President of the International Association for Mass Communication Research: "We know far more about some parts of the world than about others; we know far more about some aspects of the communication process than about others, and we have more analyses and interpretations from certain value positions than from others. An additional complication is that the implications of these imbalances are not properly understood, and as a result we not infrequently encounter universal generalizations and cross cultural applications which are just not valid." (J. D. Halloran: The Context of Mass Communication Research. CIC document No. 78).

inevitably consonant with the best interest of all individuals in a given society.

To this end, research must aim to draw closer to the emerging consideration of communication as a social process, which entails studying the media institutions not in isolation but in their relationship to other institutions in broad social, national and international contexts, i.e. conceptually in terms of structures, ownership, organization, socialization, participation, etc., potentially leading to a reappraisal of existing systems, institutions, structures and means. There is a growing awareness that alien models may be unsuitable, and that the political, cultural, social and economic features of each country must be more closely linked with its particular patterns of communication. Increasing importance has thus to be attached to creating — guided not by supposition but by research findings — appropriate, endogenous forms of communication, no less in the developing than in industrialized countries. Research must also aim at devising reliable indicators — such as exist in other fields — for communication policies and planning, so as to be able to determine what measures need to be taken, or to evaluate for example the impact of radio and television programmes within different societies. For this purpose, studies, meetings and exchanges between specialists should be organized and sponsored in order to ensure that research makes good progress and leads to positive results.

It is only when questions seem unanswerable, or when answers may be turned to practical account, that society appears to give serious support to research. Research in communications appears to be no exception to this rule. But we think expanded research in the field of communications is sorely needed. In the field which the Commission has been mandated to explore, we do not even possess adequate, or sufficiently reliable, data on a number of questions involving comparative studies, investigations in politically sensitive areas, comprehensive media impact studies, specific problems affecting developing countries — and the list is not exhaustive. Instead of basing our thinking on truly scientific investigations and surveys and pre-existing evaluations, we have had to rely most of the time on fragmentary data, random evidence, incomplete research findings and, ultimately, on personal experience and intuition. Our particular need for more comprehensive information in myriad fields leads us to a major conclusion that there are serious requirements in all societies for broad-based research in order to have solid evidence on which to formulate conclusions and well-founded decisions on communications policies and practices. Given the pivotal role of communications in the modern world, this is not an academic question, but a practical necessity.

Chapter 4

The Professional
Communicators

Along with the institutional and structural framework, and the material and technological resources, there is another essential element that calls for particular attention: human resources.

1. Difficulties of Definition

As we have seen, it is difficult to define clearly and precisely the concept of communication. As long as communication was considered merely as the transfer of information in the conventional sense of the term, and more particularly the diffusion of news, one thought mainly of those who produce the news — journalists, editors, broadcasters — as the professionals of the trade.

This is no longer so today. The field of communication has grown immensely broader, and now embraces a large number of hitherto unknown occupations and trades. Modern technology, in the form of new printing and news dissemination processes, has invaded the Gutenberg galaxy. The advent of satellites, computers, lasers and yet other technological innovations has already substantially increased and will continue to increase the number and variety of professions necessary for communication to function. The enormous extension of the cultural industry is also a source of new demands leading to the emergence of new categories of professionals. In the past decade, for example, it is estimated that in certain highly industrialized countries information and communication activities have created more jobs than the combined activities of the primary, secondary and tertiary sectors.

To this must be added another consideration. Some economic analysts today tend to situate a whole set of human activities — social, educational, cultural and economic — within the context of communication in its broadest sense. Hence the fact that the communications sector employs an ever larger proportion of the working population and makes an ever greater contribution to the national income. At the same time, the information data, and knowledge transmitted by different processes represents an increasingly important factor of development. For growth increasingly results from the conjunction of limited material resources and unlimited non-material resources (education, know-how, information). The result is that the numbers of professional communicators are soaring and the range of their skills and qualifications is constantly widening. It is difficult to quantify this phenomenon, as comparable basic statistics for different countries are lacking, and such data as are available differ too widely in their terms of reference. This is due to the fact that there is still no general agreement on the methods of computation and the criteria to be used to determine the breakdown of jobs between the information sector and the other sectors. In its broadest definition, the communication sector may be taken to embrace a large part of education and science, a part of cultural activities, health services, public administration and financial services. Moreover, many functions in the primary and secondary sectors can be considered primarily to be "communication" jobs as new technologies for information processing and informatics are invading every sector. The majority of occupations are nevertheless concentrated in the tertiary or service sector. The scale of the phenomenon varies considerably from one country to another, but the trend is uniform in all developed countries.

Various attempts, based on sound research theories, have been made to grasp the phenomenon as a whole, in all its complexity;[1] after considering the main occupations entailed in the production, processing and distribution of information, three main categories have been defined, based on the situation in the United States, and the following table drawn up:

Typology of Information Workers and Compensation [a]

	Employee Compensation ($ Millions)
Markets for information	
Knowledge producers	46,964
Scientific and technical workers	18,777
Private information services	28,187
Knowledge distributors	28,265
Educators	23,680
Public information disseminators	1,264
Communication workers	3,321
Information in markets	
Market search and coordination specialists	93,370
Information gatherers	6,132
Search and coordination specialists	28,252
Planning and control workers	58,986
Information processors	61,340
Non-electronic based	34,317
Electronic based	27,023
Information infrastructure	
Information machine workers	13,167
Non-electronic machine operators	4,219
Electronic machine operators	3,660
Telecommunication workers	5,288
Total information	243,106
Total employee compensation	454,259
Information as percentage of total	53.52%

Note: (a) Based on 440 occupational types in 201 industries. Employee compensation, calculated for 1967, includes wages and salaries and supplements.
Computed using BLS Occupation by Industry matrix and Census of Population average wages.

In a comment on this table it is pointed out that "The first category includes those workers whose output or primary activity is producing and selling knowledge. Included here are scientists, inventors, teachers, librarians, journalists, and authors.

---

(1) See Marc U. Porat, "Communication Policy in an Information Society", in *Communications for Tomorrow,* Praeger, 1978. This is only one example, albeit a very interesting one, of manpower censuses recently undertaken in developed countries.

The second major class of workers covers those who gather and disseminate information. These workers move information within firms and within markets; they search, coordinate, plan, and process market information. Included here are managers, secretaries, clerks, lawyers, brokers and typists. The last class includes workers who operate the information machines and technologies that support the previous two activities. Included here are computer operators, telephone installers and television repairers".

Similar surveys have been made in various developed countries. However, results are quite different, even not comparable. The criteria used for the categorization of professions and jobs differ widely; there is no consensus regarding the nature of human inputs in various work places, industries, enterprises, offices. It is not disputable that there is an increase of intellectual content in most of the jobs, that the border line between manual and intellectual work is gradually becoming less distinct and that many more people manage information and process data as part of their usual work. While agreeing on that, it is debatable whether all of them should be classed in the "communication sector". At present, we are unable to elucidate these questions satisfactorily but it should be stressed that in similar studies conducted in the future at the national and international levels it will not be possible to ignore problems revolving around the concept itself of the communication professionals.

2. Professionalism in Communication

Surely it is perfectly normal that professionalism should exist in communication no less than in any other domain. But, given the nature of communication, the question arises how these two concepts are to be reconciled?

Professionalism in communication is fostered by the sensitivity of all societies about news produced and diffused; by the importance information and informatics have in all branches and sectors of national life; by the rapid development of technology, demanding increased specialization. One of the effects of the scientific and technical upheavals occurring throughout the world has thus been to increase the number of professionals, who require skills which are both more technical and more diverse. So, many professionals possess unique qualifications which provide them privileged, sometimes powerful, positions in dealing with information, data and messages, all of which are sources of knowledge. This, indeed, may afford them considerable, often enviable, power.

Still, it is acknowledged that the right to collect and disseminate information is given to no one person or group in particular, but to all, individually and collectively. The exercise of this right should not therefore be monopolized by any group whatsoever, but should, in practice, be exercized by all those to whom it belongs. Passing from the concept of information to the broader concept of communication, the paradox may seem even greater. To communicate necessarily implies the active participation, on an equal footing, of partners who are actively and not passively involved. In view of this, exclusive professionalism is even harder to reconcile with the concept of communication than with that of information.

Communication, considered as a form of social exchange, is hardly compatible with an excessive professionalization[1] which, on the strength of the skills which it

---

(1) Comment by **Mr. E. Abel:** "The concern about 'exclusive professionalism' and 'excessive professionalization' lacks definition. How much professionalization, for example, is too much? The amateur-professional dichotomy can perhaps be avoided by measures that would assure access to

implies, might confer on certain members of society preponderant power vis-à-vis others in the society. On the other hand, it should be remembered that communication via different media and using all kinds of technologies is essentially a profession with its own specific, complex techniques and also, in the case of the electronic media, its own language and grammar. So the specific role to be played by the professionals can be defined and certain parameters set for their activities. It can be considered that the existence of a right belonging in principle to everyone does not necessarily mean that specialized professional categories cannot develop for the purpose of exercising this right — or helping and enabling others to make use of it — as its particular prerogative. It may indeed be wondered whether communication does not differ in this respect from other activities, in view of the special part that professional communicators, and journalists in particular, play in society owing to the impact they make and the power they have to influence the flow of information and data and the formation of ideas and opinions.

The problem of the relationship between professionalism in the communication process and democratization of communication exchange seems to be that of striking a fair and fruitful balance between professionalization and democratization. The democratization of communication, in the sense of promoting optimal exchange and involving as many actors as possible, does not mean that the development of mediated communication should be curbed or that the professionalism in this field should not be encouraged. On the other hand, the professional's role in promoting communication between peoples and nations should not restrict the process of democratizing communications or increasing users' participation.

3. Training of Professionals

The quality of any system is largely governed by the calibre of those who operate it. It may therefore be considered that training in mass communication, at all levels and in all forms, is of paramount importance. It may be regarded as fundamental to the effective operation and development of communication systems. But there is also general agreement that the lack of trained personnel and defects in training schemes are among the basic reasons for deficiencies observed all round the world. The extreme variety of communication-related activities and the ever larger range of specialized skills emerging has meant that the demand for skilled staff almost everywhere exceeds the training capacity established in each and every country.

Training for communication, in the broadest sense, involves a wide variety of specialists in a whole range of different fields. The training of journalists, as indeed of all those whose career is in the press, radio, television or the film industry, obviously occupies a prominent place in the training of communication professionals. Of particular importance, is the training and development of creative and artistic individuals and groups for all the media. In addition to the traditional requirements for skilled mass media personnel, ranging from journalists to technicians (editors, reporters, authors, script-writers, for the preparation of the content; typographers, printers, for the production of newspapers; directors, cameramen and other technicians, for television and cinema studios, and administrative and managerial personnel), numerous new needs are increasingly arising for less traditional categories of communication workers.

The development of communication makes it necessary to train engineers,

professional training for all qualified individuals, regardless of race, religion, social class or ethnic community."

technicians and maintenance staff for telecommunication networks, as well as specialists in the printing, publishing and distribution of book and periodicals. Librarians, documentalists, archivists must also be trained; moreover, the use of techniques of communication and persuasion necessitates training specialists to run information and extension work services, as well as the teachers who must learn how to use new teaching aids and techniques. Highly trained technicians, programmers and analysts are needed for data-processing and teleprocessing systems. Economists and specialists in the management of communication resources and in communication planning are also needed, as are specialists for information jobs in agriculture, family planning, health care, community development and industrialization.

There is also the problem of specialized training for a particularly important form of communication — notably in developing countries — namely, interpersonal communication, whose human channels create networks of communication for development, through a whole series of operations ranging from cooperatives to trade unions, from health care to small-scale industries, from agriculture to family planning, etc. This specialized area extends to traditional art forms and popular media, which are recognized as effective means of interpersonal communication for the transmission of educational and persuasive messages, as well as for promoting cultural identity. Such training therefore concerns all persons involved in interpersonal communication, be they teachers, agricultural authorities, social workers, health care instructors, family planning or community development counsellors. It is vital to recognize that these different categories all form an integral part of the communication community, which is interdisciplinary; hence their training must prepare them for such teamwork.

Training of all these categories of professionals is carried out in institutions of quite different kinds. In particular, what part the university should or should not play in providing this training or at least part of it is seen differently from one country to another. On the world scale, it can be said that mass media studies are a fairly recent phenomenon started only at the turn of the century; they did not develop systematically until after the Second World War. To some extent, the growth of these studies in universities is linked with the development of the media themselves and much emphasis is placed on them in such countries as the USA, Japan or the USSR. However, in the UK, for example, which has a highly developed system of mass communication, the systematic study of the mass media through teaching or research has barely begun to penetrate the universities. In most countries of Africa and Asia, mass media studies have been introduced only in the last few years. In teaching and above all in research, the field is still in its early stages of development. In Latin America, however, the picture is quite different. The region leads the developing world as to university involvement in mass media studies. The dominant activity in such studies, in universities and in other educational institutions, is journalism training. Almost every country has at least one institution which provides such training and most are associated with universities.

While universities appear to be increasingly involved in communication training, they cannot in all cases provide all the practical training which professionals need. Thus various specialized training centres and mass media organizations also play an important role. They organize training, refresher and in-service courses for professionals regardless of the qualifications acquired or not at university. Thus their role is to provide specific courses of technical and occupational instruction suitably adapted to the circumstances and demands of their work. Such courses and periods should ideally be followed by refresher courses throughout working life because of the ever-changing communication scene. Hence the importance, which cannot be too strongly emphasized, of lifelong education in this respect. It might be added that, both in education and training establishments and in research institutes, curricula and research programmes should include the study of the concept of the new world communication order, its different dimensions and implications, as well as a study of proposals intended to bring about changes in the pattern of present-day world communications.

This said, the imbalance between developed and developing countries in respect of available training facilities is aggravated by the focus of training in some countries, between senior cadres on the one hand and middle management and technical and creative workers on the other. All too frequently, training schemes are designed with the former in mind, despite the fact that there is greater need for the latter.

In this field as in others, self-reliance remains the key concept for developing countries. The desire for self-reliance does not mean isolation of communication personnel from international contacts. Decisions have to be made at each stage of the training process. The considerable experience of experts from both developed and developing countries has led to the conclusion that basic training should be conducted locally, in familiar surroundings, with training methodology suited to local conditions, cultural traditions and development strategy. Many elements of media development express a country's fundamental culture, and it is necessary to set safeguards so that the training procedure is not modelled upon an ideology borrowed from a foreign model. More advanced training may be at the regional training centres, with curriculum designed by instructors from the region, and with foreign advisors as required. Overseas training should be reserved for experienced specialists and designated trainers. With all the good-will, dedication and assistance that outside entities may be prepared to provide to developing countries, there is not much that can be achieved without those countries fulfilling their own responsibilities. This should also lead to ever more extensive, and genuine, cooperation between them. It should be noted that the involvement of advisors and teachers from developed countries serves not only to provide expertise, but also as a learning experience for the visiting instructors whose exposure to development needs and perspectives may enhance their perceptions, and be beneficial when they return to their permanent communication roles at home. Provided that it is well planned and coordinated, such cooperation should make it possible to consolidate still further the improvements already achieved. Cooperation between developing countries at the regional or inter-regional level is extremely valuable, particularly to ensure that training models correspond to local realities.

In view of the acute shortage of adequately trained personnel in many developing countries, the question of building up of manpower resources must remain a priority concern of policy-makers and planners. The need for training to be adapted to national perspectives and the close ties between communication and development both militate in favour of training provided in situ. The principle of conducting basic training locally, or regionally, in familiar cultural surroundings is widely supported today and should be adopted and extended in all regions.

Chapter 5

Rights and Responsibilities of Journalists

Although millions of people work in communication in one way or another, special attention is rightly devoted to journalists. They have not only an important social function, but their potential capacity to influence and even to shape ideas and opinions, and the problems in which they are involved by the nature of their work, makes journalism both a profession and a mission. This is particularly important since public opinion is dependent more than ever on those who supply objective, truthful and unbiased news and information; the news gatherer and news disseminator are essential to the workings of any democratic system.

1. Access to Information

Journalists claim the right to seek out information without hindrance and to transmit it safely and effectively. Some journalists also claim the right to express opinions freely, when this is the function for which they are employed as editorial writers, columnists or commentators. It is a question, on the one hand, of freedom of information and of expression; on the other hand, of the right of the reading and listening public to be informed and to hear diverse opinions, which belongs to every citizen but depends in practice on the freedom of journalists. It is of course true that the right to seek and impart information, and the right to express opinions, should be enjoyed by everyone. But journalists need to exercise these rights as a basic condition of doing their job effectively, and they are particularly vulnerable to constraints by authority. They are often placed, whether they wish it or not, among those who find themselves in the front line of defence of freedom.

Freedom of the press in its widest sense represents the collective enlargement of each citizen's freedom of expression which is accepted as a human right. Democratic societies are based on the concept of sovereignty of the people, whose general will is determined by an informed public opinion. It is this right of the public to know that is the essence of media freedom of which the professional journalist, writer and producer are only custodians. Deprivation of this freedom diminishes all others.

The press has been described as the fourth estate because full and accurate information on matters of public interest is the means by which governments, institutions, organizations and all others in authority, at whatever level, are held accountable to and by the public. Nevertheless, those in authority often tend to conceal that which is inconvenient or likely to arouse public opinion against them. Hence, one finds denial of access to information, overt or covert censorship, and deliberate attempts by official spokesmen to mislead. Despite the high-sounding principles enshrined in laws and constitutions, journalists in many countries are not free to tell the truth. For example, in several Latin American nations which were formerly democracies, martial law is in force. Measures of censorship drastically limit the journalist's capacity to do his work effectively. Journalists who incur the displeasure of the authorities, or of powerful interests, are harassed and intimidated. A climate of fear can also insidiously result in self-censorship. All such tendencies are unacceptable and must be countered. There can be many perceptions of the truth. However, the right of inquiry and expression, including dissent, is essential for establishing a more complete and rounded truth which men and nations need in a complex and diverse world. No news organ or information system is therefore worth more than the credibility it enjoys.

Active pursuit and disclosure of facts which are of public interest is one of the criteria to judge a journalist's professional capacities. The role of the investigative journalist is to question and probe the action of all those in authority and to expose them wherever there is abuse of power, incompetence, corruption or other deviations. His potential to investigate and publish matters relating to bureaucratic maladministration and corruption is of particular importance, being one of the most efficient ways of ensuring that inefficiency and dishonesty, where they exist, are not permitted to corrupt the whole system or cause injustices. Those in power therefore are very often opposed to journalists' attempts to search beyond official news releases or the normally accessible sources of information; moreover, the employer of the investigative journalist often may not be over-anxious to defend or protect his employee.

All these considerations, and also the constraints imposed by newspaper owners in certain cases, mean that the journalistic profession in various countries is going through a real crisis. This can lead to a situation in which honest journalists abandon the profession, and young people of talent decide not to enter it.

2. Protection of Journalists

The need to make provisions for the protection of journalists stems from a number of considerations that go far beyond the ensuring of personal safety, independence, and integrity of the journalists. Freedom of expression is a vital part of the essential democratic process guaranteed by the Universal Declaration of Human Rights, and by the various international instruments adopted to ensure the protection of human rights and fundamental freedoms. It flows from these guarantees that the public of every country is entitled as a right, to receive news, information and views, without interference and regardless of frontiers, and that this is an integral part of the democratic process. Accordingly, we are dealing here with two fundamental rights, namely, (a) the right to communicate news, information and views; (b) the right to receive news, information and views. These rights depend largely on the freedom of all those involved in the media to exercise objectively their role as gatherers and communicators of news, information and views, without interference and in complete security. Accordingly, the right to communicate and the right to receive communications is dependent, in the final analysis, on the provision of adequate safeguards for those engaged in the gathering and dissemination of information to the public.

The protection envisaged is not limited to physical protection of journalists, but also the protection of the professional independence and integrity of all those involved in the collection and dissemination of news, information and views to the public. It should extend not only to the journalist, but also to all other agents employed in the mass media (written and audiovisual) who have a responsibility for the collection and dissemination of news, information, images or ideas intended for the public.

Journalists, who are often embarrassing witnesses and hence become targets, face physical danger in times of conflict — in wars both declared and undeclared, in civil wars and even when covering public meetings and demonstrations which are suppressed by the forces of authority[1]. The profession has good cause to remember the eight journalists who disappeared, and never reappeared, in Cambodia; or the television reporter who was shot in cold blood by an officer of the so-called National Guard in Nicaragua. For 1977 Amnesty International recorded 104 correspondents imprisoned or missing in 25 countries. Information collated by the International Press Institute, covering a period of 15 months in 1976–78, yielded these figures: 24 journalists murdered, 57 journalists wounded, tortured or kidnapped, 13 newspapers subjected to bomb attacks.

Correspondents working in foreign countries risk retaliatory measures if they offend repressive governments, with the additional disadvantage that they may not be supported by editors or proprietors anxious to maintain representation. Admittedly, the penalty incurred by the foreign correspondent is likely to be expulsion while the journalist working in his own country may have to reckon with imprisonment, torture or even a death sentence. But in times of disturbance, foreign correspondents have been maltreated and sometimes killed by military or para-military forces. There is also this important consideration: for a people living under a dictatorship, which has crushed the freedom of the national press and media, the last remaining hope is that truthful reports will reach the outside world and arouse international opinion.

The question has therefore long been raised of whether journalists need special guarantees or special protection to ensure that they can do their work[2]. The first initiative intended to create some form of protection for journalists, which came from the professional associations themselves, dates back over 25 years. Since the adoption of the Universal Declaration of Human Rights, many suggestions and proposals have been put forward for drawing up international measures to provide such protection. The text of a convention prepared by the United Nations relating to the protection of journalists engaged in dangerous missions remains a draft only; the same is true of a Council of Europe convention concerning foreign correspondents. However, in the Additional Protocol to the Geneva Conventions of 12 August 1949, concerning the protection of victims of international armed conflicts, there is a provision relating to the protection of journalists which stipulates that journalists on dangerous professional missions in areas of armed conflict are to be considered as civilians and protected as such, under certain conditions. One can also cite the Declaration on the Mass Media adopted at the 1978 session of Unesco's General Conference, which stipulates in Article II (paragraph 4) that "if the mass media are to be in a position to promote the principles of this Declaration in their activities, it is

---

(1) **Ms. B. Zimmerman** comments that broadcast journalism sometimes raises particular problems. While a print journalist covering a story may be unidentifiable because his basic equipment (notepad and pencil) is unobtrusive, radio and TV crews making direct reports can hardly pass unnoticed with their microphones, cameras and sound equipment and sometimes attract hostile reactions from authorities or crowds. However, Ms. Zimmerman adds, "Despite the more overt danger they encounter, electronic journalists are not seeking any special protection which could lead to the diminution of press freedom."

(2) The case for measures of protection is fully discussed in *The Protection of Journalists*, by **Mr. Sean MacBride** (CIC document No. 90).

essential that journalists and other agents of the mass media, in their own country or abroad, be assured of protection guaranteeing them the best conditions for the exercise of their profession".

The question has been discussed under the auspices of our Commission, at seminars held in Stockholm in April 1978 and in Paris in May 1979. As a result, in regard to a few issues "there seems to be a general consensus among the various organizations of journalists, broadcasters and publishers that some effective measures should be adopted to ensure the better protection of journalists in the exercise of their profession in dangerous situations whether such situations arise in international or non-international armed conflicts. This could be achieved through an appropriate amendment of the Protocol to the Geneva Convention"[1].

However, reservations are also widely expressed about the desirability of a general system of protection. These are based, firstly, on the principle that journalists ought not to seek privileges or favours which accord them any unique position. Human rights for all people are the best guarantee of freedom of information; in other words, journalists will be truly protected when everyone's rights are fully recognized[2].

In addition, the view is widely held in the profession itself that measures for special protection could result in journalists being guided and watched by representatives of authority, so that it might be harder rather than easier for them to do their work. In particular, protection might be made contingent on a licensing scheme which would enable the authorities to rule on who is and who is not a journalist. This would infringe upon the principle that a journalist has a professional identity simply by the fact of his employment, or (in some countries) by membership in his trade union or professional association. Licensing schemes might well lead to restrictive regulations governing the conduct of journalists; in effect, protection would be granted only to those journalists who had earned official approval[3]. Although problems concerning the protection of journalists are real and pre-occupying, we share the anxiety aroused by the prospect of licensing and consider that it contains dangers to freedom of information.

For all these reasons, we prefer to regard the problem in the wider setting of the rights and responsibilities of journalists, and it is along these lines that we make recommendations in Part V of this Report[4]. We stress also the link between the freedom of the journalist and the freedom of the citizen, and reiterate our conviction that the former is an essential feature of a democratic society.

3. Professional Regulations

A certain number of countries have adopted special legislation regulating various aspects of the journalistic profession. In others, provisions on the subject may be contained in the general social laws, in collective conventions and also in the constitutions of certain professional organizations. Thus, there may exist complex

---

(1) See *The Protection of Journalists,* op. cit., page 28.

(2) Comment by **Mr. S. MacBride:** "I do not share the reservations expressed in this paragraph [and stress] that the factors identified in this section all point to the vital role of the journalist and the need to afford journalists and media agents a special status and protection."

(3) **Mr. S. MacBride** urges that safeguards — professional and judicial — could be provided at domestic, regional and international levels to safeguard journalists from the interferences enumerated.

(4) Comment by **Mr. S. MacBride:** "I disagree with this paragraph and regard the recommendations in Part V on these questions as wholly inadequate."

legal systems in which, in order to ascertain the journalist's status, it is necessary to consult the labour laws, a special law, a collective convention and also the statutes of certain professional associations. The respective role and importance of these different provisions naturally vary from country to country. Jurisprudence, as well as codes of professional conduct, may also have a considerable place in determining professional situation of journalists.

It may be wondered whether professional regulations for journalists are desirable. The many arguments adduced in this respect are contradictory. The multiplicity of social and economic systems existing in the world, as well as the specific needs of individual countries, obviously make it difficult to give either a generally affirmative or an overall negative answer to this question. Ultimately, this will depend on the substance of any proposed regulations[1].

In those countries in which reservations are voiced regarding the adoption of regulations, it is frequently contended that any hard-and-fast definition of the journalist may be dangerous for freedom of information. Such countries have enacted no legislation governing the journalist's profession, which in principle may be exercised by anyone.

In this connection, it is maintained that the adoption of any definition whatever generally leads to the official licensing of journalists. While it is pointed out that this practice is by no means new, but is indeed tending to spread — for example in Latin America and elsewhere — it is stressed that licensing implies government sanction of the individual exercise of the profession of journalist. Such measures would make it possible to lay down conditions of admission to the profession. A licence which is issued can also be withdrawn. The possibility of losing their means of livelihood may thus prove a deterrent to investigative journalists who have so important a role in disclosing abuses committed by the authorities. Experience shows that the granting of professional licences and all complicated accreditation procedures tend to foster government intervention in the national and international flow of news.

On the other hand, those in favour of establishing a legal definition of the professional journalist and laying down conditions of admission to the profession argue that such regulations are necessary. They may be regarded as a means of protecting the journalist including provision for various rights, guarantees and safeguards for journalists. Also, such regulations may be understood as measures favouring the public interest or media consumers. Some point out that the introduction of certain standards, combined with measures to protect journalists' interests, might give them more solid financial guarantees and greater opportunities for fulfilling their mission towards the community. Although regulations which relate to base salaries and allowances, holidays and leave of absence, conditions of dismissal and the indemnities due, promotion, hours of work, compensation payable in the case of sickness or accident, security of employment, etc., are mostly the result of collective bargaining between trade unions and management, there are countries

---

(1) Comment by **Mr. S. Losev:** "The very notion of an international statute for journalists seems to me to be wrong, since it tends to isolate journalists as a separate group from the main bulk of the public whereas to my mind, in the interests of the public and of the journalists, there should be possibly more contacts between journalists and the public. A historical analysis of the attempts to set up a statute is not in favour of statutes, since statutes existed in Mussolini's Italy and sanctified fascist regulations on journalists. The trend to treat journalists as a sect, as a separate group with a special status, as a kind of an elite seems to me to be very wrong, since it does not contribute to a wider participation of the public in journalism and in the activity of the mass media and tends to erect a Chinese wall between journalists and their audiences, which is contrary to the main stream of modern development of journalism."

where these issues are part of legislation or normative actions.

Among the potential advantages of professional regulations, mention is sometimes made of the conscience clause, under which a journalist may refuse to accomplish a professional mission or may leave his enterprise without forfeiting his severance pay on the grounds that he would otherwise jeopardize his moral interests.

Certain legislations stipulate that professional confidentiality is a right and at the same time an obligation. The purpose of confidentiality is to protect both journalists and the freedom of information, to facilitate access to sources of information and to avoid deceiving the public's trust. Moreover, many legal texts state that the journalist is not to be hampered in the exercise of his profession, and that no pressure, intimidation or influence may be used to induce him to give an incorrect or biased account of the facts.

However, whilst the law thus seeks to protect the journalist and to guarantee his rights, it also, in almost all cases, stipulates corollary duties and obligations. Thus the journalist is legally bound to refrain from divulging false or unconfirmed information, or information for advertising purposes, to uphold the dignity of his profession, comply with its professional code, refrain from publishing reports of in camera court sessions, etc. The laws of certain countries also mention more specific duties, such as that of acting in a socially responsible way, respecting human rights and the principles of cooperation between peoples, engaging in militant action and the duty to refrain from obtaining certain types of information — such as, for example, from the police or military authorities — except with their permission or in the course of a trial. Others go even further, imposing various restrictions — forbidding journalists to collaborate with any other information organ without permission from their employer, requiring them to obtain authorization from the government in order to work for a foreign organ, and so on. Moreover, provision may be made for disciplinary measures which, according to the seriousness of the offence, may even include being struck off the professional register.

The advisability of adopting legal rules defining a juridical status for the journalistic profession is viewed differently from country to country and according to the advantages and inconveniences which it may comprise. Non-statutory rules, fashioned voluntarily by the parties concerned, may suffice in certain countries. In this matter, it is not a question of adopting a half-way or arbitrary position, but diverse situations must be taken into account and attempts made to establish the best possible balance among all interests involved.

4. Professional Rights and the General Interest

In most societies, respect is paid in principle to the freedom and independence of journalists. But these ideals are frequently violated in practice, so that journalists are forced either to censor themselves or to face risks in doing their job honestly. Moreover, there is room for genuine debate about the interpretation of these broad ideals.

For journalists (and, of course, not for journalists alone) it is necessary to think of rights and responsibilities in their relationship to each other. Anyone who acts without responsibility weakens his claim to freedom, while anyone who is denied freedom cannot be called upon to exercise responsibility. The situation is most healthy when neither of these values is felt to be jeopardized.

Several international instruments have given expression to this balance of rights and responsibilities[1]. Like anyone else, journalists need to be careful not to exercise their own freedom in a way that would infringe the liberties of other people. They have an inescapable responsibility towards their fellow-citizens, the national community and other nations. In any community, there are accepted standards which ought to be respected by media organizations and by journalists individually.

Among the rights of journalists, one of the most important is the right to seek out and disseminate information freely, with access to both official and unofficial sources. It is worth noting that this right should be complemented by the responsibility of those providing information, such as official spokesmen, to supply the truth without distortion and without evasion or undue concealment.

Journalists need freedom of movement within countries and across frontiers, and freedom to transmit information without hindrance. The International Stockholm Seminar stressed the importance of the need for access to the "full range of opinion" within every country.

The right of access cannot be totally unqualified; sovereign states inevitably restrict it where military or diplomatic considerations are involved. But the rule of "official secrecy" has been invoked, even in democratic countries, where it cannot be justified by such considerations[2].

Another problem is that some media enjoy a greater right of access than others. Wealthy newspapers and broadcasting organizations not only have resources that cannot be equalled by small independent journals, but also can make use of connections with official bodies. Spokesmen and providers of information should, far more than is now the custom, treat all inquirers and journalists equally.

---

(1) Reference might first be made to the Universal Declaration of Human Rights, which expressly states: "In the exercise of his rights and freedoms, everyone shall be subject only to such limitations as are determined by law solely for the purpose of securing due recognition and respect for the rights and freedoms of others and of meeting the just requirements of morality, public order and the general welfare in a democratic society." (Article 29.)
The International Covenant on Civil and Political Rights is still more precise: "The exercise of the rights provided for in paragraph 2 of this article (freedom of expression) carries with it special duties and responsibilities. It may therefore be subject to certain restrictions, but these shall only be such as are provided by law and are necessary: (a) For respect of the rights or reputations of others; (b) for the protection of national security or of public order (ordre public), or of public health or morals (Article 19). In another article, the same covenant provides that : "Any advocacy of national, racial or religious hatred that constitutes incitement to discrimination, hostility or violence shall be prohibited by law." (Article 20). In the Convention for the Protection of Human Rights and Fundamental Freedoms (adopted by the Council of Europe, 1950), more explicit provisions are included with respect to the exercise of the freedom of expression: "The exercise of these freedoms, since it carries with it duties and responsibilities, may be subject to such formalities, conditions, restrictions or penalties as are prescribed by law and are necessary in a democratic society, in the interest of national security, territorial integrity or public safety, for the prevention of disorder or crime, for the protection of health or morals, for the protection of the reputation of rights of others, for preventing the disclosure of information received in confidence, or for maintaining the authority and impartiality of the judiciary". (Article 10). In the same line of thinking, the American Convention on Human Rights (signed in San José, 1969) stipulates: "The exercise of the right provided for in the foregoing paragraph (i.e. the right to freedom of thought and expression) shall not be subject to prior censorship but shall be subject to subsequent imposition of liability, which shall be expressly established by law. Any propaganda for war and any advocacy of national, racial, or religious hatred that constitute incitements to lawless violence or any other similar illegal action against any person or group of persons on any grounds including those of race, colour, religion, language, or national origin shall be considered as offences punishable by law." (Article 13.)

(2) Comment by **Mr. S. MacBride:** "I draw attention to the fact that there is a widespread tendency on the part of governmental agencies to withhold information on spurious grounds of "privilege", "military", "diplomatic" or "national security". Not infrequently these claims are made in order to

One of the consequences of political or economic power affecting media autonomy and of the monopoly on managerial decision-taking, which many journalists feel to be an infringement of their freedom, is reflected in their growing demand, voiced in certain countries, to be associated in the management process. Partnership in management may be regarded as a means of journalists' access to important decisions and a way of democratizing the profession of journalism. Thanks to it, journalists should be able to take part in the formulation and implementation of editorial policy and thus, at the same time, remain free to take initiatives, to determine which matters are to be covered and how they are to be covered, to present their own point of view and in general, along with the editors, to take basic decisions collectively.

The establishment in certain countries of a self-management system in production enterprises has led to the extension of this system to the media: Yugoslavia in the 1960s and Peru in the early 1970s are two cases in point which illustrate not only the trend towards collective management but also involvement of various social groups in the decision-making process[1]. In other countries, for example, France, Italy and Portugal, the setting up of associations of editors and editorial boards or committees would seem to reflect the concern of communicators to put forward other than purely material demands. The purpose of these moves is to secure a right of collective participation in the conduct and orientation of the enterprise and in the determination of the quality of the information produced.

The rights of journalists — notably the right of access to sources, the right to transmit information, and the right of interpretation and fair comment — are valuable not only to the profession but also to readers, listeners, and the entire public. Where the media enjoy adequate freedom and accept due responsibility, the result is a high standard of knowledge and informed discussion. This can be reinforced by participation in the communication process, both on the part of working journalists, and on the part of the audience through various types of public involvement and self-management systems.

---

conceal some inefficiency, corruption or other impropriety. As it is, the people who in the final analysis have to decide policies, for them the fullest freedom of information is essential. The role of the investigative journalist is paramount and must be protected."

(1) Different forms of co-management or self-management have been initiated in certain countries. In Yugoslavia, the system of self-management as an integral socio-economic order has been established in production enterprises and factories, as well as in hospitals and cultural, educational, scientific and communication institutions. Consequently, all those working in the media participate in the decision-making process. They examine matters of editorial policy and its realisation, as well as all issues of importance for their position in the media and for the development of their institutions. They also decide on matters affecting financial and material functioning, and particularly the distribution and use of income.

Unlike other enterprises, media enterprises have a specific form of management which corresponds to their special social role. For each publishing, news or broadcasting organization, a council is formed, composed not only of elected representatives of those employed by the organization, but also of representatives of different sectors of public life and delegates of socio-political, cultural, professional and other interested communities, organizations and institutions. Councils cannot interfere in current editorial affairs, but the play an important role in working out basic editorial policy and in evaluating its implementation; they transmit initiatives and proposals from the sectors which they represent, and organize public discussions on editorial programmes and development plans; they analyse the public's response, in particular complaints and criticisms.

Chapter 6
Norms of Professional Conduct

The professional conduct of journalists is conditioned by internal and external influences. One of the basic ones is the place and impact of the public in political and social affairs. Fundamental changes in the world often occur without being noticed. An instance of this has been the important change which has been taking place since World War II, in the centre of gravity of power from governments to public opinion. The combination of various elements, including higher standards of education and the mass media technology, has brought about a certain shift in the centre of gravity of political power in the world. Public opinion is now in a position to be informed and to exercise judgment on most important situations in the world. Inevitably, public opinion forms its own judgment and takes sides.

There is general recognition of the fact that journalists have responsibilities not only vis-à-vis their own convictions but also towards the public. Summarily, four kinds of responsibility may be defined: (a) contractual responsibility in relation to the media and their internal organization; (b) a social responsibility entailing obligations towards public opinion and society as a whole; (c) responsibility or liability deriving from the obligation to comply with the law; (d) responsibility towards the international community, relating to respect of universal values. These four types of responsibility may in certain respects be contradictory or even conflicting.

1. Codes of Professional Ethics

Professional ethical norms first began to be codified in the early 1920s; at present, such codes exist in some sixty countries in all regions of the world. They vary considerably both in their form and scope. In some countries, different codes govern the press, broadcasting and the cinema. Frequently, these are formulated and adopted voluntarily by the professionals themselves; in other cases, however, they are imposed by the law or by government decree. The standards of conduct found in national and regional codes are rooted in conceptions which, by and large, are universally accepted but tend to give rise to very significant variations in the formulation and interpretation of their provisions. Moreover, principles such as objectivity, impartiality, truthfulness and freedom of information are frequently formulated in rather vague and ambiguous terms. Most codes refer to such important concepts as: safeguarding freedom of information; freedom of access to information sources; objectivity, accuracy, truthfulness or the non-misrepresentation of facts; responsibility vis-à-vis the public and its rights and interests and in relation to national, racial and religious communities, the nation, the State and maintenance of peace; the obligation to refrain from a calumny, unfounded accusations, slander,

241

violations of privacy; integrity and independence; the right of reply and of correction; respect of professional confidentiality. In addition to differences in the formulation of these concepts, other variations can be found, as for example, the inclusion of special provisions relating to the cultural, social or ethnic needs of individual countries.

On the other hand, many national codes do not contain principles governing journalists' duties and responsibilities towards the international community and foreign countries, or do not give sufficient stress to such principles. This may be considered to be partly due to the fact that the codes are generally conceived in terms of an individualistic ethic concerned to regulate relations between individuals (those releasing and those receiving information) and fail to take sufficient account of the fact that the responsibilities resulting therefrom are of a social kind and affect the community as a whole, both national and international.

Professional ethics are above all important as inner directives for the individual's decisions in the various situations and dilemmas which confront him in his professional work. A conscientious journalist must carefully check all facts and, if necessary, forego publication of any doubtful or questionable news items, especially if they concern personal facts which might affect the subject's reputation if published. Thus the scope of professional ethics is much wider than the texts of legal codes. However in attempting to achieve a just balance between freedom and responsibility, the ethical aspects of this dichotomy depend not only on conscious decisions by the journalist, but also on practices in the media and the general social environment[1].

It may also be noted in relation to codes that it is not journalists who need a high standard of ethics so much as their employers, who give orders that are often repugnant to the working reporter. An example is cheque-book journalism — the practice whereby a person involved in sensational events (sometimes a criminal) is paid to give his story exclusively to one newspaper, and is shielded from questioning by other newspapers which might be more critical. Journalists' unions have attacked this practice and agreed that members should not give their cooperation, in ghost-writing the 'revelations' or in other ways; but the responsibility rests with the financial controllers who sign the cheques. More serious is the exploitation of the journalistic profession by intelligence services, who pay journalists to supply information and infiltrate the profession by securing jobs (or freelance assignments) for their agents as a cover for their real activities. This practice is clearly reprehensible and can diminish the credibility of the profession. Journalists' unions have repeatedly declared that it is unethical for members to perform services or accept remuneration from any source other than their known employers. But, while editors and proprietors have in some cases been deceived, they have in other cases consented to clandestine

---

(1) So, for different behaviour, creation of appropriate conditions is essential. A member of our Commission made the following statement in that respect: "Journalistic ethics cannot be confined to proclaiming principles and demanding that journalists respect them. What is needed are constant efforts to increase the actual opportunities for free and responsible work in the media. One of the most important conditions for this is undoubtedly the democratization of the internal relations in the mass media. The extent to which those who work in the media can develop their creativity and assert their moral and professional qualities depends on the way the institution is managed, on the financial resources made available, on the editorial policy and on many other concrete conditions. Professional ethics are expressed in the moral firmness with which a journalist stands up against various interests and pressures, when these direct him to change or distort his knowledge and findings, or to forego the publication of the truth . . . Thus professional ethics do not conflict with the principle of freedom of information. On the contrary, they give support to journalists and all those who make use of their freedom, helping them to exercise it in full consciousness of their own responsibility for the purpose of their activity." (*Professional Ethics in Mass Communication,* by **Mr. Bogdan Osolnik,** CIC document no. 90 bis).

arrangements proposed by intelligence services. Where the State, which controls the intelligence services, also controls or can intimidate the newspapers, a code of journalistic ethics is scarcely an adequate defence. Nor can it prevent intelligence services from acquiring disguised control of certain publications, which is also a practice by no means unknown in recent years.

No generalizations can be made or common denominators identified in this area; however, according to the conclusions of certain previous international consultations, codes of ethics would mainly aim at the following objectives: (a) to protect the consumer — readers, listeners, viewers, or the public in general; (b) to protect and inspire the working journalist, broadcaster or others directly concerned with the gathering, writing, processing, and presenting news and opinions; (c) to guide editors and others who take full legal responsibility for what is published and broadcast; (d) to define the responsibilities of proprietors, shareholders and governments who are in a position of absolute control over any particular form of mass media communications activity; (e) to deal with issues of advertisers and others who buy into the services of the media.

It may be concluded — a conclusion confirmed by a consultation organized by the President of the Commission — that the adoption of codes of ethics at national and regional levels is desirable, provided that such codes are prepared and adopted by the profession itself. In the elaboration of any code of ethics the Declaration on the mass media should be taken into account. Article VIII of this states: "Professional organizations, and people who participate in the professional training of journalists and other agents of the mass media and who assist them in performing their functions in a responsible manner should attach special importance to the principles of this Declaration when drawing up and ensuring application of their code of ethics." So, as far as professional deontoloty is concerned, there is a clear tendency to strengthen the ethical aspect (elaboration of meaningful codes of professional ethics) and the freedom of initiatives of the professionals themselves (voluntary nature of the codes). The Commission favours this trend with respect to professional codes of ethics.

With regard to the formulation of an international code of professional ethics this remains a controversial issue, although for its advocates the existence of such a code constitutes a major factor in the establishment of a new world information and communication order.

A number of attempts have been made by non-governmental and intergovernmental organizations to draft regional or international codes of ethics. The oldest would seem to be the Code of Journalistic Ethics adopted by the first Pan-American Press Conference held in Washington in 1926 and later by the Inter-American Press Conference held in New York in October 1950, where it was reaffirmed and adopted as the creed of the Inter-American Press Association.

Within the United Nations, the problem was first discussed nearly 30 years ago. Between 1950 and 1952, the Sub-Commission on Freedom of Information and the Press prepared a Draft International Code of Ethics for Information Personnel[1]. In

---

(1) This text contains provisions relating to freedom of information as a fundamental human right, truthfulness and accuracy of news, non-distortion of facts, refusal of personal benefits or the promotion of private interest to the detriment of the public interest, condemnation of calumny, slander, unfounded accusations and plagiary, correction of false or harmful news, right of reply, honesty and fairness towards the public and respect for private life, professional secrecy, etc. A particular provision relates to the duty of those releasing news and comment concerning foreign countries to acquire the necessary knowledge of the country to be able to write of it accurately and

1954, the General Assembly decided to take no steps with regard to the Draft, which was transmitted to information enterprises and professional associations to enable them to take such decisions as they might judge appropriate.

Several of the international associations active at present have also worked in this field. The Inter-American Association of Broadcasters (IAAB) adopted a Declaration of Ethical Principles at its Lima Assembly in 1955. A number of member organizations of the IAAB have formulated their own codes of ethics, taking into consideration the principles enunciated in the Lima Declaration. The International Federation of Journalists also dealt with the problems of professional ethics of journalists and, in Bordeaux in 1954, a declaration of journalists' duties was adopted. Six journalists' trade unions of the European Community adopted in Munich, in November 1971, a Declaration of Duties and Rights of Journalists[1]. As regards the International Organization of Journalists, it has concerned itself on several occasions with professional ethics. In a meeting organized at Unesco in November 1973, the IOJ proposed a draft concerning professional codes of ethics. The Latin American Federation of Journalists (FELAP) is also interested in these questions; FELAP does not have a code of ethics but a "Declaration of Principles", approved by 12 organizations. Lastly, a Code of professional ethics for Arab journalists was prepared by the profession under the auspices of the Arab League in August 1977.

Despite these initiatives, it is maintained both by many journalists and government authorities in charge of communication that, in a world in which so very different conceptions of the journalists' role prevail, the diversity of values likely to affect an international code would make it impossible to formulate.

In fact, what is involved is more an incompatibility between two essentially distinct conceptions of journalism than an incompatibility between the ethical proposals themselves. While it is true that it is at present difficult to formulate a code of this kind, there are no reasons to consider it unattainable or that its pursuit should be abandoned for reasons of principle. All the more so if it is acknowledged that our universe is becoming ever smaller and ever more interdependent, and that it is important to take account not only of the rights of those disseminating the messages but also of the concerns, interests and needs of those to whom they are addressed[2].

While it may well be extremely difficult, considering the different conceptions to which we have referred, to formulate agreed positive principles for journalists and the media in all countries, the Declaration on the mass media adopted by the General Conference of Unesco supplies, in our view, some basic elements for an international code[3].

---

fairly. Another provision states that it is for the professionals themselves and not for governments to ensure that the ethical principles set forth are duly respected, and that nothing in the text shall be understood to justify any intervention whatsoever on the part of the public authorities.

(1) This is a document in two parts, the first outlining the duties and responsibilities of journalists and the second defining their rights and their protection. Not all codes of ethics combine this dual purpose quite so clearly.

(2) Comment by **Mr. E. Abel:** "A planetary code for journalists of all nations is neither attainable nor desirable in present circumstances. There are indeed "two essentially distinct conceptions of journalism" in the world today. Where the press is an arm of the state, there can be no room for the exercise of independent professional judgment by journalists. A code of ethics that would be compatible with such a system of political control must necessarily be rejected by journalists who see their role as independent of the state and, indeed, as decently skeptical of governmental authority."

(3) Comment by **Ms. B. Zimmerman:** "The Commission has spoken in favour of the freedom of initiatives of the professionals themselves (the voluntary nature of journalist codes of ethics). At a

2. Press and Media Councils

There exist at present in the world some fifty press councils, media councils or other similar bodies, which are to be found in practically all regions. Most of them are concerned with the press, and only a few with broadcasting.

Though the first council was established in Sweden in 1916, the institution as such has long remained isolated, and did not begin to become generalized until the early 1960s. As an argument for the establishment of press councils, mention is often made of Sweden, where the self-regulatory system seems to function very satisfactorily, thanks mainly to the existence of an "ombudsman" and of a press council. It is worth noting that, in this country, the State has never made any attempt to turn the press council into an instrument of control by introducing its own representatives or its own regulations. The British Press Council has acquired a special reputation thanks to the integrity and firmness of which it has given proof. Press councils are essentially the brain-child of the Western media, although increasing interest in them is found in the developing countries.

As regards some European countries, France has neither press nor media councils, while in Italy a law was enacted in 1959 establishing courts of honour for the press. In Belgium, while there is as yet no press council properly so called, there exists a Council of Discipline and Arbitration. Although no press or media council exists in Japan, NSK (Nihon Shinbun Kyokai — The Japan Newspaper Publishers and Editors Association) exercises self-regulatory functions of the following codes in connexion with newspaper editing, sale, and advertisements: The Canons of Journalism; Newspaper Sales Code; Newspaper Advertising Code of Ethics and Advertising Publication Standards. Developing countries like Ghana, Indonesia, India, Kenya, Nigeria, Egypt, Tunisia and others have press councils or similar bodies.

Press and media councils have been established in various ways. Frequently, the initiative for setting them up has come from the professionals or the media themselves, even if they have not always seemed very enthusiastic about the idea[1]. In some cases, their establishment has resulted from prompting or pressure, direct or indirect, on the part of the government or the legislature. For example, councils have been directly established by the government, as in Indonesia; by the government but with independent or non-governmental appointees as in Ghana; by an act of parliament with members approved by the government, as in India; by a bill with non-governmental members, as in Italy. Voluntary bodies have been created by the publishers and journalists, as in Austria and Sweden, by proprietors and journalists, as in the Federal Republic of Germany; by a foundation, with the support of media enterprises, corporations and individuals, as in the United States (the National News

---

consultation organized by the President of the Commission, it was concluded that, amongst the professionals themselves, no agreement exists as to the necessity or practicality of an international code of ethics. The statement that "it should at least be possible to reach agreement regarding practices from which the media should abstain" indicates the implicit acceptance of the necessity of an international code of ethics, and does not reflect the findings put before the Commission nor our support of the voluntary nature of the codes."

(1) A few years ago, the position at the time was summed up in an editorial in the United States magazine *The Editor and Publisher* which observed: "Newspaper editors and publishers will never stand in the way of organizing such councils, but very few will be prime movers in setting them up". The history of the early councils shows this to have been true. Recently, however, the defensive and supportive role of media councils has been more freely recognized by media people, and this has led to greater acceptance of the idea of such councils and steps being taken to create more.

Council); by proprietors, editors and journalists as in the UK; by newspapers as in Burma, before the council was dissolved; by the publishers as in Denmark; by newspapers, radio and television as in Finland; by journalists as in the Netherlands.

Press councils fall into three main categories: (i) councils which include government representatives or whose members are all government representatives and are presided by the minister; (ii) councils which are established jointly by newspaper publishers, owners and journalists, forming in most cases a single group publishers/owners, or journalists; (iii) councils on which the general public and the profession are both represented, in varying proportions.

The composition of such bodies therefore varies quite considerably. Representation of publishers, journalists and the public, in different proportions, is provided for in Australia, Quebec and Ontario, the United Kingdom, etc., whereas no lay representation is foreseen, for example, in Austria; the Press Council of India has both professional and lay members as well as members of parliament; in Italy, courts of honour are composed of a representative of the plaintiff chosen from the legal profession and a representative of the defendant chosen among persons nominated by the Council of The Order of Journalists.

It is widely felt that a press council, as well as being free from government control, should include representatives of the public as well as of media-owners and journalists. The British Press Council, criticized as ineffective in its early days when it consisted solely of members drawn from the press industry, began to win respect when it was joined by lay members. Media proprietors tend to raise objections to lay membership, which they regard as interference with their management prerogatives; and journalists wish to be assured that lay members are genuinely representative of public opinion, rather than of a conservative elite, and moreover have some understanding of professional problems. But these anxieties are not valid reasons for abandoning the idea of lay membership, which can be an instrument of the democratization of communication. To be sure, media-owners may be reluctant to cooperate for fear of having their privileges limited; and journalists may object to being judged by representatives of the public, whom they consider incompetent. However, that is no justification for shelving the idea.

The most important concern is that of a council's functions, field of action, competence in relation to particular media, its real or alleged aims, its interpretation of ethical rules, its overall conception of the role of the journalist in society, of freedom of information, of the responsibilities incumbent on journalists and the media, etc.[1]

Moreover, it must not be forgotten that, in addition to press councils and the work which they perform, there are channels open to individuals who feel themselves to have been unfairly treated by the press. Some people are satisfied with writing letters to the editor, selections of which are published by various newspapers, or with

---

(1) Just a few examples: As regards their competence, while most councils were established to deal only with the press, a few were set up also as representatives of radio and television, as for example, in Canada (Quebec), Finland and Ghana. The function of the Council in Indonesia is to advise the minister on press matters, such as licencing of newspapers, control of newsprint import, etc. On the other hand, the Quebec Council is entirely non governmental. It does not have any legal or statutory powers. Its only real authority is a moral one and it relies on the recognition and respect accorded it by both media and journalists and by public confidence, which in the final analysis gives it strength and influence and gives it recognition in practice as well as in theory. Third parties and the public may make complaints to bodies in Belgium, Denmark, Italy, Sweden, the UK, Iceland — where the council arbitrates disputes only between newspaper men and their publishers — or in Indonesia and Japan where no machinery exists in respect of the general public.

communiqués, frequently published in the form of paid advertisements, as such means make it possible to reach large audiences. Some countries have been inspired by the Scandinavian institution of the Ombudsman[1]. All these voluntary mechanisms, while not guaranteeing perfect objectivity — in any case unattainable — are, nevertheless, infinitely preferable to government intervention limiting the freedom to publish.

As regards "Letters to the Editor", newspapers are not able to publish all they receive. The main consideration is the basis on which the letters are selected. It goes without saying that this should be done without pressure from official authorities or outside interests; but this does not exclude the possibility of bias, and the public has an interest in knowing whether the selection is fair. On issues of major public concern, it is desirable for newspapers to publish statistics of letters received which indicate majority and minority attitudes.

Libel laws are another factor affecting press standards. The loss of a libel case by a newspaper or a broadcasting station is likely to be widely publicized, and even a settlement out of court involves the publication of a correction and apology. Excessively strict libel laws can be a restraint on press freedom; but fair libel laws constitute a protection for truth.

Other questions arise when the role and significance of press and media councils are examined. In particular, it may be felt that press councils are in danger of being dominated by the "press moghuls", when they accept to adhere, and be turned into a mere defensive tool. They are also liable, in some places, to become control mechanisms in the hands of the government. Also, it is maintained that good newspapers, media and journalists have no need of press councils, whereas those less concerned with standards will always remain unaffected by them; or that, in any event, given their usual composition and meagre resources, such councils can influence neither governments nor major vested interests. Others consider that, as a result of the establishment of press councils, the notion of social responsibility has been limited, and that more confidence should be placed in the cumulative effects of individual decisions rather than in institutional experiments, which in reality are seen as being little more than a cover for official interference.

Not only the press is covered by such bodies. Some media councils, including broadcast complaints boards, have been set up by statute and are charged with adjudicating on public complaints regarding broadcast distortion, misrepresentation, unfairness and unwarranted invasions of privacy. Sweden has a radio ombudsman. The Federal Communications Commission in the United States is also required to look into complaints under a so-called Fairness Doctrine requiring balanced presentation of controversial public issues and of opposing views on them. Other countries like Canada have introduced the practice of public hearings before granting broadcast renewal licences so that the public has an opportunity of debating whether or not it has been well served by a particular station or licensee.

While variations between press and media councils certainly exist, and while their role and functions are not interpreted everywhere in the same way, they would seem

---

(1) The ombudsman in Sweden, whose function was instituted in 1969, in order to deal with breaches of professional ethics, annually handles some 400 complaints brought against the press. In 1976, for instance he received 383 complaints, and since he can himself take the initiative, has initiated more than 20 on his own account and himself reprimanded some 30 publications. Newspapers are obliged to publish the verdict whenever it goes against them. The Ombudsman can also help to obtain a private settlement with the newspaper by securing its agreement to publish a disclaimer or to correct an erroneous account of the facts.

to have at least one common denominator. Where press or broadcast councils have been set up primarily on the initiative of the media themselves, the guiding principle has been that they shall form a self-disciplinary court of honour. This idea of self-control is based on a democratic principle: the rules of behaviour as laid down by the majority within the profession have to be respected by all of them.

It is precisely this idea of rules of behaviour elaborated jointly and voluntarily, which we consider worth adopting, and which prompts us to suggest setting up similar bodies or mechanisms in all countries, regardless of the form which they take or the name given to them. We are convinced that the widespread establishment of such bodies would foster the gradual elimination of news distortion and would encourage democratic participation, both essential keys to the future of communication.

3. Right of Reply and Right of Correction

The right of reply and the right of correction are recognized at the national level, in many countries and are often guaranteed by law. But they may equally well be exercised even when not encoded in a special law. However, it should be noted that there is a distinction between these two rights. In matters of opinion, although open debate is desirable in principle, it is not practicable to require the media to afford a reply to everyone who disagrees with a published article; the importance of the issue, the degree of public interest, and available space have to be taken into consideration. By contrast, inaccurate or untruthful statements of fact should always be corrected.

There is much variation in the implementation and scope of these rights. In certain countries, such as the United Kingdom and Sweden, the codes of professional conduct contain provisions governing the exercise of them, the application of which may, in certain cases, be supervised by the press councils. Other countries are opposed to embodying these rights in legislation, and rely on the media to afford redress voluntarily. In some countries, the right of reply is available to anyone, but the right of correction is the prerogative of the authorities.

In most countries, the right of reply or correction exists only in relation to the press. However, since experience (in Yugoslavia, the Federal Republic of Germany, France, Sweden and several other countries) has demonstrated that fears that these rights applied in broadcasting might be abused are unfounded, the trend is to foster the right of reply in the case of radio and television as well as in the press.

On this subject, in which much conclusive experience has been gained at the national level, one of the main problems is whether or not the institution of the right of reply and correction should, and can, be extended to the international level. Some people think that if this right were so extended and given to governments, they might be prompted to use it in order to refute criticisms that were perfectly justified. On these grounds, the institutionalization of the right of reply at the international level is for many not acceptable. Indeed, the institution of such a right would, it is felt, constitute a threat to the independence of editorial boards. Insofar as it may entail legislating on truth and objectivity, its establishment would serve no purpose, and should be discouraged. The very diversity of the systems adopted in this respect by countries which all the same have similar traditions, cultures and values indicates that it would be neither expedient nor realistic to propose the adoption of standard international regulations for this purpose.

In support of the introduction of an international right of reply or correction, others pointed out that there already exists an international convention in this field. It is true that the right of correction is regulated, but in a most unsatisfactory manner, with the result that States and entities concerned have no effective means of correcting false or distorted information about them. The Convention on the International Right of Correction which was adopted by the United Nations General Assembly in 1952 but which has still, more than 25 years later, been ratified only by a handful of countries, is considered to be an "academic and largely ineffective instrument"[1]. Such a situation may lead not to renouncement, but to the search for a better and more effective alternative solution at the international level. It is particularly maintained that, if a right to communicate is going to be adopted — whose incorporation in international law might suitably be studied — this right should cover not only the right to be informed but also its corollary, the right to inform, to supplement incomplete information, and to correct it when false.

In the unstable world in which we live, false news may create unrest, generate or intensify social conflicts, discourage or even divert investments, and destroy other countries' confidence in the country concerned. It is of course possible in certain cases to go to law, but the process is often such a lengthy one that, by the time the verdict is given, the harm has been done and can no longer be repaired. False or distorted news of a sensational kind can do considerable harm to different countries and various political and social forces.

Here again, then, the points of view and positions adopted are very remote from one another, and it would in our view be difficult — at least in a relatively short space of time — to reconcile them and thereby achieve the adoption of more effective international instruments. The above-mentioned Unesco Declaration, though not explicitly referring to either a right to reply or a right of correction does nevertheless contain a principle "that the points of view presented by those who consider that the information published or disseminated about them has seriously prejudiced their effort to strengthen peace and international understanding, to promote human rights or to counter racialism, apartheid and incitement to war be disseminated". This is certainly a minimum that should be acceptable to everyone.

---

(1) The Convention on the International Right of Correction, opened for signing on 31 March 1953, does indeed provide for such a right; in the event of a correction requested not being published, the State making the request may apply to the United Nations Secretary-General, who is required to give appropriate publicity through the information channels at his disposal to the communiqué transmitted to him. In actual practice, the system does not operate, and some governments wonder whether a more appropriate mechanism should not be devised or the text itself be reformulated and up-dated.

Part V

Communication Tomorrow

A. CONCLUSIONS AND RECOMMENDATIONS

The survey contained in this Report has recorded a dramatic expansion of communication resources and possibilities. It is an expansion that promises great opportunities, but also raises anxieties and uncertainties. Everything will depend on the use made of the new resources — that is, on crucial decisions, and on the question of who will make the decisions. Communication can be an instrument of power, a revolutionary weapon, a commercial product, or a means of education; it can serve the ends of either liberation or of oppression, of either the growth of the individual personality or of drilling human beings into uniformity. Each society must choose the best way to approach the task facing all of us and to find the means to overcome the material, social and political constraints that impede progress.

We have already considered many suggestions for further development. Without repeating them it might be useful to begin our recommendations by summarizing previous main conclusions:

1. Our review of communication the world over reveals a variety of solutions adopted in different countries — in accordance with diverse traditions, patterns of social, economic and cultural life, needs and possibilities. This diversity is valuable and should be respected; there is no place for the universal application of preconceived models. Yet it should be possible to establish, in broad outline, common aims and common values in the sphere of communication, based on common interests in a world of interdependence. The whole human race is threatened by the arms race and by the persistence of unacceptable global inequalities, both of which generate tensions and which jeopardize its future and even its survival. The contemporary situation demands a better, more just and more democratic social order, and the realization of fundamental human rights. These goals can be achieved only through understanding and tolerance, gained in large part by free, open and balanced communications.

2. The review has also shown that the utmost importance should be given to eliminating imbalances and disparities in communication and its structures, and particularly in information flows. Developing countries need to reduce their dependence, and claim a new, more just and more equitable order in the field of communication. This issue has been fully debated in various settings; the time has now come to move from principles to substantive reforms and concrete action.

3. Our conclusions are founded on the firm conviction that communication is a basic individual right, as well as a collective one required by all communities and nations. Freedom of information — and, more specifically the right to seek, receive and impart information — is a fundamental human right; indeed, a prerequisite for many others. The inherent nature of communication means that its fullest possible exercise and potential depend on the surrounding political, social and economic conditions, the most vital of these being democracy within countries and equal, democratic relations between them. It is in this context that the democratization of communication at national and international levels, as well as the larger role of communication in democratizing society, acquires utmost importance.

253

4. For these purposes, it is essential to develop comprehensive national communication policies linked to overall social, cultural and economic development objectives. Such policies should evolve from broad consultations with all sectors concerned and adequate mechanisms for wide participation of organized social groups in their definition and implementation. National governments as much as the international community should recognize the urgency of according communications higher priority in planning and funding. Every country should develop its communication patterns in accordance with its own conditions, needs and traditions, thus strengthening its integrity, independence and self-reliance.

5. The basic considerations which are developed at length in the body of our Report are intended to provide a framework for the development of a new information and communication order. We see its implementation as an on-going process of change in the nature of relations between and within nations in the field of communications. Imbalances in national information and communication systems are as disturbing and unacceptable as social, economic, cultural and technological, both national and international disparities. Indeed, rectification of the latter is inconceivable in any true or lasting sense without elimination of the former. Crucial decisions concerning communication development need to be taken urgently, at both national and international levels. These decisions are not merely the concern of professionals, researchers or scholars, nor can they be the sole prerogative of those holding political or economic power. The decision-making process has to involve social participation at all levels. This calls for new attitudes for overcoming stereotyped thinking and to promote more understanding of diversity and plurality, with full respect for the dignity and equality of peoples living in different conditions and acting in different ways.

Thus our call for reflection and action is addressed broadly to governments and international organizations, to policy-makers and planners, to the media and professional organizations, to researchers, communication practitioners, to organized social groups and the public at large.

I. Strengthening Independence and Self-reliance

Communication Policies

All individuals and people collectively have an inalienable right to a better life which, howsoever conceived, must ensure a social minimum, nationally and globally. This calls for the strengthening of capacities and the elimination of gross inequalities; such defects may threaten social harmony and even international peace. There must be a measured movement from disadvantage and dependance to self-reliance and the creation of more equal opportunities. Since communication is interwoven with every aspect of life, it is clearly of the utmost importance that the existing "communication gap" be rapidly narrowed and eventually eliminated.

We recommend:

1. Communication be no longer regarded merely as an incidental service and its development left to chance. Recognition of its potential warrants the formulation by all nations, and particularly developing countries, of comprehensive communication policies linked to overall social, cultural, economic and political goals. Such policies should be based on inter-ministerial and inter-disciplinary consultations with broad

public participation. The object must be to utilize the unique capacities of each form of communication, from interpersonal and traditional to the most modern, to make men and societies aware of their rights, harmonize unity in diversity, and foster the growth of individuals and communities within the wider frame of national development in an interdependent world.

2. As language embodies the cultural experience of people, all languages should be adequately developed to serve the complex and diverse requirements of modern communication. Developing nations and multilingual societies need to evolve language policies that promote all national languages even while selecting some, where necessary, for more widespread use in communication, higher education and administration. There is also need in certain situations for the adaptation, simplification, and standardization of scripts and development of keyboards, preparation of dictionaries and modernized systems of language learning, transcription of literature in widely-spoken national languages. The provision of simultaneous interpretation and automated translation facilities now under experimentation for cross-cultural communication to bridge linguistic divides should also be envisaged.

3. A primary policy objective should be to make elementary education available to all and to wipe out illiteracy, supplementing formal schooling systems with non-formal education and enrichment within appropriate structures of continuing and distance learning (through radio, television and correspondence).

4. Within the framework of national development policies, each country will have to work out its own set of priorities, bearing in mind that it will not be possible to move in all directions at the same time. But, as far as resources allow, communication policies should aim at stimulating and encouraging all means of communication.

Strengthening Capacities

Communication policies should offer a guide to the determination of information and media priorities and to the selection of appropriate technologies. This is required to plan the installation and development of adequate infrastructures to provide self-reliant communications capacity.

We recommend:

5. Developing countries take specific measures to establish or develop essential elements of their communication systems: print media, broadcasting and telecommunications along with the related training and production facilities.

6. Strong national news agencies are vital for improving each country's national and international reporting. Where viable, regional networks should be set up to increase news flows and serve all the major language groups in the area. Nationally, the agencies should buttress the growth of both urban and rural newspapers to serve as the core of a country's news collection and distribution system.

7. National book production should be encouraged and accompanied by the establishment of a distribution network for books, newspapers and periodicals. The stimulation of works by national authors in various languages should be promoted.

8. The development of comprehensive national radio networks, capable of reaching

remote areas should take priority over the development of television, which, however, should be encouraged where appropriate. Special attention should be given to areas where illiteracy is prevalent.

9. National capacity for producing broadcast materials is necessary to obviate dependence on external sources over and beyond desirable programme exchange. This capacity should include national or regional broadcasting, film and documentary production centres with a basic distribution network.

10. Adequate educational and training facilities are required to supply personnel for the media and production organizations, as well as managers, technicians and maintenance personnel. In this regard, co-operation between neighbouring countries and within regions should be encouraged.

Basic Needs

All nations have to make choices in investment priorities. In choosing between possible alternatives and often conflicting interests, developing countries, in particular, must give priority to satisfying their people's essential needs. Communication is not only a system of public information, but also an integral part of education and development.

We recommend:

11. The communication component in all development projects should receive adequate financing. So-called "development support communications" are essential for mobilizing initiatives and providing information required for action in all fields of development — agriculture, health and family planning, education, religion, industry and so on.

12. Essential communication needs to be met include the extension of basic postal services and telecommunication networks through small rural electronic exchanges.

13. The development of a community press in rural areas and small towns would not only provide print support for economic and social extension activities. This would also facilitate the production of functional literature for neo-literates as well.

14. Utilization of local radio, low-cost small format television and video systems and other appropriate technologies would facilitate production of programmes relevant to community development efforts, stimulate participation and provide opportunity for diversified cultural expression.

15. The educational and informational use of communication should be given equal priority with entertainment. At the same time, education systems should prepare young people for communication activities. Introduction of pupils at primary and secondary levels to the forms and uses of the means of communication (how to read newspapers, evaluate radio and television programmes, use elementary audio-visual techniques and apparatus) should permit the young to understand reality better and enrich their knowledge of current affairs and problems.

16. Organization of community listening and viewing groups could in certain circumstances widen both entertainment and educational opportunities. Education and information activities should be supported by different facilities ranging from

mobile book, tape and film libraries to programmed instruction through "schools of the air".

17. Such activities should be aggregated wherever possible in order to create vibrant local communication resource centres for entertainment, education, information dissemination and cultural exchange. They should be supported by decentralized media production centres; educational and extension services should be location-specific if they are to be credible and accepted.

18. It is not sufficient to urge that communication be given a high priority in national development; possible sources of investment finance must be identified. Among these could be differential communication pricing policies that would place larger burdens on more prosperous urban and elite groups; the taxing of commercial advertising may also be envisaged for this purpose.

Particular Challenges

We have focused on national efforts which must be made to lead to greater independence and self-reliance. But there are three major challenges to this goal that require concerted international action. Simply put, these are paper, tariff structures and the electro-magnetic spectrum.

We recommend:

19. A major international research and development effort to increase the supply of paper. The worldwide shortage of paper, including newsprint, and its escalating cost impose crushing burdens upon struggling newspapers, periodicals and the publication industry, above all in the developing countries. Certain ecological constraints have also emerged. Unesco, in collaboration with FAO, should take urgent measures to identify and encourage production of paper and newsprint either by recycling paper or from new sources of feedstock in addition to the wood pulp presently produced largely by certain northern countries. Kenaf, bagasse, tropical woods and grasses could possibly provide alternative sources. Initial experiments are encouraging and need to be supported and multiplied.

20. Tariffs for news transmission, telecommunications rates and air mail charges for the dissemination of news, transport of newspapers, periodicals, books and audiovisual materials are one of the main obstacles to a free and balanced flow of information. This situation must be corrected, especially in the case of developing countries, through a variety of national and international initiatives. Governments should in particular examine the policies and practices of their post and telegraph authorities. Profits or revenues should not be the primary aim of such agencies. They are instruments for policy-making and planned development in the field of information and culture. Their tariffs should be in line with larger national goals. International action is also necessary to alter telecommunication tariffs that militate heavily against small and peripheral users. Current international consultations on this question may be brought to early fruition, possibly at the October 1980 session of the 154-nation International Telegraph and Telephone Consultative Committee, which should have before it specific proposals made by a Unesco-sponsored working group on "Low Telecommunication Rates" (November 1979). Unesco might, in cooperation with ITU, also sponsor an overall study on international telecommunication services by means of satellite transmission in collaboration with

Intelsat, Intersputnik and user country representatives to make proposals for international and regional coordination of geostationary satellite development. The study should also include investigation of the possibility and practicalities of discounts for transmission of news and preferential rates for certain types of transmission to and from developing countries. Finally, developing countries should investigate the possibility of negotiating preferential tariffs on a bilateral or regional basis.

21. The electro-magnetic spectrum and geostationary orbit, both finite natural resources, should be more equitably shared as the common property of mankind. For that purpose, we welcome the decisions taken by the World Administrative Radio Conference (WARC), Geneva, September–November 1979, to convene a series of special conferences over the next few years on certain specific topics related to the utilization of these resources.

II. Social Consequences and New Tasks

Integrating Communication into Development

Development strategies should incorporate communication policies as an integral part in the diagnosis of needs and in the design and implementation of selected priorities. In this respect communication should be considered a major development resource, a vehicle to ensure real political participation in decision-making, a central information base for defining policy options, and an instrument for creating awareness of national priorities.

We recommend:

22. Promotion of dialogue for development as a central component of both communication and development policies. Implementation of national policies should be carried out through three complementary communication patterns: first, from decision-makers towards different social sectors to transmit information about what they regard as necessary changes in development actions, alternative strategies and the varying consequences of the different alternatives; second, among and between diverse social sectors in a horizontal information network to express and exchange views on their different demands, aspirations, objective needs and subjective motivations; third, between decision-makers and all social groups through permanent participatory mechanisms for two-way information flows to elaborate development goals and priorities and make decisions on utilization of resources. Each one of these patterns requires the design of specific information programmes, using different communication means.

23. In promoting communication policies, special attention should be given to the use of non-technical language and comprehensible symbols, images and forms to ensure popular understanding of development issues and goals. Similarly, development information supplied to the media should be adapted to prevailing news values and practices, which in turn should be encouraged to be more receptive to development needs and problems.

Facing the Technological Challenge

The technological explosion in communication has both great potential and great danger. The outcome depends on crucial decisions and on where and by whom they are taken. Thus, it is a priority to organize the decision-making process in a participatory manner on the basis of a full awareness of the social impact of different alternatives.

We recommend:

24. Devising policy instruments at the national level in order to evaluate the positive and negative social implications of the introduction of powerful new communication technologies. The preparation of technological impact surveys can be a useful tool to assess the consequences for life styles, relevance for under-privileged sectors of society, cultural influence, effects on employment patterns, and similar factors. This is particularly important when making choices with respect to the development of communication infrastructures.

25. Setting up national mechanisms to promote participation and discussion of social priorities in the acquisition or extension of new communication technologies. Decisions with respect to the orientation given to research and development should come under closer public scrutiny.

26. In developing countries the promotion of autonomous research and development should be linked to specific projects and programmes at the national, regional and inter-regional levels, which are often geared to the satisfaction of basic needs. More funds are necessary to stimulate and support adaptive technological research. This might also help these countries to avoid problems of obsolescence and problems arising from the non-availability of particular types of equipment, related spare parts and components from the advanced industrial nations.

27. The concentration of communications technology in a relatively few developed countries and transnational corporations has led to virtual monopoly situations in this field. To counteract these tendencies national and international measures are required, among them reform of exisiting patent laws and conventions, appropriate legislation and international agreements.

Strengthening Cultural Identity

Promoting conditions for the preservation of the cultural identity of every society is necessary to enable it to enjoy a harmonious and creative inter-relationship with other cultures. It is equally necessary to modify situations in many developed and developing countries which suffer from cultural dominance.

We recommend:

28. Establishment of national cultural policies, which should foster cultural identity and creativity, and involve the media in these tasks. Such policies should also contain guidelines for safeguarding national cultural development while promoting knowledge of other cultures. It is in relation to others that each culture enhances its own identity.[1]

29. Communication and cultural policies should ensure that creative artists and

---

(1) Comment by **Mr. S. MacBride:**"I wish to add that owing to the cultural importance of spiritual and religious values and also in order to restore moral values, policy guidelines should take into account religious beliefs and traditions."

various grass-roots groups can make their voices heard through the media. The innovative uses of film, television or radio by people of different cultures should be studied. Such experiments constitute a basis for continuing cultural dialogue, which could be furthered by agreements between countries and through international support.

30. Introduction of guidelines with respect to advertising content and the values and attitudes it fosters, in accordance with national standards and practices. Such guidelines should be consistent with national development policies and efforts to preserve cultural identity. Particular attention should be given to the impact on children and adolescents. In this connection, various mechanisms such as complaint boards or consumer review committees might be established to afford the public the possibility of reacting against advertising which they feel inappropriate.

Reducing the Commercialization of Communication

The social effects of the commercialization of the mass media are a major concern in policy formulation and decision-making by private and public bodies.

We recommend:

31. In expanding communication systems, preference should be given to non-commercial forms of mass communication. Promotion of such types of communication should be integrated with the traditions, culture, development objectives and socio-political system of each country. As in the field of education, public funds might be made available for this purpose.

32. While acknowledging the need of the media for revenues, ways and means should be considered to reduce the negative effects that the influence of market and commercial considerations have in the organization and content of national and international communication flows.[1]

33. That consideration be given to changing existing funding patterns of commercial mass media. In this connection, reviews could be made of the way in which the relative role of advertising volume and costs pricing policies, voluntary contributions, subsidies, taxes, financial incentives and supports could be modified to enhance the social function of mass media and improve their service to the community.

Access to Technical Information

The flow of technical information within nations and across national boundaries is a major resource for development. Access to such information, which countries need for technical decision-making at all levels, is as crucial as access to news sources. This type of information is generally not easily available and is most often concentrated in large techno-structures. Developed countries are not providing adequate information of this type to developing countries.

---

(1) Comment by **Mr. E. Abel:** "At no time has the commission seen evidence adduced in support of the notion that market and commercial considerations necessarily exert a negative effect upon communication flows. On the contrary, the commission has praised elsewhere in this report courageous investigative journalism of the sort that can be sustained only by independent media whose survival depends upon their acceptance in the marketplace, rather than the favors of political leaders. The commission also is aware that market mechanisms play an increasingly important role today even in so-called planned economies."

We recommend:

34. Developing countries should pay particular attention to: (a) the correlation between education, scientific and communication policies, because their practical application frequently overlaps; (b) the creation in each country of one or several centres for the collection and utilization of technical information and data, both from within the country and from abroad; (c) to secure the basic equipment necessary for essential data processing activities; (d) the development of skills and facilities for computer processing and analysis of data obtained from remote sensing.

35. Developed countries should foster exchanges of technical information on the principle that all countries have equal rights to full access to available information. It is increasingly necessary, in order to reduce inequalities in this field, to promote cooperative arrangements for collection, retrieval, processing and diffusion of technological information through various networks, regardless of geographical or institutional frontiers. UNISIST, which provides basic guidelines for voluntary cooperation among and between information systems and services, should further develop its activities.

36. Developing countries should adopt national informatics policies as a matter of priority. These should primarily relate to the establishment of decision-making centres (inter-departmental and inter-disciplinary) which would inter alia (a) assess technological alternatives; (b) centralize purchases; (c) encourage local production of software; (d) promote regional and sub-regional cooperation (in various fields, including education, health and consumer services).

37. At the international level, consideration should be given to action with respect to: (a) a systematic identification of existing organized data processing infrastructures in various specialized fields; (b) agreement on measures for effective multi-country participation in the programmes, planning and administration of existing or developing data infrastructures; (c) analysis of commercial and technical measures likely to improve the use of informatics by developing countries; (d) agreement on international priorities for research and development that is of interest to all countries in the field of informatics.

38. Transnational corporations should supply to the authorities of the countries in which they operate, upon request and on a regular basis as specified by local laws and regulations, all information required for legislative and administrative purposes relevant to their activities and specifically needed to assess the performance of such entities. They should also provide the public, trade unions and other interested sectors of the countries in which they operate with information needed to understand the global structure, activities and policies of the transnational corporation and their significance for the country concerned.

III. Professional Integrity and Standards

Responsibility of Journalists

For the journalist, freedom and responsibility are indivisible. Freedom without responsibility invites distortion and other abuses. But in the absence of freedom there can be no exercise of responsibility. The concept of freedom with responsibility necessarily includes a concern for professional ethics, demanding an equitable approach to events, situations or processes with due attention to their diverse aspects. This is not always the case today.

We recommend:

39. The importance of the journalist's mission in the contemporary world demands steps to enhance his standing in society. In many countries even today, journalists are not regarded as members of an acknowledged profession and they are treated accordingly. To overcome this situation, journalism needs to raise its standards and quality for recognition everywhere as a genuine profession.

40. To be treated as professionals, journalists require broad educational preparation and specific professional training. Programmes of instruction need to be developed not only for entry-level recruits, but also for experienced personnel who from time to time would benefit from special seminars and conferences designed to refresh and enrich their qualifications. Basically, programmes of instruction and training should be conducted on national and regional levels.

41. Such values as truthfulness, accuracy and respect for human rights are not universally applied at present. Higher professional standards and responsibility cannot be imposed by decree, nor do they depend solely on the goodwill of individual journalists, who are employed by institutions which can improve or handicap their professional performance. The self-respect of journalists, their integrity and inner drive to turn out work of high quality are of paramount importance. It is this level of professional dedication, making for responsibility, that should be fostered by news media and journalists' organizations. In this framework, a distinction may have to be drawn between media institutions, owners and managers on the one hand, and journalists on the other.

42. As in other professions, journalists and media organizations serve the public directly and the public, in turn, is entitled to hold them accountable for their actions. Among the mechanisms devised up to now in various countries for assuring accountability, the Commission sees merit in press or media councils, the institution of the press ombudsman and peer group criticism of the sort practised by journalism reviews in several countries. In addition, communities served by particular media can accomplish significant reforms through citizen action. Specific forms of community involvement in decision-making will vary, of course, from country to country. Public broadcasting stations, for example, can be governed by representative boards drawn from the community. Voluntary measures of this sort can do much to influence media performance. Nevertheless, it appears necessary to develop further effective ways by which the right to assess mass media performance can be exercised by the public.

43. Codes of professional ethics exist in all parts of the world, adopted voluntarily in many countries by professional groups. The adoption of codes of ethics at national and, in some cases, at the regional level is desirable, provided that such codes are prepared and adopted by the profession itself — without governmental interference.

Towards Improved International Reporting

The full and factual presentation of news about one country to others is a continuing problem. The reasons for this are manifold: principal among them are correspondents' working conditions, their skills and attitudes, varying conceptions of news and information values and government viewpoints. Remedies for the situation will require long-term, evolutionary action towards improving the exchange of news around the world.

We recommend:

44. All countries should take steps to assure admittance of foreign correspondents and facilitate their collection and transmission of news. Special obligations in this regard, undertaken by the signatories to the Final Act of the Helsinki conference, should be honoured and, indeed, liberally applied. Free access to news sources by journalists is an indispensable requirement for accurate, faithful and balanced reporting. This necessarily involves access to unofficial, as well as official sources of information, that is, access to the entire spectrum of opinion within any country.[1]

45. Conventional standards of news selection and reporting, and many accepted news values, need to be reassessed if readers and listeners around the world are to receive a more faithful and comprehensive account of events, movements and trends in both developing and developed countries. The inescapable need to interpret unfamiliar situations in terms that will be understood by a distant audience should not blind reporters or editors to the hazards of narrow ethnocentric thinking. The first step towards overcoming this bias is to acknowledge that it colours the thinking of virtually all human beings, journalists included, for the most part without deliberate intent. The act of selecting certain news items for publication, while rejecting others, produces in the minds of the audience a picture of the world that may well be incomplete or distorted. Higher professional standards are needed for journalists to be able to illuminate the diverse cultures and beliefs of the modern world, without their presuming to judge the ultimate validity of any foreign nation's experience and traditions.

46. To this end, reporters being assigned to foreign posts should have the benefit of language training and acquaintance with the history, institutions, politics, economics and cultural environment of the country or region in which they will be serving.

47. The press and broadcasters in the industrialized world should allot more space and time to reporting events in and background material about foreign countries in general and news from the developing world in particular. Also, the media in developed countries — especially the "gatekeepers", editors and producers of print and broadcasting media who select the news items to be published or broadcast — should become more familiar with the cultures and conditions in developing countries. Although the present imbalance in news flows calls for strengthening capacities in developing countries, the media of the industrialized countries have their contribution to make towards the correction of these inequalities.

48. To offset the negative effects of inaccurate or malicious reporting of international news, the right of reply and correction should be further considered. While these

---

(1) Comment by **Mr. S. Losev:** This paragraph doesn't correspond to the Helsinki Final Act (see section 2 — information, point (c)), contradicts the interests of developing nations, and therefore is completely unacceptable and I object against it being included. I suggest to replace this recommendation by the following text: "All countries should take appropriate measures to improve the conditions for foreign correspondants to carry out their professional activities in the host countries in accordance with the provisions of the Helsinki Final Act and with due respect to the national sovereignty and the national identity of the host country".

concepts are recognized in many countries, their nature and scope vary so widely that it would be neither expedient nor realistic to propose the adoption of any international regulations for their purpose. False or distorted news accounts can be harmful, but the voluntary publication of corrections or replies is preferable to international normative action. Since the manner in which the right of reply and correction as applied in different countries varies significantly, it is further suggested that: (a) the exercise of the international right of reply and correction be considered for application on a voluntary basis in each country according to its journalistic practices and national legal framework; (b) the United Nations, in consultation with all concerned bodies, explore the conditions under which this right could be perfected at the international level, taking into account the cumbersome operation of the 1952 Convention on the International Right of Correction; (c) media institutions with an international reach define on a voluntary basis internal standards for the exercise of this right and make them publicly available.

49. Intelligence services of many nations have at one time or other recruited journalists to commit espionage under cover of their professional duties. This practice must be condemned. It undermines the integrity of the profession and, in some circumstances, can expose other journalists to unjustified suspicion or physical threat. The Commission urges journalists and their employers to be on guard against possible attempts of this kind. We also urge governments to refrain from using journalists for purposes of espionage.

Protection of Journalists

Daily reports from around the world attest to dangers that journalists are subject to in the exercise of their profession: harassment, threats, imprisonment, physical violence, assassination. Continual vigilance is required to focus the world's attention on such assaults to human rights.

We recommend:

50. The professional independence and integrity of all those involved in the collection and dissemination of news, information and views to the public should be safeguarded. However, the Commission does not propose special privileges to protect journalists in the performance of their duties, although journalism is often a dangerous profession. Far from constituting a special category, journalists are citizens of their respective countries, entitled to the same range of human rights as other citizens. One exception is provided in the Additional Protocol to the Geneva Conventions of 12 August 1949, which applies only to journalists on perilous missions, such as in areas of armed conflict. To propose additional measures would invite the dangers entailed in a licensing system since it would require some body to stipulate who should be entitled to claim such protection. Journalists will be fully protected only when everyone's human rights are guaranteed.[1]

---

(1) Comment by **Mr. S MacBride:** "I consider this paragraph quite inadequate to deal with what is a serious position. Because of the importance of the role of journalists and others who provide or control the flow of news to the media, I urge that they should be granted a special status and protection. I also urge that provisions should be made to enable a journalist to appeal against a refusal of reasonable facilities. My views on these issues are embodied in a paper entitled *The Protection of Journalists* (CIC Document No. 90) which I submitted to the Commission; I refer in particular to paragraphs 1–17 and 35–53 of this paper."

51. That Unesco should convene a series of round tables at which journalists, media executives, researchers and jurists can periodically review problems related to the protection of journalists and propose additional appropriate measures to this end.[2]

IV. Democratization of Communication

Human Rights

Freedom of speech, of the press, of information and of assembly are vital for the realization of human rights. Extension of these communication freedoms to a broader individual and collective right to communicate is an evolving principle in the democratization process. Among the human rights to be emphasized are those of equality for women and between races. Defence of all human rights is one of the media's most vital tasks.

We recommend:

52. All those working in the mass media should contribute to the fulfilment of human rights, both individual and collective, in the spirit of the Unesco Declaration on the mass media and the Helsinki Final Act, and the International Bill of Human Rights. The contribution of the media in this regard is not only to foster these principles, but also to expose all infringements, wherever they occur, and to support those whose rights have been neglected or violated. Professional associations and public opinion should support journalists subject to pressure or who suffer adverse consequences from their dedication to the defence of human rights.

53. The media should contribute to promoting the just cause of peoples struggling for freedom and independence and their right to live in peace and equality without foreign interference. This is especially important for all oppressed peoples who, while struggling against colonialism, religious and racial discrimination, are deprived of opportunity to make their voices heard within their own countries.

54. Communication needs in a democratic society should be met by the extension of specific rights such as the right to be informed, the right to inform, the right to privacy, the right to participate in public communication — all elements of a new concept, the right to communicate. In developing what might be called a new era of social rights, we suggest all the implications of the right to communicate be further explored.

Removal of Obstacles

Communication, with its immense possibilities for influencing the minds and behaviour of people, can be a powerful means of promoting democratization of society and of widening public participation in the decision-making process. This depends on the structures and practices of the media and their management and to what extent they facilitate broader access and open the communication process to a free interchange of ideas, information and experience among equals, without dominance or discrimination.

---

(1) Comment by **Mr. S. MacBride:** "I urge that such a Round Table be convened annually for a period of five years; I refer to paragraphs 50–57 of my paper on *The Protection of Journalists* (CIC Document No. 90)."

We recommend:

55. All countries adopt measures to enlarge sources of information needed by citizens in their everyday life. A careful review of existing laws and regulations should be undertaken with the aim of reducing limitations, secrecy provisions and other constraints in information practices.

56. Censorship or arbitrary control of information should be abolished.[1] In areas where reasonable restrictions may be considered necessary, these should be provided for by law, subject to judicial review and in line with the principles enshrined in the United Nations Charter, the Universal Declaration of Human Rights and the International Covenants relating to human rights, and in other instruments adopted by the community of nations.[2]

57. Special attention should be devoted to obstacles and restrictions which derive from the concentration of media ownership, public or private, from commercial influences on the press and broadcasting, or from private or governmental advertising. The problem of financial conditions under which the media operate should be critically reviewed, and measures elaborated to strengthen editorial independence.

58. Effective legal measures should be designed to: (a) limit the process of concentration and monopolization; (b) circumscribe the action of transnationals by requiring them to comply with specific criteria and conditions defined by national legislation and development policies; (c) reverse trends to reduce the number of decision-makers at a time when the media's public is growing larger and the impact of communication is increasing; (d) reduce the influence of advertising upon editorial policy and broadcast programming; (e) seek and improve models which would ensure greater independence and autonomy of the media concerning their management and editorial policy, whether these media are under private, public or government ownership.[3]

Diversity and Choice

Diversity and choice in the content of communication are a pre-condition for democratic participation. Every individual and particular groups should be able to

---

(1) Comment by **Mr. S. Losev:** "This whole problem of censorship or arbitrary control of information is within the national legislation of each country and is to be solved within the national, legal framework taking in due consideration the national interests of each country."

(2) Comment by **Mr. S. MacBride:** "I also wish to draw attention to the provisions of Article 10 of the European Convention for the Protection of Human Rights which I consider as wholly inadequate. I urge that Articles 13 and 14 of the Inter-American Convention on Human Rights (1979) are much more comprehensive and effective than the equivalent provisions of the European Convention. The matter is discussed in paragraphs 26–29 of my paper on *The Protection of Journalists* (CIC Document No. 90)."

(3) Comment by **Mr. E. Abel:** "Regarding (a) and (c), anti-monopoly legislation, whether more or less effective, is relevant only in countries where a degree of competition can be said to exist. It is a travesty to speak of measures against concentration and monopolization in countries where the media are themselves established as state monopolies, or operate as an arm of the only authorized political party. (b) Transnational corporations are expected to comply with the laws of the countries in which they do business. (d) Where it can be shown to exist, the influence of advertisers upon editorial content or broadcast programming would warrant careful study. But a sweeping demand that such influence be reduced, without pausing to examine or attempting to measure that influence in particular circumstances, is a symptom of ideological prejudice."

form judgments on the basis of a full range of information and a variety of messages and opinions and have the opportunity to share these ideas with others. The development of decentralized and diversified media should provide larger opportunities for a real direct involvement of the people in communication processes.

We recommend:

59. The building of infrastructures and the adoption of particular technologies should be carefully matched to the need for more abundant information to a broader public from a plurality of sources.

60. Attention should be paid to the communication needs of women. They should be assured adequate access to communication means and that images of them and of their activities are not distorted by the media or in advertising.

61. The concerns of children and youth, national, ethnic, religious, linguistic minorities, people living in remote areas and the aged and handicapped also deserve particular consideration. They constitute large and sensitive segments of society and have special communication needs.

Integration and Participation

To be able to communicate in contemporary society, man must dispose of appropriate communication tools. New technologies offer him many devices for individualized information and entertainment, but often fail to provide appropriate tools for communication within his community or social or cultural group. Hence, alternative means of communication are often required.

We recommend:

62. Much more attention be devoted to use of the media in living and working environments. Instead of isolating men and women, the media should help integrate them into the community.

63. Readers, listeners and viewers have generally been treated as passive receivers of information. Those in charge of the media should encourage their audiences to play a more active role in communication by allocating more newspaper space, or broadcasting time, for the views of individual members of the public or organized social groups.

64. The creation of appropriate communication facilities at all levels, leading towards new forms of public involvement in the management of the media and new modalities for their funding.

65. Communication policy-makers should give far greater importance to devising ways whereby the management of the media could be democratized — while respecting national customs and characteristics — by associating the following categories: (a) journalists and professional communicators: (b) creative artists; (c) technicians; (d) media owners and managers; (e) representatives of the public. Such democratization of the media needs the full support and understanding of all those working in them, and this process should lead to their having a more active role in editorial policy and management.

V. Fostering International Cooperation

Partners for Development

Inequalities in communication facilities, which exist everywhere, are due to economic discrepancies or to political and economic design, still others to cultural imposition or neglect. But whatever the source or reason for them, gross inequalities should no longer be countenanced. The very notion of a new world information and communication order presupposes fostering international cooperation, which includes two main areas: international assistance and contributions towards international understanding. The international dimensions of communication are today of such importance that it has become crucial to develop cooperation on a world-wide scale. It is for the international community to take the appropriate steps to replace dependence, dominance and inequality by more fruitful and more open relations of inter-dependence and complementarity, based on mutual interest and the equal dignity of nations and peoples. Such cooperation requires a major international commitment to redress the present situation. This clear commitment is a need not only for developing countries but also for the international community as a whole. The tensions and disruptions that will come from lack of action are far greater than the problems posed by necessary changes.

We recommend:

66. The progressive implementation of national and international measures that will foster the setting up of a new world information and communication order. The proposals contained in this report can serve as a contribution to develop the varied actions necessary to move in that direction.

67. International cooperation for the development of communications be given equal priority with and within other sectors (e.g. health, agriculture, industry, science, education, etc.) as information is a basic resource for individual and collective advancement and for all-round development. This may be achieved by utilizing funds provided through bilateral governmental agreements and from international and regional organizations, which should plan a considerable increase in their allocations for communication, infrastructures, equipment and programme development. Care should be taken that assistance is compatible with developing countries' priorities. Consideration should also be given to provision of assistance on a programme rather than on a strict project basis.

68. The close relationship between the establishment of a new international economic order and the new world information and communication order should be carefully considered by the technical bodies dealing with these issues. Concrete plans of action linking both processes should be implemented within the United Nations system. The United Nations, in approving the international development strategy should consider the communications sector as an integral element of it and not merely as an instrument of public information.

Strengthening Collective Self-reliance

Developing countries have a primary responsibility for undertaking necessary changes to overcome their dependence in the field of communications. The actions needed begin at the national level, but must be complemented by forceful and decisive agreements at the bilateral, sub-regional, regional, and inter-regional levels.

Collective self-reliance is the cornerstone of a new world information and communication order.

We recommend:

69. The communication dimension should be incorporated into existing programmes and agreements for economic cooperation between developing countries.

70. Joint activities in the field of communication, which are under way between developing countries should be developed further in the light of the overall analysis and recommendations of this Report. In particular, attention should be given to cooperation among national news agencies, to the further development of the News Agencies Pool and broadcasting organizations of the non-aligned countries, as well as to the general exchange on a regular basis of radio, TV programmes and films.

71. With respect to cooperation in the field of technical information, the establishment of regional and sub-regional data banks and information processing centres and specialized documentation centres should be given a high priority. They should be conceived and organized, both in terms of software and management, according to the particular needs of cooperating countries. Choices of technology and selection of foreign enterprises should be made so as not to increase dependence in this field.

72. Mechanisms for sharing information of a non-strategic nature could be established particularly in economic matters. Arrangements of this nature could be of value in areas such as multilateral trade negotiations, dealings with transnational corporations and banks, economic forecasting, and medium- and long-term planning and other similar fields.

73. Particular efforts should be undertaken to ensure that news about other developing countries within or outside their region receive more attention and space in the media. Special projects could be developed to ensure a steady flow of attractive and interesting material inspired by news values which meet developing countries' information needs.

74. Measures to promote links and agreements between professional organizations and communication researchers of different countries should be fostered. It is necessary to develop networks of institutions and people working in the field of communication in order to share and exchange experiences and implement joint projects of common interest with concrete operational contents.

International Mechanisms

Cooperation for the development of communications is a global concern and therefore of importance to international organizations, where all Member states can fully debate the issues involved and decide upon multi-national action. Governments should therefore attentively review the structures and programmes of international agencies in the communications field and point to changes required to meet evolving needs.

We recommend:

75. The Member States of Unesco should increase their support to the Organization's programme in this area. Consideration should be given to organizing a distinct

communication sector, not simply in order to underline its importance, but to emphasize that its activities are inter-related with the other major components of Unesco's work — education, science and culture.[1] In its communications activities, Unesco should concentrate on priority areas. Among these are assistance to national policy formulation and planning, technical development, organizing professional meetings and exchanges, promotion and coordination of research, and elaboration of international norms.

76. Better coordination of the various communication activities within Unesco and those throughout the United Nations System. A thorough inventory and assessment of all communications development and related programmes of the various agencies should be undertaken as a basis for designing appropriate mechanisms to carry out the necessary consultation, cooperation and coordination.

77. It would be desirable for the United Nations family to be equipped with a more effective information system, including a broadcast capability of its own and possibly access to a satellite system. That would enable the United Nations to follow more closely world affairs and transmit its message more effectively to all the peoples of the earth. Although such a proposal would require heavy investment and raise some complex issues, a feasibility study should be undertaken so that a carefully designed project could be prepared for deliberation and decision.[2][3]

78. Consideration might be given to establishing within the framework of Unesco an International Centre for the Study and Planning of Information and Communication. Its main tasks would be to: (a) promote the development of national communication systems in developing countries and the balance and reciprocity in international information flows; (b) mobilize resources required for that purpose and manage the funds put at its disposal; and (c) assure coordination among parties interested in communication development and involved in various cooperation programmes and evaluate results of bilateral and multilateral activities in this field; (d) organize round tables, seminars, and conferences for the training of communication planners, researchers and journalists, particularly those specializing in international problems; and (e) keep under review communications technology transfers between developed and developing countries so that they are carried out in the most suitable conditions. The Centre may be guided by a tripartite coordinating council composed of representatives of developing and developed countries and of interested international organizations. We suggest Unesco should undertake further study of this proposal

---

(1) Comment by **Mr. M. Lubis:** "I strongly believe that the present set-up in Unesco (Sector of Culture and Communication) is adequate to deal with the problems of Communication."

(2) Comment by **Mr. M. Lubis:** "I am of the opinion that the present communication potential of the UN system has not been effectively and efficiently used and managed. And I cannot foresee for a long time to come that the UN system will be able to speak with one voice on the really relevant issues of the world, disarmament, peace, freedom, human rights. However, I support the suggestion about a feasibility study, contained in the same paragraph."

(3) Comment by **Mr. S. MacBride:** "I would point out that the phenomenal growth of international broadcasting highlights the absence of a UN International Broadcasting System. Some thirty countries broadcast a total of *12,000 hours* per week in one hundred different languages. I urge that the UN should establish a broadcasting system of its own that would broadcast 24 hours round the clock in not less than 30 different languages. See my paper on *The Protection of Journalists* (CIC Document No. 90, paragraph 46) and the paper on *International Broadcasting* (CIC Document No. 60)."

for consideration at the 1980 session of the General Conference.[1]

Towards International Understanding

The strengthening of peace, international security and cooperation and the lessening of international tensions are the common concern of all nations. The mass media can make a substantial contribution towards achieving these goals. The special session of the United Nations General Assembly on disarmament called for increased efforts by the mass media to mobilize public opinion in favour of disarmament and of ending the arms race. This Declaration together with the Unesco Declaration on fundamental principles concerning the contribution of the mass media to strengthening peace and international understanding, to the promotion of human rights and to countering racialism, apartheid and incitement to war should be the foundation of new communication policies to foster international understanding. A new world information and communication order requires and must become the instrument for peaceful cooperation between nations.

We recommend:

79. National communication policies should be consistent with adopted international communication principles and should seek to create a climate of mutual understanding and peaceful coexistence among nations. Countries should also encourage their broadcast and other means of international communication to make the fullest contribution towards peace and international cooperation and to refrain from advocating national, racial or religious hatred, and incitement to discrimination, hostility, violence or war.

80. Due attention should be paid to the problems of peace and disarmament, human rights, development and the creation of a new communication order. Mass media both printed and audiovisual, should be encouraged to publicise significant documents of the United Nations, of Unesco, of the world peace movements, and of various other international and national organizations devoted to peace and disarmament. The curricula of schools of journalism should include study of these international problems and the views expressed on them within the United Nations.

---

(1) Comment by **Ms. B. Zimmerman:** "Although I agree that a coordinating body in the field of communication development could serve a useful purpose, I cannot support this precise recommendation. All members of the Commission did not have the opportunity to discuss thoroughly the advantages and disadvantages of various objectives and structures for such a coordinating body. As a Unesco Intergovernmental Conference is to be held in 1980 to cover that topic, I feel the Commission should welcome the careful study that the Unesco Conference is in a position to give the matter, rather than offering any recommendation at this time."

Comment by **Mr. E. Abel:** "This proposal is premature, unnecessary and unwise. The design of an appropriate mechanism for promoting and coordinating communications development demands more time and resources than this Commission possesses. Essentially the same proposal here advanced was one of two submitted to a Unesco experts meeting in November; neither one was endorsed. The question is on the agenda for an intergovernmental meeting at Unesco in April. The UN General Assembly has now taken a strong interest in the matter and has requested the Secretary-General to intervene. As it stands, this proposal can only deter the necessary cooperation of both the competent UN bodies and the developed nations whose cooperation is indispensable to further progress."

Comment by **Mr. S. MacBride:** "I suggest that if any steps are taken in this direction prior consultation and accord should be reached with journalists' organizations and other NGOs involved in the mass media."

81. All forms of co-operation among the media, the professionals and their associations, which contribute to the better knowledge of other nations and cultures, should be encouraged and promoted.

82. Reporting on international events or developments in individual countries in situations of crisis and tension requires extreme care and responsibility. In such situations the media often constitute one of the few, if not the sole, link between combatants or hostile groups. This clearly casts on them a special role which they should seek to discharge with objectivity and sensitivity.

□   □   □

The recommendations and suggestions contained in our Report do not presume to cover all topics and issues calling for reflection and action. Nevertheless, they indicate the importance and scale of the tasks which face every country in the field of information and communication, as well as their international dimensions which pose a formidable challenge to the community of nations.

Our study indicates clearly the direction in which the world must move to attain a new information and communication order — essentially a series of new relationships arising from the advances promised by new communication technologies which should enable all peoples to benefit. The awareness already created on certain issues, such as global imbalances in information flows, suggests that a process of change has resulted and is under way. The power and promise of ever-new communication technologies and systems are, however, such as to demand deliberate measures to ensure that existing communication disparities do not widen. The objective should be to ensure that men and women are enabled to lead richer and more satisfying lives.

B. ISSUES REQUIRING FURTHER STUDY

We have suggested some actions which may help lead towards a new world information and communication order. Some of them are for immediate undertaking; others will take more time to prepare and implement. The important thing is to start moving towards a change in the present situation.

However, there are other issues that require examination, but the International Commission lacked time or sufficient data or expertise to deal with them. The proposals listed below have not been approved by the Commission; several were not, in fact, even discussed. Members felt free, nevertheless, to submit individual or group proposals which, in their judgment, called for study in the future. While these suggestions have not been endorsed by the Commission, they may still indicate some preliminary ideas about issues to be pursued, if and when they arouse interest.

I. Increased Interdependence

1. Studies are necessary to define more precisely the inter-dependence of interests of rich and poor countries, as well as of countries belonging to different socio-political systems. Research undertaken to date has not adequately explored this community of interests; more substantial findings are desirable as background for eventual future measures leading to wider cooperation. Similar studies are necessary to prepare more diversified cooperative efforts among developing countries themselves.

2. For the same purpose, indicators should be worked out to facilitate comparison of the results obtained through various media in different countries.

3. As international cooperation depends on mutual understanding, language barriers are a continuing problem. There is a certain imbalance in the use of international languages and studies might be undertaken with a view to improving the situation.

II. Improved Coordination

4. A new information and communication order cannot be developed on the basis of sporadic projects and initiatives, and without a solid research base. Feasibility studies are needed to ensure better coordination of activities in many fields, particularly at an initial stage, involving (a) news collection and supply; (b) data banks; (c) broadcast programme banks for exchange purposes; (d) exchange of data gathered by remote sensing.

III. International Standards and Instruments

5. The texts of international instruments (of the League of Nations, the United Nations and UN Agencies, intergovernmental organizations, etc.) as well as draft texts which have long run up against political barriers should be reviewed in order to promote further international legislation in this area, since only by extending its scope will it be possible to overcome certain difficulties and to regulate certain aspects of

the new world communication order.

6. Studies should be undertaken to identify, if possible, principles generally recognised by the profession of journalism and which take into account the public interest. This could also encompass further consideration, by journalists' organizations themselves, of the concept of an international code of ethics. Some fundamental elements for this code might be found in the Unesco Declaration on the mass media, as well as in provisions common to the majority of existing national and regional codes.

7. Studies should be undertaken on the social, economic and cultural effects of advertising to identify problems, and to suggest solutions, at the national and international levels, possibly including study of the practicability of an international advertising code, which could have as its basis the preservation of cultural identity and protection of moral values.

IV. Collection and Dissemination of News

8. The scope of the round tables, mentioned in Recommendation 51 above, could be enlarged, after appropriate studies, to include other major problems related to the collection and dissemination of international news, particularly professional, ethical and juridical aspects.

V. Protection of Journalists

9. Further studies should be made for the safeguarding of journalists in the exercise of their profession. The possibility might be explored for setting up some mechanism whereby when a journalist is either refused or deprived of his identity card he would have a right of appeal to a professional body, ideally with adequate judicial authority to rectify the position. Such studies should also look into the possibility of the creation of an international body to which a further appeal could be made in the final resort.

VI. Greater Attention to Neglected Areas

10. The concentration of the media in the developed regions, and the control of or access to them enjoyed by the affluent categories of the population, should be corrected by giving particular attention to the needs of the less developed countries and those of rural areas. Studies should be undertaken to evaluate these needs, to determine priorities and to measure the likely rate of return of future investments. Consideration might be given for example to (a) the feasibility of generalizing sound and television broadcasting and expanding telephone networks in rural areas; (b) the efficacy of possible government measures to expand distribution of receiving sets (e.g. through special facilities, tax exemptions, low-interest loans, subsidies, etc.) and (c) technological possibilities and innovations (e.g. the production of high-power generators for areas without electricity, etc.).

VII. More Extensive Financial Resources

11. The scarcity of available resources for communication development, both at national and international levels, highlights the need for further studies in three

different areas: (a) identification of country priorities for national and international financing; (b) evaluation of the cost-effectiveness of existing investments; (c) the search for new financial resources.

12. As far as new resources are concerned, several possibilities might be explored: (a) marshalling of resources deriving from surplus profits on raw materials; (b) establishment of an international duty[1] on the use of the electromagnetic spectrum and geostationary orbit space for the benefit of developing countries; (c) levying of an international duty[2] on the profits of transnational corporations producing transmission facilities and equipment for the benefit of developing countries and for the partial financing of the cost of using international communication facilities (cable, telecommunications networks, satellites, etc.).

Responding to its wide mandate, the Commission has sought to identify major problems and trends and has recommended certain lines of action. Apart from recommendations coming from the Commission as a whole, some of its members made additional suggestions, considering that the interest for new issues will continue to grow.

It is important to realise that the new order we seek is not only a goal but a stage in a journey. It is a continuing quest for ever more free, more equal, more just relations within all societies and among all nations and peoples. This Report represents what we believe we have learned. And this, above all, is what we wish to communicate.

(1) Comment by **Mr. S. Losev:** "The idea of an international tax for whatever good reasons or causes does not seem just or justifiable to me."

(2) Comment by **Mr. S. MacBride** and **Ms. B. Zimmerman:** "The examples cited, particularly those proposing international duties, seem to have been insufficiently considered in terms of their validity or practicability in the international sphere, and indicate the need for further careful study in this area."

Appendices

General Comments

Mr. Sergei Losev

While I joined the consensus of the Commission in signing the Final Report, I would like to add to it my comments and reservations in addition to those I made on several concrete points in Parts II, III, IV and especially V.

In evaluating the Report presented by the Commission, I must say that, while in general terms the Report gives a wide and broad perspective on the development of mass media and journalism in the world today, it has its definite shortcomings and failures, which are certainly due to the great and difficult task which we all had to face.

1. The term "communication" was not properly defined and this tended to mar our Report terminologically. Communication and information, communication and mass media are often mixed up.

2. It is especially regretful that due to this too wide a definition of the term "communication" the problems of information were not adequately dealt with. In many cases still one should read "information" when it is written "communication". And it would be incorrect to translate the word "communication" into Russian otherwise than "information" in too many cases.

3. The position of developing countries has been eroded. This is especially true of the problem of sovereignty of the developing countries in the field of information and culture; the very notion of cultural invasion was not given a proper place in the Report, as was underplayed the role of Western mass culture in damaging national cultures of developing countries.

4. The recommendations are sometimes too concrete to be followed everywhere.

5. The achievements and experiences of socialist and developing countries in setting up their national systems of mass communication and of achieving self-reliance in this field were not taken into consideration by the Commission. The practical experiences of Bulgaria and Poland, of Tanzania and India, of Uzbekistan and Armenia, of Azerbaijan and Georgia, of Turkmenia and Kirghizia, of Yakutiya and Tajikistan are not in the Report and this is certainly our failure to grasp the knowhow of achieving self-reliance in this very crucial field of mass media.

6. As a result, the Final Report is a little bit too westernized in its terminology and its approaches.

7. It's unfortunate that sometimes we are catching up already old-fashioned and used trite formulas such as the notion of a free flow of information.

8. The right to communicate is too widely discussed, though this right hasn't gained any international recognition, just as it hasn't gained recognition nationally in any of the countries represented in the Commission. At the same time, the problem of developing international law in the field of information and of information exchange was not adequately dealt with.

9. As a result, the very notion of the New International Information Order has been eroded in the process of compiling the Report, whereas we all should make still more efforts to establish and develop this New International Information Order which is so needed by the world today for developing better international relations, for improving international understanding and for strengthening the national independence and sovereignty of all the countries in the world.

10. We could have a real and definitive discussion only on Part V of the Final Report. Insofar as Parts I, II, III and IV are concerned, we had actually only first readings of the texts and this certainly prevented us from a thorough discussion of each point in these parts.

Finally, I should stress once again the importance of this Report and especially its contribution towards peace and international understanding, and the due attention which has been given in it to the Helsinki Final Act.

Mr. Mustapha Masmoudi

1. I think that the reflection and work of the Commission has on the whole permitted a definition of the concept of a New World Information Order and to bring out its guiding principles, to open broad perspectives for communication and for developing the means of information in the world and to indicate within the framework of a continuing process actions which may serve as a basis for realizing this new order.

2. Nevertheless, I would have wished that the Commission had further advanced its reflection by proposing to the Director-General the text for a declaration and draft charter which might have served as a point of departure for the discussion of this important matter at the next session of Unesco's General Conference in conformity with the spirit of the resolution adopted by the 20th session of the General Conference on the role of the International Commission for the Study of Communication Problems and of the resolution on communication adopted at the 34th session of the United Nations General Assembly.

3. It also seems to me that the text of the International Convention on the Right of Correction, which was drawn up before the emergence of satellites and other vast communication means and is therefore a minimum in this regard, should have been amended and submitted for adoption and ratification by Member States and not merely taken into consideration "for voluntary application in each country in line with customary journalistic practices and national

juridical structures." The least that can be done while awaiting further action is to invite all those concerned by that convention to respect it.

4. As concerns protection problems in the field of information, it is advisable to consider, besides the protection of journalists, also that of the user (whether an individual, group, collectivity, people or nation) and, therefore, give to different users the possibility to avail themselves of varying means of protection in cases of infraction of the deontological code.

5. Finally, an observation on linguistic problems so closely linked to social and international communications. As we know, international cooperation is based essentially on mutual understanding and the exchange of scientific thought is more than ever made through the new means of communication. Now, linguistic barriers constitute a permanent obstacle to these indispendable factors for peace and progress and the imbalance between languages used on a broad international scale grows incessantly. Consequently, it is advisable to invite the international institutions concerned to give attention to the question of international languages and study adequate solutions to obviate this situation and look for new scientific communication instruments capable of disseminating and storing in the most economical way the largest amount of information.

6. Concerning the title of the Report, I would

have preferred the following: "For a New World Information and Communication Order" because it reflects the major objective of the text.

These are some of the more or less general remarks that I wish to draw to the attention of readers of our Final Report.

Mr. Gabriel Garcia Marquez and Mr. Juan Somavia

With respect to the manner in which certain issues have been presented we would like to make the following specific comments:

1. The relevance given to the issue of democratization is of the highest significance. More democratic communication structures are a national and international need of peoples everywhere promoting access, participation, decentralization, open management, and the diffusion of the power, concentrated in the hands of commercial or bureaucratic interests, is a worldwide necessity. This is particularly crucial in third world countries dominated by repressive minority regimes.

2. Communications is not just news. It is a determining factor of all social processes and a fundamental component of the way societies are organized. This approach taken by the report permits a more ample and balanced understanding of the problems involved and gives individual issues a more global perspective. This will allow the international debate on communications to be set in its proper overall political, economic and cultural context.

3. There is a tendency in different parts of the report to "glorify" technological solutions to contemporary communication problems. We want to emphasize that the "technological promise" is neither neutral nor value-free. Decisions in this field have enormous political and social implications. Each society has to develop the necessary instruments to make an evaluation of alternative choices and their impact.

4. The insistence on the need to develop communication infrastructures in third world countries is correct and necessary, but it should not be overstated. It is not possible to solve contemporary communication problems through money and training alone. The idea of a "Marshall Plan" for the development of third world communications is inappropriate and will tend to reproduce western values and transnational interests in third world societies. Actions in this field should be carefully selected so as not to reinforce minority power structures within third world countries or serve as a vehicle for cultural domination.

5. Insufficient acknowledgement is made in general of the importance research has had in making communications an issue of contemporary debate and in underpinning a number of the commission's statements. In particular, the chapter on research could have highlighted more strongly the basic importance that serious professional research will continue to have in promoting understanding of all these issues and clarifying the underlying structural phenomena.

6. The work of the commission has been a worthwhile effort to reach a certain level of consensus among participants with divergent viewpoints in the context of a United Nations body. The report is not always organic in the development of the different topics it touches upon, lacking on occasion a fully systematic and coherent style. As such, it is more a negotiated document than an academic presentation. This fact enhances its practical and political value to the extent that it reflects certain areas of common understanding upon which it may be possible to develop concrete policies and action by many social factors in different national and international settings.

Appendix 2
Notes

Definitions

Definitions of several general notions dealt with in this Report — more particularly, those of communication and information — have not been standardized nor is there a unanimity as to their meanings. In fact, the terms are used by different authors in a variety of ways, with many nuances regarding their components and significance. Nevertheless, information is often basically considered to be the signs or coded messages transmitted in one direction from a source to a receiver, while communication corresponds more to the complexity of the phenomenon of various interchanges, through signs and symbols, between individuals or communities.

Many definitions could be quoted for communication; the following may illustrate the trend towards using the term in relation to the two-way human exhanges. "Communication is . . . the broad field of human interchange of facts and opinions" (Redfield). "Communication is . . . the form of interaction which takes place through symbols. The symbols may be gestural, pictural, plastic, verbal, or any other which operate as stimuli to behaviour which would not be evoked by the symbol itself in the absence of special conditions of the person

who responds" (Lundberg). "Communication . . . encompasses all forms of expression which serve the purpose of mutual understanding" (Revesz). "Our basic purpose is to alter the original relationship between our own organism and the environment in which we find ourselves. More specifically, our basic purpose is to reduce the probability that we are solely a target of external forces, and increase the probability that we exert forces ourselves. Our basic purpose in communication is to become an affecting agent, to affect others, our physical 'environment', and ourselves, to become a determining agent, to have a vote in how things are. In short, we communicate to influence — to affect with intent." (Berlo).

It must be said that in a part of the literature, the two terms information and communication are often confused or used indiscriminately. In the preceding Report, the terms have been used as consistently as possible to refer to two different phenomena: communication as the "process" of exchanging news, facts, opinions, messages between individuals and people; information as the "product", i.e. news, data, and various other content and outputs of media, cultural activities or industries.

Some Schemes or Models
for the Study of
Communication

In the section of the Final Report concerning the functions of communication, reference is made to different theories and the significance of different components of the communication process. Without intending to elaborate conceptual models, in a text which has no pretentions to be purely scientific, it is perhaps not irrelevant to mention here in a marginal note, a few of these models in order to indicate the possible correlation between preoccupations of researchers and orientations of bodies such as the International Commission.

The models presented here belong to varying categories depending on the scientific inspiration of their authors. Thus, they are complementary and not mutually exclusive.

I. The model derived from the concept of the discrete communication system

This model was first designed in 1947, but was given its definitive formulation in 1949 by Claude E. Shannon and Warren Weaver. As the diagram below indicates, this communication model comprises four elements: a source of information, with a greater or lesser number of messages to communicate; a transmitter or sender with the capacity to transform a message into a signal; a receiver which decodes the signal in order to retrieve the initial message; and, finally, the destination, a person (or thing) for whom the message is intended.

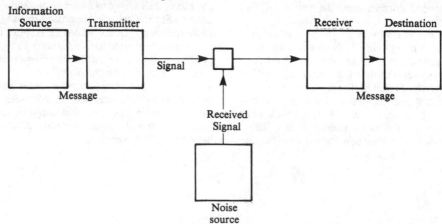

SCHEMATIC DIAGRAM OF A GENERAL COMMUNICATION SYSTEM.*

*Source: The Mathematical Theory of Communication, C. Shannon and W. Weaver, University of Illinois Press, 1949.

284

II. Models derived
from psycho-sociological inspiration

It was Harold Lasswell who first precisely delineated the various elements which constitute a "communication fact". According to him, one cannot suitably describe a "communication action" without answering the following questions: who said what, by what channel, to whom and with what effect?

Identification of transmitters, analysis of message content, study of transmission channels, audience identification and evaluation of effects; these are the five parameters of communications studies. Michael Bühler represents the Lasswell model with this diagram:

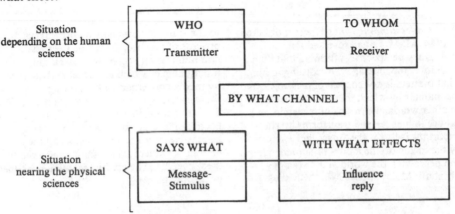

Based on the findings of diverse studies carried out during electoral campaigns (notably that opposing Roosevelt and Wilkie in 1940), Elihu Katz and Paul Lazarsfeld in 1955 elaborated a concept known as the two-step theory of communication. According to them media messages first reached persons more involved and more influential than others; then, opinion leaders retransmitted

and amplified the received information within the framework of small group, face-to-face relations.

Later observations showed that the opinion leaders did not always constitute such a simple relay between the media and the public at large; influence networks are complex and varied. Here is how Bühler represents the Katz-Lazarsfeld theory:

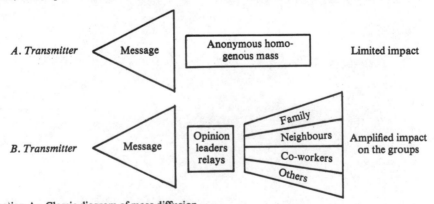

Situation A: Classic diagram of mass diffusion
Situation B: Model of the modifications made in the message by opinion relays. These changes comprise, on the one hand, sifting of the message and, on the other, amplification of the news retained.

In another view, John W. and Matilda Riley adopt an intentionally sociological perspective: they put the accent on the diverse influences which prevail upon the "communicator", the message sender, as well as on its receiver, each of them immerged in primary groups (family, working environment, etc.), themselves integral parts of a broader social structure. Therefore, "in such an all-encompassing system, the mass communication process appears . . . as a component of a wider social process, which affects it and is in turn affected by it."

III. Models with a cultural or anthropological inspiration

With *Understanding Mass Media*, published in 1964, M. McLuhan reversed the customary perspective, affirming that "the medium is the message". According to him, what matters is not content of messages, but the manner by which these are transmitted. In other words, the means of transmitting a culture influences and transforms it. The important factor is the "massage" exercized by the media on the modes of apprehending and perceiving the world and its realities. Abraham Moles applies cybernetic diagrams to the study of communication; and the process of cultural, artistic or scientific communication is presented as circuit, functioning of which is permanently assured by media concerned with renewing themselves. According to him, there is a double socio-cultural cycle: one is long, because it is relayed from the creators to society by micro-environments and the media; the other is short for it goes directly from events to society by the unique channel of the media.

IV. "Institutional" approaches inspired by the political sciences

The "general communication model" proposed by George Gerbner in 1958 led him to define the different roles of the "communicator" and to identify the diverse sources which had influence on him. These he divides into two categories: first "internal" powers, second, "external" powers.

The table opposite illustrates this conception:

Power roles within the media	Characteristic Power sources	Characteristic Functions
1. Clients	Availability of funds for investments and subsidies	Specify conditions for allocation of capital, for diverse facilities, for operational credits
2. Superiors	Authority	Formulate programmes and supervise their execution
3. Colleagues	Solidarity	Establish norms; self-dcfcnce
4. Competitors	Scarcity	Establish norms; oversight
5. Auxiliaries	Services	Supply, distribute
outside the media		
6. Authorities	Legislation and application of laws	Regulate social order, including communications
7. Organizations	Outlets to authorities, private interests and the public for support and protection	Solicit favorable attention
8. Experts	Specialized knowledge	Give consultations, lend talents, establish norms
9. Members of public	Reception of messages	Validate the media to their audience

In his *Communication: A Plea for a New Approach* (CIC Document No. 40, 1979), Francis Balle departs from an assumption in the form of a double inequality. Communication is more than simply techniques labelled media. But it is less than the totality of social exchanges. This dual inequality invites the researcher to bring to light the multiple relationships of influences, complementarities, exclusions or reciprocal substitutions between different means of social exchange, as well as inviting concentration on different means of social communication: interpersonal, institutional (between institutions, between governments and the governed, etc.) and through the media.

It is this last approach which seems closest to the "global approach" suggested and adopted by the International Commission throughout its Report.

International Satellite
Systems

Intelsat

The Intelsat global satellite system is made up of two elements: the space segment, consisting of satellites owned by Intelsat; and the ground segment, consisting of the earth stations owned by telecommunications entities in the countries in which they are located.

At 31 March 1979, the space segment consisted of 12 satellites in synchronous orbit at an altitude of approximately 35,780 km (22,240 miles). Global service was being provided through a combination of Intelsat IV and IV–A satellites over the Atlantic and Indian Ocean regions and Intelsat IV satellites over the Pacific Ocean region.

Each Intelsat IV–A has a nominal capacity of 6,000 voice circuits and two television channels, while the Intelsat IVs have a nominal capacity of 4,000 voice circuits plus two television channels each.

The ground segment of the global system for international service consisted of 249 communications antennas at 203 earth stations sites in 97 countries. The combined system of satellites and earth stations was providing over 670 earth station-to-earth station communications pathways.

In addition to the international voice circuits in full-time use (more than 12,000) Intelsat satellites were also providing facilities for a wide variety of telecommunications services including data transmission and television, to more than 130 countries, territories and possessions.

As of March 1979, Intelsat was providing satellite capacity for national domestic services in 15 countries (Algeria, Brazil, Chile, Colombia, France, Malaysia, Nigeria, Norway, Oman, Peru, Saudi Arabia, Spain, Sudan, Uganda and Zaire). Other countries which will soon be initiating or which are actively considering the use of Intelsat satellites for their domestic services include Denmark, Egypt, India and Iraq.

The Intelsat V era is scheduled to begin in 1980 with the launching of the first in this new series of advanced communications satellites.

Each Intelsat V will have a nominal capacity of 12,000 simultaneous two-way telephone circuits, plus two television channels.

In part, the additional capacity has been achieved by increased employment of frequency reuse techniques, as well as the use of a new frequency band. For instance, the 6/4 GHz frequency band is used four times, twice through geographic isolation by means of east and west hemispherical beams and twice through dual polarization, and the new 14/11 GHz band is used twice, through physically separated east and west spot beams.

It is anticipated that the capacity of the Intelsat V series will be able to cope with the growing demand for international satellite communications facilities until well into the 1980s.

(Source: *Intelsat Report,* 1979)

Intersputnik

The international space communication system and organization "Intersputnik" was set up in 1971 on an initiative of socialist countries — Bulgaria, Hungary, the GDR, the Republic of Cuba, Mongolia, Poland, Rumania, the Soviet Union, and Czechoslovakia — to ensure requirements for telephone and telegraph communication, exchanges of radio and telegraph communication, exchanges of radio and television programmes as well as for the transmission of other types of information via the earth's artificial satellites. The Government of the Socialist Republic of Vietnam acceded to the agreement in 1979.

The agreement on the "Intersputnik" is based on the universality principle which was determined by the resolutions of the UN General Assembly and the Treaty of January 27, 1967 on the Principles Governing the Activities of States in Exploration and Use of Outer Space, which point out that outer space is open to exploration and use by all the States without any discrimination whatsoever.

Cooperation is maintained on the basis of respect for the sovereignty and independence of States, equality and non-interference in internal affairs as well as on the basis of mutual assistance and mutual advantage.

The "Intersputnik" is an open international organization. The Government of any State which will declare accession to the agreement may become its member.

The agreement does not limit the sovereign rights of countries to participation in other international space communication organizations and gives an opportunity to use the communication channels of the "Intersputnik" system for non-member countries on a par with the "Intersputnik" members.

In its activities, the "Intersputnik" seeks to broaden and deepen cooperation in the field of space communication with other international organizations.

The "Intersputnik" communication systems includes a space complex, consisting of communications satellites with control systems and earth-based systems which maintain mutual contact via the communications satellites.

The space complex is the property of the organization or is leased from its members. Earth-based stations are the property of the States that built them or of the recognized organizations that operate them.

The first earth-based stations for operation in the "Intersputnik" system to begin international exchange of information in 1973 were built in the Soviet Union and the Republic of Cuba. Earlier, in 1967, an earth-based station in Mongolia was brought into operation, but its function was only to receive Soviet television programmes telecast in the USSR to the national network of orbital stations. In subsequent years, earth-based stations have been built in Czechoslovakia and Poland (1974), the GDR (1975), Hungary and Bulgaria (1976), and in Algeria (1979). Earth-based stations are under construction in Vietnam, Laos and Afghanistan (1980). Stations are to be brought into operation in Angola, Ethiopia, Iraq, the People's Democratic Republic of Yemen, and a number of other countries.

The USSR's communications satellites "Molnia–2" and "Molnia–3", circling the earth in an elliptical orbit, were used at the first stages of the functioning of the "Intersputnik" system. Those satellites used two radio-frequency channels for telephone and telegraph communications and exchanges of radio and television programmes. Since 1979 new satellites "Statsionar" in a geostationary orbit have been in use in the "Intersputnik" system. The satellites are located above the Atlantic and Indian Oceans and make it possible to ensure communication practically between all countries.

Each "Statsionar" satellite has six general-purpose radio-frequency broad-band channels which can be used both for telephone and telegraph communication, and for exchanges of radio and television programmes.

The "Intersputnik" system will use the capacities on board those satellites, proceeding from the countries' requirements for communication channels. Thus, during the summer Olympic Games in 1980, the "Statsionar" satellites will have eight broad-band channels functioning; one of them will be for telephone and telegraph communication, and seven for the transmission of Olympic television and radio broadcasting programmes to many countries and continents.

The "Intersputnik" ensures to an increasing extent the countries' requirements for international exchange of information and the circle of countries using the channels of this communication system is expanding.

(Source: "Intersputnik" representatives in Moscow)

International Organizations
Active in Various
Communication Fields*

I. International Intergovernmental Organizations

United Nations: General Assembly; ECOSOC; related organs including the International Law Commission; the Committee on the Peaceful Uses of Outer Space; the regional commissions for Europe (ECE), Asia and the Pacific (ESCAP), Latin America (ECLA), Africa (ECA), Western Asia (ECWA); the UNDP; UNCTAD; Unicef.

Specialized and other UN Agencies: ILO; ITU; Unesco; UPU; World Intellectual Property Organization (WIPO); GATT; FAO; WHO; ICAO; IMCO; WMO; the World Bank.

II. Regional Intergovernmental Organizations

Europe: Council of Europe; European Economic Communities (EEC); Council for Mutual Economic Assistance (COMECON); Conference on Security and Cooperation in Europe (CSCE); Nordic Council.

The Americas: Organization of American States (OAS) and related institutions — Inter-American Commission on Human Rights, Inter-American Council for Education, Science and Culture, Inter-American Development Bank; Andean Pact.

Africa: Organization for African Unity (OAU).

Arab Region: League of Arab States; Arab League Educational, Cultural and Scientific Organization (ALECSO) and Arab Regional Literacy Organization attached to it.

Asia and the Pacific: Association of South-East Asian Nations (ASEAN).

III. Other Organizations

Organization for Economic Cooperation and Development (OECD); Non-Aligned Conferences.

---

*In a *Survey of International Structures for Policy and Decision-making in the Communications Field*, prepared for the Commission by the International Institute of Communications (CIC Document No. 29), a number of such organizations and institutions have been referred to as indicated in this appendix.

IV. Operational Agencies and Professional Organizations
(inter-governmental and non-governmental)

Regional Telecommunications Organizations: European Conference of Postal and Telecommunications Administrations (CEPT); Arab Telecommunications Union (ATU); Pan African Telecommunications Union (PATU); Asia Pacific Telecommunity; Inter-American Telecommunications Commission (CITEL).

Satellite Communications: International Telecommunications Satellite Organization (Intelsat); Intersputnik; International Maritime Satellite Organization (INMARSAT); European Space Agency (ESA); Arab Space Communications Organization (ASO).

Broadcasting Organizations: European Broadcasting Union (EBU); International Radio and Television Organization (OIRT); Union of National Radio and Television Organizations of Africa (URTNA); Asia Pacific Broadcasting Union (ABU); Arab States Broadcasting Union (ASBU); Ibero-American Television Organization (OTI); Inter-American Association of Broadcasters (AIR); Caribbean Broadcasting Union; Commonwealth Broadcasting Association; Communauté de télévision francophone; Communauté radiophonique de programmes de langue française; Catholic Broadcasting Organization (UNDA); Islamic Broadcasting Union; World Association for Christian Communication.

V. Professional Media Organizations

There are a large number of non-governmental international organizations in the communications field, including the following:
- —Association internationale pour la recherche et la diffusion des méthodes audio-visuelles et structuro-globales
- —Commonwealth Press Union
- —Confederation of Asean Journalists
- —European Alliance of Press Agencies
- —Federación Latinoamericana de Periodistas
- —Inter-American Press Association
- —Intergovernmental Bureau for Informatics
- —International Association for Mass Communication Research
- —International Catholic Film Organization
- —International Catholic Union of the Press
- —International Community of Booksellers Associations
- —International Confederation of Societies of Authors and Composers
- —International Council on Archives
- —International Documentation and Communication Centre
- —International Federation for Documentation
- —International Federation for Information Processing
- —International Federation of Chief Editors
- —International Federation of Journalists
- —International Federation of Library Associations
- —International Federation of Newspaper Publishers
- —International Federation of the Periodical Press
- —International Federation of Producers of Phonograms and Videograms
- —International Film and Television Council
- —International Institute of Communications
- —International Organization of Journalists
- —International PEN
- —International Press Institute
- —International Press Telecommunications Council
- —International Publishers Association
- —Organization of Asian News Agencies
- —Press Foundation of Asia
- —Universal Esperanto Association

There are many other international organizations in these and similar fields and new organizations are being created, especially at the regional and sub-regional levels, as awareness of the many communication problems at all levels increases and the need for non-official cooperation among professionals becomes apparent.

Appendix 3

International Commission
for the Study
of Communication Problems

Origin and Mandate

1. Following the general policy debate which took place during the nineteenth session of Unesco's General Conference (Nairobi, October-November 1976) where a great emphasis was placed on fundamental issues of communication between peoples and nations — as well as following a difficult discussion of a draft declaration on the fundamental principles governing the use of mass media in strengthening peace and international understanding and in combating war propaganda, racialism and apartheid — many delegates felt that the discussion of such questions would have been facilitated and the controversies attenuated had a more thorough analysis of all communication and information problems been available.

2. After a lengthy debate, it was generally agreed that "the highest priority should be given to measures aiming at reducing the communication gap existing between the developed and the developing countries and at achieving a freer and more balanced international flow of information" and that "a review should be undertaken of the totality of the problems of communication in modern society".

3. In the light of these considerations, the Director-General decided to entrust an international commission, composed of sixteen members with the task of carrying out a study of all communication problems in present-day society. The Commission was established in December 1977.

4. The Commission's mandate was defined by the Director-General. Its terms and main lines of inquiry are quoted in the Report itself (Part I, Chapter 3, Section 4).

Composition

5. The nomination of Commission members was guided by demands of pluralism and the need for unity and homogeneity; by the need to ensure the experience and qualifications, involvement of currents of thought, intellectual trends, cultural traditions, and the diversity of economic and social systems in the major regions of the world.

President:

Sean MacBride (Ireland), journalist, barrister and politician, President of the International Peace Bureau, former Minister for Foreign Affairs, founding member of Amnesty International, United Nations Commissioner for Namibia, holder of the Nobel and Lenin Peace Prizes.

Members:

Elie Abel (U.S.A.), journalist, and broadcaster, Harry and Norman Chandler Professor of Communication, Stanford University.

295

Hubert Beuve-Méry (France), journalist, founder of the newspaper *Le Monde,* president of the Centre de formation et de perfectionnement des journalistes, Paris.

Elebe Ma Ekonzo (Zaire), journalist, Director of National Press, Director-General of Agence Zaire-Presse.

Gabriel Garcia Marquez (Colombia), journalist and author.

Sergei Losev (U.S.S.R.) Director-General of TASS News Agency.

Mochtar Lubis (Indonesia), journalist, President of the Press Foundation of Asia.

Mustapha Masmoudi (Tunisia), Permanent Delegate of Tunisia to Unesco, formerly Secretary of State for Information, President of the Intergovernmental Coordinating Council for Information of the Non-Aligned Countries.

Michio Nagai (Japan), journalist and sociologist, former Minister of Education, editorialist of the newspaper *Assahi Shimbun.*

Fred Isaac Akporuaro Omu (Nigeria), Research Professor, University of Benin, previously Commissioner for Information, Social Development and Sport, Bendel State.

Bogdan Osolnik (Yugoslavia), journalist, politician, member of the National Assembly.

Gamal El Oteifi (Egypt), former Minister for Information and Culture, honorary professor, Cairo University, journalist, lawyer and legal adviser.

Johannes Pieter Pronk (Netherlands), economist and politician.

Juan Somavia (Chile), Executive Director, Instituto Latinoamericano de Estudios Transnacionales (Mexico City).

Boobli George Verghese (India), journalist and Gandhi Peace Foundation Fellow.

Betty Zimmerman (Canada), broadcaster, Director, Radio Canada International.

6. The Commission was assisted during the course of its work by a small Secretariat of Unesco staff members. The Executive Secretary was Asher Deleon.

Activities

7. The Commission had full intellectual autonomy in carrying out its mandate and it enjoyed complete freedom in the organization and execution of its work and in establishing the contents of its Report.

8. From December 1977 to November 1979, the Commission held eight sessions, for a total of 42 days; four of the meetings were in Paris, the others in Sweden (April, 1978), Yugoslavia (January, 1979), India (March, 1979), Mexico (June, 1979). In connection with the Stockholm session, an international seminar on the infrastructures of news collection and dissemination was organized in collaboration with the Swedish Government. Similarly, on the occasion of other meetings outside Paris, round tables were organized by the host Governments on major themes of particular importance relating to links between communication and

society, development, technology and culture.

9. During the course of its work, the President and other members of the Commission participated in numerous conferences, meetings, seminars and discussion groups organized by international organizations and professional associations and various regional and national institutions.

10. Additional substantive inputs into the work of the Commission were the papers prepared on specific aspects of communication by specialists from around the world (see list annexed) and numerous hearings, research findings, topical documentation and analytical commentaries generously provided by dozens of international, regional and national

institutions — research and documentation centres, journalism schools, universities, professional associations and similar bodies.

11. The Commission also had the benefit of hundreds of individual, institutional and governmental comments on its Interim Report, which was published, circulated to more than 7,000 addressees and submitted in 1978 to the 20th session of Unesco's General Conference.

12. The President of the Commission transmitted the Final Report to the Director-General in February 1980.

List of Documents
of The International Commission
For The Study of Communication Problems

1. Membership of the International Commission (CIC) (Orig. and Rev.)

2. Origin and mandate

3. Methods of work

4. Director-General's inaugural address at the first Commission's session (Mr. A. M. M'Bow)

5. Chairman's address at the inaugural meeting of the Commission (Mr. S. MacBride)

6. A glimpse into communications statistics

7. A selected bibliography on communication

8. From freedom of information to the free flow of information — From the free flow of information to the free and balanced flow of information

9. Communication: what do we know?

10. Communication: what do we know? (II)

□ □ □

11. The world of news agencies

12. News agencies multilateral cooperation

13. Monographs (I)
    AFP — Agence France-Presse
    ANSA — Agenzia Nazionale Stampa Associata
    AP — Associated Press
    APS — Agence de Presse Sénégalaise
    AZAP—Agence Zaire Presse
    BERNAMA — Pertubuhan Berita Nasional Malaysia

Where author is not indicated, the document has been prepared by the CIC Secretariat or the Unesco Secretariat.

14. Monographs (II)
    CANA — Caribbean News Agency
    DPA — Deutsche Presse Agentur
    GNA — Ghana News Agency
    INA — Iraqi News Agency
    IPS — Inter Press Service
    KYODO — Kyodo Tsushin News Service
    LATIN — Agencia Latinoamericana de Informacion

15. Monographs (III)
    MENA — Middle East News Agency
    PRENSA LATINA
    REUTER
    TANJUG — Telegrafska Agencija Nova Jugoslavija
    TASS — Telegrafnoie Agenstvo Sovietskavo Soyusa
    UPI — United Press International

16. Collaboration between news agencies in Nordic countries (G. Naesselund, Denmark)

17. A national policy for balance and freedom of information (T. Hammarberg, Sweden)

18. An approach to the study of transnational news media in a pluralistic world (L. Sussman, USA)

19. Infrastructures of news collection and dissemination in the World (International seminar in Stockholm, 24–27 April 1978) Organization — Discussions — Conclusions

20. Extracts from deontological codes of journalists

□ □ □

21. List of international instruments concerning different aspects of communication

22. Communication: extracts from international instruments

23. Survey of national legislation (1)
    Constitutional provisions

24. Survey of national legislation (2)
    Media enterprises
    I. The press
    II. News agencies

25. Survey of national legislation (3)
    Media enterprises
    III. Radio
    IV. Cinema

26. Survey of national legislation (4)
    V. News content

27. Survey of national legislation (5)
    VI. Information personnel

27. National legislation on information:
bis   Latin America (O. Capriles, Venezuela)

28. Comparative account of national structures for policy and decision-making in the communication field (prepared by the International Institute of Communication)

29. Survey of international structures for policy and decision-making in the communication field (prepared by the International Institute of Communication)

30. Role and activities of the UN and its Agencies in the field of communication

□ □ □

31. The new world information order (M. Masmoudi, Tunisia, member of CIC)

32. Aims and approaches to a new international communication order (B. Osolnik, Yugoslavia, member of CIC)

33. Communication for an interdependent, pluralistic world (E. Abel, USA, member of CIC)

33. Call for a new international information order:
bis Preliminary remarks (G. El-Oteifi, Egypt, member of CIC)

33. Shaping a new world information order
ter (Speech of the President of the International Commission at the "Forum 1979")

34. The new international economic order and the new international information order (C. Hamelink, Netherlands)

35. Some remarks on the relation between the new international information order and the new international economic order (J. Pronk, Netherlands, member of CIC)

36. The right to communicate (J. D'Arcy, France)

37. The right to communicate
        1. Concept (L. S. Harms, USA)
        2. Towards a definition (D. Fisher, Ireland)

38. The right to communicate
        3. Legal foundation (A. A. Cocca, Argentina)
        4. Relationship with mass media (J. Richstad, USA)

39. The right to communicate
        5. A socialist approach (J. Pastecka, Poland)

39. Relation between the right to communicate and planning of communication
bis G. El-Oteifi, Egypt, member of CIC)

39. Right to communicate and the New International
ter Communication Order (Tomo Martelanc, Yugoslavia)

40. Communication: a plea for a new approach (F. Balle, France)

□ □ □

41. Communication and international development: some theoretical considerations (M. Tehranian, Iran)

42. Mass media and national development — 1979 (W. Schramm, USA)

43. Towards a national policy on communication in support of development (G.N.S. Raghawan and V. S. Gopalakrishnan, India)

44. A philosophy for development communications: the view from India (B. G. Verghese, India, member of CIC)

45. Readings on the relationship between development and communication

46. Mass media ownership (R. Cruise O'Brien, USA)

47. Communication accompanies capital flows (H. Schiller, USA)

48. Farewell to Aristotle: "Horizontal" Communication (L. Ramiro Beltran, Colombia)

49. Rural development and the flow of communication (H. Cassirer, USA)

50. Advertising and public relations in the arms industries: their role in the mass media (P. Lock, Federal Republic of Germany)

□ □ □

51. Typology of restrictions upon freedom of information: from evident, recognised violations to hidden impediments (J. Louy, France)

52. Obstructions to the free flow of information (F. Giles, UK)

53. Responsibility and obstacles in journalism (prepared by the International Organization of Journalists)

54. Imbalance in the field of communication (I)
    Asia

55. Imbalance in the field of communication (II)
    Latin America and the Caribbean (L. Anibal Gomez, Venezuela)

56. Export–import flows of news:
    1. Foreign news on foreign terms: Finland (U. Kivikuru, Finland)
    2. Flows of culture and information: Hungary (T. Szecsko, Hungary)

57. The image reflected by mass media: Distortions
    a) The image of Southern Africa in certain Western countries (R. Lefort, France)
    b) Study of five reports on Ethiopia (R. Lefort, France)

58. The image reflected by mass media: Manipulations
    The nuclear axis: a case study in the field of investigative reporting (B. Rogers, UK)

59. The image reflected by mass media: Stereotypes
    a) Race relations (C. Jones, UK)

59. The image reflected by mass media: Stereotypes
bis   b) Images of women (M. Gallagher, Ireland)

60. International broadcasting (B. Bumpus, UK)

61. Communication planning

62. Communications and communities: a North-American perspective (J. Halina, Canada)

63. A national policy for purposeful use of information: mass media in USSR (Y.A. Poliakov, USSR)

64. A national policy for socialisation and self-management of information (V. Mićović, Yugoslavia)

65. Access and participation in communication (F. Berrigan, Australia)

66. Readings on participation in communication

67. Alternative experiences (I)
    Local radio and television stations in Italy (G. Richeri, Italy)

68. Alternative experiences (II)
    Communication practices in Latin America (F. Reyes Matta, Chile)

69. Democratization of communication (J. Somavia, Chile, member of CIC)

70. The true problem: democratizing information (J. Schwoebel, France)

□□□

71. Education and learning innovations: use of communication technologies and facilities

72. Mass media education or education for communication (J. Dessaucy, France)

73. Strengthening the press in the Third World (prepared by the International Press Institute)

74. Communication and training: an indicative international review of facilities and resources

75. Culture and communication (V. Flores Olea, Mexico)

76. Interaction between culture and communication (M. Lubis, Indonesia, member of CIC)

77. Cultural industry (H. Gutierrez, Mexico)

78. The context of mass communication research (J. Halloran, UK)

79. Readings on trends in communication research (1)

80. Readings on trends in communication research (2)

□□□

81. Communication technologies of the 1980s (I)
    1. The implications (K. Schaefer and A. Rutkowski, USA)
    2. The future of computer communications (D. Parkhill, Canada)

82. Communication technologies of the 1980s (II)
     3. Development of television broadcasting technology (M. Krivosheev, USSR)
     4. Recent progress and its impact upon communication policy and development (R. Gazin, Yugoslavia)

83. Communication technologies of the 1980s (III)
     5. The social implications (S. Komatsuzaki, Japan)
     6. Future trends (Yash Pal, India)

84. Technology and change in modern communication (I. de Sola Pool, USA)

85. Contribution of scientific and technological progress to the development of communication (V. S. Korobeynikov, USSR)

86. New technological developments in the print media (A. Smith, UK)

87. International allocation of frequencies to national broadcasting services (M. Chaffai, Tunisia)

88. Institutional configuration for large space communications structures: a basis for the development of international space communications norms (D. Smith, USA)

89. The protection of the individual, his freedom and privacy, in particular in the computer field (J. Freese, Sweden)

90. The protection of Journalists (S. MacBride, Ireland, President of CIC)

90. Professional Ethics in Mass Communication
bis (B. Osolnik, Yugoslavia, member of CIC)

90. Freedom and responsibility of journalists
ter (Hubert Beuve-Méry, Member of CIC)

□□□

91. Main forms of traditional communication: Africa (M. Diabaté, Mali)

92. Not a thing of the past: functional and cultural status of traditional media in India (H.K. Ranganath, India)

93. Main forms of traditional communication: Egypt (S. M. Hussein, Egypt)

94–100. Communications: Readings

Index

Note: National or geographical references are not included in the index; they are too numerous and, also, so many of the situations described, analyses made or comments given in the Report are based on examples from or refer to several countries, groups of countries or regions that it would be repetitive and uninformative to list them in detail.